mine

Anne Arundel Community College
READING 023 & 024

THIRD EDITION

Meribeth Allman, Kathy Mills,
Rebekah Nutter, and Kerry Taylor

Taken from

Efficient & Flexible Reading, Sixth Edition, by Kathleen T. McWhorter

Academic Reading, Fourth Edition, by Kathleen T. McWhorter

Bridging the Gap: College Reading, Seventh Edition, by Brenda D. Smith

Building Strategies for College Reading: A Text with Thematic Reader, Third Edition, by Jane L. McGrath

Steps to College Reading, Second Edition, by Dorothy U. Seyler

Reading Skills for College Students, Fifth Edition, by Ophelia H. Hancock

Reading Across the Disciplines: College Reading and Beyond by Kathleen T. McWhorter

D1511861

PEARSON

Custom
Publishing

Taken from:

Efficient & Flexible Reading, Sixth Edition
by Kathleen T. McWhorter
Copyright © 2002 by Kathleen T. McWhorter
Published by Longman Publishers
A Pearson Education Company
Boston, Massachusetts 02116

Academic Reading, Fourth Edition
by Kathleen T. McWhorter
Copyright © 2001 by Addison Wesley Longman, Inc.
A Pearson Education Company
Boston, Massachusetts 02116

Bridging the Gap: College Reading, Seventh Edition
by Brenda D. Smith
Copyright © 2003 by Pearson Education, Inc.
Published by Longman Publishers

Building Strategies for College Reading: A Text with Thematic Reader, Third Edition
by Jane L. McGrath
Copyright © 2001, 1998, 1995 by Prentice-Hall, Inc.
A Pearson Education Company
Upper Saddle River, New Jersey 07458

Steps to College Reading, Second Edition
by Dorothy U. Seyler
Copyright © 2001, 1998 by Allyn & Bacon
A Pearson Education Company
Boston, Massachusetts 02116

Reading Skills for College Students, Fifth Edition
by Ophelia H. Hancock
Copyright © 2001, 1998, 1995, 1991, 1987 by Prentice-Hall, Inc.

Reading Across the Disciplines: College Reading and Beyond
by Kathleen T. McWhorter
Copyright © 2002 by Kathleen T. McWhorter
Published by Longman Publishers

This special edition published in cooperation with Pearson Custom Publishing.

Printed in the United States of America

10 9 8 7 6 5

Please visit our web site at www.pearsoncustom.com

ISBN 0–536–75087-4

BA 998392

PEARSON CUSTOM PUBLISHING
75 Arlington Street, Suite 300, Boston, MA 02116
A Pearson Education Company

Contents

Section I

Critical Reading 023

CHAPTER 1

UNDERSTAND THE VOCABULARY THE AUTHOR USES

CHAPTER OBJECTIVES

✔ Formulate an overall strategy for defining unfamiliar words.

✔ Understand how to use context to help define a word.

✔ Understand how to use the parts of the word to help define it.

✔ Identify other resources for defining unfamiliar words.

✔ Recognize the difference between the denotation and connotation of a word.

✔ Recognize when words are chosen by the author for a special purpose.

✔ Recognize and understand figurative language.

KEY VOCABULARY

✔ context
✔ context clues
✔ prefix
✔ root
✔ suffix
✔ word analysis
✔ literal meaning
✔ denotation
✔ connotation
✔ figurative language
✔ simile
✔ metaphor

Our English language has over one million words. Words that inform us, tell us stories, paint pictures of things we've never seen, make us fall in love and go to war.

With so many possibilities, it's not surprising that you encounter unfamiliar and confusing words in reading assignments.

As you develop your plan for reading this chapter, think about what you do when you run into a word you don't know. Perhaps you stop and look it up in the dictionary or find someone you can ask. What else have you tried? What strategies have you used when the definition you found in the dictionary didn't make sense in the context of the sentence or paragraph you were reading?

As you preview this chapter, jot down preliminary answers to each of the main heading questions (e.g., "What Is My Basic Strategy for Understanding the Author's Vocabulary?"; "How Can I Use the Context to Help Define a Word?"; and so on). Then, as you read and gain new information, revise your answers.

WHAT IS MY BASIC STRATEGY FOR UNDERSTANDING THE AUTHOR'S VOCABULARY?

As You Plan:

1. Review words that are highlighted—i.e., words in **boldface** or *italic* and words that are defined in footnotes or marginal notes.

As You Read:

2. Identify unfamiliar words.
3. Use context clues:

    Look at the surrounding words: Do they offer any clues?

    Look at the rest of the sentences or paragraphs: Do they offer any clues?

    Look for other clues, such as punctuation, the author's purpose, or setting.

4. Analyze word parts:

    Look at the word: Is it related to a known word?

5. Use your own experience.
6. Predict the possible meaning.
7. Try out the meaning in the sentence and see if it makes sense.
8. Decide if the definition makes sense, if you should try again, or if you should consult a dictionary or an expert.
9. Check for meanings beyond the literal definition.

As You Review:

10. Clarify any remaining definitions.
11. If it is important to your purpose, determine a way to review and remember the new words.

HOW CAN I USE THE CONTEXT TO HELP DEFINE A WORD?

Most of these words are familiar: *option, trading, call, put, uncovered, naked,* and *covered.* Yet in this paragraph from the stockbroker's newsletter you read in Chapter 1, your definitions for the words probably didn't help you understand the paragraph.

> Writing or selling *Options* against stock you already own is a strategy that is conservative and usually works well in a *trading* market. An Option is either a *call* (a right to buy 100 shares of stock at a specified price in the future) or a *put* (a right to sell 100 shares of stock at a specified price in the future). Thus an Option buyer or seller who owns no stock (called *uncovered* or *naked*) is a speculator who is looking at making large percentage returns on a small amount of invested capital in a short time. This individual would be paying the Option premium to us, the *covered* writer. (Schneider, Kirk's Quotes)

This is because words do not have just one isolated meaning. Words take on meaning from their context—how they are used in conjunction with other words.

When you read this paragraph, you could either skip over the words you didn't know or try to figure out their meanings. Fortunately, active readers—readers thinking about and looking for related information—can often use clues the author provides to help them understand unfamiliar words. In fact, I just used a context clue: I defined what I meant by "active reader" and set it off with a dash (—) as your clue.

For other examples of context clues, look in the stockbroker's paragraph. For the first two words—*Options* and *trading*—are there any words or information in the paragraph that help? Not really, so if you don't recognize them from your own experience, come back to them later. The next words—*call, put, uncovered, naked*—are defined for you (parentheses are your clue). To define the final word—*covered*—the author gives the definition for its opposite—*uncovered*—as your clue.

USING CONTEXT CLUES

Assume you are reading your astronomy text and come to the unfamiliar words *perihelion* and *aphelion*. To comprehend the passage, you must understand the words. See how you can use the context clues the author provides.

> *Perihelion* is the point in the earth's orbit when the distance between the earth and the sun is at its minimum, as opposed to *aphelion*.

Here, the author defined *perihelion* directly (the point in the earth's orbit when the distance between the earth and the sun is at its minimum) and has clued you to the definition of *aphelion* by stating it is the opposite (therefore, *aphelion* must be the point in the earth's orbit when the distance between the earth and the sun is at its maximum).

In addition to using punctuation, stating a definition, or an opposite, an author can provide clues such as giving an example or explanation, or restating the thought in more simple terms.

Making use of context clues to help define unfamiliar words is much like the work you did in Chapter 2 to infer the author's purpose. You combine all the information an author provides to figure out the meaning the word has in this context. The meanings you construct through context clues are not wild guesses; they are thoughtful suppositions supported by the author's information.

Unless the passage is extremely difficult with too many unfamiliar words, using context clues can save you time and assure that you have the best definition for the context.

See how author John Macionis uses a variety of context clues in these passages from his text *Sociology*. As you read, look for words, phrases, and punctuation that relate to or seem to point to the unknown word.

Gives a Specific Definition of an Important Word (*sociology*):

A distinctive perspective is central to the discipline of *sociology*, which is defined as the scientific study of human social activity. As an academic discipline, sociology is continually learning more about how human beings as social creatures think and act.

Provides an Explanation of a New Word (*replication*):

One way to limit distortion caused by personal values is through the *replication* of research. When the same results are obtained by subsequent studies there is increased confidence that the original research was conducted objectively.

Uses Punctuation as a Clue to Meaning of Words (*experiment, hypothesis*):

The logic of science is clearly expressed in the *experiment*—a research method that investigates cause-and-effect relationships under highly controlled conditions. Experimental research tends to be explanatory, meaning that it is concerned not with just what happens but with why. Experiments are typically devised to test a specific *hypothesis*—an unverified statement of a relationship between any facts or variables. In everyday language, a hypothesis is simply a hunch or educated guess about what the research will show.

Gives Clue to Unknown Term (*ethnography*) by Comparison to Known Term (*case study*):

Cultural anthropologists describe an unfamiliar culture in an *ethnography*; a sociologist may study a particular category of people or a particular setting as a *case study*.

Gives Clue to New Term (*secondary analysis*) by Stating Its Opposite:

Each of the methods of conducting sociological investigation described so far involves researchers personally collecting their own data. Doing so is not always possible, however, and it is often not necessary. In many cases, sociologists engage in *secondary analysis*.

Gives Clue to New Word (*subculture*) with Examples:

When describing cultural diversity, sociologists often use the term *subculture*. Teenagers, Polish-Americans, homeless people, and "southerners" are all examples of subcultures within American societies. Occupations also foster subculture differences, including specialized ways of speaking, as anyone who has ever spent time with race-car drivers, jazz musicians, or even sociologists can attest.

PRACTICE: DEFINING WORDS USING CONTEXT CLUES

Use the author's context clues to unlock the meaning of the italicized words and phrases in these passages. Describe the context clues you used.

1. The *World Wide Web* (WWW or Web) is a collection of standards and protocols used to access information available on the Internet. This information is in the form of documents linked together in what is called a *hypermedia* system. Hypermedia is combined-use multimedia (text, images, video, and sound) in a Web presentation page. (Leshin, *Student Resource Guide to the Internet*)

2. *Like terms* are terms that have the same variables with the same exponents. (Angel, *Elementary Algebra for College Students*)

3. Despite extensive media attention since the summer of 1988, global climate change remains a challenge to *lay comprehension*. One study found that 12 of 14 ordinary citizens surveyed had heard of global warming, but all held fundamental misconceptions about the process (Kempton, 1990). (Wilson and Henson, *Learning about Global Warming: A Study of Students and Journalists*)

4. A composer often provides a marking for *tempo*, or overall speed, to help convey the character of a composition. (Politoske, *Music*)

5. *Computerphobia*, the fear of computers, is apparently affecting more and more people as microcomputers continue to be plugged into more and more homes, schools, and offices throughout the land. This relatively recent phenomenon, also known as *cyberphobia*, occurs in a large proportion of students and professionals. (Fuori and Gioia, *Computers and Information Processing*)

6. A magazine is custom-designed for its special audience. For example, *Redbook* and *Cosmopolitan* are both primarily women's magazines and may have articles on similar topics but their *slant*—their approach to the topic—is very different. Each must answer the questions and provide the information their readers expect. (McGrath, *Magazine Article Writing Basics Handbook*)

HOW CAN I USE THE WORD ITSELF AS A CLUE TO ITS MEANING?

You can't always rely on context clues; there may not be any or they may be confusing. Another strategy you can use to define an unfamiliar word is to analyze the parts of the word—its root and any prefixes and/or suffixes—as clues to the meaning of the entire word.

The root is the basic part of a word. Additional words are made by adding a prefix at the beginning of a root word and/or a suffix at the end of a root word. Prefixes and suffixes change the meaning of the root word. A suffix can also change the way a word can be used in a sentence and its part of speech. Combining the meanings of the word parts can help you understand the whole word.

When you learn the meaning of a few common word parts, you have a head start on defining other words that contain those parts. In fact, researchers estimate that for every word part you know, you have the key to unlock the meaning of about seven more words.

USING WORD PARTS

Let's assume you are reading a different astronomy text, this one with no context clues, and you come to the unfamiliar words *perihelion* and *aphelion*. If you know, or can discover the meanings of the basic word parts, you can define the words as easily as with context clues:

> *perihelion*: *peri* from the Greek meaning *near* + *helios* from the Greek meaning *the sun* = near the sun
>
> *aphelion*: *apo* from the Greek meaning *away from* + *helios* from the Greek meaning *the sun* = away from the sun

We arrive at similar meanings for perihelion and aphelion as when there were context clues. We just used a different strategy.

As another example, if you know that *apolune* means the point in the path of a body orbiting the moon that is farthest from the center of the moon, what does *perilune* mean? By combining what you already knew about peri (near) with the new information (lune means moon), you know that perilune means the point in the path of a body orbiting the moon that is nearest the center of the moon.

Use word parts to help define each of these words.

un = not	*able* = capable of
retro = backward	*spec* = see
trans = across	*anti* = against

a. un•read•able (not capable of being read)
b. retro•spec•tive (looking backward)
c. trans•atlantic (across the Atlantic ocean)
d. anti•inflammatory (against, or counteracting inflammation)

PRACTICE: DEFINING WORDS USING WORD PARTS

The table on page 46 lists some common word parts and their definitions. Use them to help you define the italicized words in the numbered passages at the top of page 47.

ROOTS

aud, aur	hear	*literate, literatus*	able to read/write
annus (ennal)	year	*manus*	by hand
carcin	cancer	*mille*	1,000
cardio	heart	*mit*	send
chrono	time	*mor, mort*	die
cred	belief	*nom, nomen*	name
demos	the people	*pathy*	feeling
derma	skin	*phob*	fear
divers	different	*psycho*	mind, soul
duc, duct	lead, make, shape	*port*	carry
geron, geras	aging, old age	*scribe, script*	write
graph, graphy	writing, record	*spec*	see
hydro	water	*vox*	voice

PREFIXES

ante-	before	*micro-*	small
anti-, contra-	against	*mal-*	badly, inadequate
auto-	self	*mis-*	wrongly
bi-	two, both	*mono-*	one, single
bio-	living organisms	*neo-*	new
circum-	around	*multi-*	many
con-	with	*para-*	beside, beyond
contra-	against	*phren-, phreno-*	mind
dis-	not or away	*poly-*	many
dys-	difficult, painful	*post-*	after, behind
ec-, eco-	habitat	*pre-*	before, in front of
ecto-	outside	*pro-*	in favor of, ahead of
em-, im-	to give	*proto-*	original; chief
endo-	inside, within	*pseudo-*	false
en-	to make; cause	*re-*	again
ex-	out of	*retro-*	backward
hemi-	half	*quadri-, quadr-*	four
hyper-	excessive, more than	*schizo- or chiz-*	split
hypo-	low, less than	*semi-*	half
il-, in-, ir-	in/into or not	*sub-*	under, below
inter-	among, between	*super-, supra*	above
intra-	within, inside	*tele-, trans*	across, over a distance
macro-	large	*ultra-*	super, excessive
mega-	large	*un-, non-*	not
mal-	bad	*uni-, mono-*	one

SUFFIXES

-graphy	writing or science	*-ism*	manner of action
-able, -ible	able to	*-itis*	inflammation
-al	characterized by	*-ity*	condition, state
-algia	pain	*-ine*	having the nature of
-ance, -ancy	action, quality, amount	*-less*	without
-ectomy	surgical removal	*-logy*	oral/written expression
-ence, -ency	action, quality of	*-ly*	like
-er, -or, -ist	one who	*-ment*	action
-ese	native to; originating in	*-ology*	study of
-fy	make, form into	*-ulent*	abounding in
-ful	full of		

1. It is the loss of this *biodiversity* and the loss of *irreplaceable* ancient forests that most concern environmentalists about the issue of logging in national forests. (Scott, "Hoots to Blame?")

2. In the industrialized countries, 3.3 percent of the adult population is *illiterate*. For the developing countries as a whole, the figure is 35 percent, and rises as high as 60 percent in the 47 least developed countries. (Bequette, *UNESCO Courier*)

3. In *telecommunications* we are moving to a single worldwide information network, just as economically we are becoming one global marketplace. (Naisbitt and Aburdene, *Megatrends 2000*)

4. Baca recalls her role in the beginning of the Chicano Mural Movement when she was searching for a way to express her own experience as a Hispanic American artist. Greatly influenced by the Mexican muralists, Baca discovered a means of community *empowerment*. (Estrada, "Judy Baca's Art for Peace")

5. Moving from our analysis of the term communication, we now examine the process of communication. We begin by studying a communication model and the three types of communication important to our study in this text: *intrapersonal, interpersonal*, and mass communication. (Bittner, *Each Other*)

6. The compost pile is really a teeming *microbial* farm. (Office of Environmental Affairs, *Backyard Composting*)

IF I STILL CAN'T FIGURE OUT THE MEANING, WHAT OTHER RESOURCES CAN I USE?

There will be times when you can't piece together any helpful information from the context or the structure of the word. When this happens, take the time to look the word up in the book's glossary or a dictionary, or ask one of your resource people (someone you identified in Chapter 1 as being a resource).

A glossary is a quick, easy-to-use resource because it only lists the specific meaning of the word as it is used in the book. Not all books provide a glossary (and even those that do sometimes won't provide enough information—such as how to pronounce the word), so sometimes you will need to consult a dictionary.

A dictionary is a reliable source of all the definitions for a word, plus correct spelling variations, pronunciations, parts of speech, and derivations. Since you will often find several definitions for a word, you must always fit the meaning you select back into the original context to be certain it makes sense.

USING A DICTIONARY

Assume that this time you come across *perihelion* and *aphelion* in your text and you don't have any context clues and you don't know the meaning of the word parts. Looking up the words in a dictionary gives you literal meanings similar to when you used context clues or word parts.

aphe·li·on (ə fēʹlē ən, -fēlʹyən) *n., pl.* **-li·ons** or **-li·a** (-ə) [ModL, altered (as if Gr) by Johannes KEPLER < earlier *aphelium* < Gr *apo-*, from + *hēlios*, SUN¹; modeled on L *apogaeum*, APOGEE] the point farthest from the sun in the orbit of a planet or comet, or of a man-made satellite in orbit around the sun: opposed to PERIHELION

In this passage from the editors of *Syllabus*, you may have conflicting ideas about the meaning of *rudimentary*—does it mean low or high?

The increasing power of the personal computer is making it possible to develop applications that are smarter and more responsive to the user.... Anyone who has used a spelling or grammar checker has experienced this type of application at a very *rudimentary* level. ("Advanced Technologies Lead the Way to the Future of Educational Computing," *Syllabus*)

If *rudimentary* is an unfamiliar word, your best resource is the dictionary.

ru·di·men·ta·ry (rōō′də men′tər ē, -men′trē) *adj.* of, or having the nature of, a rudiment or rudiments; specif., *a*) elementary *b*) incompletely or imperfectly developed *c*) vestigial

Unfortunately, finding the correct meaning of a word in the dictionary is not always this clear-cut. Many words have more than one meaning and can be used as more than one part of speech. Each time you look up a word in the dictionary, your job is to sort through the definitions and select the one definition that best fits the context.

For example, if you look up the word *base* in a dictionary, you find a variety of definitions.

base¹ (bās) *n., pl.* **bas′es** (-iz) ⟦ME < OFr *bas* < L *basis,* BASIS⟧ **1** the thing or part on which something rests; lowest part or bottom; foundation **2** the fundamental or main part, as of a plan, organization, system, theory, etc. **3** the principal or essential ingredient, or the one serving as a vehicle [paint with an oil *base*] **4** anything from which a start is made; basis **5** *Baseball* any of the three sand-filled bags (*first base, second base,* or *third base*) that must be reached safely one after the other to score a run **6** the point of attachment of a part of the body [the *base* of the thumb] **7** a center of operations or source of supply; headquarters, as of a military operation or exploring expedition **8** *a*) the bottommost layer or coat, as of paint *b*) a makeup cream to give a desired color to the skin, esp. in the theater **9** *Archit.* the lower part, as of a column, pier, or wall, regarded as a separate unit **10** *Chem.* any compound that can react with an acid to form a salt, the hydroxyl of the base being replaced by a negative ion: in modern theory, any substance that produces a negative ion and donates electrons to an acid to form covalent bonds: in water solution a base tastes bitter, turns red litmus paper blue, and, in dissociation theory, produces free hydroxyl ions: see pH **11** *Dyeing* a substance used for fixing colors **12** *Geom.* the line or plane upon which a figure is thought of as resting [the *base* of a triangle] **13** *Heraldry* the lower portion of a shield **14** *Linguis.* any morpheme to which prefixes, suffixes, etc. are or can be added; stem or root **15** *Math. a*) a whole number, esp. 10 or 2, made the fundamental number, and raised to various powers to produce the major counting units, of a number system; radix *b*) any number raised to a power by an exponent (see LOGARITHM) *c*) in business, etc., a starting or reference figure or sum upon which certain calculations are made

Select the best definition of *base* for each of the following each sentences.

1. In the expression 4^2, the 4 is called the *base*, and the 2 is called the exponent.
2. The Ionic order's most striking feature is the column, which rests on an ornately profiled *base* of its own.
3. The closing of the military *base* in the region prompted a quick economic decline.

4. Today's experiment will show whether the compound is *base* or acid.

5. Both investigation teams were working from the same *base* information.

PRACTICE: SELECTING THE BEST DICTIONARY DEFINITION

Each of the italicized words or phrases has multiple meanings listed in the dictionary. Select the definition that best fits the context.

1. Your career depends not only on your efforts, but also on the efforts of many other people. You cannot be successful by yourself. You can only be successful as part of a joint effort by many different people, by acting in *harmony* with other people. All through your career, you will find yourself interdependent with other people. (Johnson, *Human Relations and Your Career*)

> **har·mo·ny** (här′mə nē) *n., pl.* **-nies** ⟦ME *armony* < OFr *harmonie* < L *harmonia* < Gr < *harmos*, a fitting < IE base *ar- >* ART, ARM¹⟧ **1** a combination of parts into a pleasing or orderly whole; congruity **2** agreement in feeling, action, ideas, interests, etc.; peaceable or friendly relations **3** a state of agreement or orderly arrangement according to color, size, shape, etc. **4** an arrangement of parallel passages of different authors, esp. of the Scriptures, so as to bring out corresponding ideas, qualities, etc. **5** agreeable sounds; music **6** *Music a)* the simultaneous sounding of two or more tones, esp. when satisfying to the ear *b)* structure in terms of the arrangement, modulation, etc. of chords (distinguished from MELODY, RHYTHM) *c)* the study of this structure

2. The growth of the Sun Belt and the decline of the Snow Belt were tied to new resource problems facing the United States in the 1970s. For the first time in its history the country faced an *acute* energy crisis. (Unger, *These United States*)

> **a·cute** (ə kyo̅o̅t′) *adj.* ⟦L *acutus*, pp. of *acuere*, sharpen: see ACUMEN⟧ **1** having a sharp point **2** keen or quick of mind; shrewd **3** sensitive to impressions *[acute* hearing*]* **4** severe and sharp, as pain, jealousy, etc. **5** severe but of short duration; not chronic: said of some diseases **6** very serious; critical; crucial *[an acute* shortage of workers*]* **7** shrill; high in pitch **8** of less than 90 degrees *[an acute* angle*]*: see ANGLE¹, illus. **9** INTENSIVE (sense 3)

3. Science is an important foundation of all sociological research and, more broadly, helps us to *critically* evaluate information we encounter every day. (Macionis, *Sociology*)

> **crit·i·cal** (krit′i kəl) *adj.* **1** tending to find fault; censorious **2** characterized by careful analysis and judgment *[a sound critical* estimate of the problem*]* **3** of critics or criticism **4** of or forming a crisis or turning point; decisive **5** dangerous or risky; causing anxiety *[a critical* situation in international relations*]* **6** of the crisis of a disease **7** designating or of important products or raw materials subject to increased production and restricted distribution under strict control, as in wartime **8** *a)* designating or of a point at which a change in character, property, or condition is effected *b)* designating or of the point at which a nuclear chain reaction becomes self-sustaining —**crit′i·cal·ly** *adv.* —**crit′i·cal′i·ty** (-kal′ə tē) or **crit′i·cal·ness** *n.*

4. A *front* usually is in constant motion, shifting the position of the boundary between the air masses but maintaining its function as a barrier between them. Usually one air mass is actively displacing the other; thus the *front* advances in the direction dictated by the movement of the more active air mass. (Bergman and McKnight, *Introduction to Geography*)

front (frunt) *n.* ⟦ ME < OFr < L *frons* (gen. *frontis*), forehead, front < IE *bhren-*, to project > OE *brant*, steep, high ⟧ **1** *a*) the forehead *b*) the face; countenance **2** *a*) attitude or appearance, as of the face, indicating state of mind; external behavior when facing a problem, etc. /to put on a bold *front*/ *b*) [Colloq.] an appearance, usually pretended or assumed, of social standing, wealth, etc. **3** [Rare] impudence; effrontery **4** the part of something that faces forward or is regarded as facing forward; most important side; forepart **5** the first part; beginning /toward the *front* of the book/ **6** the place or position directly before a person or thing **7** a forward or leading position or situation ☆**8** the first available bellhop or page, as in a hotel: generally used as a call **9** the land bordering a lake, ocean, street, etc. **10** [Brit.] a promenade along a body of water **11** the advanced line, or the whole area, of contact between opposing sides in warfare; combat zone **12** a specified area of activity /the home *front*, the political *front*/ **13** a broad movement in which different groups are united for the achievement of certain common political or social aims ☆**14** a person who serves as a public representative of a business, group, etc., usually because of his or her prestige ☆**15** a person or group used to cover or obscure the activity or objectives of another, controlling person or group **16** a stiff bosom, worn with formal clothes **17** *Archit.* a face of a building; esp., the face with the principal entrance **18** *Meteorol.* the boundary between two air masses of different density and temperature —*adj.* **1** at, to, in, on, or of the front **2** *Phonet.* articulated with the tongue toward the front of the mouth: said of certain vowels, as (i) in *bid* —*vt.* **1** to face; be opposite to **2** to be before in place **3** to meet; confront **4** to defy; oppose **5** to supply or serve as a front, or facing, of —*vi.* **1** to face in a certain direction /a castle *fronting* on the sea/ ☆**2** to act as a FRONT (senses 14 & 15): with *for*

5. The effects created by different intensities of sound, or dynamics, are basic to all musical expression. In traditional music, we often first become aware of the impact of dynamic effects upon hearing very sudden changes from soft to loud, or vice versa. For some of us, the first awareness of musical dynamics is very obvious, as in the so-called "Surprise" Symphony of Franz Joseph Haydn (1732–1809). Here, the surprise is a *radical* change in volume, a very loud chord coming on the heels of a gentle melody. (Politoske, *Music*)

rad|i·cal (rad′i kəl) *adj.* ⟦ ME < LL *radicalis* < L *radix* (gen. *radicis*), ROOT¹ ⟧ **1** *a*) of or from the root or roots; going to the foundation or source of something; fundamental; basic /a *radical* principle/ *b*) extreme; thorough /a *radical* change in one's life/ **2** *a*) favoring fundamental or extreme change; specif., favoring basic change in the social or economic structure *b*) [R-] designating or of any of various modern political parties, esp. in Europe, ranging from moderate to conservative in program **3** *Bot.* of or coming from the root **4** *Math.* having to do with the root or roots of a number or quantity —*n.* **1** *a*) a basic or root part of something *b*) a fundamental **2** *a*) a person holding radical views, esp. one favoring fundamental social or economic change *b*) [R-] a member or adherent of a Radical party **3** *Chem.* a group of two or more atoms that acts as a single atom and goes through a reaction unchanged, or is replaced by a single atom: it is normally incapable of separate existence **4** *Math. a*) the indicated root of a quantity or quantities, shown by an expression written under the radical sign *b*) RADICAL SIGN

PRACTICE: DEFINING WORDS USING OUTSIDE RESOURCES

Define each of the italicized words or phrases and tell what resource you used to find your definition.

1. A piece of rock no bigger than a potato has awakened a *somnolent* American space program and inspired planetary scientists, *spacecraft*

designers and the NASA leadership with what may become a new sense of mission. Tantalizing clues in the meteorite have *emboldened* them to think that if they are clever and persistent, they may yet find on Mars the first evidence of extraterrestrial life. (Wilford, *New York Times*)

2. Since before the first *Gutenberg revolution*, paper has served as an indispensable all-purpose catalyst for much of one abstraction of what universities are all about: the creation, preservation, dissemination, and interpretation of data, information, and knowledge. (Lynn, "Publish Electronically or Perish," *Higher Education Product Companion*)

3. Few people could imagine that in a decade or so television would become a *preemptory* force in American culture, defining the news, reshaping politics, reorienting family life, and remaking the cultural expectations of several generations of Americans. (Gilder, *Life After Television*)

4. Water has transformed Colorado from *sere* cactus country into green miles covered by melon vines in the Arkansas Valley; into lush emerald fairways at the Hyland Hills Golf Course in Westminster; into manicured crayon-green lawns in the Durango West subdivision; and into lines of dusty green grapevines twisting along acres of trellises under the shadow of Mount Garfield in Palisade. (Lofholm, "Finite resource jars state's vision of infinite promise," *Denver Post*)

5. Our institutions of family, religion, education, business, labor, and community are attempting to keep afloat while wrestling with both internal and external combatants. Each group's *raison d'être* is challenged constantly while it seeks acceptable canons in which to function in modern society. (Rauch, "A Quality Life Should Be Full of Values," *USA Today*)

How Can I Use the Strategies Together While I'm Reading?

Real reading tasks don't have the obvious look of these isolated samples. To successfully read (remember that reading and understanding are synonymous terms) the variety of material required in an academic setting requires that you use these strategies flexibly.

When you encounter a word that hinders your understanding, you may first check to see if there are any context clues you can use. On the other hand, if you recognize the parts of the word, perhaps that is all the clue you need. You work smarter, not harder. But you also realize that if context clues, word analysis, and your experience don't yield a probable meaning for the word, you must take time to consult an outside resource, like the dictionary.

For example, read this sentence from *Megatrends 2000*, by John Naisbitt and Patricia Aburdene. "Conceived under the influence of the next millennium, these new megatrends are the gateways to the 21st century." Perhaps you read the passage by combining three strategies:

1. Noting the context relationships between millennium and 21st century and between megatrends and gateways

2. Using knowledge of word parts—mille = 1,000 and mega = big

3. Remembering some prior knowledge—perhaps you've heard of megatrends.

Even if you used a slightly different set of strategies, when you fit the meanings together you understood that Naisbitt and Aburdene were saying "after thinking about the next thousand years—the 21st century—these are the big trends or ideas that will get us there successfully."

For a strategy to help remember new words, see the section entitled "Improving Vocabulary" on the companion web site http://www.prenhall.com/mcgrath

PRACTICE: DEFINING WORDS USING CONTEXT CLUES, WORD PARTS, AND OTHER RESOURCES

Use your word sleuthing strategies to define the italicized words in the selection below.

Endangered Species: Endangered Means There's Still Time
U.S. Department of the Interior, U.S. Fish and Wildlife Service

---

¹Since life began on this planet, countless creatures have come and gone—*rendered extinct* by naturally changing *ecological* conditions, and more recently by humans and their activities.

²If *extinction* is part of the natural order, and if so many species still remain, some people ask, "Why save *endangered species*? What makes a relatively few animals and plants so special that effort and money should be spent to preserve them?"

WHY SAVE ENDANGERED SPECIES?

³Saving species is important to many people for a variety of reasons. People care about saving species for their beauty and the thrill of seeing them, for scientific and educational purposes, and for their ecological, historic, and cultural values.

⁴A *compelling reason* to preserve species is that each one plays an important role in an *ecosystem*—an intricate network of plant and animal communities and the associated environment. When a species becomes endangered, it indicates that something is wrong with the ecosystems we all depend on. Like the canaries used in coal mines whose deaths warned miners of bad air, the increasing numbers of endangered species warn us that the health of our environment has declined. The measures we take to save endangered species will help *ensure* that the planet we leave for our children is as healthy as the planet our parents left for us.

⁵Some species provide more immediate value to humans. For example, cancer fighting drugs have been *derived* from the bark of a *yew* that is native to the Pacific Northwest. Chemicals used to treat diseases of nerve tissue were found in an endangered plant in Hawaii. Valuable resources such as these could be lost forever if species go extinct.

CAUSES OF DECLINE

⁶We can no longer attribute the *accelerating loss* of our wild animals and plants to "natural" processes. *Habitat destruction* is the single most serious worldwide threat to wildlife and plants, followed by *exploitation* for commercial or other purposes. Disease, *predation*, inadequate conservation laws, pollution, and introduction of non-native species, or a combination of these can contribute to a species' decline.

THE LISTING PROCESS

⁷The U.S. Fish and Wildlife Service maintains the List of Endangered and Threatened Wildlife and Plants, which identifies species protected under the Endangered Species Act. The Act defines an "endangered" species as one that is in danger of extinction throughout all or a significant portion of its range. A "threatened" species is one likely to become endangered within the foreseeable future.

To understand the meaning of the selection above you had to use several strategies together. For example,

- *rendered extinct* (¶1): Check surrounding words for clues. Prior phrase "have come and gone" clue to general meaning. I already know extinct means gone. Predict possible meaning: "made to disappear." Fit meaning into sentence. It makes sense.
- *ecological* (¶1): Check surrounding words; no strong clues. Read ahead; no specific clues. Consider topic, and that *eco* means habitat. Predict possible meaning "environmental." Fit meaning into sentence. It makes sense, but since this appears to be an important word, I should also check for a dictionary definition.

- *extinction* (¶2): Check surrounding words for clues. Following phrase "and if so many species still remain" seems to be opposite to meaning of extinction. Consider it has the same root as *extinct*. Predict possible meaning: "disappearing." Fit meaning into sentence. It makes sense.
- *endangered species* (¶2): Check surrounding words; no strong clues. Read ahead; locate specific definition in last paragraph. Fit meaning into sentence. It makes sense.
- *compelling reason* (¶4): Check surrounding words for clues. No direct restatement but phrase "each one plays an important role" makes me think it means "good reason." Fit meaning into sentence. It makes sense.
- *ecosystem* (¶4): Check surrounding clues; punctuation indicates definition follows.
- *ensure* (¶4): Check surrounding words for clues. No direct word clues but the sentence, taken as a whole, seems to suggest it is positive action. Consider the root *sure*. Predict possible meaning: "make sure." Fit meaning into sentence. It makes sense.
- *derived* (¶5): Check surrounding words for clues. No direct clues but phrase "from the bark" makes me think it means "taken from or made out of." Fit meaning into sentence. It makes sense.
- *yew* (¶5): Check surrounding words for clues. Prior phrase "from the bark of a" suggests it's a tree. Fit meaning into sentence. It makes sense.

Define these words from paragraph 6.

- *accelerating loss*
- *habitat destruction*
- *exploitation*
- *predation*

How Can a Word Mean More Than Its Definition?

In this chapter we've concentrated on finding an exact literal, or denotative, meaning of a word. But words often mean more than what it says in the dictionary. Words can also suggest meanings that trigger an assortment of feelings and emotions. These associated meanings are called connotations—what the word implies to the reader. Because of these meanings beyond the literal, authors can subtly influence readers with the words they select. You should be especially wary of connotations when the author's primary purpose is to persuade. For example, which of these descriptions do you think I prefer?

> Dr. McGrath is petite, has reddish-brown hair, and a good sense of humor.
>
> Dr. McGrath is a runt, has reddish-brown hair, and a good sense of humor.

Yes, even though I have a good sense of humor, I do prefer being called petite. Why? Because even though both petite and runt mean "short" in the dictionary, they make me feel differently because of their connotations. For me, the connotation of petite is positive: small and delicate. The connotation of runt, is negative: unnaturally short.

For example, consider the similarities and differences between the denotative and connotative meanings of the italicized words in each pair of passages.

Jeff was very *confident* he would get the job because he scored well on the written exam.

Jeff was very *cocky* about getting the job because he scored well on the written exam.

Because they felt so strongly about the issue, Karen and Bill took part in a *rally* at the capital.

Because they felt so strongly about the issue, Karen and Bill took part in a *demonstration* at the capital.

In everyday reading, however, you don't have two versions of the same passage to compare. Therefore, once you have determined the literal meaning, ask yourself if the word or phrase makes you feel or react—positively or negatively—beyond its meaning. Determine whether the word seems to soften the impact of the message (*anti-personnel weapon* instead of *bomb*) or intensify your reaction to the message (*guerrilla fighters* instead of *freedom fighters*). Authors choose words for their maximum impact—including their connotative meaning. You must understand both the denotative and connotative meaning of the words to fully understand the author's message. We'll take another look at how authors influence us by their choice of words in Chapter 6.

PRACTICE: CONSIDERING BOTH THE CONNOTATIVE AND DENOTATIVE MEANINGS

Read each pair of words. List their literal definitions and then describe their connotations.

1. a. jock   b. athlete
2. a. reserved   b. inhibited
3. a. collect   b. hoard
4. a. impertinent b. bold

Read each passage with special attention to the italicized phrases. Why do you think the author selected those words? What message does the author want to convey? What other words or phrases could be used that would be more neutral?

5. After *unsuccessfully peddling his idea to every monarch of Western Europe*, Columbus finally interested the rulers of Spain. (Unger, *These United States*)

6. By *crushing black leaders*, while *inflating the images of Uncle Toms* and celebrities from the world of sport and play, the mass media were *able to channel and control the aspirations and goals of the black masses*. (Cleaver, *Soul On Ice*)

7. To many minds, Hillary Clinton [was] *the quintessential yuppie mother* of the 1990s, juggling career and family with remarkable skill. (Editorial, *The Arizona Republic*)

8. Exemptions from ESA (the Endangered Species Act) can be granted by the *so-called God Squad*, which is convened at the request of the U.S. Secretary of the Interior. (Berke, "The Audubon View," *Audubon*)

WHAT IS FIGURATIVE LANGUAGE?

> From my drifting hot air balloon, the Hawaiian Islands looked like bread crumbs floating in a bowl of soup.

> Enthusiasm bubbled out of petite 22-year old Chrissy Oliver with the effervescence of a just-opened split of champagne.

> Homelessness is a rusty blade cutting through the soul of humanity.

Each of these statements is an example of figurative language: using words in an imaginative way to help the reader comprehend the message more clearly. Certainly, I could have written the statements literally: "The Hawaiian Islands look small," "Chrissy Oliver was happy to win the race," or "Homelessness causes untold problems," but I would have taken the risk that you could not picture exactly what I wanted you to understand.

Although figurative language may not make sense literally, it does help you form a mental image, or picture, of what an author is talking about. Figurative expressions often compare something the author thinks you already know about to what he or she wants you to understand. The most basic of these comparisons are called similes (direct comparisons using the words "like" or "as") and metaphors (implied comparisons).

When a passage doesn't make sense to you at the literal level, check to see if the author is using figurative language. If so, use the author's words to draw a mental picture definition and fit that back into the context.

For example, what does historian John Lukacs compare the problems of America to in this paragraph? What does he want you to picture and understand from the figurative expressions in this passage?

> As the great French thinker Georges Beranos once wrote: "The worst, the most corrupting lies are problems wrongly stated." To put this in biological terms: without an honest diagnosis there can be no therapy, only further decay and perhaps even death. So I must sum up seven deadly sins of misdiagnosis: seven deadly problems that now face this country because of their intellectual misstatements. (Lukacs, *Our Seven Deadly Sins of Misdiagnosis*)

Lukacs wants you to picture the nation as a sick person to whom the doctor has given the wrong diagnosis. Before the person (the nation) can be cured, the illness (the problem) has to be correctly identified.

In this paragraph, training and development specialist Ron Zemke employs two comparisons. What does he want you to picture and understand from the figurative expressions?

> The auditorium lights grow dim. A diffusion of sunrise hues washes languidly across a sweep of rear-projection screens. From beneath stage level, rising in single file like a septet of hunter's moons, come the seven letters of the sacred rite: Q-U-A-L-I-T-Y. (Zemke, "Faith, Hope and TQM" *Training*)

In the second sentence Zemke compares the slides coming on the screen to a slow, colorful sunrise. Then he compares the appearance of the seven (septet) letters of the word QUALITY to the wondrous appearance of large, bright (hunter's) moons. (Note: When you have difficulty understanding a part of the figurative comparison, like "Hunter's moons," check with one of your resources to get the literal meaning of the expression. You must understand the literal before the figurative will make sense.)

PRACTICE: UNDERSTANDING FIGURATIVE LANGUAGE

Describe what the author is comparing, and what you should picture and understand from the figurative language in each of these passages.

1. This is our hope. This is the faith that I go back to the South with. With this faith we will be able to hew out of the mountain of despair a stone of hope. With this faith we will be able to transform the jangling discords of our nation into a beautiful symphony of brotherhood. (Martin Luther King Jr., "I Have A Dream," speech delivered in Washington, D.C., August 28, 1963)

2. The performance improvement efforts of many companies have as much impact on operational and financial results as a ceremonial rain dance has on the weather. (Schaffer and Thompson, "Successful Change Begins with Program Results," *Harvard Business Review*)

3. "Whatever women do—even just wiggling their thumbs—their neuron activity is more greatly distributed throughout the brain," says Dr. Mark George, a psychiatrist and neurologist at the Medical University of South Carolina.

   When a man puts his mind to work, neurons turn on in highly specific areas of the brain. When a woman does, her brain cells light up such a patchwork that the scans look like a night view of Las Vegas. (Hales, "If You Think We Think Alike, Think Again," *Ladies' Home Journal*)

4. Their great love, in which she lived completely immersed, seemed to be ebbing away, like the water of a river that was sinking into its own bed; and she saw the mud at the bottom. (Flaubert, *Madame Bovary*)

5. The flowering of Etruscan civilization coincides with the Archaic age in Greece. During this period, especially near the end of the sixth and early in the fifth century B.C., Etruscan art showed its greatest vigor. (Janson and Janson, *A Basic History of Art*)

6. But time has proven that R. E. "Ted" Turner—Captain Outrageous to the press—is crazy like a fox. (Griffin and Ebert, *Business*)

REVIEW QUESTIONS

1. Discuss your overall strategy for defining unfamiliar words.
2. Explain how to use context clues to help define a word and list two types of clues that authors use.
3. Explain what it means to use the parts of the word to help define it. Give one example.
4. List two other resources for defining unfamiliar words and when you might use them.
5. State the difference between the denotation and connotation of a word. Give an example of how a word can have a connotative meaning beyond its dictionary meaning.
6. Explain why it is important to understand both the denotative and connotative meanings of words and phrases.
7. Explain the purpose of figurative language and give an example.

THINK AND CONNECT QUESTIONS

8. Reread "Computers: The Essentials," by Larry Long and Nancy Long, Chapter 1, Exercise #4. Identify three unfamiliar words you came across when you first read it and describe the strategies you used to figure them out. Now that you have some additional strategies, would you go about defining them any differently? Why or why not?

9. Reread "Wild Things," by Nick Taylor, Chapter 2, Exercise #4. Identify two figurative expressions and explain what the author wanted you to picture.

APPLICATION EXERCISES

10. From recent newspapers or magazines, select an article you think uses a word or phrase for its connotative meaning. Explain why you think the author used the language. Rewrite the word or phrase keeping the literal meaning but changing the connotation.

WEB EXERCISE

11. Log onto one of these dictionary sites or use a search directory/engine to locate a dictionary.

http://www.m-w.com/netdict.htm
http://www.dictionary.com/
http://www.facstaff.bucknell.edu/rbeard/diction.html

Find these three words: (1) *cliché*, (2) *thesaurus*, (3) *jargon*. Write down their definitions and turn them in to your professor.

USE YOUR STRATEGIES—EXERCISE #1

Jimmy Tomlin writes columns and features for the *High Point North Carolina Enterprise* and various national magazines. "Mistletoe" is from Delta Airlines' *Sky* magazine.

Mistletoe: Harmless Holiday Sprig? Or Something Far Worse?

Jimmy Tomlin

[1]This season, if you chance to catch a comely member of the opposite sex beneath a sprig of mistletoe, try not to think, as I now do, about white-robed priests running around in the woods, kissing one another.

[2]Before I started researching this article, I innocently viewed a peck under the mistletoe as a quaint custom—a notion shared by no less an authority than Michael Christian, who wrote *The Art of Kissing* (under the pen name William Cane). "Some women have told me they like to buy a lot of mistletoe because they like to get a lot of kisses," Christian told me, "and they hang it all over the place, as sort of a way to encourage friendly contact."

[3]I could have spent the rest of my life blithely ignorant of the origins of the custom. But no. I had to set off on a quest for knowledge that led to the forests of Olde England and to tales of mischievous Norse gods.

[4]How did mistletoe—considered a parasite in the plant world—become a mild aphrodisiac? Why not, say, holly or hemp?

[5]The short answer is, we're not sure.

[6]We do know, however, that through the ages in many cultures mistletoe has been held in high esteem as a potent plant.

[7]Some peoples, for example, believed mistletoe guaranteed fertility; others used it as a birth-control substance. Its medicinal powers have been said to cure everything from epilepsy, vertigo and tremors to toothaches, measles and dog bites. My advice? Don't try this at home.

[8]Soldiers of some cultures have even worn sprigs of the plant into battle, believing it offered them some sort of mystical protection. Similarly, during the Middle Ages, the superstitious hung branches of mistletoe from their ceilings to ward off evil spirits. They also believed a sprig of mistletoe in a baby's cradle would protect the child from fairies.

[9]The Druids, a class of priests among the Celts of ancient Britain, regarded both mistletoe and the oak tree, on which mistletoe grew, as sacred. During late-night rituals that included animal sacrifices, the white-robed Druids used golden sickles to cut down sprigs of mistletoe. Then they distributed the plant among the people, believing that it would protect their homes from thunder and lightning.

[10]During those pagan ceremonies, the Druid priests embraced and kissed one another, which some folklorists say is the origin of kissing under mistletoe.

[11]A more charming explanation of the tradition can be traced to Norse mythology. In a story of myth, mistletoe, madness and murder, the Norse god Balder, son of the chief god, Odin, began having terrible nightmares about his own death. He confided his fears to his mother, Frigg, who procured a solemn oath from all things in heaven and earth never to harm her precious son. All except mistletoe, which Frigg found too harmless-looking to bother with.

[12]The gods made a sport of throwing things at Balder. Sticks and stones fell short of striking him; swords bounced off him—until the blind god Hoder, prodded by the prankster Loki, threw some mistletoe at him, which pierced Balder's body and killed him instantly.

[13]Interesting story, you might say, but what does it have to do with kissing, other than mistletoe being the kiss of death for Balder?

[14]Well, in at least one version of the myth, the shaft of mistletoe was removed and Balder came back to life. Frigg was so thankful that she made mistletoe a symbol of love and good will, and she promised a kiss to anyone passing beneath it.

[15]How we made the leap from Druids and Norse gods to kissing under mistletoe isn't clear. It does appear, however, that the custom became popular in such countries as England and Germany, where families and friends gathered under the "kissing ball" to sing holiday carols and kiss. Charles Dickens even includes a mistletoe-inspired kiss in *The Pickwick Papers*.

[16]Traditionally, the proper procedure was for the gent to bestow upon the lass a single kiss for each berry removed from the mistletoe until there were no more berries. Time—and, no doubt, the introduction of artificial greenery—has for the most part ended that tradition.

[17]And whereas a kiss beneath the mistletoe these days is usually considered nothing more than a sign

of friendship and good cheer, it was once regarded as a promise to marry. By the same token, it was believed a young woman not kissed under the mistletoe would not be married before the following Christmas.

[18]So kiss as you will, dear readers, but keep your lips off the mistletoe itself. While some people still believe the plant has medicinal benefits, health experts warn that mistletoe can stimulate the central nervous system, increase blood pressure and cause nausea.

[19]Of course, kissing under it can have precisely the same effects.

EXERCISE #1 QUESTIONS

1. What is Tomlin's purpose?
2. Do you think Tomlin is knowledgeable on this topic? Why or why not?
3. Write the meanings of these words and phrases:
   a. comely (¶1)
   b. quaint (¶2)
   c. pen name (¶2)
   d. blithely ignorant (¶3)
   e. parasite (¶4)
   f. aphrodisiac (¶4)
   g. potent (¶6)
   h. pagan ceremonies (¶10)

USE YOUR STRATEGIES—EXERCISE #2

Pulitzer Prize winning historian Irwin Unger has been teaching American history for over twenty-five years on both coasts. He now teaches at New York University. "The Knowledge Industries" is excerpted from Chapter 28, "The Dissenting Sixties" of *These United States*, Volume II: Since 1865.

The Knowledge Industries

Irwin Unger

[1]The accumulation and diffusion of knowledge helped fuel the decade's [the 1960s] economic boom. In some ways this knowledge explosion was the pay-off from years of previous scientific advances. It also owed much to the great postwar outlays for research and higher education. In 1950 Congress had established the National Science Foundation to encourage research, especially in areas related to national defense. By 1957 outlays for research and development (R&D) by public and private organizations had reached almost $10 billion annually. Meanwhile, the country's higher education system surged dramatically. In 1940, the last full peacetime year, there were 1.5 million college students; by 1950 there were 2.6 million. From the mid-1950s on, the country's support of what would later be called the "knowledge industries" was dazzling by any previous standard.

[2]Some Americans complained that the public schools were not teaching children to read or to calculate and blamed it on John Dewey's disciples, the "progressive educators." But most citizens were proud of the job the nation was doing. Their complacency was suddenly shattered when, in October 1957, the Russians put a hollow steel ball called "Sputnik" into orbit around the earth. Having long considered their nation the world's scientific and technological leader, Americans were dismayed to discover that they had been abruptly pushed off their pinnacle by their chief international rival.

[3]For the next few years Americans subjected themselves to one of their periodic agonizing reappraisals of education. A dozen books were soon echoing the complaints of earlier critics about American educational failings. Public dismay over Sputnik induced Congress in 1958 to pass the National Defense Education Act, providing large federal outlays for scientific and language training for college students. By 1970 federal appropriations for research had almost tripled, and federal funding of higher education was four times as high as it had been ten years earlier. Industrial firms, universities, and foundations also invested billions in basic scientific research and the development of new products.

[4]Booming research and industrial growth made a college education even more valuable than in the past, and with the postwar "baby-boom" generation reaching their late teens, there were also more eligible college-age students. By 1970, some 7 million young men and women were enrolled in colleges and universities, an increase of nearly 500 percent in little more than a generation.

EXERCISE #2 QUESTIONS

1. What is Unger's purpose for this section?
2. Do you think Unger is knowledgeable on this topic? Why or why not?
3. Write the meaning of these words and phrases:
   a. accumulation and diffusion of knowledge (¶1)
   b. outlays (¶1)
   c. system surged dramatically (¶2)
   d. complacency was suddenly shattered (¶2)
   e. abruptly pushed off their pinnacle (¶2)
   f. periodic agonizing reappraisals of education (¶3)
   g. echoing the complaints (¶3)
   h. induced (¶3)

Robert McGrath is a freelance writer. His work appears in numerous national publications. This selection, "Hummingbirds," is from *FEDCO Reporter*.

Hummingbirds: Jewels On Wings
Robert L. McGrath

[1]You've probably enjoyed watching those tiny rainbow-pinioned helicopters hover at the feeder in your backyard—or perhaps at your neighbor's. But how much do you really know about these jewels on wings?

[2]Hummingbirds come in a variety of colors, though mostly in the same diminutive size that makes them stand out as among nature's most remarkable creatures.

[3]There are more than 300 kinds, but amazingly, only the ruby-throated hummingbird is found east of the Mississippi River. Western states are home to as many as 18 different types, with the bulk of the others in the family inhabiting Central and South America. None are found outside the Western Hemisphere.

[4]Their kaleidoscopic plumage has no solid color. Instead, there are tiny barbs on each feather, placed so they break and refract light, just as a mirror or a diamond will do. While the male hummingbird is more colorful than his mate, underparts of both male and female are usually gray or a variety of other shades, while head and back are often a glowing green.

[5]The birds sport so many patches of different tints, they're often named after precious jewels—ruby, topaz, emerald, amethyst-throated.

[6]Those whirring wing-beats are made possible by special hinges within their bone-structure that permit helicopter-like rapid vibrating and feathering. Suspended or backward flight requires about 54 wing-beats per second, while normal dodging, darting flight reaching 50 miles per hour takes up to 75 beats of its narrow wings.

[7]Because it uses so much energy in flight, a hummingbird goes into a state resembling hibernation at night when it rests from a constant labor of gathering food. When awake, its normal temperature is over 100 degrees; it falls to as low as 64 degrees when it's asleep. The hummingbird's heartbeat, however, is super fast. While human beings average 72 beats a minute, the hummer's regular rate is 615 beats a minute when in flight.

[8]The territorial-minded male hummingbird vigorously defends his space against other birds, cats, or even snakes. Yet, once he has selected his mate and courtship is complete, the male leaves everything else to his partner. She alone builds the solid little nest—so small a quarter placed on top of it would stick out over the edges—using plant fibers, lichens, and bark, then cementing this miniature cup with saliva glue and spider webs.

[9]It takes 21 days for the female to hatch her two pea-sized pearly eggs. She then begins the endless duty of feeding the helpless, ever-hungry chicks by herself, a task lasting three weeks, when the fledglings are ready to fly.

[10]Anyone with a hummingbird feeder can enjoy a thrill a minute watching these winged wonders display their aerial antics—the most exciting in the world of birds.

EXERCISE #3 QUESTIONS

1. What is McGrath's purpose?
2. Do you think McGrath is knowledgeable on this topic? Why or why not?
3. Write the meanings of these words and phrases:
   a. hover (¶1)
   b. diminutive size (¶2)
   c. state resembling hibernation (¶7)
   d. territorial-minded (¶8)
   e. fledglings (¶9)
   f. aerial antics (¶10)
4. Identify and explain:
   a. 2 figurative phrases in paragraph 1
   b. 2 figurative phrases in paragraph 4
   c. 1 figurative phrase in paragraph 9

Ellen Goodman is an internationally syndicated columnist. This selection, "Drop the Ball on Sports Metaphors in Political Coverage," first appeared in the *Boston Globe*.

Drop the Ball on Sports Metaphors in Political Coverage

Ellen Goodman

¹The crocuses are a-blooming, the Ides of March and the Ides of Super Tuesday are here. So, by all these portents, it must be time for my quadrennial plea against the use of sports metaphors in writing, speaking and thinking about politics.

²This has been a long, personal and so far entirely futile attempt on my part to have an impact on the rhetoric of democracy. By my calculations, politics has been described as the great American sport ever since the first election was called a race and the candidate became a winner.

PLAY-BY-PLAY ANALYSIS

³But sports reached a saturation point in the '80s when politicians began to sound like the Wide World of Sports, and the media turned from analysis to play-by-play. One favorite mixed sports metaphor came in 1984 from Lawton Chiles, now the governor of Florida, who described the "game plan" for the presidential debates this way: "It's like a football game.... Mondale can't get the ball back with one big play. But the American people love a horse race. I would advise him not to knock Reagan out."

⁴Well, as expected, the 1992 campaign began with the usual assortment of slam-dunks, knockout punches, end runs and hard balls. But something happened after the campaign left New Hampshire and relative civility. While I was trying to get out of the locker room, we ended up in the trenches.

⁵The metaphors switched from sports to war. The political coverage reads less like "Sports Illustrated" than "Soldier of Fortune."

⁶We have campaign "assaults" and "attacks." The Super Tuesday states are "battlegrounds." The candidates "snipe" and "take aim" at each other. Jerry Brown is accused of using "slash-and-burn" tactics. Paul Tsongas is "under fire." And Pat Buchanan is a man who will "take no prisoners."

PLAYING FIELD TO KILLING FIELD

⁷How did this primary get off the playing field and onto the killing field? Kathleen Jamieson, political wordsmith and dean of the University of Pennsylvania's Annenberg School of Communication, says that war images creep in as a campaign gets, well, hostile.

⁸"When you are playing fairly within the rules of the game, the sports metaphors fit. The war metaphor is much more negative. It doesn't assume fair play or a referee."

⁹If words are the way we frame our ideas, the war metaphor is more than rhetoric. It forces us to talk and think about elections as if they were lethally combative events in which the object was to kill the enemy and declare victory. In the end, the war metaphor produces a victor or a commander-in-chief. But not necessarily a governor, or a leader, or a problem-solver.

¹⁰War talk doesn't allow the candidates to describe or stand on common ground. "It doesn't assume the goodwill and integrity of the other side," says Ms. Jamieson, "It doesn't talk about common good and collective ends. It assumes one person is right and the other's wrong."

SEARCH-AND-DESTROY MISSION

¹¹As for the media and the metaphor, fighting words frame the campaign as a search-and-destroy mission. It is not a coincidence that attack ads make the headlines. Nor is it a coincidence, says Ms. Jamieson, that men are much more likely to talk like warriors and write like war correspondents.

¹²Ms. Jamieson herself has been trying to elaborate a different political campaign language. She first played with a courtship metaphor since the candidates do woo the electorate and pledge forms of fidelity. That was, to put it mildly, fraught with sexual undertones.

¹³In New Hampshire, a focus group came up with the metaphor of an orchestra. The government is, after all, a collective entity that needs a leader to keep things in harmony. This had a nice ring, but it didn't hit all the right notes.

¹⁴Now Ms. Jamieson is toying with a metaphor that would picture the campaign as a quest. In the vernacular of the "quest" metaphor, the candidates would overcome "tests" that reveal their "character."

[15]The campaign would become a "search" for answers, not for the soft underbelly of an opponent.

[16]The point is to shift the verbal focus from strategy—"Is he doing what's necessary to win?"—to problems—"Does he understand them, can he solve them?" Her own quest for this "quest" metaphor has just begun. Any ideas are welcome in our metaphor mailbag.

[17]In the meantime, in the spirit of candidates and those who cover them, block that war metaphor. Tackle it if you must. There are already enough bodies on the combat field, careers blown to smithereens and land mines planted for the fall election. All we have learned so far this election year is that politics is hell.

EXERCISE #4 QUESTIONS

1. What is Goodman's purpose?
2. Explain these words and phrases:
   a. portents (¶1)
   b. quadrennial plea against the use of sports metaphors (¶1)
   c. futile (¶2)
   d. rhetoric of democracy (¶2)
   e. mixed sports metaphor (¶3)
   f. relative civility (¶4)
   g. political coverage reads less like "Sports Illustrated" than "Soldier of Fortune." (¶5)
   h. the war metaphor is more than rhetoric (¶9)
   i. lethally combative events (¶9)
   j. courtship metaphor (¶12)
   k. metaphor of an orchestra (¶13)
   l. vernacular (¶14)
   m. soft underbelly of an opponent (¶15)
   n. block that war metaphor (¶17)

USE YOUR STRATEGIES—EXERCISE #5

Mary Lynn Hendrix is a science writer in the Office of Scientific Information, National Institute of Mental Health (NIMH). Scientific review was provided by NIMH staff members Thomas R. Insel, M.D.; Dennis L. Murphy, M.D.; Teresa A. Pigott, M.D.; Judith L. Rapoport, M.D.; Barry Wolfe, Ph.D.; and Joseph Zohar, M.D.

Obsessive-Compulsive Disorder

Mary Lynn Hendrix

WHAT IS OCD?

[1]In the mental illness called OCD (obsessive-compulsive disorder), a person becomes trapped in a pattern of repetitive thoughts and behaviors that are senseless and distressing but extremely difficult to overcome. The following are typical examples of OCD:

[2]Troubled by repeated thoughts that she may have contaminated herself by touching doorknobs and other "dirty" objects, a teenage girl spends hours every day washing her hands. Her hands are red and raw, and she has little time for social activities.

[3]A middle-aged man is tormented by the notion that he may injure others through carelessness. He has difficulty leaving his home because he must first go through a lengthy ritual of checking and rechecking the gas jets and water faucets to make certain that they are turned off.

[4]If OCD becomes severe enough, it can destroy a person's capacity to function in the home, at work, or at school. That is why it is important to learn about the disorder and the treatments that are now available.

HOW COMMON IS OCD?

[5]For many years, mental health professionals thought of OCD as a very rare disease because only a small minority of their patients had the condition. But it is believed that many of those afflicted with OCD, in efforts to keep their repetitive thoughts and behaviors secret, fail to seek treatment. This has led to underestimates of the number of people with the illness. However, a recent survey by the National Institute of Mental Health (NIMH)—the Federal agency that supports research nationwide on the brain, mental illness, and mental health—has provided new understanding about the prevalence of OCD. The NIMH survey shows that this disorder may affect as much as 2 percent of the population, meaning that OCD is more common than schizophrenia and other severe mental illnesses.

EXERCISE #5 QUESTIONS

1. What is Hendrix's purpose?
2. Do you think Hendrix is knowledgeable on this topic? Why or why not? What impact does the scientific review panel have on your view?
3. Write the meanings of these words and phrases and what strategies you used to get each one.
   a. OCD (¶1)
   b. repetitive (¶1)
   c. contaminated (¶2)
   d. tormented (¶3)
   e. ritual (¶3)
   f. capacity to function (¶4)
   g. afflicted (¶5)
   h. underestimates (¶5)
   i. prevalence (¶5)
   j. affect (¶5)
   k. schizophrenia (¶5)

A. Think about the reading demands you have this semester. Discuss how important you think your ability to understand the author's language is to successful comprehension. How important do you think understanding vocabulary is when you are listening to a lecture?

B. Describe a time when you used a particular word, in writing or speaking, because of its connotation. What was your purpose? Were you successful? Has anyone successfully convinced you to do or not do something by their choice of words?

Main Idea Chapter 2

- What is a topic?
- What is a main idea?
- What are supporting details?
- What is a summary?

Kabuki Theater by Utagawa Toyokuni (1795–1825). Color woodblock print, 38.5 × 26.0 cm. Musée des Arts Asiatiques-Guimet, Paris, France. Photo: Arnaudet. Copyright Réunion des Musées Nationaux/Art Resource, NY.

What Is a Main Idea?

The **main idea** of a passage is the central message that the author is trying to convey about the material. It is a sentence that condenses thoughts and details into a general, all-inclusive statement of the author's message.

Comprehending the main idea is crucial to your comprehension of text, and many experts believe that it is the most important reading skill. In fact, if all reading comprehension techniques were combined and reduced to one essential question, that question might be, "What is the main idea the author is trying to get across to the reader?" Whether you read a single paragraph, a chapter, or an entire book, your most important single task is to understand the main idea of what you read.

Labels for Main Idea

Reading specialists use various terms when referring to the main idea. In classroom discussions, all of the following words are sometimes used to help students understand the meaning of *main idea:*

main point

central focus

gist

controlling idea

central thought

thesis

The last word on the list, *thesis,* is a familiar word in English composition classes. Students usually have had practice in stating a thesis sentence for English essays, but they have not had as much practice in stating the main idea of a reading selection. Recognizing the similarity between a thesis and a main idea statement will help to clarify the concept.

Importance of Prior Knowledge in Main Idea

Research has been done investigating the processes readers use to construct main ideas. One researcher, Peter Afflerbach,[1] asked graduate students and uni-

---

[1] P. Afflerbach, "How Are Main Idea Statements Constructed? Watch the Experts!," *Journal of Reading* 30 (1987): 512–518; and "The Influence of Prior Knowledge on Expert Readers' Main Idea Construction Strategies," *Reading Research Quarterly* 25 (1990): 31–46.

versity professors to "think aloud" as they read passages on both familiar and unfamiliar topics. These expert readers spoke their thoughts to the researcher before, during, and after reading. From these investigations, Afflerbach concluded that expert readers use different strategies for familiar and unfamiliar materials.

This research showed that *already knowing something about the topic is the key* to easy reading. When readers are familiar with the subject, constructing the main idea is effortless and, in many cases, automatic. These readers quickly assimilate the unfolding text into already well-developed knowledge networks. They seem to organize text into chunks for comprehension and later retrieval. These "informed" readers do not have to struggle with an information overload.

By contrast, expert readers with little prior knowledge of the subject are absorbed in trying to make meaning out of unfamiliar words and confusing sentences. Because they are struggling to recognize ideas, few mental resources remain for constructing a main idea. These "uninformed" experts were reluctant to guess at a main idea and to predict a topic. Instead, they preferred to read all the information before trying to make sense of it. Constructing the main idea was a difficult and deliberate task for these expert readers.

Main Idea Strategies

The following strategies for getting the main idea were reported by Afflerbach's expert readers. Can you see the differences in the thinking processes of the informed and uninformed experts?

"Informed" Expert Readers

Strategy 1: The informed expert readers skimmed the passage before reading and took a guess at the main idea. Then they read for corroboration.

Strategy 2: The informed experts automatically paused while reading to summarize or reduce information. They frequently stopped at natural breaks in the material to let ideas fall into place.

"Uninformed" Expert Readers

Strategy 1: Expert readers who did not know about the subject were unwilling to take a guess at the main idea. Instead they read the material, decided on a topic, and then looked back to pull together a main idea statement.

Strategy 2: The uninformed experts read the material and they reviewed it to find key terms and concepts. They tried to bring the key terms and concepts together into a main idea statement.

Strategy 3: The uninformed experts read the material and then proposed a main idea statement. They double-checked the passage to clarify or revise the main idea statement.

What differences do you see in these approaches? Since introductory college textbooks address many topics that are new and unfamiliar, freshmen readers will frequently need to use the strategies of uninformed expert readers to comprehend the main ideas of their college texts. Until prior knowledge is built for the different college courses, main idea construction for course textbooks is likely to be a *conscious effort* rather than an automatic phenomenon.

What Is a Topic?

The **topic** of a passage is like a title. It is a word, name, or phrase that labels the subject but does not reveal the specific contents of the passage. The topic is a general rather than specific term and forms an umbrella under which the specific ideas or details in the passage can be grouped. For example, what general term would pull together and unify the following items?

Items: carrots

            lettuce

            onions   Topic? _____

            potatoes

Exercise 4.1

Identifying Topics

Each of the following lists includes four specific items or ideas that could relate to a single topic. At the end of each list, write a general topic that could form an umbrella under which the specific ideas can be grouped.

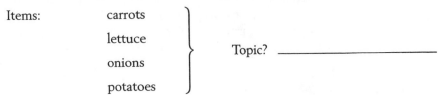

1. shirt	2. psychology	3. democracy	4. Bermuda	5. coffee
pants	history	autocracy	Cuba	tea
jacket	sociology	oligarchy	Haiti	cola
sweater	political science	monarchy	Tahiti	chocolate
_____	_____	_____	_____	_____

How Do Topics and Main Ideas Differ?

Topics are general categories, like titles, but they are not main ideas. In the previous list, caffeine is a general term or topic that unifies the items, *coffee, tea, cola,* and *chocolate.* If those items were used as details in a paragraph, the main idea could not be expressed by simply saying "caffeine." The word *caffeine* would answer the question, "What was the passage about?" but not the second question, "What is the author's main idea?"

A writer could actually devise several very different paragraphs about caffeine using the same four details as support. If you were assigned to write a paragraph about caffeine, using the four items as details, what would be the main idea or thesis of your paragraph?

Topic: Caffeine

Main idea or thesis: _____

Read the following examples of different main ideas that could be developed in a paragraph about caffeine.

1. Consumption of caffeine is not good for your health. (Details would enumerate health hazards associated with each item.)
2. Americans annually consume astonishing amounts of caffeine. (Details would describe amounts of each consumed annually.)
3. Caffeine can wake up an otherwise sluggish mind. (Details would explain the popular use of each item as a stimulant.)
4. Reduce caffeine consumption with the decaffeinated version of popular caffeine-containing beverages. (Details would promote the decaffeinated version of each item.)

EXAMPLE Below are examples of a topic, main idea, and supporting detail.

Topic ————➤ **Early Cognitive Development**

Main Idea ————➤ { Cognitive psychologists sometimes study young children to observe the very beginnings of cognitive activity. For example, when children first be-

Detail ————➤ gin to utter words and sentences, they overgeneralize what they know and make language more consistent than it actually is.

Christopher Peterson, *Introduction to Psychology*

EXPLANATION The topic pulls our attention to a general area, and the main idea provides the focus. The detail offers elaboration and support.

Exercise 4.2

Differentiating Topic, Main Idea, and Supporting Details

This exercise is designed to check your ability to differentiate statements of the main idea from topic and specific supporting details. Compare the items within each group and indicate whether each one is a statement of the main idea *(MI)*, a topic *(T)*, or a specific supporting detail *(SD)*.

Group 1

_____ a. For poor farm families, life on the plains meant a sod house or a dugout carved out of the hillside for protection from the winds.

_____ b. One door and usually no more than a single window provided light and air.

_____ c. Sod houses on the plains

James W. Davidson et al., *Nation of Nations*

Group 2

_____ a. She was the daughter of English poet Lord Byron and of a mother who was a gifted mathematician.

_____ b. Babbage and the Programming Countess

_____ c. Ada, the Countess of Lovelace, helped develop the instructions for doing computer programming computations on Babbage's analytical engine.

_____ d. In addition, she published a series of notes that eventually led others to accomplish what Babbage himself had been unable to do.

H. L. Capron, *Computers*, 5th ed. (adapted)

Group 3

_____ a. As a group, for instance, Generation Xers try harder to work around employees' childcare needs by creating flexible schedules, and many encourage workers to bring their children—and even their pets—to the workplace for visits.

_____ b. Generation X entrepreneurs differ

_____ c. Generation Xers are choosing to run their companies differently from how their parents might have done.

_____ d. Their goal is to recognize and reward people for the contributions they make rather than for their titles in the corporate hierarchy.

From Ronald Ebert and Ricky Griffin, *Business Essentials*, 2nd ed. (adapted)

Group 4

_____ a. Mexican American Political Gains

_____ b. During the 1960s four Mexican Americans—Senator Joseph Montoya of New Mexico and representatives Eligio de la Garza and Henry B. Gonzales of Texas and Edward R. Roybal of California—were elected to Congress.

_____ c. In 1974 two Chicanos were elected governors—Jerry Apodaca in New Mexico and Raul Castro in Arizona—becoming the first Mexican-American governors since early in this century.

_____ d. Since 1960 Mexican Americans have made important political gains.

James Kirby Martin et al., *America and Its Peoples*, 4th ed., vol. 2, pp. 898–99

Questioning for the Main Idea

To determine the main idea of a paragraph, an article, or a book, follow the three basic steps listed in the box on page 131. The order of the questions may vary depending on your prior knowledge of the material. If the material is familiar, main idea construction may be automatic and thus a selection of significant supporting details would follow. If the material is unfamiliar, as frequently occurs in textbook reading, identifying the details through key terms and concepts would come first and from them you would form a main idea statement.

 Reader's Tip

Finding the Main Idea

* **Establish the topic.** Who or what is this about? What general word or phrase names the subject? The topic should be broad enough to include all the ideas, yet restrictive enough to focus on the direction of the details. For example, identifying the topic of an article as "politics," "federal politics," or "corruption in federal politics" might all be correct, but the last may be the most descriptive of the actual contents.

* **Identify the key supporting terms.** What are the major supporting details? Look at the details that seem to be significant to see if they point in a particular direction. What aspect of the subject do they address? What seems to be the common message? Details such as kickbacks to senators, overspending on congressional junkets, and lying to the voters could support the idea of "corruption in federal politics."

* **Focus on the message of the topic.** What is the main idea the author is trying to convey about the topic?

This statement should be

A complete sentence

Broad enough to include the important details

Focused enough to describe the author's slant

The author's main idea about corruption in federal politics might be that voters need to ask for an investigation of seemingly corrupt practices by federal politicians.

Read the following example, and answer the questions for determining the main idea.

EXAMPLE

New high-speed machines also brought danger to the workplace. If a worker succumbed to boredom, fatigue, or simple miscalculation, disaster could strike. Each year of the late nineteenth century some 35,000 wage earners were killed by industrial accidents. In Pittsburgh iron and steel mills alone, in one year 195 men died from hot metal explosions, asphyxiation, and falls, some into pits of molten metal. Men and women working in textile mills were poisoned by the thick dust and fibers in the air; similar toxic atmospheres injured those working in anything from twine-making plants to embroidery factories. Railways, with their heavy equipment and unaccustomed speed, were especially dangerous. In Philadelphia over half the railroad workers who died between 1886 and 1890 were killed by accidents. For injury or death, workers and their families could expect no payment from employers, since the idea of worker's compensation was unknown.

James W. Davidson et al., *Nation of Nations*

1. Who or what is this about? _____

2. What are the major details? _____

3. What is the main idea the author is trying to convey about the topic?

_____

EXPLANATION The passage is about injuries from machines. The major details are 35,000 killed, 195 died from explosions, etc., poisoned by dust, and half of rail workers killed. The main idea is that new high-speed machines brought danger to the workplace.

What Do Details Do?

Look at the details in the picture on page 133 to decide what message the photographer is trying to communicate. Determine the topic of the picture, propose a main idea using your prior knowledge, and then list some of the significant details that support this point.

What is the topic? _____

_____

What are the significant supporting details? _____

_____

What is the point the photograph is trying to convey about the topic?

_____

The topic of the picture is baseball. The details show a player, whose name is Jones, making a giant leap into the stands to catch the ball, but the ball is too high and too well hit. The fans are concentrating on the ball while moving back to avoid being hit. One fan, however, reaches with his mitt to catch the ball. This prepared fan also holds a target sign in his lap, indicating the place to hit a homerun ball. To make the photograph even more visually interesting, Jones's body is centered in the middle of the letters POW, as if he were stepping on the letter O. The main idea of the picture is the fielder has failed to

AP/Wide World Photos

catch a homerun hit. For baseball fans who want the exact details that are not disclosed in the picture, left fielder Jacque Jones (11) of the Minnesota Twins missed the homerun hit by Chicago White Sox's Ray Durham in the first inning in Minneapolis, Tuesday, June 26, 2001.

Details support, develop, and explain a main idea. Specific details can include reasons, incidents, facts, examples, steps, and definitions. The task of a reader is to recognize the major supporting details and to pull them together into a main idea. Being able to pick out major details implies that the reader has some degree of prior knowledge on the subject and has probably already begun to form some notion of the main idea.

Textbooks are packed full of details, but fortunately all details are not of equal importance. Major details tend to support, explain, and describe main ideas, whereas minor details tend to support, explain, and describe the major details. Ask the following questions to determine which details are major in importance and which are not:

1. Which details logically develop the main idea?
2. Which details help you understand the main idea?
3. Which details make you think the main idea you have chosen is correct?

Noticing key words that form transitional links from one idea to another can sometimes help the reader distinguish between major and minor details.

Stated and Unstated Main Ideas

Like paragraphs, pictures also suggest main ideas. Artists compose and select to communicate a message. Look at the picture shown here and then answer the questions that follow.

Association of American Publishers

What is the general topic of the picture? _____

What details seem important? _____

What is the main idea the artist is trying to convey about the topic?

_____

The topic of the picture is reading. The details show the actress Whoopi Goldberg sitting in an empty corridor on an improvised seat reading a book. The book title, *Peter Pan*, is written on the book as well as at the bottom of the page. We can assume that she is reading *Peter Pan* for pleasure, since it is fanciful and seldom required reading. We can also assume she has escaped to a quiet place for a few minutes of pleasurable reading. She is having fun and wants to be alone, but the camera has caught her. The main idea, "Get caught reading," is written at the bottom of the picture. The message is that we should copy this noted comedian and escape to enjoy a good book.

Now look at the picture below, which does not include a slogan or directly stated appeal. Again, answer the questions that follow.

AP/Wide World Photos

What is the general topic of the picture? _____

What details seem important? _____

What is the main idea the artist is trying to convey about the topic?

_____

The topic of the picture is a disaster. The building has collapsed and rescue workers with hard hats are moving rocks and looking for survivors and victims. Emergency personnel carry an orange body bag with the remains of a victim. The American flag at the top of the rubble indicates that this is in the United States. A fireman in uniform stands under the flag as smoke still rises from still-simmering fires in the rubble. The disaster is recent, and the site is dangerous. The main idea of this picture is that emergency rescue workers are trying to sort through this enormous disaster for possible pockets of life, as well as for victims. From the details and your prior knowledge, you will recognize that this is the World Trade Center disaster that occurred on September 11, 2001, when two hijacked airliners crashed into the towers in New York and destroyed both buildings.

As in the pictures, an author's main point can either be directly stated in the material or it can be unstated. When the main idea is stated in a sentence, the statement is called a **topic sentence** or **thesis statement.** Such a general statement is helpful to the reader because it provides an overview of the material. It does not, however, always express the author's opinion of the subject. For that reason, although helpful in overviewing, the topic sentence may not always form a complete statement of the author's main point.

Frequency of Stated Main Idea. Research shows that students find passages easier to comprehend when the main idea is directly stated within the passage. How often do stated main ideas appear in college textbooks? Should the reader expect to find that most paragraphs have stated main ideas?

For psychology texts, the answer seems to be about half and half. In a recent study,[2] stated main ideas appeared in *only 58 percent* of the sampled paragraphs in introductory psychology textbooks. In one of the books, the main idea was directly stated in 81 percent of the sampled paragraphs, and the researchers noted that the text was particularly easy to read.

Given these findings, we should recognize the importance of being skilled in locating and, especially, in constructing main ideas. In pulling ideas together to construct a main idea, you will be looking at the big picture and not be bound to the text in search of any single suggestive sentence.

Examples of Stated Main Idea

EXAMPLE

Managers can regain control over their time in several ways. One is by meeting whenever possible in someone else's office, so that they can leave as soon as their business is finished. Another is to start meetings on time without waiting for late-comers. The idea is to let late-comers adjust their schedules rather than everyone else adjusting theirs. A third is to set aside a block of time to work on an important project without interruption. This may require ignoring the telephone, being protected by an aggressive secretary, or hiding out. Whatever it takes is worth it.

Joseph Reitz and Linda Jewell, *Managing*

1. Who or what is this about? _____

2. What are the major details? _____

3. What is the main idea the author is trying to convey about the topic?

_____

EXPLANATION The passage is about managers controlling their time. The major details are *meet in another office, start meetings on time,* and *block out time to work.* The main idea, stated in the first sentence, is that managers can do things to control their time.

---

[2]B. Smith and N. Chase, "The Frequency and Placement of Main Idea Topic Sentences in College Psychology Textbooks." *Journal of College Reading and Learning* 24 (1991): 46–54.

Location of Stated Main Ideas. Should college readers wish for all passages in all textbooks to begin with stated main ideas? Indeed, research indicates that when the main idea is stated at the beginning of the passage, the text tends to be comprehended more easily. In their research, however, Smith and Chase found only 33 percent of the stated main ideas to be positioned as the first sentence of the paragraph.

Main idea statements can be positioned at the beginning, in the middle, or at the end of a paragraph. Both the beginning and concluding sentences of a passage can be combined for a main idea statement. The following examples and diagrams demonstrate the different possible positions for stated main ideas within paragraphs.

1. **An introductory statement of the main idea is given at the beginning of the paragraph.**

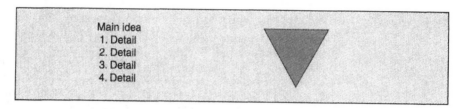

EXAMPLE

Under hypnosis, people may recall things that they are unable to remember spontaneously. Some police departments employ hypnotists to probe for information that crime victims do not realize they have. In 1976, twenty-six young children were kidnapped from a school bus near Chowchilla, California. The driver of the bus caught a quick glimpse of the license plate of the van in which he and the children were driven away. However, he remembered only the first two digits. Under hypnosis, he recalled the other numbers and the van was traced to its owners.

David Dempsey and Philip Zimbardo, *Psychology and You*

2. **A concluding statement of the main idea appears at the end of the paragraph.**

EXAMPLE

Research is not a once-and-for-all-times job. Even sophisticated companies often waste the value of their research. One of the most common errors is not providing a basis for comparisons. A company may research its market, find a need for a new advertising campaign, conduct the campaign, and then neglect to research the results. Another may simply feel the need for a new campaign, conduct it, and research the results. Neither is getting the full benefit of the research. When you fail to research either the results or your position *prior* to the campaign, you cannot know the effects of the campaign. *For good evaluation you must have both before and after data.*

Edward Fox and Edward Wheatley, Modern Marketing

3. Details are placed at the beginning to arouse interest, followed by a statement of the main idea in the middle of the paragraph.

EXAMPLE

What happens when foreign materials do enter the body by breaking through the skin or epithelial linings of the digestive, circulatory, or respiratory systems and after the clotting process is complete? The next line of defense comes into action. Phagocytic cells (wandering and stationary) may engulf the foreign material and destroy it. But there is another and very complicated aspect of the process. *This is the production of specific antibody molecules. Antibodies may circulate in the blood as mentioned or they may be bound to cells;* less is known about these cell-bound antibodies. Antibodies inactivate or destroy the activity of antigens by combining with them. The reaction is a manifestation of the immune response, and the discipline primarily devoted to its study is immunology. Generally immunity is considered to be peculiar to the vertebrates, but recent evidence suggests that a form of immunity occurs in invertebrate animals also.

Willis H. Johnson et al., Essentials of Biology

4. Both the introductory and concluding sentences state the main idea.

EXAMPLE

A speech of tribute is designed to create in those who hear it a sense of appreciation for the traits or accomplishments of the person or group to whom tribute is paid. If you cause your audience to realize the essential worth or importance of the person or group, you will have succeeded. But you may go further than this. You may, by honoring a person, arouse deeper devotion to the cause he or she represents. Did this person give distinguished service to community or country? Then strive to enhance the audience's sense of patriotism and service. Was this individual a friend to young people? Then try to arouse the conviction that working to provide opportunities for the young deserves the audience's support. Create a desire in your listeners to emulate the person or persons honored. *Make them want to develop the same virtues, to demonstrate a like devotion.*

Douglas Ehninger et al., Principles of Speech Communication

Unfortunately, readers cannot always rely on a stated main idea being provided. For example, fiction writers rarely, if ever, use stated main ideas. The following is an example of a paragraph with an unstated main idea.

5. Details combine to make a point but the main idea is not directly stated.

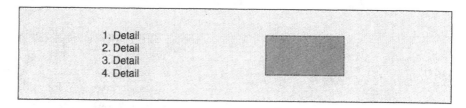

1. Detail
2. Detail
3. Detail
4. Detail

EXAMPLE   This creature's career could produce but one result, and it speedily followed. Boy after boy managed to get on the river. The minister's son became an engineer. The doctor's sons became "mud clerks"; the wholesale liquor dealer's son became a bar-keeper on a boat; four sons of the chief merchant, and two sons of the county judge, became pilots. Pilot was the grandest position of all. The pilot, even in those days of trivial wages, had a princely salary—from a hundred and fifty to two hundred and fifty dollars a month, and no board to pay. Two months of his wages would pay a preacher's salary for a year. Now some of us were left disconsolate. We could not get on the river—at least our parents would not let us.

Mark Twain, Life on the Mississippi

EXPLANATION   Main idea: Young boys in the area have a strong desire to leave home and get a job on the prestigious Mississippi River.

Exercise 4.3

Identifying Stated Main Ideas

Read the following passages and apply the three-question system. Select the letter of the author's topic, identify major and minor details, and underline the main idea. For each passage in this exercise, the answer to the third question will be stated somewhere within the paragraph.

Passage A

The term vegetarian means different things to different people. Strict vegetarians, or *vegans*, avoid all foods of animal origins, including dairy products and eggs. Far more common are *lacto-vegetarians*, who eat dairy products but avoid flesh foods. Their diets can be low in cholesterol, but only if they consume skim milk and other low- or nonfat products. **Ovo-vegetarians** add eggs to their diet, while *lact-ovo-vegetarians* eat both dairy products and eggs. *Pesco-vegetarians* eat fish, dairy products, and eggs. Some people in the semivegetarian category prefer to call themselves "non-red meat eaters."

Rebecca J. Donatelle, *Health: The Basics*, 4th ed.

_____ 1. The topic of the passage is
    a. Vegetarians Without Dairy Products
    b. Becoming a Vegetarian
    c. Different Vegetarian Categories
    d. Health Issues for Vegetarians

2. Indicate whether each of the following details is major or minor in support of the author's topic.
    _____ a. Pesco-vegetarians eat fish.
    _____ b. Lacto-vegetarians can have low cholesterol if they consume skim milk.
    _____ c. Ovo-vegetarians add eggs to their diet.

3. Underline the sentence that best states the main idea of this passage.

Passage B

Building and equipping the pyramids focused and transformed Egypt's material and human resources. Artisans had to be trained, engineering and transportation problems solved, quarrying and stone-working techniques perfected, and laborers recruited. In the Old Kingdom, whose population has been estimated at perhaps 1.5 million, more than 70,000 workers at a time were employed in building the great temple-tombs. No smaller work force could have built such a massive structure as the Great Pyramid of Khufu.

Mark Kishlansky et al., *Civilization in the West*, 4th ed.

_____ 1. The topic of the passage is
    a. Training Laborers for the Pyramids
    b. Resources Needed for Building Pyramids
    c. Pyramid Building Problems
    d. The Pyramids

2. Indicate whether each of the following details is major or minor in support of the author's topic.
    _____ a. The Old Kingdom had an estimated population of 1.5 million.
    _____ b. More than 70,000 workers at a time were employed in building the great temple-tombs.
    _____ c. Artisans had to be trained.

3. Underline the sentence that best states the main idea of this passage.

Passage C

If you're upset or tired, you're at risk for an emotion-charged confrontation. If you ambush someone with an angry attack, don't expect her or him to be in a productive frame of mind. Instead, give yourself time to cool off before you try to resolve a conflict. In the case of the group project, you could call a meeting for later in the week. By that time, you could gain control of your feelings and think things through. Of course, sometimes issues need to be discussed on the spot; you may not have the luxury to wait. But whenever it's practical, make sure your conflict partner is ready to receive you and your message. Select a mutually acceptable time and place to discuss a conflict.

Steven A. Beebe, Susan J. Beebe, and Diana K. Ivy, *Communication* (adapted)

_____ 1. The topic of the passage is
  a. Planning for Conflict Resolution
  b. Confrontation
  c. Being Productive
  d. Solving Problems

2. Indicate whether each of the following details is major or minor in support of the author's topic.
  _____ a. Give yourself time to cool off before you try to resolve a conflict.
  _____ b. If you are upset, you are at risk for a confrontation.
  _____ c. Call a meeting a week later for a group project.

3. Underline the sentence that best states the main idea of this passage.

Passage D

In a Utah case, the defendant fell asleep in his car on the shoulder of the highway. Police stopped, smelled alcohol on his breath, and arrested him for driving while intoxicated. His conviction was reversed by the Utah Supreme Court, because the defendant was not in physical control of the vehicle at the time as required by the law. In freeing the defendant, the Supreme Court judged that the legal definition of sufficiency was not established in this case because the act observed by the police was not *sufficient* to confirm the existence of a guilty mind. In other words, the case against him failed because he was not violating the law at the time of the arrest and because it was also possible that he could have driven while sober, then pulled over, drank, and fell asleep.

Jay S. Albanese, *Criminal Justice, Brief Edition* (adapted)

_____ 1. The topic of the passage is
  a. Driving Drunk
  b. The Utah Supreme Court
  c. Sleeping Behind the Wheel
  d. Establishing Sufficiency for Drunken Driving

2. Indicate whether each of the following details is major or minor in support of the author's topic.

_____ a. Police arrested the defendant for driving while intoxicated.

_____ b. The defendant was not violating a law at the time of the arrest.

_____ c. The case was tried in Utah.

3. Underline the sentence that best states the main idea of this passage.

Exercise 4.4

Writing Stated Main Ideas

Read the following passages and use the three-question system to determine the author's main idea. For each passage in this exercise, the answer to the third question will be stated somewhere within the paragraph.

Passage A

Time is especially linked to status considerations, and the importance of being on time varies with the status of the individual you are visiting. If the person is extremely important, you had better be there on time or even early just in case he or she is able to see you before schedule. As the person's status decreases, so does the importance of being on time. Junior executives, for example, must be on time for conferences with senior executives, but it is even more important to be on time for the company president or the CEO. Senior executives, however, may be late for conferences with their juniors but not for conferences with the president. Within any hierarchy, similar unwritten rules are followed with respect to time. This is not to imply that these "rules" are just or fair; they simply exist.

Joseph DeVito, *Interpersonal Communication*, 6th ed.

1. Who or what is this about? _____

2. What are the major details? _____

_____

_____

3. What is the main idea the author is trying to convey about the topic?

_____

_____

Underline the main idea.

Passage B

Courting behavior in birds is also believed to be instinctive. In one experiment Daniel Lehrman of Rutgers University found that when a male blond ring dove was isolated from females, it soon began to bow and coo to a stuffed model of a female—a model that it had previously ignored. When the model was replaced by a rolled-up cloth, he began to court the cloth; and when this was removed the sex-crazed dove directed his attention to a corner of the cage, where it could at least focus its gaze. It seems that the threshold for release of the behavior pattern became increasingly lower as time went by without the sight of a live female dove. It is almost as though some specific "energy" for performing courting behavior were building up within the male ring dove.

Robert Wallace, *Biology: The World of Life*

1. Who or what is this about? _____

2. What are the major details? _____

_____

_____

3. What is the main idea the author is trying to convey about the topic?

_____

Underline the main idea.

Passage C

To retrieve a fact from a library of stored information, you need a way to gain access to it. In recognition tests, retrieval cues (such as photographs) provide reminders of information (classmates' names) we could not otherwise recall. Retrieval cues also guide us where to look. If you want to know what the pyramid on the back of a dollar bill signifies, you might look in *Collier's Encyclopedia* under "dollar," "currency," or "money." But your efforts would be futile. To get the information you want, you would have to look under "Great Seal of the United States." Like information stored in encyclopedias, memories are inaccessible unless we have cues for retrieving them. The more and better learned the retrieval cues, the more accessible the memory.

David G. Myers. *Psychology*

1. Who or what is this about? _____

2. What are the major details? _____

_____

3. What is the main idea the author is trying to convey about the topic?

_____

_____

Underline the main idea.

Passage D

Most of the Plains Indians believed that land could be utilized, but never owned. The idea of owning land was as absurd as owning the air people breathed. To some, the sacredness of the land made farming against their religion. Chief Somohalla of the Wanapaun explained why his people refused to farm. "You ask me to plow the ground! Shall I take a knife and tear my mother's bosom? . . . You ask me to cut grass and make hay and sell it, and be rich like white men! But how dare I cut off my mother's hair?"

James Kirby Martin et al., *America and Its Peoples*, 4th ed.

1. Who or what is this about? _____

   _____

2. What are the major details? _____

   _____

3. What is the main idea the author is trying to convey about the topic?

   _____

Underline the main idea.

Passage E

A crab lives at the bottom of its ocean of water and looks upward at jellyfish drifting above it. Similarly, we live at the bottom of our ocean of air and look upward at balloons drifting above us. A balloon is suspended in air and a jellyfish is suspended in water for the same reason: each is buoyed upward by a displaced weight of fluid equal to its own weight. In one case the displaced fluid is air, and in the other case it is water. In water, immersed objects are buoyed upward because the pressure acting up against the bottom of the object exceeds the pressure acting down against the top. Likewise, air pressure acting up against an object immersed in air is greater than the pressure above pushing down. The buoyancy in both cases is numerically equal to the weight of fluid displaced. **Archimedes' principle** holds for air just as it does for water: An object surrounded by air is buoyed up by a force equal to the weight of the air displaced.

Paul Hewitt, *Conceptual Physics*, 8th ed.

1. Who or what is this about? _____

2. What are the major details? _____

   _____

3. What is the main idea the author is trying to convey about the topic?

   _____

Underline the main idea.

Examples of Unstated Main Idea

EXAMPLE Michael Harner proposes an ecological interpretation of Aztec sacrifice and cannibalism. He holds that human sacrifice was a response to certain diet deficiencies in the population. In the Aztec environment, wild game was getting scarce, and the population was growing. Although the maize-beans combination of food that was the basis of the diet was usually adequate, these crops were subject to seasonal failure. Famine was frequent in the absence of edible domesticated animals. To meet essential protein requirements, cannibalism was the only solution. Although only the upper classes were allowed to consume human flesh, a commoner who distinguished himself in a war could also have the privilege of giving a cannibalistic feast. Thus, although it was the upper strata who benefited most from ritual cannibalism, members of the commoner class could also benefit. Furthermore, as Harner explains, the social mobility and cannibalistic privileges available to the commoners through warfare provided a strong motivation for the "aggressive war machine" that was such a prominent feature of the Aztec state.

Serena Nanda, *Cultural Anthropology*, 4th ed.

1. Who or what is this about? _____

2. What are the major details? _____

3. What is the main idea the author is trying to convey about the topic?

_____

EXPLANATION The passage is about Aztec sacrifice and cannibalism. The major details are: *diet deficiencies occurred, animals were not available*, and *members of the upper class and commoners who were war heroes could eat human flesh*. The main idea is that *Aztec sacrifice and cannibalism met protein needs of the diet and motivated warriors to achieve.*

| Exercise 4.5 | Identifying Unstated Main Ideas |

Read the following passages and apply the three-question system. Select the letter of the author's topic, identify major and minor details, and choose the letter of the sentence that best states the main idea.

Passage A

Until recently, the U.S. census, which is taken every ten years, offered only the following categories: Caucasian, Negro, Indian, and Oriental. After years of complaints from the public the list was expanded. In the year of 2000 census, everyone had to declare that they were or were not "Spanish/Hispanic/Latino." They had to mark "one or more races" that they "considered themselves to be." Finally, if these didn't do it, you could check a box called "Some Other Race" and then write whatever you wanted. For example, Tiger Woods, one of the top golfers of all time, calls himself Cablinasian. Woods invented this term as a boy to try to explain to himself just who he was—a combination of Caucasian, Black, Indian, and Asian. Woods wants to embrace both sides of his family.

James M. Henslin, *Sociology*, 5th ed. (adapted)

_____ 1. The topic of the passage is
   a. Tiger Woods Speaks Out
   b. The U.S. Census
   c. Identify Your Race
   d. The Emerging Multiracial Identity

2. Indicate whether each of the following details is major or minor in support of the author's topic.
   _____ a. Tiger Woods is one of the top golfers of all time.
   _____ b. Tiger Woods wants to embrace both sides of his family.
   _____ c. Until recently, the U.S. census offered only four racial categories.

_____ 3. The sentence that best states the main idea of this passage is
   a. Citizens complained about the four categories of the previous census.
   b. The 2000 census took a new approach and allowed citizens to identify themselves as being of more than one race.
   c. Tiger Woods considers himself a combination of Caucasian, Black, Indian, and Asian.
   d. Information from the 2000 census will be more useful than data gathered from the previous census.

Passage B

The rate of incarceration in prison increased from 27 per 100,000 women in 1985 to 57 per 100,000 in 1998. Men still outnumber women in the inmate population by a factor of about 14 to 1, but the gap is narrowing—from 17 to 1 a decade ago. Women constituted only 4 percent of the total prison and jail population in the United States in 1980 but more than 6 percent in 1998.

Jay S. Albanese, *Criminal Justice*

_____ 1. The topic of the passage is
   a. Men Versus Women in Jail
   b. Incarceration in America
   c. The Increasing Number of Women in Jail
   d. Overcrowded Prisons

2. Indicate whether each of the following details is major or minor in support of the author's topic.

_____ a. The rate of incarceration of women in prison in 1985 was 27 per 100,000.

_____ b. The rate of incarceration of women in prison in 1998 was 57 per 100,000.

_____ c. A decade ago men outnumbered women 17 to 1.

_____ 3. Which sentence best states the main idea of this passage?

a. Men continue to outnumber women in the prison and jail population.

b. The rate of incarceration is increasing for both men and women.

c. In the last decade the rate of women incarcerated has doubled.

d. The role of women in society has changed in the last decade.

Passage C

Each year in the United States approximately 50,000 miscarriages are attributed to smoking during pregnancy. On average, babies born to mothers who smoke weigh less than those born to nonsmokers, and low birth weight is correlated with many developmental problems. Pregnant women who stop smoking in the first three or four months of their pregnancies give birth to higher-birth-weight babies than do women who smoke throughout their pregnancies. Infant mortality rates are also higher among babies born to smokers.

Rebecca J. Donatelle, *Health: The Basics*, 4th ed.

_____ 1. The topic of the passage is

a. Infant Mortality

b. Smoking

c. Smoking and Pregnancy

d. Smoking and Miscarriages

2. Indicate whether each of the following details is major or minor in support of the author's topic.

_____ a. Low birth weight is correlated with many developmental problems.

_____ b. Infant mortality rates are also higher among babies born to smokers.

_____ c. Babies born to mothers who smoke weigh less than those born to nonsmokers.

_____ 3. Which sentence best states the main idea of this passage?
   a. Smoking during pregnancy increases the chance of miscarriages, low-weight babies, and infant mortality.
   b. Smoking during pregnancy causes many miscarriages.
   c. Ceasing smoking during pregnancy can increase infant birth weight.
   d. Smoking is a major contributor to infant mortality.

Passage D

The young reporter with the slow Missouri drawl stamped the cold of the high Nevada desert out of his feet as he entered the offices of the Virginia City *Territorial Enterprise*. It was early in 1863. The newspaper's editor, Joseph T. Goodman, looked puzzled at seeing his Carson City correspondent in the home office, but Samuel Clemens came right to the point: "Joe, I want to sign my articles. I want to be identified to a wider audience." The editor, already impressed with his colleague of six months, readily agreed. Then came the question of a pen name, since few aspiring writers of the time used their legal names. Clemens had something in mind: "I want to sign them 'Mark Twain,'" he declared. "It is an old river term, a leadsman's call, signifying two fathoms—twelve feet. It has a richness about it; it was always a pleasant sound for a pilot to hear on a dark night; it meant safe water."

Roderick Nash and Gregory Graves, *From These Beginnings*, 6th ed., vol. 2.

_____ 1. The topic of the passage is
   a. Becoming a Reporter
   b. How Mark Twain Got His Name
   c. Safe Water on the River
   d. Working for the Virginia City *Territorial Enterprise*

2. Indicate whether each of the following details is major or minor in support of the author's topic.
   _____ a. Clemens had worked for the newspaper for six months.
   _____ b. The newspaper's editor was Joseph T. Goodman.
   _____ c. Clemens wanted to sign his articles in order to be known to a wider audience.

_____ 3. Which sentence best states the main idea of this passage?
   a. Samuel Clemens worked as a young reporter for the Virginia City *Territorial Enterprise*.
   b. The newspaper's editor, Joseph T. Goodman, was impressed with the young reporter, Samuel Clemens.
   c. "Mark Twain" is a river term that means two fathoms—twelve feet.
   d. The young reporter, Samuel Clemens, decided to take the pen name "Mark Twain."

| Exercise 4.6 | **Writing Unstated Main Ideas** |

Read the following passages and use the three-question system to determine the author's main idea. Pull the ideas together to state the main ideas in your own words.

Passage A

According to the U.S. Department of the Census, the demographic shift in the population will be "profound" in the next 50 years. By 2050, Hispanics will make up 24.5 percent of the population, up from 10.2 percent in 1996. The annual growth rate of the Hispanic population is expected to be 2 percent through the year 2030. To put this growth in perspective, consider the fact that even at the height of the baby boom explosion in the late 1940s and early 1950s, the country's annual population increase never reached 2 percent. Demographers, it seems, are alerting us to the enormous importance of such change. Says Gregory Spencer, Director of the Census Bureau's Population Projections Branch, "The world is not going to be the same in thirty years as it is now."

Ronald Ebert and Ricky Griffin, *Business Essentials*, 2nd ed.

1. Who or what is this about? _____

2. What are the major details? _____

_____

3. What is the main idea the author is trying to convey about the topic?

_____

_____

Passage B

Prior to the time of Jan Baptiste van Helmont, a Belgian physician of the 17th century, it was commonly accepted that plants derived their matter from materials in the soil. (Probably, many people who haven't studied photosynthesis would go along with this today.) We aren't sure why, but van Helmont decided to test the idea. He carefully stripped a young willow sapling of all surrounding soil, weighed it, and planted it in a tub of soil that had also been carefully weighed. After five years of diligent watering (with rain water), van Helmont removed the greatly enlarged willow and again stripped away the soil and weighed it. The young tree had gained 164 pounds. Upon weighing the soil, van Helmont was amazed to learn that it had lost only 2 ounces.

Robert Wallace et al., *Biology: The Science of Life*, 3rd ed.

1. Who or what is this about? _____

2. What are the major details? _____

_____

3. What is the main idea the author is trying to convey about the topic?

_____

_____

Passage C

The Aswan High Dam, built in Egypt with Russian support, was supposed to provide hydroelectric power and to increase Egypt's food supply by controlling the unpredictable Nile River. The project meant that great art treasures were flooded as submerged land was drained for cultivation. However, only one-tenth of an acre of land was made available for each person added to Egypt's population during the period of construction. One result of the dam was that the Nile no longer flooded the delta farm-lands annually. These annual floods served to restore the farmland fertility with deposited silt. This no longer the case, the quality of the farmland decreased. The dam also cut off the nutrients that had been washed to the Mediterranean Sea as a result of the annual floodings. Because of this, or the change in the salinity of the sea that the dam produced, the sardine catch dropped from 18,000 tons per year to 500 tons per year. The stable lake created by the dam allowed aquatic snails to flourish. The snails serve as an intermediate host to a blood fluke that bores into humans causing the dreaded disease, schistosomiasis. The construction of the dam had important political implications at the time.

Robert Wallace, *Biology: The World of Life*

1. Who or what is this about? _____

2. What are the major details? _____

_____

_____

3. What is the main idea the author is trying to convey about the topic?

_____

_____

Passage D

If using sunscreen, apply it at least 30–45 minutes before exposure, then reapply it periodically, especially after you swim or sweat. It is especially important to protect children. One or more severe sunburns with blisters in childhood or adolescence can double the risk of the skin cancer melanoma later in life. Additional protection can be provided by a wide-brimmed hat to protect your head and face, and opaque clothing to cover those body areas you wish to protect. Any fabric or material you can see through, including some beach umbrellas, does not give full protection. You should stay out of the sun between 10 A.M. and 2 P.M. when the rays are strongest.

Curtis O. Byer and Louis W. Shainberg, *Living Well: Health in Your Hands*, 2nd ed.

1. Who or what is this about? _____

2. What are the major details? _____

_____

_____

3. What is the main idea the author is trying to convey about the topic?

_____

_____

Passage E

In 1979 when University of Minnesota psychologist Thomas Bouchard read a newspaper account of the reuniting of 39-year-old twins who had been separated from infancy, he seized the opportunity and flew them to Minneapolis for extensive tests. Bouchard was looking for differences. What "the Jim twins," Jim Lewis and Jim Springer, presented were amazing similarities. Both had married women named Linda, divorced, and married women named Betty. One had a son James Alan, the other a son James Allan. Both had dogs named Toy, chainsmoked Salems, served as sheriff's deputies, drove Chevrolets, chewed their fingernails to the nub, enjoyed stock car racing, had basement workshops, and had built circular white benches around trees in their yards. They also had similar medical histories: Both gained 10 pounds at about the same time and then lost it; both suffered what they mistakenly believed were heart attacks, and both began having late-afternoon headaches at age 18.

Identical twins Oskar Stohr and Jack Yufe presented equally striking similarities. One was raised by his grandmother in Germany as a Catholic and a Nazi, while the other was raised by his father in the Caribbean as a Jew. Nevertheless, they share traits and habits galore. They like spicy foods and sweet liqueurs, have a habit of falling asleep in front of the television, flush the toilet before using it, store rubber bands on their wrists, and dip buttered toast in their coffee. Stohr is domineering toward women and yells at his wife, as did Yufe before he was separated.

David G. Myers, *Psychology*

1. Who or what is this about? _____

2. What are the major details? _____

_____

_____

3. What is the main idea the author is trying to convey about the topic?

_____

_____

Interpreting Longer Selections

Understanding the main idea of longer selections requires a little more thinking than finding the main idea of a single paragraph. Since longer selections such as articles or chapters involve more material, the challenge of tying the ideas together can be confusing and complicated. Each paragraph of a longer selection usually represents a new aspect of a supporting detail. In addition, several major ideas may contribute to developing the overall main idea. The reader, therefore, must fit the many pieces together under one central theme.

For longer selections, the reader needs to add an extra step between the two questions, "What is the topic?" and "What is the main idea the author is trying to convey?" The step involves organizing the material into manageable subunits and then relating those to the whole. Two additional questions to ask are, "Under what subsections can these ideas be grouped?" and "How do these subsections contribute to the whole?"

Use the suggestions in the box below to determine the main idea of longer selections. The techniques are similar to those used in previewing and skimming, two skills that also focus on the overall central theme.

Reader's Tip

Getting the Main Idea of Longer Selections

* **Think about the significance of the title.** What does the title suggest about the topic?

* **Read the first paragraph or two for a statement of the topic or thesis.** What does the selection seem to be about?

* **Read the subheadings and, if necessary, glance at the first sentences of some of the paragraphs.** Based on these clues, what does the article seem to be about?

* **Look for clues that indicate how the material is organized.** Is the purpose to define a term, to prove an opinion or explain a concept, to describe a situation, or to persuade the reader toward a particular point of view?
  Is the material organized into a list of examples, a time order or sequence, a comparison or contrast, or a cause-and-effect relationship?

* **As you read, organize the paragraphs into subsections.** Give each subsection a title. These become your significant supporting details.

* **Determine how the overall organization and subsections relate to the whole.** Answer the question, "What is the main idea the author is trying to convey in this selection?"

Summary Writing: A Main Idea Skill

A **summary** is a series of brief, concise statements in your own words of the main idea and the significant supporting details. The first sentence should state the main idea or thesis, and subsequent sentences should incorporate the significant details. Minor details and material irrelevant to the learner's purpose should be omitted. The summary should be in paragraph form and should always be shorter than the material being summarized.

Why Summarize?

Summaries can be used for textbook study and are particularly useful in anticipating answers for essay exam questions. For writing research papers, summarizing is an essential skill. Using your own words to put the essence of an article into concise sentences requires a thorough understanding of the material. As one researcher noted, "Since so much summarizing is necessary for writing papers, students should have the skill before starting work on research papers. How much plagiarism is the result of inadequate summarizing skills?"[3]

Writing a research paper may mean that you will have to read as many as thirty articles and four books over a period of a month or two. After each reading, you want to take enough notes so you can write your paper without returning to the library for another look at the original reference. Since you will be using so many different references, the notetaking should be done carefully. The complete sentences of a summary are more explicit than underscored text or the highlighted topic-phrase format of an outline. Your summary should demonstrate a synthesis of the information.

EXAMPLE Read the following excerpt on political authority as if you were researching for a term paper and writing a summary on a note card. Mark key terms that you would include in your summary. Before reading the example provided, anticipate what you would include in your own summary.

Types of Authority

Where is the source of the state's authority? Weber described three possible sources of the right to command, which produce what he called traditional authority, charismatic authority, and legal authority.

Traditional Authority

In many societies, people have obeyed those in power because, in essence, "that is the way it has always been." Thus, kings, queens, feudal lords, and tribal chiefs did not need written rules in order to govern. Their authority was based on tradition, on long-standing customs, and it was handed down from parent to child, maintaining traditional authority from one generation to the next. Often, traditional authority has been

---

[3]K. Taylor, "Can College Students Summarize?" *Journal of Reading* 26 (March 1983): 540–44.

58

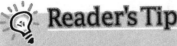

Reader's Tip

How to Summarize

* **Keep in mind the purpose of your summary.** Your projected needs will determine which details are important and how many should be included.

* **Decide on the main idea the author is trying to convey.** Make this main idea the first sentence in your summary.

* **Decide on the major ideas and details that support the author's point.** Mark the key terms and phrases. Include in your summary the major ideas and as many of the significant supporting details as your purpose demands.

* **Do not include irrelevant or repeated information in your summary.**

* **Use appropriate transitional words and phrases to show relationships between points.**

* **Use paragraph form.**

* **Do not add your personal opinion as part of the summary.**

justified by religious tradition. For example, medieval European kings were said to rule by divine right, and Japanese emperors were considered the embodiment of heaven.

Charismatic Authority

People may also submit to authority, not because of tradition, but because of the extraordinary attraction of an individual. Napoleon, Gandhi, Mao Tse-tung, and Ayatollah Khomeini all illustrate authority that derives its legitimacy from *charisma*—an exceptional personal quality popularly attributed to certain individuals. Their followers perceive charismatic leaders as persons of destiny endowed with remarkable vision, the power of a savior, or God's grace. Charismatic authority is inherently unstable. It cannot be transferred to another person.

Legal Authority

The political systems of industrial states are based largely on a third type of authority: legal authority, which Weber also called *rational authority*. These systems derive legitimacy from a set of explicit rules and procedures that spell out the ruler's rights and duties. Typically, the rules and procedures are put in writing. The people grant their obedience to "the law." It specifies procedures by which certain individuals hold offices of power, such as governor or president or prime minister. But the authority is vested in those offices, not in the individuals who temporarily hold the offices. Thus, a political system based on legal authority is often called a "government of laws, not of men." Individuals come and go, as American presidents have come and gone, but the office, "the presidency," remains. If individual officeholders overstep their authority, they may be forced out of office and replaced.

Alex Thio, *Sociology*, 3rd ed.

1. To begin your summary, what is the main point? _____

_____

2. What are the major areas of support? _____

_____

3. Should you include an example for each area? _____

_____

EXPLANATION Begin your summary with the main point, which is that Weber describes the three sources of authority as traditional, charismatic, and legal. Then define each of the three sources but do not include examples.

Read the summary below and notice how closely it fits your own ideas.

> *Political Authority*
> *Weber describes the three command sources as traditional, charismatic, and legal authority. Traditional authority is not written but based on long-standing custom such as the power of queens or tribal chiefs. Charismatic authority is based on the charm and vision of a leader such as Gandhi. Legal authority, such as that of American presidents, comes from written laws and is vested in the office rather than the person.*

Exercise 4.7

Summarizing

Read the following passages and mark the key terms and phrases. Begin your summary with a statement of the main point and add the appropriate supporting details. Use your markings to help you write the summary. Be brief but include the essential elements.

Passage A: Prosecutors

The task of prosecutors is to represent the community in bringing charges against an accused person. The job of the prosecutor is constrained by political factors, caseloads, and relationships with other actors in the adjudication process.

First, most prosecutors are elected (although some are appointed by the governor), so it is in their interests to make "popular" prosecution decisions—and in some cases these may run counter to the ideals of justice. For example, prosecution "to the full extent of the law" of a college student caught possessing a small amount of marijuana may be unwarranted, but failure to prosecute may be used by political opponents as evidence that the prosecutor is "soft on crime."

A second constraint is caseload pressures, which often force prosecutors to make decisions based on expediency rather than justice. A prosecutor in a jurisdiction where many serious crimes occur may have to choose which to prosecute to the full extent of the law and which ones to plea-bargain.

Third, prosecutors must maintain good relationships with the other participants in the adjudication process: police, judges, juries, defense attorneys, victims, and witnesses. Cases typically are brought to prosecutors by the police, and police officers usually serve as witnesses.

Jay S. Albanese, *Criminal Justice*

Use your marked text to write a summary.

Passage B: Suicide Among College Students

Compared to nonstudents of the same age, the suicide rate among college students is somewhat higher. Why is this so? For one thing, among the younger college students who commit suicide (ages 18–22), a common thread is the inability to separate themselves from their family and to solve problems on their own. College presents many of these younger students with the challenge of having to be independent in many ways while remaining dependent on family in other ways, such as financially and emotionally.

Several other characteristics of the college experience may relate to suicide. A great emphasis is put on attaining high grades and the significance of grades may be blown out of proportion. A student may come to perceive grades as a measurement of his or her total worth as a person, rather than just one of many ways a person can be evaluated. If a student is unable to achieve expected grades, there may be a total loss of self-esteem and loss of hope for any success in life.

In the college setting, where self-esteem can be tenuous, the end of a relationship can also be devastating. A student who has recently lost a close friend or lover can become so deeply depressed that suicide becomes an attractive alternative. The problem can be compounded when depression interferes with coursework and grades slip.

Curtis O. Byer and Louis W. Shainberg, *Living Well: Health in Your Hands*, 2nd ed.

Use your marked text to write a summary.

Passage C: Alcohol Advertising and College Students

The alcohol industry knows a receptive market when it sees it. Each year, college students spend a reported $5.5 billion ($446 per student) on alcohol, consuming some 4 billion cans' worth of alcohol and accounting for 10 percent of total beer sales. For brewers, student drinking spells not just current sales, but future profits as well, because most people develop loyalty to a specific beer between the ages of 18 and 24. To secure this lucrative market, brewers and other alcohol producers spend millions of dollars each year promoting their products to college students. One conservative estimate places annual expenditures for college marketing between $15 million and $20 million. According to one survey, alcohol advertising of local specials in many college newspapers has increased by more than half over the past decade, stymieing college and community efforts to reduce binge drinking.

Rebecca J. Donatelle, *Health: The Basics*, 4th ed.

Use your marked text to write a summary.

Summary Points

● **What is a topic?**

The topic of a passage is the general term that forms an umbrella for the specific ideas presented.

● **What is a main idea?**

The main idea is the point the author is trying to convey about the topic. In some passages the main idea is stated in a sentence, and in others it is unstated.

● **What are significant details?**

Details support, develop, and explain the main idea. Some details are of major significance and others are only of minor significance in supporting the main idea.

● **What is a summary?**

Summaries condense material and include the main ideas and major details.

Selection 1 PSYCHOLOGY

CONTEMPORARY FOCUS

Humans owe a debt to animals whose lives are manipulated and sacrificed for the sake of knowledge. Is there a line that marks the point when animal research is acceptable and when it is unethical?

BRAIN RESEARCH ON MONKEYS

Gail Schontzler

From *Bozeman Daily Chronicle* (MT), December 3, 2000

Tall and bearded, Charlie Gray looks like a rugged outdoorsman, not like what you might expect of a research scientist, and not like a man afraid to be photographed.

Gray, 42, is doing research at Montana State University, trying to unlock the mysteries of the brain. He is excited about his work, and proud that his knowledge has already helped provide a cure for patients suffering the uncontrollable tremors of Parkinson's disease.

"I'm incredibly fascinated by the brain," Gray said. "It's an incredibly mysterious and fascinating thing to learn about. It's probably the greatest mystery there is. Everything we are is what goes on inside our head."

Yet Gray advances scientific knowledge by drilling holes in the skulls of rhesus monkeys and cats and poking electrodes into their brains. When the research is completed after one to five years, the animals must be euthanized. It's a use of animals that could incense animal-rights activists. That is why he refuses to be photographed.

Collaborative Activity

Collaborate on responses to the following questions:

- What are the positive and negative arguments for a university conducting research on animals?
- How do animal-rights activists apply pressure for animal protection?
- Why are students invited to participate in research projects in psychology and education?

Skill Development—Stage 1: Preview

Preview the next selection to predict the purpose and your learning plan.

The author's main purpose is to describe the infant-mother relationship.
Agree ☐   Disagree ☐

After reading this selection, I will need to know the meaning of contact comfort.   Agree ☐   Disagree ☐

Activate Schema

Do parents who were abused as children later abuse their own children?

As a child, what did you use as a "security blanket"?

Learning Strategy

Explain the psychological needs of an infant monkey and the effect that deprivation of those needs can have on the whole pattern of psychological development.

Word Knowledge

What do you know about these words?

surrogate   functional   anatomy   tentatively   novel

desensitized   ingenious   deprived   persisted   deficient

Your instructor may give a true-false vocabulary review before or after reading.

Stage 2: Integrate Knowledge While Reading

Predict   Picture   Relate   Monitor   Correct

MONKEY LOVE

From James V. McConnell, *Understanding Human Behavior*

The scientist who has conducted the best long-term laboratory experiments on love is surely Harry Harlow, a psychologist at the University of Wisconsin. Professor Harlow did not set out to study love—it happened by accident. Like many other psychologists, he was at first primarily interested in how organisms

5   learn. Rather than working with rats, Harlow chose to work with monkeys.

Since he needed a place to house and raise the monkeys, he built the Primate Laboratory at Wisconsin. Then he began to study the effects of brain lesions on monkey learning. But he soon found that young animals reacted somewhat differently to brain damage than did older monkeys, so he and his wife Margaret de-

10   vised a breeding program and tried various ways of raising monkeys in the laboratory. They rapidly discovered that monkey infants raised by their mothers often caught diseases from their parents, so the Harlows began taking the infants away from their mothers at birth and tried raising them by hand. The baby monkeys had been given cheesecloth diapers to serve as baby blankets. Almost from the

15   start, it became obvious to the Harlows that their little animals developed such strong attachments to the blankets that, in the Harlows' own terms, it was often hard to tell where the diaper ended and the baby began. Not only this, but if the Harlows removed the "security" blanket in order to clean it, the infant monkey often became greatly disturbed—just as if its own mother had deserted it.

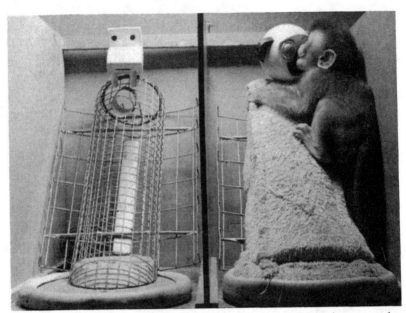

Although the baby monkey receives milk from Harlow's wire mother, it spends most of its time with the terry-cloth version and clings to the terry-cloth mother when frightened.
Harlow Primate Library, University of Wisconsin

The Surrogate Mother

20   What the baby monkeys obviously needed was an artificial or *surrogate* mother—something they could cling to as tightly as they typically clung to their own mother's chest. The Harlows sketched out many different designs, but none really appealed to them. Then, in 1957, while enjoying a champagne flight high over the city of Detroit, Harry Harlow glanced out of the airplane
25   window and "saw" an image of an artificial monkey mother. It was a hollow wire cylinder, wrapped with a terry-cloth bath towel, with a silly wooden head at the top. The tiny monkey could cling to this "model mother" as closely as to its real mother's body hair. This surrogate mother could be provided with a functional breast simply by placing a milk bottle so that the nipple
30   stuck through the cloth at an appropriate place on the surrogate's anatomy. The cloth mother could be heated or cooled; it could be rocked mechanically or made to stand still; and, most important, it could be removed at will.

While still sipping his champagne, Harlow mentally outlined much of the research that kept him, his wife, and their associates occupied for many years
35   to come. And without realizing it, Harlow had shifted from studying monkey learning to monkey love.

Infant-Mother Love

The chimpanzee or monkey infant is much more developed at birth than the human infant, and apes develop or mature much faster than we do. Almost

from the moment it is born, the monkey infant can move around and hold
40 tightly to its mother. During the first few days of its life the infant will approach and cling to almost any large, warm, and soft object in its environment,
particularly if that object also gives it milk. After a week or so, however, the
monkey infant begins to avoid newcomers and focuses its attentions on
"mother"—real or surrogate.

45 During the first two weeks of its life warmth is perhaps the most important
psychological thing that a monkey mother has to give to its baby. The Harlows
discovered this fact by offering infant monkeys a choice of two types of
mother-substitutes—one wrapped in terry cloth and one that was made of
bare wire. If the two artificial mothers were both the same temperature, the
50 little monkeys always preferred the cloth mother. However, if the wire model
was heated, while the cloth model was cool, for the first two weeks after birth
the baby primates picked the warm wire mother-substitutes as their favorites.
Thereafter they switched and spent most of their time on the more comfortable cloth mother.

55 Why is cloth preferable to bare wire? Something that the Harlows called
contact comfort seems to be the answer, and a most powerful influence it is. Infant monkeys (and chimps too) spend much of their time rubbing against
their mothers' skins, putting themselves in as close contact with the parent as
they can. Whenever the young animal is frightened, disturbed, or annoyed, it
60 typically rushes to its mother and rubs itself against her body. Wire doesn't
"rub" as well as does soft cloth. Prolonged "contact comfort" with a surrogate
cloth mother appears to instill confidence in baby monkeys and is much more
rewarding to them than is either warmth or milk. Infant monkeys also prefer a
"rocking" surrogate to one that is stationary.

65 According to the Harlows, the basic quality of an infant's love for its
mother is *trust*. If the infant is put into an unfamiliar playroom without its
mother, the infant ignores the toys no matter how interesting they might be. It
screeches in terror and curls up into a furry little ball. If its cloth mother is now
introduced into the playroom, the infant rushes to the surrogate and clings to
70 it for dear life. After a few minutes of contact comfort, it apparently begins to
feel more secure. It then climbs down from the mother-substitute and begins
tentatively to explore the toys, but often rushes back for a deep embrace as if
to reassure itself that its mother is still there and that all is well. Bit by bit its
fears of the novel environment are "desensitized" and it spends more and more
75 time playing with the toys and less and less time clinging to its "mother."

Good Mothers and Bad

The Harlows found that, once a baby monkey has come to accept its mother
(real or surrogate), the mother can do almost no wrong. In one of their studies,
the Harlows tried to create "monster mothers" whose behavior would be so abnormal that the infants would desert the mothers. Their purpose was to deter-
80 mine whether maternal rejection might cause abnormal behavior patterns in
the infant monkeys similar to those responses found in human babies whose
mothers ignore or punish their children severely. The problem was—how can

you get a terry-cloth mother to reject or punish its baby? Their solutions were ingenious—but most of them failed in their main purpose. Four types of "monster mothers" were tried, but none of them was apparently "evil" enough to impart fear or loathing to the infant monkeys. One such "monster" occasionally blasted its babies with compressed air; a second shook so violently that the baby often fell off; a third contained a catapult that frequently flung the infant away from it. The most evil-appearing of all had a set of metal spikes buried beneath the terry cloth; from time to time the spikes would poke through the cloth making it impossible for the infant to cling to the surrogate.

The baby monkeys brought up on the "monster mothers" did show a brief period of emotional disturbance when the "wicked" temperament of the surrogates first showed up. The infants would cry for a time when displaced from their mothers, but as soon as the surrogates returned to normal, the infant would return to the surrogate and continue clinging, as if all were forgiven. As the Harlows tell the story, the only prolonged distress created by the experiment seemed to be that felt by the experimenters!

There was, however, one type of surrogate that uniformly "turned off" the infant monkeys. S. J. Suomi, working with the Harlows, built a terry-cloth mother with ice water in its veins. Newborn monkeys would attach themselves to this "cool momma" for a brief period of time, but then retreated to a corner of the cage and rejected her forever.

From their many brilliant studies, the Harlows conclude that the love of an infant for its mother is *primarily a response to certain stimuli the mother offers.* Warmth is the most important stimulus for the first two weeks of the monkey's life, then contact comfort becomes paramount. Contact comfort is determined by the softness and "rub-ability" of the surface of the mother's body— terry cloth is better than are satin and silk, but all such materials are more effective in creating love and trust than bare metal is. Food and mild "shaking" or "rocking" are important too, but less so than warmth and contact comfort. These needs—and the rather primitive responses the infant makes in order to obtain their satisfaction—are programmed into the monkey's genetic blueprint. The growing infant's requirement for social and intellectual stimulation becomes critical only later in a monkey's life. And yet, if the baby primate is deprived of contact with other young of its own species, its whole pattern of development can be profoundly disturbed.

Mother-Infant Love

The Harlows were eventually able to find ways of getting female isolates pregnant, usually by confining them in a small cage for long periods of time with a patient and highly experienced normal male. At times, however, the Harlows were forced to help matters along by strapping the female to a piece of apparatus. When these isolated females gave birth to their first monkey baby, they turned out to be the "monster mothers" the Harlows had tried to create with mechanical surrogates. Having had no contact with other animals as they grew up, they simply did not know what to do with the furry little strangers that suddenly appeared on the scene. These motherless mothers at first totally ignored their children, although if the infant persisted, the mothers occasionally gave in and provided the baby with some of the contact and comfort it demanded.

130   Surprisingly enough, once these mothers learned how to handle a baby, they did reasonably well. Then, when they were again impregnated and gave birth to a second infant, they took care of this next baby fairly adequately.

Maternal affection was totally lacking in a few of the motherless monkeys, however. To them the newborn monkey was little more than an object to be 135   abused the way a human child might abuse a doll or a toy train. These motherless mothers stepped on their babies, crushed the infant's face into the floor of the cage, and once or twice chewed off their baby's feet and fingers before they could be stopped. The most terrible mother of all popped her infant's head into her mouth and crunched it like a potato chip.

140   We tend to think of most mothers—no matter what their species—as having some kind of almost divine "maternal instinct" that makes them love their children and take care of them no matter what the cost or circumstance. While it is true that most females have built into their genetic blueprint the tendency to be interested in (and to care for) their offspring, this inborn tendency is always ex-145   pressed in a given environment. The "maternal instinct" is strongly influenced by the mother's past experiences. Humans seem to have weaker instincts of all kinds than do other animals—since our behavior patterns are more affected by learning than by our genes, we have greater flexibility in what we do and become. But we pay a sometimes severe price for this freedom from genetic control.

150   Normal monkey and chimpanzee mothers seldom appear to inflict real physical harm on their children; human mothers and fathers often do. Serapio R. Zalba, writing in a journal called *Trans-action*, estimated in 1971 that in the United States alone, perhaps 250,000 children suffer physical abuse by their parents each year. Of these "battered babies," almost 40,000 may be very 155   badly injured. The number of young boys and girls killed by their parents annually is not known, but Zalba suggests that the figure may run into the thousands. Parents have locked their children in tiny cages, raised them in dark closets, burned them, boiled them, slashed them with knives, shot them, and broken almost every bone in their bodies. How can we reconcile these facts 160   with the much-discussed maternal and paternal "instincts"?

The research by the Harlows on the "motherless mothers" perhaps gives us a clue. Mother monkeys who were themselves socially deprived or isolated when young seemed singularly lacking in affection for their infants. Zalba states that most of the abusive human parents that were studied turned out to have been 165   abused and neglected *themselves* as children. Like the isolated monkeys who seemed unable to control their aggressive impulses when put in contact with normal animals, the abusive parents seem to be greatly deficient in what psychologists call "impulse control." Most of these parents also were described as being socially isolated, as having troubles adjusting to marriage, often deeply in 170   debt, and as being unable to build up warm and loving relationships with other people—including their own children. Since they did not learn how to love from their own parents, these mothers and fathers simply did not acquire the social skills necessary for bringing up their own infants in a healthy fashion.

Stage 3: Recall

Stop to self-test, relate, and react.
Your instructor may choose to give you a true-false comprehension review.

Thinking About "Monkey Love"

Explain and give examples of findings from Harlow's experiment that you believe are applicable to human infants.
Response Suggestion: Describe the experimental finding and use examples to relate it to the psychological needs of human infants.

Contemporary Link

Why might some people feel that Harlow's animal research is less acceptable than Gray's research on the brain? Give specific examples to support your statement.

Skill Development: Summarizing

Using this selection as a source, summarize on index cards the information that you might want to include in a research paper entitled "Animal Rights: Do Scientists Go Too Far?"

Skill Development: Main Idea

Answer the following with *T* (true) or *F* (false).

_____ 1. The main point of the first four paragraphs is that Harlow's shift to studying monkey love occurred by accident.

_____ 2. In the second section titled "Infant-Mother Love," the main point is that an infant monkey needs the "contact comfort" of the mother to give it a feeling of security while interacting with the environment.

_____ 3. In the beginning of the section titled "Good Mothers and Bad," the main point is that baby monkeys will reject monster mothers.

_____ 4. In the beginning of the section titled "Mother-Infant Love," the main point is that the maternal instinct is not influenced by the mother's past experiences.

Comprehension Questions

After reading the selection, answer the following questions with *a*, *b*, *c*, or *d*. In order to help you analyze your strengths and weaknesses, the question types are indicated.

Main Idea

1. Who or what is the topic? _____

_____

What is the main idea the author is trying to convey about the topic?

_____

_____

Inference

_____ 2. When Harry Harlow originally started his experiments with monkeys, his purpose was to study
a. love.
b. breeding.
c. learning.
d. disease.

Inference

_____ 3. The reason that the author mentions Harry Harlow's revelations on the airplane is to show
a. that he had extrasensory perception.
b. that he liked to travel.
c. that he was always thinking of his work.
d. in what an unexpected way brilliant work often starts.

Detail

_____ 4. In his experiments Harlow used all of the following in designing his surrogate mothers except
a. a terry-cloth bath towel.
b. real body hair.
c. a rocking movement.
d. temperature controls.

Detail

_____ 5. Harlow manipulated his experiments to show the early significance of warmth by
a. heating wire.
b. changing from satin to terry cloth.
c. equalizing temperature.
d. creating "monster mothers."

Inference

_____ 6. Harlow feels that for contact comfort the cloth mother was preferable to the wire mother for all of the following reasons except
a. the cloth mother instilled confidence.
b. the wire mother didn't "rub" as well.
c. the wire mother was stationary.
d. with the cloth mother, the infant felt a greater sense of security when upset.

Detail	_____	7. Harlow's studies show that when abused by its mother, the infant will a. leave the mother. b. seek a new mother. c. return to the mother. d. fight with the mother.
Detail	_____	8. For an infant to love its mother, Harlow's studies show that in the first two weeks the most important element is a. milk. b. warmth. c. contact comfort. d. love expressed by the mother.
Inference	_____	9. In Harlow's studies with motherless monkeys, he showed that the techniques of mothering are a. instinctive. b. learned. c. inborn. d. natural.
Inference	_____	10. The Harlows feel that child abuse is caused by all of the following problems except a. parents who were abused as children. b. socially isolated parents. c. parents who cannot control their impulses. d. parents who are instinctively evil.

Answer the following with *T* (true) or *F* (false).

Inference	_____	11. The author feels that love in infant monkeys has a great deal of similarity to love in human children.
Inference	_____	12. The author implies that isolated monkeys have difficulty engaging in normal peer relationships.
Detail	_____	13. After learning how to handle the first baby, many motherless mothers became better parents with the second infant.
Inference	_____	14. Zalba's studies support many of the findings of the Harlow studies.
Detail	_____	15. Harlow had initially planned to perform drug experiments on the monkeys.

Vocabulary

According to the way the italicized word was used in the selection, indicate *a, b, c,* or *d* for the word or phrase that gives the best definition. The number in parentheses indictes the line nmber of the passage in which the word is located.

1. "the *surrogate* mother" (20–21)
   a. mean
   b. thoughtless
   c. loving
   d. substitute

2. "a *functional* breast" (29)
   a. mechanical
   b. operational
   c. wholesome
   d. imitation

3. "on the surrogate's *anatomy*" (30)
   a. body
   b. head
   c. offspring
   d. personality

4. "begins *tentatively* to explore" (71–72)
   a. rapidly
   b. hesitantly
   c. aggressively
   d. readily

5. "fears of the *novel* environment" (74)
   a. hostile
   b. literary
   c. dangerous
   d. new

6. "fears . . . are *desensitized*" (74)
   a. made less sensitive
   b. made more sensitive
   c. electrified
   d. communicated

7. "solutions were *ingenious*" (83–84)
   a. incorrect
   b. noble
   c. clever
   d. honest

8. "*deprived* of contact" (116)
   a. encouraged
   b. denied
   c. assured
   d. ordered into

9. "if the infant *persisted*" (127)
   a. stopped
   b. continued
   c. fought
   d. relaxed

10. "to be greatly *deficient*" (167)
    a. lacking
    b. supplied
    c. overwhelmed
    d. secretive

Search the Net

- Conduct a search on the signs of child abuse. List five indicators that a child may be suffering from abuse or neglect. List three agencies that can be contacted to report suspected abuse. Plan your own search or begin by trying the following:

  National Foundation for Abused and Neglected Children: http://www.gangfreekids.com/index.html

- Conduct a search on the causes of delinquency among children and teenagers. List the different types of abuse and neglect that can cause delinquency. List steps that can be taken to prevent delinquency. Plan your own search or begin by trying the following:

  Coordinating Council on Juvenile Justice and Delinquency: http://ojjdp.ncjrs.org/council/index.html

Concept Prep

for Psychology

What is classical conditioning?

Classical conditioning is the learning that takes place when a subject is taught, or conditioned, to make a new response to a neutral stimulus. This is illustrated by the research of **Ivan Pavlov**, a Russian scientist in the late nineteenth century. Pavlov was studying the basic processes of digestion, focusing on salivation in dogs. Since salivation is a **reflex**, it is an unlearned, automatic response in dogs. When food is presented, dogs will automatically salivate. As his research progressed, Pavlov noticed that the dogs would salivate at the sight of the assistant who delivered the food. At this point, Pavlov decided to investigate learning.

Pavlov reasoned that no learning was involved in the dog's automatic salivation (the **unconditioned response**) when presented with food (the **unconditioned stimulus**). He wondered, however, if he could teach the dogs to salivate at the sound of a bell. To investigate this, Pavlov decided to pair the sound of a bell with the presentation of the food, sound first and food second. The bell alone was a **neutral stimulus** that had never before caused salivation. After a number of **trials** (presenting sound and food together), the dogs became conditioned to associate the sound of the bell with the food. The dogs soon would salivate at the sound, even when the food was withheld. Learning had taken place; Pavlov had taught the dogs to react to a neutral stimulus. Once learning or conditioning had taken place, the sound became a **conditioned stimulus** and the salivation became a **conditioned response**. To take this experiment a step further, if the sound is consistently presented without food, the salivation response will gradually weaken until the dogs completely stop salivating at the sound of the bell (**extinction**). Pavlov's work on animals and learning laid the groundwork for the American behaviorists of the twentieth century.

What is behaviorism?

At the beginning of the twentieth century, many American psychologists disagreed with Freud's psychoanalytical approach (see page 46). They wanted to measure behavior in the laboratory and explain personality in terms of learning theories

Two pigeons seek food in a box developed by psychologist B. F. Skinner as part of his operant conditioning research.
Bettmann/CORBIS

and observable behaviors. **B. F. Skinner** was a leader in this new movement. He borrowed from Pavlov's work and conducted research on operant conditioning.

Skinner posed questions such as, What are your beliefs about rewards and punishments? Do consequences affect your behaviors? Are you a reflection of your positive and negative experiences? Skinner believed that consequences shape behavior and that your personality is merely a reflection of your many learned behaviors.

Skinner demonstrated **operant conditioning** (behaviors used to operate something) by putting a rat inside a small box that came to be known as a **"Skinner box."** The rat explored the box until eventually it found that by pressing a lever, it could make food appear. The rat enjoyed the food and dramatically increased the lever-pressings. The food was a **positive reinforcer** for the lever-pressing. In other words, the food reinforced the behavior and increased it. To stop the lever-pressing behavior **(extinction)**, the rat was given a shock each time the lever was touched. The shock is a **negative reinforcer.** Rewards are positive reinforcers, and punishments are negative reinforcers.

Behavior modification, a type of **behavior therapy,** uses the principles of classical and operant conditioning to increase desired behaviors and decrease problem behaviors. You can use these principles to train a pet, stop a smoking habit, or overcome a fear of flying. Does the desire to make a good grade (reward) affect your studying behavior? Skinner would say, "Yes."

REVIEW QUESTIONS

Study the material and answer the following questions.

1. Who was Ivan Pavlov? _____
   _____

2. What is a reflex? _____
   _____

3. What is a neutral stimulus? _____
   _____

4. Why is the response to the food called unconditioned? _____
   _____

5. What is a conditioned stimulus? _____
   _____

6. What is extinction? _____
   _____

7. How did B. F. Skinner differ from Freud? _____
   _____

8. How does operant conditioning differ from classical conditioning? ___
   _____

9. What is the role of a positive reinforcer? _____
   _____

10. In behavior modification, what makes you want to change behaviors? ___
    _____

Your instructor may choose to give a true-false review of these psychology concepts.

Selection 2 ART HISTORY

CONTEMPORARY FOCUS

What drives the price of a painting to astronomical levels? Is it the potential for pleasure in viewing the work or the potential for profit?

A BLUE PERIOD FOR ART BUYERS

Thane Peterson

Reprinted from the December 25, 2000 issue of *Business Week* by special permission. Copyright © 2000 by The McGraw-Hill Companies.

Londoner Michael G. Wilson, a producer of James Bond movies, is a renowned photo collector. But these days, when he peruses the offerings of dealers, he's often shocked to find classic works by such artists as Man Ray or Gustave Le Gray priced at $500,000 or more. "I used to say a good photo cost the price of a used car," Wilson says. "Then it was a new car, and then a condo. Now, it's measured in houses."

Prices for top modern works are astonishing. *Woman with Crossed Arms*, an ultra-rare canvas from Picasso's Blue Period, went for $55 million at Christie's International, an all-time record for the artist. An Alberto Giacometti sculpture, *Grande Femme Debout*, fetched $14.3 million.

Serious collectors never stop buying. But with prices so high, many are taking precautions. The first rule—always—is don't buy art solely as an investment. Rather, buy works you enjoy living with. And don't be afraid to wait if you don't find exactly what you want.

Collaborative Activity

Collaborate on responses to the following questions:

- What makes a photograph worth a half million dollars?
- Is the greatest profit on art made by the artists or the art dealers?
- How does the phrase "art is subjective" apply to a $55 million Picasso?

Skill Development—Stage 1: Preview

Preview the next selection to predict the purpose and your learning plan.

What is the purpose of writing about art?

What painting is analyzed in the passage?

Activate Schema

What style are Picasso's most famous paintings?

Who is your favorite artist?

Learning Strategy

Understand the questions that you ask when writing about art and see how the example illustrates a way of answering.

Word Knowledge

What do you know about these words?

eluding   bourgeois   enhance   prominence   wisps

wedded   stubble   ponderously   sensate   untainted

Your instructor may give a true-false vocabulary review before or after reading.

Stage 2: Integrate Knowledge While Reading

Predict   Picture   Relate   Monitor   Correct

WHY WRITE ABOUT ART?
From Sylvan Barnet, *A Short Guide to Writing About Art*, 5th ed.

We write about art in order to clarify and to account for our responses to works that interest or excite or frustrate us. In putting words on paper we have to take a second and a third look at what is in front of us and at what is within us. Picasso said, "To know what you want to draw, you have to begin drawing"; simi-
5   larly, writing is a way of finding what you want to write, a way of learning. The last word is never said about complex thoughts and feelings—and works of art, as well as our responses to them, embody complex thoughts and feelings. But when we write about art we hope to make at least a little progress in the difficult but rewarding job of talking about our responses. As Arthur C. Danto says in the
10   introduction to *Embodied Meanings* (1994), a collection of essays about art:

> Until one tries to write about it, the work of art remains a sort of aesthetic blur. . . . After seeing the work, write about it. You cannot be satisfied for very long in simply putting down what you felt. You have to go further. (p. 14)

15   When we write, we learn; we also hope to interest our reader by communicating our responses to material that for one reason or another is worth talking about.

The Function of Critical Writing

In everyday language the most common meaning of criticism is "finding fault," and to be critical is to be censorious. But a critic can see excellences as well as faults. Because we turn to criticism with the hope that the critic has seen some-
20   thing we have missed, the most valuable criticism is not that which shakes its

finger at fault but that which calls attention to interesting matters going on in the work of art.

Getting Ideas: Asking Questions to Get Answers

The painter Ad Reinhardt once said that "Looking is not as simple as it looks."
25 What are some of the basic things to look for in trying to acquire an understanding of the languages of art; that is, in trying to understand what a work of art expresses?

Basic Questions

One can begin a discussion of the complex business of expression in the arts almost anywhere, but let's begin with some questions that can be asked of almost any work of art—whether a painting or a drawing or a sculpture or even
30 a building.

- **What is my first response to the work?** Later you may modify or even reject this response, but begin by trying to study it. Jot down your responses—even your free associations. Do you find the work puzzling, boring, pretty, ugly, offensive, sexy, or what? The act of jotting down a response may help you to deepen the response, or to move beyond it to a different response.

- **When and where was the work made?** Does it reveal the qualities that your textbook attributes to the culture? (Don't assume that it does; works of art have a way of eluding easy generalization.)

- **Where would the work originally have been seen?** Perhaps in a church or a palace, or a bourgeois home, or (if the work is an African mask) worn by a costumed dancer, but surely not in a museum (unless it is a contemporary work) or in a textbook. For Picasso, "The picture-hook is the ruination of a painting. . . . As soon as a painting is bought and hung on a wall, it takes on quite a different significance, and the painting is done for." If the work is now part of an exhibition in a museum, how does the museum's presentation of the work affect your response?

- **What purpose did the work serve?** To stimulate devotion? To impress the viewer with the owner's power? To enhance family pride? To teach? To delight? Does the work present a likeness, or express a feeling, or illustrate a mystery?

- **In what condition has the work survived?** Is it exactly as it left the artist's hands, or has it been damaged, repaired, or in some way altered? What evidence of change can be seen?

- **What is the title?** Does it help to illuminate the work? Sometimes it is useful to ask yourself, "What would I call the work?" Picasso called one of his early self-portraits *Yo Picasso* (i.e., "I, Picasso"), rather than, say, *Portrait of the Artist*, and indeed his title goes well with the depicted self-confidence.

A Sample Essay

The following essay on Jean-François Millet's *The Gleaners*, written by Robert Herbert, was originally a note in the catalog issued in conjunction with the art exposition at the Canadian World's Fair, Expo 67.

35 In this brief essay, in fact, Herbert skillfully sets forth material that might have made half a dozen essays: Millet's life, the background of Millet's thought, Millet's political and social views, the composition of *The Gleaners*, Millet's depiction of peasants, Millet's connection with later painters. But the aim is always to make us see. In *The Gleaners* Millet tried to show us certain
40 things, and now Robert Herbert tries to show us—tries to make us see—what Millet was doing and how he did it.

"Millet's *The Gleaners*"

by Robert Herbert

The Gleaners, *by Jean-François Millet, 1857. Oil on canvas, 83.6 × 111 cm. Musée d'Orsay, Paris, France. Photo: Jean Schormans/Réunion des Musées Nationaux/Art Resource, NY.*

Jean-François Millet, born of well-to-do Norman peasants, began his artistic training in Cherbourg. In 1837 he moved to Paris where he lived until 1849, except for a few extended visits to Normandy. With the sounds of
45 the Revolution of 1848 still rumbling, he moved to Barbizon on the edge of the Forest of Fontainebleau, already noted as a resort of landscape painters, and there he spent the rest of his life. One of the major painters of what came to be called the Barbizon School, Millet began to celebrate the labors of the peasant, granting him a heroic dignity which expressed the aspira-
50 tions of 1848. Millet's identification with the new social ideals was a result not of overtly radical views, but of his instinctive humanitarianism and his

rediscovery in the actual peasant life of the eternal rural world of the Bible and of Virgil, his favorite reading since youth. By elevating to a new prominence the life of the common people, the revolutionary era released the stimulus which enabled him to continue this essential pursuit of his art and of his life.

The Gleaners, exhibited in the Salon of 1857, presents the very poorest of the peasants who are fated to bend their backs to gather with clubbed fingers the wisps of overlooked grain. That they seem so entirely wedded to the soil results from the perfect harmony of Millet's fatalistic view of man with the images which he created by a careful disposition of lines, colors, and shapes. The three women are alone in the bronzed stubble of the foreground, far removed from the bustling activity of the harvesters in the distance, the riches of whose labors have left behind a few gleanings. Millet has weighted his figures ponderously downward, the busy harvest scene is literally above them, and the high horizon line which the taller woman's cap just touches emphasizes their earth-bound role, suggesting that the sky is a barrier which presses down upon them, and not a source of release.

The humility of primeval labor is shown, too, in the creation of primitive archetypes rather than of individuals. Introspection such as that seen in Velazquez's *Water Carrier of Seville*, in which the three men are distinct individuals, is denied by suppressing the gleaners' features, and where the precise, fingered gestures of La Tour's *Saint Jerome* bring his intellectual work toward his sensate mind, Millet gives his women clublike hands which reach away from their bent bodies toward the earth.

It was, paradoxically, the urban-industrial revolution in the nineteenth century which prompted a return to images of the preindustrial, ageless labors of man. For all their differences, both Degas and Van Gogh were to share these concerns later, and even Gauguin was to find in the fishermen of the South Seas that humble being, untainted by the modern city, who is given such memorable form in Millet's *Gleaners*.

Stage 3: Recall

Stop to self-test, relate, and react.

Your instructor may choose to give you a true-false comprehension review.

Thinking About "Why Write About Art?"

What does the author mean in referring to Millet's "instinctive humanitarianism" and the paradox of the urban-industrial revolution in the nineteenth century prompting a return to images of the labors of man?

Response Suggestion: Define instinctive humanitarianism, paradox, and urban-industrial revolution. Relate the meanings to Millet's historical times and to his painting.

Contemporary Link

In order to write about art and clarify your understanding, the author suggests six basic questions to guide your thinking. Expand on this concept from a purchaser's point of view. List six additional questions that you think a collector should ask before paying $15 million for a work of art.

Skill Development: Main Idea

Answer the following with *T* (true) or *F* (false).

_____ 1. The main idea of the first paragraph is that writing about art helps us understand art.

_____ 2. The main idea of the paragraph beginning with "In everyday language" is that art does not deserve criticism.

_____ 3. The main idea of the last paragraph is that Millet was a greater painter than Degas or Van Gogh.

Comprehension Questions

After reading the selection, answer the following questions with *a, b, c,* or *d.* In order to help you analyze your strengths and weaknesses, the question types are indicated.

Main Idea _____ 1. The best statement of the main idea is
a. the act of writing to explore and answer basic questions about art helps us clarify our responses and learn.
b. in *The Gleaners*, Millet depicts poor peasants who are harvesting grain.
c. Picasso believed that you have to experience in order to appreciate.
d. the purpose of writing about art is to learn and to find flaws.

Inference _____ 2. The author believes that the ultimate goal of criticism is to
a. find fault.
b. be censorious.
c. contrast and thus highlight excellences.
d. uncover new aspects of interest.

Inference _____ 3. The author uses Ad Reinhardt's quotation, "Looking is not as simple as it looks," to suggest that
a. most people are ignorant of good art.
b. guidelines for examining art are needed.
c. what you see does not control what you feel.
d. Reinhardt did not understand art.

Detail _____ 4. The author believes that our initial responses to art
  a. are never valid.
  b. may change with study.
  c. only reveal our own biases.
  d. demonstrate our own ignorance.

Inference _____ 5. In Picasso's statement about the "picture-hook," he implies that taking a painting from its origins and hanging it on a wall
  a. gives more people an opportunity to view it.
  b. enhances the painting.
  c. allows for a greater appreciation of the painting.
  d. changes the painting for the worse.

Inference _____ 6. The author suggests that Millet moved to Barbizon because
  a. he wanted to attend college there and become a land-scape painter.
  b. he wanted to work with the peasants and learn their ways.
  c. it was an artistic colony that was somewhat sheltered from the conflicts of war.
  d. it was located in Normandy where the artist was born.

Inference _____ 7. Herbert suggests that the women in Millet's *The Gleaners* are
  a. searching for leftovers for personal use.
  b. harvesting grain for the wealthy landowner.
  c. working with the harvesters.
  d. stealing something they should not be taking.

Inference _____ 8. According to Herbert, Millet depicts the three women as
  a. independently in charge of their own destinies.
  b. sinners being punished.
  c. tied to the earth.
  d. reaching toward heaven.

Detail _____ 9. According to Herbert, Millet's portrayal of peasants
  a. was similar to La Tour's *Saint Jerome*.
  b. gave them heroic dignity.
  c. ridiculed primeval labor.
  d. was a result of his radical politics.

Detail _____ 10. According to the passage, an artist who created primitive archetypes similar to Millet's three women was
  a. Picasso.
  b. Velazquez.
  c. La Tour.
  d. Gauguin.

Answer the following with *T* (true) or *F* (false).

Inference   _____ 11. The author suggests that the one who benefits most from writing about art is the writer.

Detail   _____ 12. Herbert's essay was originally written as an explanation for attendees at the Canadian World's Fair.

Detail   _____ 13. Herbert suggests that the three women in Millet's painting are portrayed in a similar manner to the three men in Velazquez's *Water Carrier of Seville*.

Detail   _____ 14. Millet was born into a very poor family.

Detail   _____ 15. According to Herbert, the hands of Millet's gleaners are slim and agile.

Vocabulary

According to the way the italicized word was used in the selection, select *a*, *b*, *c*, or *d* for the word or phrase that gives the best definition. The number in parentheses indicates the line number of the passage in which the word is located.

_____ 1. "*eluding* easy generalizations" (30, item 2)
    a. generating
    b. skillfully avoiding
    c. capturing
    d. copying

_____ 2. "*bourgeois* home" (30, item 3)
    a. peasant
    b. middle class
    c. modern
    d. decorated

_____ 3. "*enhance* family pride" (30, item 4)
    a. mimic
    b. increase
    c. validate
    d. insure

_____ 4. "new *prominence*" (53–54)
    a. era
    b. importance
    c. art form
    d. style of interpretation

_____ 5. "*wisps* of overlooked grain" (59)
    a. small fragments
    b. bundles
    c. handfuls
    d. buckets

_____ 6. "*wedded* to the soil" (59–60)
    a. indebted
    b. contrasted
    c. removed
    d. joined

_____ 7. "bronzed *stubble*" (62)
    a. oil painting
    b. rough growth
    c. dim light
    d. smooth grass

_____ 8. "*ponderously* downward" (65)
    a. heavily
    b. curved
    c. carelessly
    d. needlessly

9. "his *sensate* mind" (75)
   a. logical
   b. relating to the senses
   c. narrow
   d. curious

10. "*untainted* by the modern city" (81)
    a. uncontaminated
    b. uncontrolled
    c. unimpressed
    d. unmatched

Search the Net

■ Search for and print a picture of a piece of art by an artist of your choice, such as Paul Cezanne, Georgia O'Keeffe, or Diego Rivera. Describe your first response to the work, where and when the work was created, where the work may have originally been seen, and the purpose that the work originally had. Begin your own search, or start with one of the following:

Constable.net: http://www.constable.net/index.html

Art Without Artifice—The Truth About Famous Paintings: http://painting.netfirms.com/

Internet Art Museum: http://library.thinkquest.org/29313/

■ Search for and print two different pictures of pieces of artwork that illustrate different styles of painting. Compare and contrast your first response to each work, where each work may have originally been seen, and the original purpose of each piece. Begin your own search, or start with one of the following:

Museum Suite: http://www.museum.suite.dk/

National Museum of Women in the Arts Permanent Collection Tour: http://dir.yahoo.com/Arts/Art_History/Collections/

El Museo del Barrio: http://www.elmuseo.org/

Concept Prep

for Art

When we say "the arts," what do we mean?

The **arts** and the **fine arts** refer to creative works in painting, sculpture, literature, architecture, drama, music, opera, dance, and film. A work that is exceptionally well crafted is said to aspire to the level of fine art.

Museums, a word derived from Greek to mean places presided over by the Muses, display fine arts in paintings and sculpture. Some of the greatest museums in the world are the **Louvre** in Paris, the **Prado** in Madrid, and the **Metropolitan Museum of Art** in New York. Art tells us about people and their culture as illustrated in the earliest primitive cave drawings depicting animals and hunters or in the elaborately decorated tombs in the Egyptian pyramids built for the ascension of pharaohs into heaven.

Who are considered some of the greatest artists?

- One of the most extraordinary artists was **Leonardo da Vinci** (1452–1519). He was considered a **Renaissance man** because of his genius, insatiable curiosity, and wide interests in art, engineering, anatomy, and aeronautics. He painted the **Mona Lisa,** the world's most famous painting. This woman with the mysterious smile whose eyes seem to follow you is displayed in the Louvre behind several layers of bulletproof glass.

- **Michelangelo** (1475–1564) was a sculptor, painter, architect, and poet. Before he was thirty years old, he created the famous marble statue of **David,** which portrays the biblical king in his youth. Michelangelo was commissioned by the Pope to paint the ceiling of the **Sistine Chapel** in the Vatican in Rome. For four years, the artist worked on his back in the chapel to complete the biblical story, **The Creation of Adam,** which contains more than 400 individual figures.

- The founder and leading artist of the **Impressionists** was **Claude Monet** (1840–1926). Critics said the feathery brushstrokes and play of light in his works conveyed the "impression" of a particular moment. Monet advocated getting out of the studio and painting outdoors facing the sub-

This self portrait of Vincent van Gogh was painted in 1887, three years before he died.
Self Portrait, 1887 by Vincent van Gogh, Musée d'Orsay, Paris, France. Copyright Réunion des Musées Nationaux/Art Resource, NY.

ject. He painted many scenes of the gardens and water lily ponds surrounding his home in **Giverny** near Paris.

- **Van Gogh** (1853–1890) borrowed from the Impressionists but achieved another dimension in the swirling brushstrokes of his work to convey his unique vision. His sunflower paintings and **Starry Night** are among his most famous works, now popularized in mass reproductions, but in his lifetime Van Gogh sold only one painting. He suffered from depression and spent his last years in a mental institution. In an argument with another artist, he cut off his own ear, which he later sent to a prostitute.

- **Pablo Picasso** (1881–1973) is one of the most influential of all modern artists. Because traditional skills in painting were so easy for him, he looked for new modes of expres-sion. He was the originator of Cubism, an abstract style of painting that displays several perspectives of an object si-multaneously. One of his most acclaimed paintings is **Guer-nica,** a haunting visual protest against the savagery of war.

REVIEW QUESTIONS

Study the material and answer the following questions.

1. What do works included in "the arts" have in common? _____
   _____

2. Where is the Louvre? _____
   _____

3. What is a Renaissance Man? _____
   _____

4. What is unusually engaging about Mona Lisa's face? _____
   _____

5. What story is painted on the ceiling of the Sistine Chapel? _____
   _____

6. How did the Impressionists get the name? _____
   _____

7. What scenes did Monet paint at Giverny? _____
   _____

8. Which painter advocated painting outdoors? _____
   _____

9. How did Van Gogh disfigure himself? _____
   _____

10. Why did Picasso turn to Cubism? _____

Your instructor may choose to give a true-false review of these art concepts.

Selection 3 **SOCIOLOGY**

CONTEMPORARY FOCUS

The world is becoming increasingly urban as people leave rural areas and seek economic opportunity in cities. The new immigrants congregate in shantytowns, overcrowded settlements that lack basic city services. How can individuals and governments solve these squatter problems?

LETTER FROM BRAZIL

Robert Neuwirth

The Nation, New York, July 10, 2000

Many Brazilians will tell you that the favelas are slums or shantytowns, but that is simply the dictionary definition. The favelas may once have been urban wastelands, but over the past two decades favelados have transformed their junkyard colonies into desirable neighborhoods, achieving something most illegal settlers can only dream of: permanence. Their new brand of self help urban development could become a model for the rest of the world. Here are its two simple steps: Let the poor build, then work with them to stabilize their self built communities.

Other countries have huge squatter populations, of course, but Brazil is one of the few places where squatters have transformed their domains into thriving neighborhoods. Here are some of the reasons why the favelados have succeeded where most other squatters have not.

The favelados defy many stereotypes. They aren't anarchists or punks or people raging against the system; most favelados are simply trying to create a better life for themselves and their kids.

The squatters are shrewd and strategic. Early on, they recognized that one of the legacies of authoritarian rule was that there was a huge amount of fallow land under government control. So they tended to invade these parcels.

The favelados also understand the need for coordinated action. Since a single person has a hard time erecting a house, the favelas became natural collectives. The residents united in *mutiroes*—cooperative building associations—and erected their communities collectively.

The squatters realized they had to work inside the system. Some favelas cut deals with local politicians—promising support if the officials helped them get city services like running water, sanitation or access to mass transit.

The favelados have also been aided in their quest by a marvelous quirk of Brazilian law and by responsive governments. In contrast to the United States, where property rights are king, Brazil's Constitution explicitly protects squatters.

Collaborative Activity

Collaborate on responses to the following questions:

- Why didn't Brazilian cities outlaw the favelas?
- How has the human spirit and cooperation changed the favelas?
- What happens to new immigrants who go to the favelas?

Skill Development—Stage 1: Preview

Preview the next selection to predict its purpose, organization, and your learning plan.

The author probably describes the problems of city slums.
Agree ☐   Disagree ☐

After reading this selection, I will need to know the ten major cities in the world.   Agree ☐   Disagree ☐

Activate Schema

Why do so many people flock to Mexico City?

Why do so many people prefer city life to farm life?

Learning Strategy

Seek to understand the reasons for urbanization and the problems.

Word Knowledge

What do you know about these words?

pursuits	endeavors	transcends	serene	pastoral
spigot	distort	deteriorating	dismal	enclaves

Your instructor may give a true-false vocabulary review before or after reading.

Stage 2: Integrate Knowledge While Reading

Predict   Picture   Relate   Monitor   Correct

URBANIZATION
From James M. Henslin, *Sociology*, 5th ed.

The key to the origin of cities is the development of more efficient agriculture (Lenski and Lenski 1987). Only when farming produces a surplus can some people stop being food producers and gather in cities to spend time in other pursuits. A **city,** in fact, can be defined as a place in which a large number of
5   people are permanently based and do not produce their own food. The invention of the plow between five and six thousand years ago created widespread agricultural surpluses, stimulating the development of towns and cities (Curwin and Hart 1961).

Slum houses on the hillside in Mexico are built with brick walls and wooden boards.
Jonathan Nourok/PhotoEdit

The Industrial Revolution and the Size of Cities

Most early cities were tiny by comparison with those of today, merely a collection of a few thousand people in agricultural centers or on major trade
routes. The most notable exceptions are two cities that reached 1 million
for a brief period of time before they declined—Changan in China about
A.D. 800 and Bagdad in Persia about A.D. 900 (Chandler and Fox 1974).
Even Athens at the peak of its power in the fifth century B.C. had less than
200,000 inhabitants. Rome, at its peak, may have had a million or more
(Flanagan 1990).

Even 200 years ago, the only city in the world that had a population of
more than a million was Peking (now Beijing), China (Chandler and Fox
1974). Then in just 100 years, by 1900, the number of such cities jumped to
sixteen. The reason was the Industrial Revolution, which drew people to cities
by providing work. The Industrial Revolution also stimulated rapid transportation and communication, and allowed people, resources, and products to
be moved efficiently—all essential factors (called infrastructure) on which
large cities depend. Today about 300 cities have a million or more people
(Frisbie and Kasarda 1988).

City Life

Cities are intended to be solutions to problems. They are the result of human
endeavors that seek to improve life collectively, to develop a way of life that
transcends the limitations of farm and village. Cities hold out the hope of jobs,
education, and other advantages. The perception of opportunity underlies
mass migration to cities throughout the world.

City Slums in the Least Industrialized Nations

Images of the Least Industrialized Nations that portray serene pastoral scenes distort today's reality. In these nations, poor rural people have flocked to the cities in such numbers that these nations now contain most of the world's largest cities. Each year the cities of the Least Industrialized Nations grow by 62 million people (Annez 1998). That's more than all the Italians who live in Italy, the equivalent of adding twice the population of Canada every year. In the Most Industrialized Nations, industrialization usually preceded urbanization, but here *urbanization is preceding industrialization.*

The settlement patterns are also different. When rural migrants and immigrants move to U.S. cities, they usually settle in deteriorating houses near the city's center. The wealthy reside in suburbs and luxurious city enclaves. Migrants to cities of the Least Industrialized Nations, in contrast, establish illegal squatter settlements outside the city. There they build shacks from scrap board, cardboard, and bits of corrugated metal. Even flattened tin cans are used for building material. The squatters enjoy no city facilities—roads, public transportation, water, sewers, or garbage pickup. After thousands of squatters have settled an area, the city acknowledges their right to live there and adds bus service and minimal water lines. Hundreds of people use a single spigot. About 5 *million* of Mexico City's residents live in such conditions, with hundreds of thousands more pouring in each year.

This story is repeated throughout South America, Africa, India, and the rest of the so-called underdeveloped world. Why this vast rush to live in the city under such miserable conditions? The explanation lies in the many "push" factors that arise from the breakdown of traditional rural life. With the importation of modern medicine, a safer water supply, and better transportation and distribution of food, the death rate has dropped, and the rural populations are multiplying. There is not enough land for everyone, and rural life can no longer support so many people. "Pull" factors also draw people to the cities—the hope of jobs, education, better housing, and even a more stimulating life.

At the bottom of a ravine near Mexico City is a dismal bunch of shacks. Some of the families living in them have 14 children.

"We used to live up there," Senora Gonzalez gestured toward the mountain, "in those caves. Our only hope was one day to have a place to live. And now we do." She smiled with pride at the jerry-built shacks . . . each one had a collection of flowers planted in tin cans. "One day, we hope to extend the water pipes and drainage—perhaps even pave . . ."

And what was the name of her community? Senora Gonzalez beamed. "Esperanza!" (McDowell 1984:172)

Esperanza is the Spanish word for hope. This is what lies behind the rush to these cities—the hope of a better life. And this is why the rush won't slow down. In 1930, only one Latin American city had more than a million people—now fifty do! The world's cities are growing by one million people each week (Brockerhoff 1996).

Will the Least Industrialized Nations adjust to this vast, unwanted migration? They have no choice. Authorities in Brazil, Guatemala, Venezuela, and

other countries have sent in the police and the army to evict the settlers. It doesn't work. It just leads to violence, and the settlers keep streaming in. The adjustment will be painful. The infrastructure (roads, water, sewers, electricity, and so on) must be built, but these poor countries don't have the resources to
80 build them. As the desperate flock to the cities, the problems will worsen.

Stage 3: Recall

Stop to self-test, relate, and react.

Your instructor may choose to give you a true-false comprehension review.

Thinking About "Urbanization"

What is the relationship of cities to farming?

Response Suggestion: Describe historically how one must come before the other and how one supports the other.

Contemporary Link

How can other cities solve urban slum problems by using the success of the favelas? Explain the conditions that are necessary for the favela model to work.

Skill Development: Main Idea

Answer the following with *T* (true) or *F* (false).

_____ 1. The main idea of the selection is stated in the first sentence of the second paragraph.

_____ 2. The topic of the third paragraph is the Industrial Revolution in China.

_____ 3. The main topic for the entire selection is the failure of the farms to support the people.

_____ 4. The need for cities to have adequate infrastructure to serve new rural migrants is a major detail in support of the main idea of this selection.

Comprehension Questions

After reading the selection, answer the following questions with *a, b, c,* or *d.* In order to help you analyze your strengths and weaknesses, the question types are indicated.

Main Idea   _____ 1. Which is the best statement of the main idea?
   a. City slums in the Least Industrialized Nations lack sewage and sanitation.
   b. Without efficient agriculture and industrialization to support the development of cities, city slums are now emerging in underdeveloped countries.
   c. A surplus of farm produce is the key factor in the development of the many cities that now have over a million people.
   d. Cities offer solutions to problems and attract mass migrations of people looking for opportunities.

Detail   _____ 2. In 1900, how many cities had over a million people?
   a. 2
   b. 4
   c. 16
   d. 300

Detail   _____ 3. Infrastructure includes all of the following except
   a. roads.
   b. migrants.
   c. water.
   d. electricity.

Inference   _____ 4. By using the word *perception* in the phrase, "The perception of opportunity underlies mass migration," the author suggests that
   a. the opportunity is not always a reality for migrants.
   b. migrants usually get what they expect.
   c. migrants have developed clear goals for their migrations.
   d. mass migrations are usually caused by famine in underdeveloped countries.

Detail   _____ 5. The pattern of migrants to the cities in the Least Industrialized Nations is
   a. to move to the inner city.
   b. to move to the luxurious city enclaves.
   c. to settle in deteriorating housing near the city's center.
   d. to settle outside the city.

Inference   _____ 6. The author suggests that all of the following nations are included in the Least Industrialized Nations except
   a. Canada.
   b. Mexico.
   c. India.
   d. Brazil.

Detail   _____ 7. The author attributes the breakdown of traditional rural life and the move to city slums to all of the following except
     a. reduced death rate.
     b. the urban infrastructure readily available to the new squatters.
     c. safer water supply.
     d. better transportation.

Inference   _____ 8. The primary reason the author includes the story of Senora Gonzalez is to
     a. argue for better transportation for the squatters.
     b. explain why violence is prevalent in squatter communities.
     c. show that most squatters will leave the community and find jobs.
     d. dramatize the hope, pride, and determination of the squatters.

Inference   _____ 9. In the statement, "urbanization is preceding industrialization," the author means that
     a. the people are needed for the jobs in the cities.
     b. the people are coming before the jobs.
     c. the people come to the cities and do not want to work.
     d. the people who are coming are not trained to fill the jobs.

Inference   _____ 10. The reader can conclude that
     a. cities encourage migrants to locate in squatter communities.
     b. cities can regulate the flow of migrants into the squatter communities.
     c. cities have little control over the establishment of squatter communities.
     d. cities first provide the land, water, and electricity and then the squatter communities are built.

Answer the following with *T* (true) or *F* (false).

Detail   _____ 11. The author attributes the development of cities to the creation of the plow.

Detail   _____ 12. The author defines a "pull" factor as a positive motivation to migrate to a city.

Detail   _____ 13. According to the passage, every year each of the major cities in the Least Industrialized Nations grows by 62 million people.

Detail   _____ 14. According to the passage, the first city in history to reach a million in population was Athens.

Detail   _____ 15. Senora Gonzalez lives in a shack in a ravine near Mexico City.

Vocabulary

According to the way the italicized word was used in the selection, select *a*, *b*, *c*, or *d* for the word or phrase that gives the best definition. The number in parentheses indicates the line of the passage in which the word is located.

_____ 1. "in other *pursuits*" (3–4)
    a. communities
    b. occupations
    c. locations
    d. environments

_____ 2. "human *endeavors*" (26–27)
    a. efforts
    b. mysteries
    c. misfortunes
    d. miseries

_____ 3. "*transcends* the limitations" (28)
    a. combines
    b. changes
    c. rises above
    d. compares

_____ 4. "portray *serene* pastoral scenes" (31)
    a. peaceful
    b. unsanitary
    c. lonely
    d. shameful

_____ 5. "portray serene *pastoral* scenes" (31)
    a. religious
    b. mountainous
    c. small town
    d. country

_____ 6. "*distort* today's reality" (32)
    a. confirm
    b. describe
    c. compliment
    d. twist

_____ 7. "*deteriorating* houses" (40)
    a. antique
    b. remodeled
    c. falling apart
    d. vacant

_____ 8. "luxurious city *enclaves*" (41)
    a. exclusive enclosed areas
    b. houses
    c. country clubs
    d. apartment buildings

_____ 9. "use a single *spigot*" (48)
    a. water hose
    b. sink
    c. faucet
    d. shower

_____ 10. "*dismal* bunch of shacks" (60)
    a. newly erected
    b. dreadful
    c. dangerous
    d. illegal

Search the Net

■ List the names and locations of three different shantytowns. Briefly describe the living conditions, the population, and some of the factors that led to the creation of each shantytown. Start your own search, or begin with one of the following:

Gypsy Journal: http://www.gypsyjournal.com/Chapter.asp?ChapterID=346

Scriptnet2000: http://www.scriptnet2000.org.uk/ghana/ghcities.html

Caritas.org: http://www.caritas.org.au/what_we_do/where_la1.htm

- While industrialization draws people to urban areas, cities are not always prepared to serve the needs of a growing population. Discuss five of the problems that arise as a result of overpopulation. Provide Web site addresses for each source of your information. Start your own search, or begin with one of the following:

Facing the Future; People and the Planet: http://www.facingthefuture.org/

Negative Population Growth: http://www.npg.org/

Population Action: http://www.populationaction.org/

Concept Prep

for Sociology

What is sociology?

While psychology focuses on the individual, **sociology** focuses on explaining group behaviors and society. **Sociologists** use logic and the scientific method to observe and explain interpersonal interaction, group membership, and social institutions. Students majoring in sociology may concentrate on family and community services, social justice, cultural issues, urban issues, or gerontology (the study of issues of aging).

What is a counterculture movement?

In the late 1950s the **Beat Generation** began to question the accepted American values. These **beatniks** scorned materialism, traditional family life, religion, and politics. They embraced radical politics and exotic music, art, and literature. Their slang included words like *chick, Big Apple,* and *square,* and their appeal on college campuses scattered the seeds for change in the next decade.

By the 1960s, young people were beginning to see themselves as a social force for change. Many protested and demonstrated for civil rights, women's rights, gay and lesbian rights, and abortion. They declared a **generation gap** between themselves and the decision makers, feeling that no one over thirty years of age could be trusted. These young people rejected the traditional dreams of success and values of conservative Middle America. They rebelled against the expected path to success and chose an alternative lifestyle. They became **hippies** or **flower children,** wearing unconventional clothing, using drugs, and practicing free love and communal living. By the late 1960s they were protesting U.S. military involvement in Vietnam. To celebrate their new culture or **counterculture,** 400,000 young people gathered near **Woodstock,** a small town in New York state, for a rock music festival in 1969. They listened to music, took drugs, and made love.

What is feminism?

Feminism is a political movement for women's rights, asserting that women and men should have equal legal, economic, social, and political rights. In 1963 **Betty Friedan's** book, *The Feminine Mystique,* launched this new movement that was to

Counterculture groups join the Fourth of July celebration in 1968 in El Rito, N.M.
Lisa Law/The Image Works

redefine female roles in American society. Basing her information on interviews and questionnaires, Friedan wrote about the sense of discontent, frustration, and exhaustion felt by educated American women. She criticized educators and the mass media for thinking women could only be mothers and housewives. **Gloria Steinem,** founder of *Ms.* magazine, was also a leader in the women's liberation movement.

What is an environmentalist?

An **environmentalist** is a person dedicated to protecting our natural resources from destruction and pollution. **Rachel Carson,** a marine biologist, popularized a mass movement for environmental protection in 1962 with the publication of her book, *Silent Spring.* In the book, she described how DDT and other pesticides contaminated the food chain, killed birds and fish, and caused human illnesses.

Study the material and answer the following questions.

1. What *is* sociology? _____
   _____

2. Who were the beatniks? _____
   _____

3. What is a counterculture? _____
   _____

4. Who were the hippies? _____
   _____

5. What was the significance of Woodstock? _____
   _____

6. What *is* feminism? _____
   _____

7. What was the point of *The Feminine Mystique?* _____
   _____

8. Who is Gloria Steinem? _____
   _____

9. What was the significance of *Silent Spring?* _____
   _____

10. What *is* DDT? _____
    _____

Your instructor may choose to give a true-false review of these sociology concepts.

READER'S JOURNAL

Name _____ Date _____

CHAPTER 4

Answer the following questions to reflect on your own learning and progress. Use the perforations to tear the assignment out for your instructor.

1. When trying to determine the author's point, why is it important to determine the topic first? _____

   _____

2. Why is prior knowledge important in stating the main idea? _____

   _____

3. Why should the main idea be stated in a complete sentence? _____

   _____

4. When you write a term paper, where do you usually state the main idea? Why? _____

   _____

5. For what purpose have you written a summary as part of your school work? What was difficult about writing it? _____

   _____

6. Reflect on the multiple-choice items in the longer selections. How were your errors similar to or different from your errors in the last chapter?

   _____

7. Compare your concentration on the psychology, art history, and sociology selections. Which did you feel most focused on and why? _____

   _____

8. How many of the thirty vocabulary items did you answer correctly?

   _____

C h a p t e r **3**

Organizational Patterns

Most college students take courses in several different disciplines each semester. You may study psychology, anatomy and physiology, mathematics, and English composition all in one semester. During one day you may read a poem, solve math problems, and study early developments in psychology.

What few students realize is that a biologist and a psychologist, for example, think about and approach their subject matter in similar ways. Both carefully define terms, examine causes and effects, study similarities and differences, describe sequences of events, classify information, solve problems, and enumerate characteristics. The subject matter and language they use differ, but their approaches to the material are basically the same. Researchers, textbook authors, and your professors use standard approaches, or **organizational patterns,** to express their ideas.

In academic writing, commonly used organizational patterns include definition, classification, order or sequence, cause and effect, comparison and contrast, and listing/enumeration. Other important patterns include statement and clarification, summary, generalization and example, and addition.

These patterns can work for you in several ways:

- Patterns help you anticipate the author's thought development and thus, focus your reading.
- Patterns help you remember and recall what you read.
- Patterns are useful in your own writing; they help you organize and express your ideas in a more coherent, comprehensible form.

The following section describes each pattern listed above. In subsequent chapters, you will see how these patterns are used in specific academic disciplines.

| 4a | **DEFINITION** |

Each academic discipline has its own specialized vocabulary. One of the primary purposes of introductory textbooks is to introduce students to this new language. Consequently, definition is a commonly used pattern throughout most introductory-level texts.

Suppose you were asked to define the word *comedian* for someone unfamiliar with the term. First, you would probably say that a comedian is a person who entertains. Then you might distinguish a comedian from other types of entertainers by saying that a comedian is an entertainer who tells jokes and makes others laugh. Finally, you might mention, by way of example, the names of several well-known comedians who have appeared on television. Although you may have presented it informally, your definition would have followed the standard, classic pattern. The first part of your definition tells what general class or group the term belongs to (entertainers). The second part tells what distinguishes the term from other items in the same class or category. The third part includes further explanation, characteristics, examples, or applications.

You can visualize the definition pattern as follows:

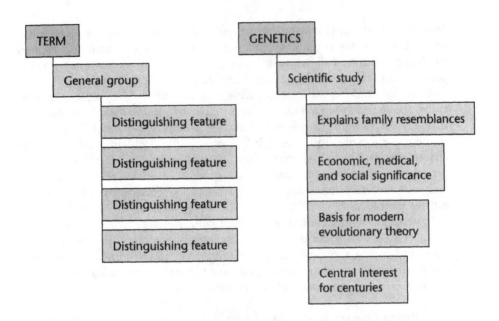

See how the term *genetics* is defined in the following paragraph, and notice how the term and the general class are presented in the first sentence. The remainder of the paragraph presents the distinguishing characteristics.

> Genetics is the scientific study of heredity, the transmission of characteristics from parents to offspring. Genetics explains why offspring resemble their parents and also why they are not identical to them. Genetics is a subject that has considerable economic, medical, and social significance and is partly the basis for the modern theory of evolution. Because of its importance, genetics has been a topic of central interest in the study of life for centuries. Modern concepts in genetics are fundamentally different, however, from earlier ones.
>
> —Mix, Farber, and King, *Biology, The Network of Life,* p. 262

Writers often provide clues called **transitions** that signal the organizational pattern being used. These signals may occur within single sentences or as connections between sentences. (Transitional words that occur in phrases are italicized here to help you spot them.)

TRANSITIONS FOR THE DEFINITION PATTERN

genetics *is* . . .

bureaucracy *means* . . .

patronage *refers to* . . .

aggression *can be defined* as . . .

deficit is *another term* that . . .

balance of power *also means* . . .

4b | **CLASSIFICATION**

If you were asked to describe types of computers, you might mention mainframes, minicomputers, and microcomputers. By dividing a broad topic into its major categories, you are using a pattern known as *classification*.

This pattern is widely used in many academic subjects. For example, a psychology text might explain human needs by classifying them into two categories: primary and secondary. In a chemistry textbook, various compounds may be grouped and discussed according to common characteristics, such as the presence of hydrogen or oxygen. The classification pattern divides a topic into parts, on the basis of common or shared characteristics.

Here are a few examples of topics and the classifications or categories into which each might be divided.

- Movies: comedy, horror, mystery
- Motives: achievement, power, affiliation, competency
- Plant: leaves, stem, roots

Note how the paragraph that follows classifies the various types of cancers.

The name of the cancer is derived from the type of tissue in which it develops. Carcinoma (carc = cancer; omo = tumor) refers to a malignant tumor consisting of epithelial cells. A tumor that develops from a gland is called an adenosarcoma (adeno = gland). Sarcoma is a general term for any cancer arising from connective tissue. Osteogenic sarcomas (osteo = bone; genic = origin), the most frequent type of childhood cancer, destroy normal bone tissue and eventually spread to other areas of the body. Myelomas (myelos = marrow) are malignant tumors, occurring in middle-aged and older people, that interfere with the blood-cell-producing function of bone marrow and cause anemia. Chondrosarcomas (chondro = cartilage) are cancerous growths of cartilage.

—Tortora, *Introduction to the Human Body,* p. 56

You can visualize the classification pattern as follows:

TOPIC	CANCER
Part or Type 1	Carcinoma
Part or Type 2	Adenosarcoma
Part or Type 3	Sarcoma
Part or Type 4	Osteogenic sarcomas
Part or Type 5	Myelomas
Part or Type 6	Chondrosarcomas

TRANSITIONS FOR THE CLASSIFICATION PATTERN

There are *several kinds* of chemical bonding . . .
There are *numerous types of* . . .
Reproduction can be *classified as* . . .
the human skeleton is *composed of* . . .
muscles *comprise* . . .
one type of communication . . .
another type of communication . . .
finally, there is . . .

4c ORDER OR SEQUENCE

If you were asked to summarize what you did today, you probably would mention key events in the order in which they occurred. In describing how to write a particular computer program, you would detail the process step by step. In each case, you are presenting information in a particular sequence or order. Each of these examples illustrates a form of the organizational pattern known as *order* or *sequence*. Let's look at several types of order.

Chronology

Chronological order refers to the sequence in which events occur in time. This pattern is essential in the academic disciplines concerned with the interpretation of events in the past. History, government, and anthropology are prime examples. In various forms of literature, chronological order is evident; the narrative form, used in novels, short stories, and narrative essays, relies on chronological order.

You can visualize the chronological order pattern as follows:

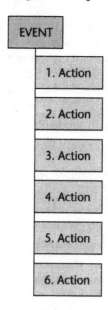

The following paragraph uses chronology to describe how full-scale intervention in Vietnam began.

> The pretext for full-scale intervention in Vietnam came in late July 1964. On July 30 South Vietnamese PT (patrol torpedo) boats attacked bases in the Gulf of Tonkin inside North Vietnamese waters. Simultaneously, the *Maddox,* an American destroyer, steamed into the area to disrupt North Vietnamese communication facilities. On August 2, possibly seeing the two separate missions as a combined maneuver against them, the North Vietnamese sent out several PT boats to attack the destroyer. The *Maddox* fired, sinking one of the attackers, then radioed the news to Washington. Johnson ordered another ship into the bay. On August 3 both destroyers reported another attack, although somewhat later, the commander of the *Maddox* radioed that he was not sure. Nonetheless, the president ordered American planes to retaliate by bombing inside North Vietnam.
>
> —Wilson, et al., *The Pursuit of Liberty,* p. 493

TRANSITIONS FOR CHRONOLOGICAL ORDER

in ancient times . . .
at the start of the battle . . .
on September 12 . . .
the *first* primate species . . .
later efforts . . .
Other chronological transitions are *then, before, during, by the time, while, afterward, as, after, thereafter, meanwhile,* and *at that point.*

Process

In disciplines that focus on procedures, steps, or stages by which actions are accomplished, the process pattern is often employed. These subjects include mathematics, natural and life sciences, computer science, and engineering. The pattern is similar to chronology, in that the steps or stages follow each other in time. Transitional words and phrases often used in conjunction with this pattern are similar to those used for chronological order. You can visualize the process pattern as follows:

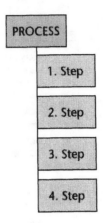

Note how this pattern is used in a paragraph explaining what occurs in the brain during sleep.

> Let us track your brain waves through the night. As you prepare to go to bed, an EEG records that your brain waves are moving along at a rate of about 14 cycles per second (cps). Once you are comfortably in bed, you begin to relax and your brain waves slow down to a rate of about 8 to 12 cps. When you fall asleep, you enter your *sleep cycle,* each of whose stages shows a distinct EEG pattern. In Stage 1 sleep, the EEG shows brain waves of about 3 to 7 cps. During Stage 2, the EEG is characterized by *sleep spindles,* minute bursts of electrical activity of 12 to 16 cps. In the next two stages (3 and 4) of sleep, you enter into a very deep state of relaxed sleep. Your brain waves slow to about 1 to 2 cps, and your breathing and heart rate decrease. In a final stage, the electrical activity of your brain increases; your EEG looks very similar to those recorded during stages 1 and 2. It is during this stage that you will experience REM sleep, and you will begin to dream.
>
> —Zimbardo and Gerrig, *Psychology and Life,* p. 115

Order of Importance

The pattern of ideas sometimes expresses order of priority or preference. Ideas are arranged in one of two ways: from most to least important, or from least to most important. In the following paragraph, the causes of the downward trend in the standard of living are arranged in order of importance.

The United States' downward trend in standard of living has many different causes, of which only a few major ones can be identified here. Most important is probably deindustrialization, the massive loss of manufacturing jobs as many U.S. corporations move their production to poor, labor-cheap countries. But deindustrialization hurts mostly low-skilled manufacturing workers. Most of the well-educated, high-skilled employees in service industries are left unscathed. Deindustrialization alone is therefore not enough to explain the economic decline. Another major factor is the great increase in consumption and decrease in savings. Like their government, people spend more than they earn and become deeply in debt. Those who do practice thrift still have an average rate of savings significantly lower than in countries with fast-growing economies. The habits of high consumption and low saving may have resulted from the great affluence after the Second World War up until the early 1970s (Harrison, 1992).

—Thio, *Sociology*, p. 255

Order of importance is used in almost every field of study.

> ## TRANSITIONS FOR ORDER OF IMPORTANCE
> is *less* essential than . . .
> *more* revealing is . . .
> of *primary* interest is . . .
> Other transitions that show the order of importance are *first, next, last, most important, primarily,* and *secondarily*.

Spatial Order

Information organized according to its physical location, or position or order in space, exhibits a pattern that is known as *spatial order*. Spatial order is used in academic disciplines in which physical descriptions are important. These include numerous technical fields, engineering, and the biological sciences.

You can see how the following description of a particular type of blood circulation relies on spatial relationships.

Pulmonary circulation conducts blood between the heart and the lungs. Oxygen-poor, CO_2-laden blood returns through two large veins (venae cavae) from tissues within the body, enters the right atrium, and is then moved into the right ventricle of the heart. From there, it is pumped into the pulmonary artery, which divides into two branches, each leading to one of the lungs. In the lung, the arteries undergo extensive branching, giving rise to vast networks of capillaries where gas exchange takes place, with blood becoming oxygenated while CO_2 is discharged. Oxygen-rich blood then returns to the heart via the pulmonary veins.

—Mix, Farber, & King, *Biology: The Network of Life*, pp. 663–664

Diagramming is of the utmost importance in working with this pattern; often, a diagram accompanies text material. For example, a diagram makes the functions of the various parts of the human brain easier to understand. Lecturers often refer to a visual aid or chalkboard drawing when providing spatial descriptions.

TRANSITIONS FOR SPATIAL ORDER

the *left side* of the brain . . .
the *lower* portion . . .
the *outer* covering . . .
beneath the surface . . .
Other spatial transitions are *next*
to, beside, to the left, in the center,
and *externally.*

4d   CAUSE AND EFFECT

The cause-and-effect pattern expresses a relationship between two or more actions, events, or occurrences that are connected in time. The relationship differs, however, from chronological order in that one event leads to another by *causing* it. Information that is organized in terms of the cause-and-effect pattern may:

- explain causes, sources, reasons, motives, and action
- explain the effect, result, or consequence of a particular action
- explain both causes and effects

You can visualize the cause and effect pattern as follows:

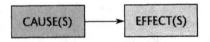

Cause and effect is clearly illustrated by the following passage, which gives the sources of fashions or the reasons why fashions occur.

Why do fashions occur in the first place? One reason is that some cultures, like ours, *value change:* what is new is good, even better. Thus, in many modern societies clothing styles change yearly, while people in traditional societies may wear the same style for generations. A second reason is that many industries promote quick changes in fashion to increase sales. A third reason is that fashions usually trickle down from the top. A new style may occasionally originate from lower-status groups, as blue jeans did. But most fashions come from upper-class people who like to adopt some style or artifact as a badge of their status. But they cannot monopolize most status symbols for long. Their style is adopted by the middle class, maybe copied or modified for use by lower-status groups, offering many people the prestige of possessing a high-status symbol.

—Thio, *Sociology*, p. 534

The cause-and-effect pattern is used extensively in many academic fields. All disciplines that ask the question "Why" employ the cause-and-effect thought pattern. It is widely used in the sciences, technologies, and social sciences.

Many statements expressing cause-and-effect relationships appear in direct order, with the cause stated first and the effect following: "When demand for a product increases, prices rise." However, reverse order is sometimes used, as in the following statement: "Prices rise when a product's demand increases."

The cause-and-effect pattern is not limited to an expression of a simple one-cause, one-effect relationship. There may be multiple causes, or multiple effects, or both multiple causes and multiple effects. For example, both slippery road conditions and your failure to buy snow tires (causes) may contribute to your car sliding into the ditch (effect).

In other instances, a chain of causes or effects may occur. For instance, failing to set your alarm clock may force you to miss your 8:00 A.M. class, which in turn may cause you not to submit your term paper on time, which may result in a penalty grade.

TRANSITIONS FOR THE CAUSE-AND-EFFECT PATTERN

stress *causes* . . .
aggression *creates* . . .
depression *leads to* . . .
forethought *yields* . . .
mental retardation *stems from* . . .
life changes *produce* . . .
hostility *breeds* . . .
avoidance *results in* . . .
Other cause-and-effect transitions are *therefore,*
consequently, hence, for this reason, and *since.*

4e COMPARISON AND CONTRAST

The comparison organizational pattern is used to emphasize or discuss similarities between or among ideas, theories, concepts, or events, whereas the contrast pattern emphasizes differences. When a speaker or writer is concerned with both similarities and differences, a combination pattern is used. You can visualize these three variations of the pattern as follows:

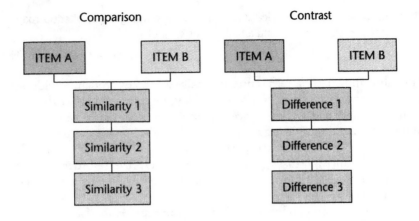

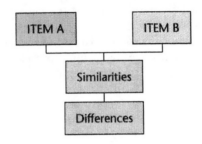

The comparison-and-contrast pattern is widely used in the social sciences, where different groups, societies, cultures, or behaviors are studied. Literature courses may require comparisons among poets, among several literary works, or among stylistic features. A business course may examine various management styles, compare organizational structures, or contrast retailing plans.

A contrast is shown in the following paragraph, which describes the purchasing processes of small and large businesses.

> Small businesses are likely to have less formal purchasing processes. A small retail grocer might, for example, purchase a computer system after visiting a few suppliers to compare prices and features, while a large grocery store chain might collect bids from a specified number of vendors and then evaluate those bids on pre-established criteria. Usually, fewer individuals are involved in the decision-making process for a small business. The owner of the small business, for example, may make all decisions, and a larger business may operate with a buying committee of several people.
>
> —Kinnear, Bernhardt, and Krentler, *Principles of Marketing,* p. 218

Depending on whether a speaker or writer is concerned with similarities, differences, or both similarities and differences, the pattern might be organized in different ways. Suppose a professor of American literature is comparing the work of two American poets, Walt Whitman and Robert Frost. Each of the following organizations is possible:

1. Compare and then contrast the two. That is, first discuss how Frost's poetry and Whitman's poetry are similar, and then discuss how they are different.
2. Discuss by author. Discuss the characteristics of Whitman's poetry, then discuss the characteristics of Frost's poetry, then summarize their similarities and differences.
3. Discuss by characteristic. For example, first discuss the two poets' use of metaphor, next discuss their use of rhyme, and then discuss their common themes.

TRANSITIONS THAT SHOW CONTRAST

unlike Whitman, Frost . . .
less wordy than Whitman . . .
contrasted with Whitman, Frost . . .
Frost *differs from* . . .
Other transitions of contrast are *in contrast, however, on the other hand, as opposed to,* and *whereas.*

TRANSITIONS THAT SHOW COMPARISON

similarities between Frost and Whitman . . .
Frost is *as powerful as* . . .
like Frost, Whitman . . .
both Frost and Whitman . . .
Frost *resembles* Whitman in that . . .
Other transitions of comparison are *in a like manner, similarly, likewise, correspondingly,* and *in the same way.*

4f LISTING/ENUMERATION

If asked to evaluate a film you saw, you might describe the characters, plot, and technical effects. These details about the film could be arranged in any order; each detail provides further information about the film, but they have no specific relationship to one another. This arrangement of ideas is known as *listing* or *enumeration*—giving bits of information on a topic by stating them one after the other. Often there is no particular method of arrangement for those details.

You can visualize the listing/enumeration patterns as follows:

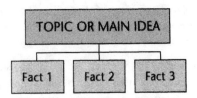

The following list of managers' difficulties in problem solving could have been presented in any order without altering the meaning of the paragraph.

> Although accurate identification of a problem is essential before the problem can be solved, this stage of decision making creates many difficulties for managers. Sometimes managers' preconceptions of the problem prevent them from seeing the situation as it actually is. They produce an answer before the proper question has ever been asked. In other cases, managers overlook truly significant issues by focusing on unimportant matters. Also, managers may mistakenly analyze problems in terms of symptoms rather than underlying causes.

—Pride, Hughes, and Kapoor, Business, p. 189

This pattern is widely used in college textbooks in most academic disciplines. In its loosest form, the pattern may be simply a list of items: factors that influence light emission, characteristics of a particular poet, a description of an atom, a list of characteristics that define poverty.

Somewhat tighter is the use of listing to explain, support, or provide evidence. Support may be in the form of facts, statistics, or examples. For instance, the statement, "The incidence of white collar crime has dramatically increased over the past ten years" would be followed by facts and statistics documenting the increase.

TRANSITIONS FOR LISTING

one aspect of relativity . . .

a second feature of relativity . . .

also, relativity . . .

there are several characteristics of . . .

(1) . . . , (2) . . . , and (3) . . . ,

(a) . . . , (b) . . . , and (c) . . . ,

Other transitional words and phrases are *in addition, first, second, third, finally,* and *another.*

4g   MIXED PATTERNS

Organizational patterns are often combined. In describing a process, a writer may also give reasons why each step must be followed in the prescribed order. A lecturer may define a concept by comparing it to something similar or familiar. Suppose an essay in your political science textbook opens by stating, "The distinction between 'power' and 'power potential' is an important one in considering the balance of power." You might expect a definition pattern (where the two terms are defined), but you also might anticipate that the essay would discuss the difference between the two terms (contrast pattern).

➤ **NOW PRACTICE . . . USING ORGANIZATIONAL PATTERNS 1**

For each of the following topic sentences, anticipate what organizational pattern(s) the paragraph is likely to exhibit. Record your prediction in the space provided.

1. The Enlightenment celebrated the power of reason; however, an opposite reaction, Romanticism, soon followed.

   Pattern: _____

2. Psychogenic amnesia—a severe and often permanent memory loss—results in disorientation and the inability to draw on past experiences.

   Pattern: _____

3. Several statistical procedures are used to track the changes in the divorce rate.

   Pattern: _____

4. The GNP (gross national product) is an economic measure that considers the total value of goods and services that a country produces during a given year.

   Pattern: _____

5. Large numbers of European immigrants first began to arrive in the United States in the 1920s.

   Pattern: _____

6. There are sources of information about corporations that might help an investor evaluate them. One of the most useful is the Value Line Investment Survey.

   Pattern: _____

7. Diseases of the heart and blood vessels—cardiovascular diseases—are the leading cause of death in the United States today.

   Pattern: _____

8. The spinal cord is located within the spinal column; it looks like a section of rope or twine.

   Pattern: _____

9. Think of the hardware in a computer system as the kitchen in a short-order restaurant: It's equipped to produce whatever output a customer (user) requests, but sits idle until an order (command) is placed.

   Pattern: _____

10. The purpose of a resumé is to sell the qualities of the person writing it; it should include several important kinds of information.

    Pattern: _____

➤ NOW PRACTICE . . . USING ORGANIZATIONAL PATTERNS 2

Read each of the following paragraphs and identify the primary organizational pattern used in each.

Paragraph 1

Ours is an ethnically, religiously, and racially diverse society. The white European Protestants, black slaves, and Native Americans who made up the bulk of the U.S. population when the first census was taken in 1790 were joined by Catholic immigrants from Ireland and Germany in the 1840s and 1850s. In the 1870s, Chinese migrated to America, drawn by jobs in railroad construction. Around the turn of the twentieth century, most immigration was from eastern, central, and southern Europe, with its many ethnic, linguistic, and religious groups. Today, most immigration is from Asia and Latin America.

—Greenberg and Page, *The Struggle for Democracy*, p. 71

Pattern: _____

Paragraph 2

Skeletal muscle tissue is named for its location—attached to bones. Skeletal muscle tissue is also *voluntary* because it can be made to contract by conscious control. A single skeletal muscle fiber (cell) is cylindrical and appears *striated* (striped) under a microscope; when organized in a tissue, the fibers are parallel to each other. Each muscle fiber has a plasma membrane, the **sarcolemma,** surrounding the cytoplasm, or **sarcoplasm.** Skeletal muscle fibers are multinucleate (more than one nucleus), and the nuclei are near the sarcolemma.

—Tortora, *Introduction to the Human Body*, p. 77

Pattern: _____

Paragraph 3

Once you know someone's e-mail address, you're ready to send a mail message. If you want to experiment without risking embarrassment, try sending a test message to yourself before you send a message to someone else. Just put your own user id in the To: field; the mail will be sent to you. All mailers have a command that puts you in a mode for creating and sending your own mail messages. Look for a New Message command in a pull-down menu or perhaps a special "new message" icon on a tool bar. After issuing the command for starting a new message, you will be put into a mode for constructing an e-mail message. You'll be given an opportunity to enter the To: header, the Subject: header, and the optional Cc: header. The From: header will be filled in for you automatically. You will probably be given a window display in which all of these items can be filled by moving your mouse around and clicking the field you want to complete. If you don't want to put something in a given field, just press Return or Enter to leave it blank. The only header field that can't be left blank is the To: field.

—Lehnert, *Light on the Internet, Essentials of the Internet and the World Wide Web*, 1999, p. 34.

Pattern: _____

Paragraph 4

By far the most important committees in Congress are the standing committees. Currently 16 standing committees in the Senate and 22 in the House receive the bills that are introduced in Congress. The standing committees are assigned subject-matter jurisdiction by the rules of their respective house, and their titles reflect their general area of expertise. Hence, we have the Senate Finance Committee, the House Agriculture Committee, the Senate Budget Committee, the House Judiciary Committee, and so on. The authority of the standing committees includes the power to study legislation, to subpoena witnesses or information, to remand bills to subcommittees, to vote bills dead, to table bills (putting them aside, thus allowing them to die quietly at the end of the congressional term), to amend bills, to write bills (amending a bill or writing an entirely new version of a bill is called **marking-up**), or to report the bill to the floor.

—Baradat, *Understanding American Democracy*, p. 202

Pattern: _____

Paragraph 5

When considering the relationship of Congress and the president, the basic differences of the two branches must be kept in mind. Members of Congress are elected from narrower constituencies than is the president. The people usually expect the president to address general concerns such as foreign policy and economic prosperity, while Congresspersons are asked to solve individual problems. There are structural differences as well. Congress is a body composed of hundreds of independent people, each with a different power base, and it is divided along partisan lines. Thus, it is difficult for Congress to act quickly or to project unity and clear policy statements.

—Baradat, *Understanding American Democracy*, p. 300

Pattern: _____

Although the patterns presented in the previous section are the most common, writers do not limit themselves to these six patterns. Especially in academic writing, you may also find statement and clarification, summary, generalization and example, and addition. Transitions associated with these different patterns are listed in the "Summing It Up" table on page 64–65.

Statement and Clarification

Many writers make a statement of fact and then proceed to clarify or explain that statement. For instance, a writer may open a paragraph by stating that "The best education for you may not be the best education for someone else." The remainder of the paragraph would then discuss that statement and make its meaning clear by explaining how educational needs are individual and based on one's talents, skills, and goals.

Summary

A summary is a condensed statement that provides the key points of a larger idea or piece of writing. The summaries at the end of each chapter of this text provide a quick review of the chapter's contents. Often writers summarize what they have already said or what someone else has said. For example, in a psychology textbook you will find many summaries of research. Instead of asking you to read an entire research study, the textbook author will summarize the study's findings. Other times a writer may repeat in condensed form what he or she has already said as a means of emphasis or clarification.

Generalization and Example

Examples are one of the best ways to explain something that is unfamiliar or unknown. Examples are specific instances or situations that illustrate a concept or idea. Often writers make a general statement, or generalization, and then explain it by giving examples to make its meaning clear. In a social problems textbook, you may find the following generalization: Computer theft by employees is on the increase. The section may then go on to offer examples from specific companies in which employees insert fictitious information into the company's computer program and steal company funds.

Addition

Writers often introduce an idea or make a statement and then supply additional information about that idea or statement. For instance an education textbook may introduce the concept of home schooling and then provide in-depth information about its benefits. This pattern is often used to expand, elaborate, or discuss an idea in greater detail.

► NOW PRACTICE . . . USING ORGANIZATIONAL PATTERNS 3

For each of the following statements, identify the pattern that is evident and write its name in the space provided. Choose from among the following patterns: process, statement and clarification, summary, generalization and example, addition, and spatial order.

1. If our criminal justice system works, the recidivism rate—the percentage of people released from prison who return—should decrease. In other words, in a successful system, there should be a decrease in the number of criminals who are released from prison and become repeat offenders.

   Pattern: _____

2. Students who are informed about drugs tend to use them in greater moderation. Furthermore, they tend to help educate others.

   Pattern: _____

3. A successful drug addiction treatment program would offer free or very cheap drugs to addicts. Heroin addicts, for example, could be prescribed heroin when under a physician's care.

   Pattern: _____

4. In conclusion, it is safe to say that crime by women is likely to increase as greater numbers of women assume roles traditionally held by men.

   Pattern: _____

5. The pollutants we have just discussed all involve chemicals; we can conclude that they threaten our environment and our well-being.

   Pattern: _____

6. Sociologists study how we are socialized into sex roles, the attitudes expected of males and females. Sex roles, in fact, identify some activities and behaviors as clearly male and others as clearly female.

   Pattern: _____

7. Patients often consult a lay referral network to discuss their medical problems. Cancer patients, for instance, can access Internet discussion groups that provide both information and support.

   Pattern: _____

Patterns and Transitions

PATTERN	CHARACTERISTICS	TRANSITIONS
Definition	Explains the meaning of a word or phrase	Is, refers to, can be defined as, means, consists of, involves, is a term that, is called, is characterized by, occurs when, are those that, entails, corresponds to, is literally
Classification	Divides a topic into parts based on shared characteristics	Classified as, is comprised of, is composed of, several varieties of, different stages of, different groups that, includes, one, first, second, another, finally, last
Chronological Order	Describes events, processes, procedures	First, second, later, before, next, as soon as, after, then, finally, meanwhile, following, last, during, in, on, when, until
Process	Describes the order in which things are done or how things work	First, second, next, then, following, after that, last, finally

Order of Importance

PATTERN	CHARACTERISTICS	TRANSITIONS
Spatial Order	Describes physical location or position in space	Above, below, besides, next to, in front of, behind, inside, outside, opposite, within, nearby
Cause-Effect	Describes how one or more things cause or are related to another	*Causes:* because, because of, for, since, stems from, one cause is, one reason is, leads to, causes, creates, yields, produces, due to, breeds, for this reason
		Effects: consequently, results in, one result is, therefore, thus, as a result, hence
Comparison–Contrast	Discusses similarities and/or differences among ideas, theories, concepts, objects, or persons	*Similarities:* both, also, similarly, like, likewise, too, as well as, resembles, correspondingly, in the same way, to compare, in comparison, share
		Differences: unlike, differs from, in contrast, on the other hand, instead, despite, nevertheless, however, in spite of, whereas, as opposed to

(continued)

Listing/Enumeration	Organizes lists of information: characteristics, features, parts, or categories	The following, several, for example, for instance, one, another, also, too, in other words, first, second, numerals (1., 2.), letters (a., b.), most importantly, the largest, the least, finally importantly
Statement and Clarification	Indicates that information explaining an idea or concept will follow	In fact, in other words, clearly, evidently, obviously
Summary	Indicates that a condensed review of an idea or piece of writing is to follow	In summary, in conclusion, in brief, to summarize, to sum up, in short, on the whole
Generalization and Example	Provides examples that clarify a broad, general statement	For example, for instance, that is, to illustrate, thus
Addition	Indicates that additional information will follow	Furthermore, additionally, also, besides, further, in addition, moreover, again

CHAPTER 4

Techniques for Learning Textbook Material

IN THIS CHAPTER YOU WILL LEARN:

1. To use highlighting effectively.
2. To make marginal annotations.
3. To paraphrase text.
4. To use outlining to organize ideas.
5. To summarize information.
6. To draw concept maps.

As a college student, you are expected to learn large amounts of textbook material. Rereading to learn is *not* an effective strategy. Writing *is* an effective strategy. In fact, writing is an excellent means of improving both your comprehension and your retention. Many successful students almost always read with a pen in hand ready to highlight, mark, annotate, or paraphrase ideas. Some students use writing to study and review the material after reading. They outline to organize information, write summaries to condense ideas, or draw maps to show relationships.

Writing during and after reading has numerous advantages:

1. **Writing focuses your attention.** If you are writing as well as reading, you are forced to keep your mind on the topic.
2. **Writing forces you to think.** By highlighting or writing you are forced to decide what is important and understand relationships and connections.
3. **Writing tests your understanding.** One of the truest measures of understanding is your ability to explain an idea in your own words. When you have understood an idea, you will be able to write about it, but when an idea is unclear or confusing, you will be at a loss for words.

4. **Writing facilitates recall.** Research studies indicate that information is recalled more easily if it is elaborated on. Elaboration involves expanding and thinking about the material by drawing connections and associations, seeing relationships, and making applications. As you will see throughout the chapter, writing is a form of elaboration.

This chapter describes six learning strategies that use writing as a learning tool: highlighting, annotating, paraphrasing, outlining, summarizing, and mapping.

HIGHLIGHTING TECHNIQUES

When reading factual material, the easiest and fastest way to mark important facts and ideas is to highlight them using a pencil, pen, or marker. Many students are hesitant to mark their texts because they want to sell them at the end of the semester. However, highlighting makes the book more useful to you, so try not to let your interest in selling the book prevent you from reading and studying in the most efficient manner.

How to Highlight Effectively

Your goal in highlighting is to identify and mark those portions of an assignment that are important to reread when you study that chapter. Here are a few suggestions on how to highlight effectively:

1. **Read a paragraph or section first and then go back and highlight what is important.** If you highlight as you read, you run the risk of highlighting an idea that you think is important, only to find out later in the passage that it is less important than you originally thought.

2. **Use your knowledge of paragraph structure to guide your highlighting.** Try to highlight important portions of the topic sentence and any supporting details that you want to remember. Use signal words to locate changes or divisions of thought.

3. **Use headings to guide your highlighting.** Earlier in this book you learned that headings could be used to establish a purpose for reading. In Chapter 8 you saw that turning headings into questions to guide your reading is the Q step in the SQ3R reading-study system. A logical extension of these uses of headings is to use questions to help you identify what to highlight. As you read, you should be looking for the answer to your questions; when you find information that answers the questions, highlight it.

4. **Use a system for highlighting.** You can use a number of systems. They include
   - using two or more colors of ink or highlighters to distinguish between main ideas and details or more and less important information.
   - using single underscoring for details and highlighting for main ideas.
   - placing brackets around the main idea and using a highlighter to mark important details.

   Because no system is the most effective for everyone, develop a system that works well for you. Once you develop that system, however, use it consistently. If you vary systems, your chances for confusion and error while reviewing are greater.

5. **Highlight just enough words to make the meaning clear when rereading.** Avoid highlighting a whole sentence. Usually the core parts of the sentence, along with an additional phrase or two, are sufficient. Notice that you can understand the meaning of the following sentence by reading only the highlighted parts.

   Fad diets disregard the necessity for balance among the various classes of nutrients.

   Now, read only the highlighted parts of the following paragraph. Can you understand what the paragraph is about?

   ### PLEA BARGAINING

   When a plea agreement is made, for whatever reason, most states now require that the agreement be in writing and signed by all parties involved. This protects the lawyers, the judge, and the defendant, and ensures that there is a record that can be produced in court should the agreement be denied or contested. In signing the agreement, the defendant is also attesting to the fact that he or she entered a guilty plea voluntarily and knowingly.

   Barlow, *Criminal Justice in America.*

   Most likely you were able to understand the basic message by reading only the highlighted words. You were able to do so because the highlighted words were core parts of each sentence or modifiers that directly explained those parts.

6. **Be sure that your highlighting accurately reflects the content of the passage.** Incomplete or hasty highlighting can mislead you as you review the passage and cause you to miss the main point. As a safeguard against this, occasionally test your accuracy by rereading only what you have highlighted. Does your highlighting tell what the paragraph or passage is about? Does it express the most important idea in the passage?

Highlighting the Right Amount

If you highlight either too little or too much, you will defeat its purpose. If you highlight too little, you will miss valuable information and your review and study of the material will be incomplete. If you highlight too much, you are not identifying and highlighting the most important ideas. The more you highlight, the more you will have to reread when studying, and the less of a timesaver the procedure will be.

Here is a passage highlighted in three ways. Read the entire passage and then examine each version of the highlighting. Try to decide which version would be most useful if you were rereading it for study purposes.

Version 1

THE FUNCTIONS OF EYE MOVEMENTS

With eye movements you can serve a variety of functions. One such function is to seek feedback. In talking with someone, we look at her or him intently, as if to say, "Well, what do you think?" As you might predict, listeners gaze at speakers more than speakers gaze at listeners. In public speaking, you might scan hundreds of people to secure this feedback.

A second function is to inform the other person that the channel of communication is open and that he or she should now speak. You see this regularly in conversation when one person asks a question or finishes a thought and then looks to you for a response.

Eye movements may also signal the nature of a relationship, whether positive (an attentive glance) or negative (eye avoidance). You can also signal your power through "visual dominance behavior." The average speaker, for example, maintains a high level of eye contact while listening and a lower level while speaking. When people want to signal dominance, they may reverse this pattern—maintaining a high level of eye contact while talking but a much lower level while listening.

By making eye contact you psychologically lessen the physical distance between yourself and another person. When you catch someone's eye at a party, for example, you become psychologically close, though physically far apart.

DeVito, *Messages.*

Version 2

THE FUNCTIONS OF EYE MOVEMENTS

With eye movements you can serve a variety of functions. One such function is to seek feedback. In talking with someone, we look at her or him intently, as if to say, "Well, what do you think?" As you might predict, listeners gaze at speakers more than speakers gaze at listeners. In public speaking, you might scan hundreds of people to secure this feedback.

A second function is to inform the other person that the channel of communication is open and that he or she should now speak. You see this regularly in conversation when one person asks a question or finishes a thought and then looks to you for a response.

Eye movements may also signal the nature of a relationship, whether positive (an attentive glance) or negative (eye avoidance). You can also signal your power through "visual dominance behavior." The average speaker, for example, maintains a high level of eye contact while listening and a lower level while speaking. When people want to signal dominance, they may reverse this pattern—maintaining a high level of eye contact while talking but a much lower level while listening.

By making eye contact you psychologically lessen the physical distance between yourself and another person. When you catch someone's eye at a party, for example, you become psychologically close, though physically far apart.

Version 3

THE FUNCTIONS OF EYE MOVEMENTS

With eye movements you can serve a variety of functions. One such function is to seek feedback. In talking with someone, we look at her or him intently, as if to say, "Well, what do you think?" As you might predict, listeners gaze at speakers more than speakers gaze at listeners. In public speaking, you might scan hundreds of people to secure this feedback.

A second function is to inform the other person that the channel of communication is open and that he or she should now speak. You see this regularly in conversation when one person asks a question or finishes a thought and then looks to you for a response.

Eye movements may also signal the nature of a relationship, whether positive (an attentive glance) or negative (eye avoidance). You can also signal your power through "visual dominance behavior." The average speaker, for example, maintains a high level of eye contact while listening and a lower level while speaking. When people want to signal dominance, they may reverse this pattern—maintaining a high level of eye contact while talking but a much lower level while listening.

By making eye contact you psychologically lessen the physical distance between yourself and another person. When you catch someone's eye at a party, for example, you become psychologically close, though physically far apart.

This passage on eye movements lists five functions of eye movements and briefly explains each. In evaluating the highlighting done in Version 1, you can see that it does not contain enough information. Only four of the five functions are highlighted and practically none of the explanations are highlighted.

Version 2, on the other hand, has too much highlighting. Although all of the important details are highlighted, many less important details are also highlighted. For instance, in the first paragraph, the first function and an explanation are highlighted (though using more text than is necessary), but also additional information about how often speakers and listeners gaze at each other. In fact, nearly every sentence is highlighted, and for review purposes it would be almost as easy to reread the entire passage as it would be to read only the highlighting.

Version 3 is an example of effective highlighting. If you reread only the highlighting, you will see that each of the five functions of eye movements and brief explanations of them have been highlighted.

As a general rule of thumb, try to highlight no more than 20 to 30 percent of the passage. Once you exceed this range, you begin to lose effectiveness. Of course, if a particular section or passage is very factual or detailed it may require more detailed highlighting. However, if you find that an entire assignment or chapter seems to require 60 to 70 percent highlighting, you should consider using one of the other notetaking methods suggested later in this chapter.

EXERCISE 9-1

DIRECTIONS: Read and highlight the following excerpt from a zoology textbook using the guidelines for highlighting. When you have finished, compare your highlighting to that in the sample on page 382.

Excerpt

RODS AND CONES OF THE EYE

Among the most complex receptor cells are the photoreceptor cells of vertebrates. These are called rods or cones, depending on their shapes (Fig. 1). Rods have cylindrical outer segments that contain approximately 2000 disc-shaped membranes bearing light-absorbing pigments. This pigment is rhodopsin, a yellow substance that absorbs a broad range of wavelengths. Rhodopsin combines a vitamin-A derivative called **retinal** with a protein called **opsin**. Cones are similar, except that their outer segments are cone-shaped, and the opsins differ. Vertebrates typically have several types of cones with different opsins that enable them to perceive different colors. In addition, lungfishes, many reptiles, and birds have colored drops of oil in the cones, which narrow the color sensitivity. Mammals have cones with three different opsins, each of which absorbs light most effectively at a different wavelength from the other two. In humans these three wavelengths are perceived as red, blue, and green. Although we have only three kinds of cones, any color can be perceived from the combination of cones it stimulates. For example, stimulation of both red-sensitive and blue-sensitive cones would indicate the color purple.

Rods and cones also differ in their sensitivity. Rods are so sensitive that they can respond to individual photons, but they become blinded in bright daylight. They are therefore useful mainly at night and in heavy shadow. Cones are not sensitive enough to work in darkness, but the different color sensitivities enable them to transmit information about color in bright light. Good vision in the dark requires a large number of rods, while color vision in daylight requires numerous cones. The retinas of most mammals, especially nocturnal ones, have primarily rods. The retinas of humans and other primates have a mixture of rods and cones in peripheral areas and have only cones in the center of focus, called the fovea. Humans have a total of about 100 million rods and 3 million cones.

Harris, *Concepts in Zoology.*

Sample Highlighting

RODS AND CONES OF THE EYE

Among the most complex receptor cells are the photoreceptor cells of vertebrates. These are called rods or cones, depending on their shapes (Fig. 1). Rods have cylindrical outer segments that contain approximately 2000 disc-shaped membranes bearing light-absorbing pigments. This pigment is rhodopsin, a yellow substance that absorbs a broad range of wavelengths. Rhodopsin combines a vitamin-A derivative called **retinal** with a protein called opsin. Cones are similar, except that their outer segments are cone-shaped, and the opsins differ. Vertebrates typically have several types of cones with different opsins that enable them to perceive different colors. In addition, lungfishes, many reptiles, and birds have colored drops of oil in the cones, which narrow the color sensitivity. Mammals have cones with three different opsins, each of which absorbs light most effectively at a different wavelength from the other two. In humans these three wavelengths are perceived as red, blue, and green. Although we have only three kinds of cones, any color can be perceived from the combination of cones it stimulates. For example, stimulation of both red-sensitive and blue-sensitive cones would indicate the color purple.

Rods and cones also differ in their sensitivity. Rods are so sensitive that they can respond to individual photons, but they become blinded in bright daylight. They are therefore useful mainly at night and in heavy shadow. Cones are not sensitive enough to work in darkness, but the different color sensitivities enable them to transmit information about color in bright light. Good vision in the dark requires a large number of rods, while color vision in daylight requires numerous cones. The retinas of most mammals, especially nocturnal ones, have primarily rods. The retinas of humans and other primates have a mixture of rods and cones in peripheral areas and have only cones in the center of focus, called the fovea. Humans have a total of about 100 million rods and 3 million cones.

EXERCISE 9–2

DIRECTIONS: Choose one of the reading selections at the end of this chapter. Assume that you are reading it as part of a class reading assignment on which you will be tested. As you read, highlight the important ideas. Tomorrow, reread what you have highlighted and then answer the multiple-choice questions that follow the selection.

ANNOTATING AND MAKING MARGINAL NOTATIONS

If you were reading the want ads in a newspaper in search of an apartment to rent, you would probably mark certain ads. As you phoned for more information, you might make notes about each apartment. These notes would help you decide which apartments to visit. Similarly, in many types of academic reading, making notes, or *annotating,* is a useful strategy. Annotating is a means of keeping track of your impressions, ideas, reactions, and questions as you read. Then, after reading, reviewing your annotations will help you form a final impression of the work. If a writing assignment accompanies the reading, your annotations will serve as an excellent source of ideas for a paper. Annotating should be used in conjunction with highlighting. Highlighting is a means of identifying important information; annotating is a method of recording *your* thinking about these key ideas.

There are no fixed rules about how or what to annotate. In general, try to mark or note any ideas about the assignment that come to mind as you read or reread. Write your annotations in the margins. Use annotations to

- write questions about the material
- condense important points
- identify ideas with which you disagree
- mark good or poor examples of supporting data
- jot down inconsistencies
- locate key terms or definitions
- consider contrasting points of view
- summarize arguments
- mark words with strong connotative meanings
- identify the author's viewpoints or feelings

Several methods of annotation are discussed in the following sections.

Using Symbols to Annotate

Symbols can be used to distinguish different types of information, to emphasize material to be studied, or to show relationships among ideas. They can be very convenient, for instance, in calling attention to examples or definitions, portions of an assignment that you feel are particularly important to study, or contrasting ideas and opinions.

Develop your own set of symbols and use them consistently. Here is a sample list of commonly used symbols and their meanings.

Symbol	Meaning
ex	an example is included
def	an important term is defined
▭	unknown word to look up in dictionary later
T	good test question
?	confusing idea
*	very important
sum	summary statement
⟋	relates to another idea

Now read the following passage, paying particular attention to the use of symbols.

3 factors
①
def {
ex {
②
def {
③ def {
∘∘

Three key factors are commonly subsumed within the concept of modernization: industrialization, urbanization, and bureaucratization. **Industrialization** refers to a shift from human to nonhuman sources of energy and the rise of the factory system of economic production. An example would be the process by which shoes, previously made by hand in small shops, came to be manufactured in factories by electrically powered machines. **Urbanization** means the movement of people from rural areas into towns and cities (where factories tend to be located). **Bureaucratization** refers to the rise of large-scale formal organizations. These three components of modernization, in turn, lead to changes in such social institutions as religion, politics, and the family.

Popenoe, *Sociology.*

Annotating to Condense Information

Annotating is a helpful technique to use when you work through complicated or lengthy explanations. Often a few marginal notes can be used to summarize an entire paragraph, as shown in the following example.

estimated demand = number of possible buyers × how much each will buy × market share percent

The first step in estimating demand for a particular product is to identify demand for an entire product category in the markets that the company serves. PepsiCo, for example, will estimate the entire demand for soft drinks in domestic and international markets. A small business, such as a start-up premium coffee supplier, will estimate demand only in markets it expects to reach. Marketers predict total demand by first identifying the number of buyers or potential buyers and then multiplying that estimate times the average amount each member of the target market is likely to purchase. For example, the coffee entrepreneur may estimate that there are 10,000 consumer households in his market who would be willing to buy his premium coffee and that each household would purchase approximately 25 pounds of coffee a year. The total annual demand for the product is 250,000 pounds.

Once the marketer estimates total demand, the next step is to predict what the company's market share is likely to be. The company's estimated demand is then its share of the whole (estimated) pie. In our coffee example, the entrepreneur may feel that he can gain 5 percent of this market, or 12,500 pounds or about 1,000 pounds a month—not bad for a new start-up business. Of course, such projections need to take into consideration other factors that might affect demand, such as new competitors entering the market, the state of the economy, and changing consumer tastes.

Solomon and Stuart, *Marketing.*

You can see that annotations are a useful timesaving device when ideas are complicated and cannot be reviewed quickly by highlighting.

Annotating to Record Reactions

Annotations are particularly useful when reading literature, essays, controversial articles, arguments, or persuasive material. Because each type of work is intended to provoke a reader's response, record your reactions and feelings as you read.

The poem "Anecdote of the Jar" follows. Read the poem first, then study the annotations. Notice how the annotations reveal the reader's thinking about the poem.

ANECDOTE OF THE JAR   *symbol—worldliness - material*
                                                      artificial vs. nature
I placed a (jar) in Tennessee,
And round it was, upon a hill.
It made the (slovenly) wilderness   *careless*
Surround that hill.   *unkempt*

The wilderness rose up to it,
And sprawled around, no longer wild.——— *wilderness is changed*
The jar was round upon the ground
And tall and of a port in air.
                                                      authority
It took (dominion) everywhere.   *ruling power*
The jar was gray and bare.
It did not give of bird or bush.——— *wildlife absent*
Like nothing else in Tennessee.——— *jar unlike nature*

— Wallace Stevens

DIRECTIONS: Refer to the same reading selection used for Exercise 9–2. Review your highlighting and add annotations that clarify or summarize content or record your reactions. Add at least two annotations that reflect your thinking.

| EXERCISE 9-4 | *DIRECTIONS:* Highlight and annotate a section from a current chapter in one of your textbooks using the suggestions for effective highlighting and annotating presented earlier in this chapter. ■ |

PARAPHRASING

A paraphrase restates a passage's ideas in your own words. You retain the author's meaning, but you use your own wording. In speech we paraphrase frequently. For example, when you relay a message from one person to another, you convey the meaning but do not use the person's exact words. A paraphrase makes a passage's meaning clearer and often more concise.

Paraphrasing is a useful technique in several situations.

1. **Paraphrasing is a means of recording information from reference sources in note form for later use in writing a research paper.**

2. **Paraphrasing is also useful when dealing with material for which exact, detailed comprehension is required.** For instance, you might paraphrase the steps in solving a math problem or the procedures for a lab set-up in chemistry.

3. **Paraphrasing is also helpful for understanding extremely difficult or complicated passages that must be worked out word by word.**

4. **Paraphrasing is useful when reading material that is stylistically complex, or with an obvious slant, bias, strong tone, or detailed description.**

Study the following example of a paraphrase of the stylistically complex preamble of the United States Constitution. Notice that it restates in different words the intent of the preamble.

PREAMBLE

We the people of the United States, in order to form a more perfect union, establish justice, insure domestic tranquillity, provide for the common defense, promote the general welfare, and secure the blessings of liberty to ourselves and our posterity, do ordain and establish this Constitution of the United States of America.

PARAPHRASE

The citizens of the United States established the Constitution to create a better country, to provide rightful treatment, peace, protection, and well-being for themselves and future citizens.

Notice first how synonyms were substituted for words in the original—*citizens* for *people, country* for *union, protection* for *defense,* and so forth. Next, notice that the order of information was rearranged.

Use the following suggestions to paraphrase effectively:

1. **Read slowly and carefully.** You must understand exactly what is said before you can paraphrase.

2. **Read the entire material before writing anything.**

3. **As you read, focus on both exact meanings and relationships between ideas.**

4. **Begin paraphrasing sentence by sentence.**

5. **Read each sentence and identify its core meaning.** Use synonyms, replacing the author's words with your words. Look away from the original sentence and write in your own words what it means. Then reread the original and add any additional or qualifying information.

6. **Don't try to paraphrase word by word.** Instead, work with clauses and phrases (idea groups).

7. **For words or phrases about which you are unsure of the meaning, check a dictionary to locate a more familiar meaning.**

8. **You may combine several original sentences into a more concise paraphrase.** It is also acceptable to present ideas in a different order than in the original.

9. **Compare your paraphrase with the original for completeness and accuracy.**

EXERCISE 9–5

DIRECTIONS: Provide synonyms for the underlined words or phrases in the following excerpt from Sartre's essay on existentialism. Discuss and compare choices in a class discussion.

The existentialist, on the contrary, thinks it very <u>distressing</u> that God does not exist, because all possibility of finding values in a heaven of ideas disappears along with Him; there can no longer be an *a priori* Good, since there is no <u>infinite</u> and perfect consciousness to think it. Nowhere is it written that the Good exists, that we must be honest, that we must not lie; because the fact is we are on a <u>plane</u> where there are only men. Dostoievsky said, "If God didn't exist, everything would be possible." That is the very <u>starting point</u> of existentialism. Indeed, everything is <u>permissible</u> if God does not exist, and as a result man is <u>forlorn,</u> because neither within him nor without does he find anything to cling to. He can't start making excuses for himself.

Sartre, Existentialism.

EXERCISE 9–6

DIRECTIONS: Write a paraphrase of the second paragraph of the following selection from a sociology text.

_____

_____

_____

_____

_____

_____

_____

THE HOME SCHOOLING MOVEMENT

It is difficult to estimate the number of youngsters involved in **home schooling,** *where children are not sent to school and receive their formal education from one or both parents.* Legislation and court decisions have made it legally possible in most states for parents to educate their children at home, and each year more people take advantage of that opportunity. Some states require parents or a home tutor to meet teacher certification standards, and many require parents to complete legal forms and affidavits to verify that their children are receiving instruction in state-approved curricula.

Supporters of home education claim that it is less expensive and far more efficient than mass public education. Moreover they cite several advantages: alleviation of school overcrowding, added curricular and pedagogical alternatives not available in the public schools, strengthened family relationships, lower dropout rates, the fact that students are allowed to learn at their own rate, increased motivation, higher standardized test scores, and reduced discipline problems. Proponents of home schooling also believe that it provides the parents with the opportunity to reinforce their moral values through education—something they are not satisfied that the public schools will do.

Critics of the home schooling movement contend that it creates as many problems as it solves. They acknowledge that, in a few cases, home schooling offers educational opportunities superior to those found in most public schools, but few parents can provide such educational advantages. Some parents who withdraw their children from the schools in favor of home schooling have an inadequate educational background and insufficient formal training to provide a satisfactory education for their children. Typically, parents have fewer, not more, technological resources at their disposal than do schools. However, . . . the relatively inexpensive computer technology that is readily available today is causing some to challenge the notion that home schooling is in any way inferior to more highly structured classroom education.

Finally, a sociological concern is the restricted social interaction experienced by children who are educated at home. Patricia Lines, a U. S. Department of Education policy analyst, believes that the possibilities provided by technology and the promise of home schooling are greatly exaggerated and insisted that "technology will never replace the pupil-teacher relationship." Also, while relationships with parents and siblings may be enhanced, children taught at home may develop a distorted view of society. Children who live in fairly homogeneous neighborhoods, comprising people of the same race, socioeconomic status, and religious background, do not experience the diversity that can be provided in the social arena of the schools. They may be ill equipped to function successfully in the larger multicultural world.

Thompson and Hickey, *Society in Focus: An Introduction to Sociology.*

EXERCISE 9–7

DIRECTIONS: Write a paraphrase of the excerpt on page 384 ("The first step . . . "). When you have finished, compare your paraphrase with that of another student.

OUTLINING

Outlining is an effective way to organize information and discover relationships between ideas. It forces you to select what is important from each paragraph and determine how it is related to key ideas in other paragraphs. Outlining enables you to learn and remember what you read because the process of selecting what is important and expressing it in your own words requires thought and comprehension and provides for repetition and review. Outlining is particularly effective for pragmatic learners who can learn material that is orderly and sequential.

Outlining is particularly useful in the following situations:

- When reading material that seems difficult or confusing, outlining forces you to sort ideas, see connections, and express them in your own words.

- When you are asked to write an evaluation or a critical interpretation of an article or essay, it is helpful to outline the factual content. The outline reflects development and progression of thought and helps you analyze the writer's ideas.

- In subject matter where order or process is important, an outline is particularly useful. For example, in a data processing course in which various sets of programming commands must be performed in a specified sequence, an outline is a good way to organize the information.

- In the natural sciences, in which classifications are important, outlines help you record and sort information. In botany, for example, one important focus is the classification and description of various plant groups. An outline enables you to list subgroups within each category and to keep track of similar characteristics.

Developing an Outline

To be effective, an outline must show the relative importance of ideas and the relationship between ideas. The easiest way to achieve this is to use the following format:

I. **First Major Topic**
   A. First major idea
      1. First important detail
      2. Second important detail
   B. Second major idea

1. First important detail

   a. Minor detail or example

   b. Minor detail or example

2. Second important detail

II. Second Major Topic

  A. First major idea

Notice that the more important ideas are closer to the left margin, and less important details are indented toward the middle of the page. A quick glance at an outline indicates what is most important and how ideas support or explain one another.

Use the following suggestions to write effective outlines:

1. **Read a section completely before writing.**

2. **Be brief and concise; do not write in complete sentences.** Unless the outline is to be submitted to your instructor, use abbreviations, symbols, or shorthand words as you would in lecture notetaking.

3. **Use your own words rather than those in the text.**

4. **Be certain that all information beneath a heading supports or explains it.**

5. **Every heading that is aligned vertically should be of equal importance.**

To illustrate further the technique for outlining, read the following passage and then study the outline that follows it.

NONBIODEGRADABLE POLLUTANTS

Heavy metals, such as mercury, cadmium, and arsenic, and manufactured chemicals, such as PCBs and some pesticides, are examples of nonbiodegradable pollutants. These chemicals are highly toxic, so that low levels of exposure or low concentrations of these compounds are poisonous. Such chemicals are so foreign to living organisms that they are not metabolized and remain in the ecosystem basically unchanged. Worse than that, if eaten, they may be stored within the body. Each time chemicals such as PCBs, mercury, or dioxin are taken into the body they are added to the existing stock. If this accumulation continues, a toxic level is reached. The Romans were great poisoners, and they knew the toxic value of gradually administering poisons such an antimony or arsenic. Each meal was safe to eat, but the steady diet of a little poison time after time led to the death of the victim. Even though nonbiodegradable pollutants may be relatively rare, they are stored in the bodies of an organism and passed on up the food chain in a process called **biological amplification** (also referred to as biological magnification). A predator absorbs all the stored pollutants in the hundreds or thousands of prey items that it eats, and each meal provides a dose of the toxin. The chemical is stored in the body of the predator, where the successive doses accumulate and become more concentrated. If the predator then falls prey to a larger carnivore, the entire dose of toxicity is taken to the next step in the food chain. Thus, the concentration of the toxin is amplified at each link in the food chain.

Bush, *Ecology of a Changing Planet.*

Here is the outline for the above selection:

I. Nonbiodegradable Pollutants
  A. examples
    1. heavy metals
      a. mercury
      b. cadmium
    2. manufactured chemicals
      a. PCBs
      b. pesticides
  B. highly toxic
    1. poisonous at low exposure and concentrations
    2. not metabolized; remain in ecosystem unchanged
  C. stored within body when eaten
    1. added to existing stock in body
    2. can eventually reach toxic level
  D. biological amplification (magnification)
    1. predator eats many prey with stored pollutants
    2. doses accumulate and become more concentrated
    3. carnivore eats predator
    4. toxicity taken up food chain

By reading the passage and then reviewing the outline, you can see that it represents, in briefest form, the contents of the passage. Reading an outline is an effective way to reacquaint yourself with the content and organization of a chapter without taking the time that reading, highlighting, or marginal notation requires.

How Much Information to Include

Before you begin to outline, decide how much information to include. An outline can be very brief and cover only major topics, or at the other extreme, it can be very detailed, providing an extensive review of information.

The purpose of your outline should determine how much detail you include. For example, if you are outlining a reading assignment for which your instructor asked that you be familiar with the author's viewpoint and general approach to a problem, little detail is needed. On the other hand, if you are outlining a section of an anatomy and physiology text for an upcoming objective exam, a much more detailed outline is needed. To determine the right amount of detail, ask yourself: "What do I need to know? What type of test situation, if any, am I preparing for?"

EXERCISE 9-8

DIRECTIONS: Read the following excerpt from Brian Fagan's *People of the Earth: An Introduction to World Prehistory,* an archaeology textbook, and write a brief outline.

For hundreds of thousands of years, *Homo erectus* flourished in the tropical and temperate regions of the Old World. Except for an overall increase in brain size, *H. erectus* remained remarkably stable in evolutionary terms for more than a million years, until less than 500,000 years ago. Eventually, *H. erectus* evolved into early *H. sapiens,* but we do not even know when the gradual transition began or how it took place. Some researchers believe it began as early as 400,000 years ago; others, much later, sometime around or after 200,000 years ago.

For hundreds of thousands of years, both *H. erectus* and early *H. sapiens* survived and evolved with the aid of what Steven Mithen calls multiple intelligences separated by walls analogous to those dividing the chapels of a medieval cathedral. As Mithen says (1996), the thoughts in one chapel could barely be heard in another. Archaic humans lacked one vital component of the modern mind: cognitive flexibility, the ability to bridge the walls between their many intelligences. Such flexibility appears to have been the prerogative of modern humans, *Homo sapiens sapiens.*

Homo sapiens sapiens means "wise person," and the controversies surrounding the origins of modern humanity—of ourselves—rank among the most vigorous in archaeology. What is it that separates us from earlier humans, scientists wonder? First and foremost must be our ability to speak fluently and articulately. We communicate, we tell stories, we pass on knowledge and ideas—all through the medium of language. Consciousness, cognition, self-awareness, foresight, and the ability to express oneself and one's emotions—these are direct consequences of fluent speech. They can be linked with another attribute of the fully fledged human psyche: the capacity for symbolic and spiritual thought, concerned not only with subsistence and technology but also with defining the boundaries of existence and the relationship among the individual, the group, and the universe.

EXERCISE 9-9

DIRECTIONS: Write an outline of "The Home Schooling Movement" on page 388.

MAPPING TO SHOW RELATIONSHIPS

Mapping is a process of drawing diagrams to describe how a topic and its related ideas are connected. It is a means of organizing and consolidating information by using a visual format. Maps facilitate learning because they group and consolidate information. Although mapping appeals to visual learners, verbal learners will also find it to be effective in organizing information. This section discusses two types of maps: concept maps and thought pattern maps.

Concept Maps

Concept maps are visual outlines; they show how ideas within a passage are related. Maps can take different forms. You can draw them in any way that shows the relationships among the ideas. Sketching rather than exact, careful drawing is appropriate. When drawing maps feel free to abbreviate, add lines to show relationships, add notes, or redraw to make changes. Figure 9.1 shows two sample maps. Each was drawn to show the organization of Chapter 2 of this text. Refer to Chapter 2, pages 65–95, then study each map.

Think of a map as a diagram that shows how ideas are connected. Maps, like outlines, can vary in the amount of detail included, ranging

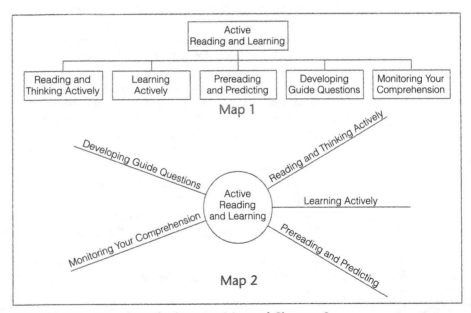

FIGURE 9.1   Two Sample Concept Maps of Chapter 2

from very general to highly specific. The maps shown in Figure 9.1 only provide an overview of the chapter and reflect its general organization. A more detailed map of one of the topics, prereading, included in Chapter 2 (p. 76), is shown in Figure 9.2. Use the following steps in drawing a map.

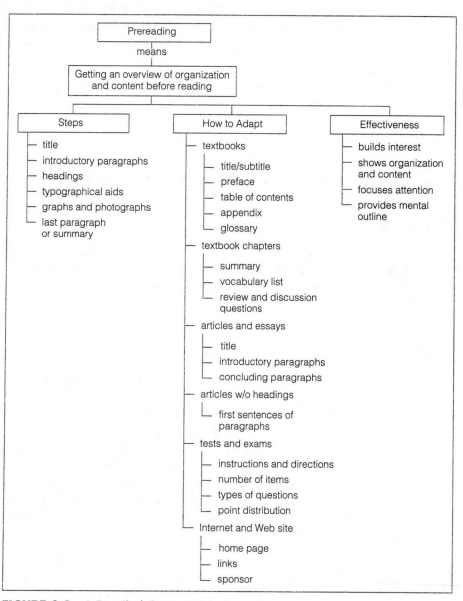

FIGURE 9.2 A Detailed Concept Map

1. **Identify the overall subject and write it in the center or at the top of the page.** How you arrange your map will depend on the subject matter and its organization. Circles or boxes are useful but not absolutely necessary.

2. **Identify the major supporting information that relates to the topic.** State each fact or idea on a line connected to the central topic.

3. As you discover details that further explain an idea already mapped, **draw a new line branching from the idea it explains.**

EXERCISE 9–10

DIRECTIONS: Draw a map that reflects the overall organization of this chapter.

EXERCISE 9–11

DIRECTIONS: Draw a map that reflects the organization of one of the end-of-chapter readings in this book that you have read this semester.

EXERCISE 9–12

DIRECTIONS: Select a section from one of your textbooks. Draw a concept map that reflects its organization.

Academic Application

Thought Pattern Maps

When a particular thought pattern is evident throughout a passage, you may wish to draw a map reflecting that pattern. Maps for each common thought pattern are shown in Chapter 5. Now that you are familiar with the idea of mapping, review Chapter 5, paying particular attention to the diagrams shown for each pattern. When reading a history text, for example, you may find it helpful to draw time lines (see p. 200) to organize events within historical periods. Or, when reading a text that compares two works of philosophy or two key political figures, you may find one of the maps shown on pages 208–209 helpful in distinguishing similarities and differences.

EXERCISE 9–13

DIRECTIONS: Draw a concept map showing the overall organization of Chapter 8, "Learning and Retention Strategies."

**EXERCISE
9-14**

*Academic
Application*

DIRECTIONS: Conduct an experiment to see whether outlining or mapping is a better way for you to show relationships between ideas. Choose and read a substantial section from one of your textbooks. Write a brief outline of it, then draw a map of this same section. Which of these two methods was easier for you to do? Which of these will be most useful for you? Why?

SUMMARIZING INFORMATION

A summary is a compact restatement of the important points of a passage. You might think of it as a shortened version of a longer message. Unlike a paraphrase, a summary does not include all information presented in the original. Instead, you must select what to include. A summary contains only the gist of the text, with limited background, explanation, or detail. Although summaries vary in length, they are often one quarter or less of the length of the original.

Summaries are useful in a variety of reading situations in which a condensed overview of the material is needed. You might summarize information in preparation for an essay exam or key points of news articles required in an economics class. Some class assignments also require summarization. Lab reports for science courses include a summary of results. A literature instructor may ask you to summarize the plot of a short story.

Use the following steps as a guide when writing a summary.

1. **Read the entire original work first.** Do not write anything until you understand it completely and have a complete picture of the work.

2. **Reread and highlight key points.** Look in particular for topic sentences and essential details.

3. **Review your highlighting.** Cross out all but vital phrases. Eliminate repetitious information.

4. **Write sentences to include all remaining highlighted information.** Condense and combine information wherever possible.

5. **Present ideas in the summary in the same order in which they appeared in the original,** unless you are purposely regrouping ideas.

6. **Revise your summary.** Try to make your summary more concise by eliminating repetition and combining ideas.

Read this selection by Joyce Cary, and study the sample summary.

Art and Education

A very large number of people cease when quite young to add anything to a limited stock of judgments. After a certain age, say 25, they consider that their education is finished.

It is perhaps natural that having passed through that painful and boring process, called expressly education, they should suppose it over, and that they are equipped for life to label every event as it occurs and drop it into its given pigeonhole. But one who has a label ready for everything does not bother to observe any more, even such ordinary happenings as he has observed for himself, with attention, before he went to school. He merely acts and reacts.

For people who have stopped noticing, the only possible new or renewed experience, and, therefore, new knowledge, is from a work of art. Because that is the only kind of experience which they are prepared to receive on its own terms, they will come out from their shells and expose themselves to music, to a play, to a book, because it is the accepted method of enjoying such things. True, even to plays and books they may bring artistic prejudices which prevent them from seeing *that* play or comprehending *that* book. Their artistic sensibilities may be as crusted over as their minds.

But it is part of an artist's job to break crusts, or let us say rather that artists who work for the public and not merely for themselves, are interested in breaking crusts because they want to communicate their intuitions.

Carey, *On the Function of the Novelist.*

Sample Summary

Many people consider their education to be complete at an early age, and at that time, cease to observe and react to the world around them. Art forces people to think and react. For some people, their artistic sensibility may be as stagnant as their minds. It is the artist's responsibility to intervene in order to communicate.

EXERCISE 9–15

DIRECTIONS: Read and summarize the following essay by James Thurber.

A Dog's Eye View of Man

If Man has benefited immeasurably by his association with the dog, what, you may ask, has the dog got out of it? His scroll has, of course, been heavily charged with punishments: he has known the muzzle, the leash, and the tether; he has suffered the indignities of the show bench, the tin can on the tail, the ribbon in the hair; his love life with the other sex of his species has been regulated by the frigid hand of authority, his digestion ruined by the macaroons and marshmallows of doting women. The list of his woes could be continued indefinitely. But he has also had his fun, for he has been privileged to live with and study at close range the only creature with reason, the most unreasonable of creatures.

The dog has got more fun out of Man than Man has got out of the dog, for the clearly demonstrable reason that Man is the more laughable of the two animals. The dog has long been bemused by the singular activities and the curious practices of men, cocking his head inquiringly to one side, intently watching and listening to the strangest goings-on in the world. He has seen men sing together and fight one another in the same evening. He has watched them go to bed when it is time to get up, and get up when it is time to go to bed. He has observed them destroying the soil in vast areas, and nurturing it in small patches. He has stood by while men built strong and solid houses for rest and quiet, and then filled them with lights and bells and machinery. His sensitive nose, which can detect what's cooking in the next township, has caught at one and the same time the bewildering smells of the hospital and the munitions factory. He has seen men raise up great cities to heaven and then blow them to hell.

Thurber, *Thurber's Dogs.*

_____

_____

_____

_____

EXERCISE 9–16

DIRECTIONS: Write a summary of "The Home Schooling Movement" on page 388. Use the outline you constructed in Exercise 9–9 to guide your writing.

_____

_____

_____

_____

_____

_____

_____

_____

Critical Thinking Tip #9

Annotating and Critical Thinking

Annotating is a way of identifying and summarizing key information. It is also a way to facilitate critical thinking. Annotating helps you record your reactions as you read. You might

- jot down questions
- highlight emotionally charged words
- note opposing ideas
- mark ideas you question or disagree with
- note places where you feel further information is needed
- mark sections you feel are particularly strong or weak

Here is a sample annotation in which a reader recorded her thinking about the passage:

HATE SPEECH ON CAMPUS

definition?

why?

In recent years, a rise in verbal abuse and violence directed at people of color, lesbians and gay men, and other historically persecuted groups has plagued the United States. Among the settings of these expressions of intolerance are college and university campuses, where bias incidents have occurred sporadically since the mid-1980s. Outrage, indignation and demands for change have greeted such incidents—understandably, given the lack of racial and social diversity among students, faculty and administrators on most campuses.

guidelines or rules?

Many universities, under pressure to respond to the concerns of those who are the objects of hate, have adopted codes or policies prohibiting speech that offends any group based on race, gender, ethnicity, religion or sexual orientation.

opinion

That's the wrong response, well-meaning or not. The First Amendment to the United States Constitution protects speech no matter how offensive its content. Speech codes adopted by government-financed state colleges and universities amount to government censorship, in violation of the Constitution. And the ACLU [American Civil Liberties Union] believes that all campuses should adhere to First Amendment principles because academic freedom is a bedrock of education in a free society.

isn't some response necessary?

Tischler, ed., *Debating Points: Race and Ethnic Relations.*

As you learn more about critical thinking throughout the text, you will get more ideas about what to mark and annotate.

EXERCISE 9-17

DIRECTIONS: Select a section of at least five substantial paragraphs from one of your current textbook chapters. Write a paraphrase of its first paragraph; then write a summary of the entire section.

Academic Application

EXERCISE 9-18

DIRECTIONS: Choose one of the reading selections at the end of this chapter. Read the selection, highlight, and annotate it. Then write a brief outline and summary of its content. Be sure to show the relationships between ideas as well as record the most important ideas.

SUMMARY

1. Why is writing during and after reading an effective learning strategy?

Writing during and after reading enhances both your comprehension and recall. Writing activities such as highlighting, annotating, paraphrasing, outlining, summarizing, and mapping can
- focus your attention
- force you to think
- test your understanding
- aid your recall

2. How can you highlight more effectively?

To make highlighting an efficient means of identifying what is important within each paragraph you should
- read first, then highlight
- use paragraph structure to guide you
- use headings as a guide
- develop your own highlighting system
- highlight as few words as possible
- reread your highlighting to test its accuracy

3. Why should you annotate and make marginal notations in conjunction with your highlighting?

Annotating involves recording ideas, reactions, impressions, and questions as you read. Using symbols and brief phrases as marginal notes is useful in condensing, supplementing, and clarifying passage content because you are adding your own thinking to the highlighted material.

4. Why is paraphrasing a useful study strategy?

Paraphrasing is the restatement of a passage's ideas in your own words. It is a particularly useful strategy for recording the meaning and checking your comprehension of detailed, complex, precise, difficult, or unusually written passages. Using your own words rather than the author's expresses the meaning of the passage clearer and more concisely, thereby making study and review easier.

5. What is an outline and what are its advantages?

Outlining is a form of organizing information that provides you with a structure that indicates the relative importance of ideas and shows the relationships among them. When done well, it helps you sort out ideas, improves your concentration, and aids your recall.

6. What is mapping?

Mapping is a process of drawing diagrams to show the connection between a topic and its related ideas. Both concept maps and thought pattern maps enable you to adjust to both the type of information being recorded and its particular organization. Grouping and consolidating information in this way makes it easier to learn and remember.

7. What is involved in summarizing?

Summarizing involves selecting a passage's most important ideas and recording them in a condensed abbreviated form. A summary provides a brief overview of a passage that can be useful in completing writing assignments and reports, preparing for class participation, or in reviewing for exams.

Reading Selection 17

The Supreme Court in Action

Edward S. Greenberg and Benjamin I. Page
From *The Struggle for Democracy*

The Supreme Court of the United States is an important and powerful part of our democratic system. Read this excerpt from an American government textbook to learn the traditions and rules the court follows and how it decides which cases to hear.

— · —

1   The Supreme Court meets from the first Monday in October (set by statute) until late June or early July, depending on the press of business. Let's see how it goes about deciding cases.

Norms of Operation

2   The Court is a tradition-bound institution defined by many rituals and long-standing norms. Brass spittoons still stand next to each justice's chair; quill pens and inkwells still grace the desks of competing counsel. Pages only gave up knickers in 1963; required formal wear (with tails) for lawyers was only recently abandoned. When the justices meet in public session to hear oral arguments or to announce decisions, they enter the courtroom in the same way: the chief justice is the first to emerge from behind the curtain that is draped behind the bench; the remainder enter in order of seniority.

3   More important than rituals are norms, unwritten but clearly understood ways of behaving. One norm is *secrecy*, which keeps the conflicts between justices out of the public eye and elevates the stature of the Court. Justices do not grant interviews very often. Reporters are not allowed to stalk the corridors for a story. Clerks are expected to keep all memos, draft opinions, and conversations with their justices confidential. Justices are not commonly seen on the frantic Washington, D.C., cocktail party circuit. When meeting in conference to argue and decide cases, the justices meet alone, without secretaries or clerks. While a breach of secrecy has occurred on occasion, allowing "insider" books like *The Brethren* to be published, they are the exceptions. As a result, we know less about the inner workings of the Court than about any other branch of government.

4   *Courtesy* is another norm. Though justices may sometimes express their displeasure and distaste for each other in private, in public they treat each other with great formality and respect. The justices shake hands before court sessions and conferences. They refer to each other as "my brother" or my "dissenting brother." Differences of opinion are usually respected; justices are allowed every opportunity to make their case to their fellow justices.

5   *Seniority* is another important norm. Seniority determines the assignment of office space, the seating arrangements in open court (the most junior are at the ends), the order of speaking in conference (the chief justice, then the most senior, etc.), and the order of voting (the most junior goes first).

6   Finally, the justices are expected to stick very closely to *precedent* when they are reaching a decision. When the Court departs from precedent, it is essentially overruling its own past actions, exercising judicial review of itself. In most cases, departure from precedent comes in only very small steps over many years, for example, several decisions chipped away at the "separate but equal" doctrine of *Plessy* v. *Ferguson* before it was decisively reversed in *Brown* v. *Board of Education*. If there is a significant ideological

Oral argument and the announcement of decisions happen here in the main courtroom of the Supreme Court building.

turnover on the court, however, change can come more quickly. The Rehnquist Court has been particularly aggressive in overturning precedents on the civil rights, criminal justice, and abortion fronts.

Controlling the Agenda

7   The Court has a number of screening mechanisms to control its agenda and to focus its attention on cases that involve important federal or constitutional questions.

8   Several technical rules help keep down the numbers. Cases must be real and adverse, meaning that they must involve a real dispute between two parties. The Court will not provide "advisory" opinions to guide the other branches. Disputants in a case must have standing, meaning that they must have a real and direct interest in the issues that are raised. The Court sometimes changes the definition of *standing* to make access easier or more difficult. The Warren Court favored a broad definition of *standing*, inviting litigation. The Rehnquist court tightened the definition, making it harder for people suing in the name of some larger group of affected people—consumers, racial minorities, and so on—to bring cases. Cases must also be ripe,

meaning that all other avenues of appeal have been exhausted and that injury has already taken place (it will not accept hypothetical or predicted injury cases). Appeals must also be filed within a specified time limit, paperwork must be proper and complete, and a filing fee of $200 must be paid. The fee can be waived if a petitioner is indigent and files an affidavit *in forma pauperis* (in the manner of a pauper). One of the most famous cases in American history, *Gideon* v. *Wainwright* (1963), which established the right to counsel in criminal cases, was submitted *in forma pauperis* on a few pieces of lined paper by a Florida State Penitentiary inmate named Clarence Earl Gideon.

9   The most powerful tool that the Court has for controlling its own agenda is the power to grant or not to grant a **writ of certiorari.** A grant of cert is a decision of the Court that an appellate case raises an important federal or constitutional issue that it is prepared to consider. Law clerks in the chief justice's office prepare a brief summary of each petition for the justices, along with a recommendation on whether or not to grant cert. The clerks, in consultation with the chief justice, prepare a "discuss list" of cases that they are recommending for cert. Under the **rule of four,** petitions are granted cert if at least four justices

vote in favor. There are several reasons why a petition may not command four votes, even if the case involves important constitutional issues: it may involve a particularly controversial issue that the Court would like to avoid, or the Court may not yet have developed a solid majority and wishes to avoid a split decision. Few petitions survive all of these hurdles. Of the 5,000 or so cases that are filed in each session, the Court grants cert for only a little more than 200. For cases denied cert, the decision of the lower court stands.

10   Deciding how freely to grant "cert" is tricky business for the Court. Used too often, it threatens to inundate the Court with cases. Used too sparingly, it leaves in place the decisions of 12 different circuit courts on substantial federal and constitutional questions.

EXAMINING READING SELECTION 17

Checking Your Vocabulary

Directions: Using context, word parts, or a dictionary if necessary, circle the letter of the meaning for each word as it is used in the reading.

1. seniority (paragraphs 2 and 5)
   a. order by length of service
   b. arrangement by degrees held
   c. order by importance
   d. arrangement by age

2. precedent (paragraph 6)
   a. a judicial decision that came before
   b. a judicial decision that was overruled
   c. a judicial decision that is in question
   d. a judicial decision that follows another

3. adverse (paragraph 8)
   a. created new legal requirements
   b. causes harm or danger
   c. meets a set of specified criteria
   d. involves a controversy or dispute

4. indigent (paragraph 8)
   a. unfamiliar with court procedures
   b. poor
   c. without an attorney
   d. unqualified

5. inundate (paragraph 10)
   a. to mystify
   b. to separate
   c. to overwhelm
   d. to cause ruin financially

Checking Your Comprehension

Directions: Circle the letter of the best answer.

1. This reading focuses on
   a. how justices behave.
   b. how the Supreme Court operates under a code of secrecy.
   c. how the Supreme Court selects cases.
   d. the operations of the Supreme Court.

2. The Supreme Court could best be described as
   a. self-regulating and efficient.
   b. innovative and adaptable.
   c. independent and tradition bound.
   d. eccentric and self-interested.

3. Little is known about the functioning of the Court because
   a. books like *The Brethren* are inaccurate.
   b. the justices maintain secrecy.
   c. the press does not consider the Court's operation newsworthy.
   d. the justices never meet in public session.

4. When cert is granted, the court
   a. reverses a lower court decision.
   b. agrees to consider an important federal or constitutional issue.
   c. recommends whether or not to consider an important issue.
   d. prepares a discuss list.

5. An adverse case is one
   a. that has exhausted all appeals.
   b. for which a cert has been denied.
   c. to which the rule of four does not apply.
   d. that involves a real dispute.

6. Which statement best describes the organization of this reading selection?
   a. The writers focus on causes and effects of court decisions.
   b. The writers emphasize differences among the justices.
   c. The writers present the court's operation chronologically.
   d. The writers list norms and operating procedures.

Thinking Critically

7. What would you expect the attitude of the justices to be toward the author of the book *The Brethren,* which gave "inside" information about the workings of the court?
   a. respect and admiration
   b. disapproval
   c. hate
   d. indifference

8. Which one of the following cases would the Supreme Court most likely consider?
   a. a convicted murderer just about to file an appeal in federal court
   b. a case in which a woman requests that a law be written that prohibits all pregnant women from smoking to prevent possible injury to fetuses
   c. a racial discrimination case that has not yet come to trial
   d. a personal injury case in which the victim has exhausted all appeals

9. The tone of this reading could best be described as
   a. distant.
   b. informational.
   c. argumentative.
   d. critical.

10. Which of the following statements can be inferred from the reading?
    a. The Court at times has chosen to avoid controversial issues.
    b. The justices frequently have personality disputes.
    c. The court is unwilling to try cases for which appeals have been exhausted.
    d. The court welcomes theoretical cases that concern possible injury.

Questions for Discussion

1. Identify and discuss a current legal issue leading to a hypothetical case in which you believe the court might seriously consider departing from a precedent. On what do you base your hypothetical case?

2. The article states that "the Court sometimes changes definition of standing to make access easier or more difficult." What is the definition of standing? Do you think it is fair for the Court to change this definition seemingly at random? Support your position.

3. Why do you think that granting "cert"—a writ of certiorari—places the Supreme Court in a particularly precarious position?

4. Why do you think the Court will hear cases that are "ripe" as opposed to predicted or hypothetical cases?

Selection 17:		1029 words	
Finishing Time:	_____	_____	_____
	HR.	MIN.	SEC.
Starting Time:	_____	_____	_____
	HR.	MIN.	SEC.
Reading Time:		_____	_____
		MIN.	SEC.
WPM Score:		_____	
Comprehension Score:		_____	%

READING SELECTION 18

ARE WE ALONE IN THE UNIVERSE?

Jeffrey Bennet, et al.
From *The Cosmic Perspective*

Is life on earth unique, or does life exist on other planets? This reading reports efforts to answer these long-standing questions and describes plans for our continuing quest to locate those like ourselves.

— · —

1   The study of the Earth can teach us much about other worlds. In particular, it teaches us about the conditions for life and may help us answer what is surely one of the deepest philosophical questions of all time: Are we alone in the universe? . . .

2   In the time between the Copernican revolution and the space age, many people expected the other planets in our solar system to be Earth-like and to harbor intelligent life. In fact, a reward was supposedly once offered for the first evidence of intelligent life on another planet *other than Mars*. Venus, a bit closer to the Sun than Earth, was often pictured as a tropical paradise. Such expectations were dashed by the bleak images of Mars returned by spacecraft and the discovery of the runaway greenhouse effect on Venus. Many scientists began to believe that only Earth has the right conditions for life, intelligent or otherwise. Recently, the pendulum has begun to swing the other way, spurred primarily by two developments. First, biologists are learning that life thrives under a much wider range of conditions than once imagined. Second, planetary scientists are developing a much better understanding of conditions on other worlds. It now seems quite likely that conditions in at least some places on other worlds might be conducive to life.

The Hardiness, Diversity, and Probability of Life

3   Even on Earth, biologists long assumed that many environments were uninhabitable. But recent discoveries have found life surviving in a remarkable range of conditions. The teeming life surviving at temperatures as high as 125°C near underwater volcanic vents and in hot springs is only one of many surprises. Biologists have found microorganisms living deep inside rocks in the frozen deserts of Antarctica and inside basaltic rocks buried more than a kilometer underground. Some bacteria can even survive radiation levels once thought lethal—apparently, they have evolved cellular machinery that repairs mutations as fast as they occur. The newly discovered diversity of microscopic life has forced scientists to redraw the "tree of life," crowding familiar plants and animals into one corner. The majority of these microorganisms need neither sunlight, oxygen, nor "food" in the form of other organisms. Instead, they tap a variety of chemical reactions for their survival.

4   The new view of terrestrial biology forces us to rethink the possibility of life elsewhere. First, life on Earth thrives at extremes of temperature, pressure, and atmospheric conditions that overlap conditions found on other worlds. The Antarctic valleys, for example, are as dry and cold as certain parts of Mars, and the conditions found in terrestrial hot springs may have been duplicated on a number of planets and moons at certain times in the past. Second, life harnesses energy sources readily available on other planets.

The basalt-dwelling bacteria, for example, would probably survive if they were transplanted to Mars. Third, life on Earth has evolved from a common ancestor into every imaginable ecological niche (and some unimaginable ones as well). The diversification of life on Earth has basically tested the limits of our planet, and there is no reason to doubt that it would do so on other planets. Thus, if life ever had a foothold on any other planet in the past, some organisms might still survive in surprising ecological niches today even if the planet has undergone substantial changes. The only real question is whether life ever got started elsewhere in the first place.

5 What is the probability of life arising from nonliving ingredients? This is probably the greatest unknown in exobiology. The fact that we exist and are asking the question does not tell us the probability; it merely tells us that it happened once. But the rapidity with which life arose on Earth may provide a clue. As we've discussed, we find fossil evidence for life dating almost all the way back to the end of the period of early bombardment in the solar system, suggesting that life arises easily and perhaps inevitably under the right conditions. Some people even speculate that primitive life arose many times during the heavy bombardment, only to be extinguished by violent impacts just as many times. If life indeed arises easily given the right conditions, we must search the solar system for those conditions, past or present.

6 **Time Out to Think** *The preceding discussion implies that the rapid appearance of life on Earth means that life is highly probable. Do you agree with this logic? What alternative conclusions could you reach?*

Life in the Solar System

7 Speculation about life in the solar system usually begins with Mars, for good reason. Before it dried out billions of years ago, its early atmosphere gave the surface hospitable conditions that rivaled those on Earth, with ample running water, the necessary raw chemical ingredients for life, and a variety of familiar energy sources. Many of Earth's organisms would have thrived under early Martian conditions, and some could even survive in places in today's Martian environment. Our first attempt to search for life on Mars came with the Viking missions to Mars in the 1970s, which included two landers equipped to search for the chemical signs of life. No life was found. But the landers sampled only two locations on the planet and tested soils only very near the surface. If life once existed on Mars, it either has become extinct or is hiding in other locations.

8 Today, a renewed debate about Martian life is under way, thanks in part to the study of a Martian meteorite found in Antarctica in 1984. The meteorite apparently landed in Antarctica 13,000 years ago, following a 16-million-year journey through space after being blasted from Mars by an impact. The rock itself dates to 4.5 billion years ago, indicating that it solidified shortly after Mars formed and therefore was present during the time when Mars was warmer and wetter. Painstaking analysis of the meteorite reveals indirect evidence of past life on Mars, including layered carbonate minerals and complex molecules (called polycyclic aromatic hydrocarbons), both of which are associated with life when they are found in Earth rocks. Even more intriguing, highly magnified images of the meteorite reveal eerily lifelike forms (Figure 1). These forms bear a superficial resemblance to terrestrial bacteria, although they are about a hundred times smaller—about the same size as recently discovered terrestrial "nanobacteria" and viruses. Nevertheless, many scientists dispute the conclusion that these features suggest the past existence of life on Mars, claiming that nonbiological causes can also explain many of the meteorite's unusual features.

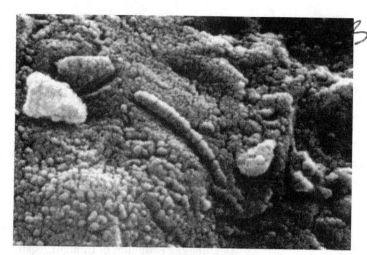

FIGURE 1 Microscopic view of seemingly lifelike structures in a Martian meteorite.

Life Around Other Stars

9   Only a few places in our solar system seem hospitable to life, but many more hospitable worlds may be orbiting some of the hundred billion other stars in the Milky Way Galaxy or stars in some of the billions of other galaxies in the universe. Might some of the stars be orbited by planets that are as hospitable as our own Earth?

10   The bottom line is that, according to our theories of solar system formation, planets with all the necessities for life should be quite common in the universe. The only major question is whether these ingredients combine to form life.

The fact that life arose very early in Earth's history suggests that it may be very easy to produce life under Earth-like conditions, but we will not know for sure unless and until we find other life-bearing planets. NASA is currently developing plans for orbiting telescopes that may be able to detect ozone in the spectra of planets around other stars—and, at least in our solar system, substantial ozone implies life. In addition, radio astronomers are searching the skies in hopes of receiving a signal from some extraterrestrial civilization. Perhaps, in a decade or two, we will discover unmistakable evidence of life. On that day, if it comes, we will know that we are not alone.

11   **Time Out to Think** *Consider the following statements: (1) We are the only intelligent life in the entire universe. (2) Earth is one of many planets inhabited by intelligent life. Which do you think is true? Do you find either philosophically troubling?*

Looking outward to the blackness of space, sprinkled with the glory of a universe of lights, I saw majesty—but no welcome. Below was a welcoming planet. There, contained in the thin, moving, incredibly fragile shell of the biosphere is everything that is dear to you, all the human drama and comedy. That's where life is; that's where all the good stuff is.

Loren Acton, U.S. Astronaut

EXAMINING READING SELECTION 18*

Checking Your Vocabulary

Directions: Complete each of the following items; refer to a dictionary if necessary.

1. Discuss the connotative meanings of the phrase *extraterrestrial civilization.*

2. Define each of the following words:
   a. harbor (paragraph 2)

   _____

   b. conducive (paragraph 2)

   _____

   c. lethal (paragraph 3)

   _____

*Multiple-choice questions are contained in Part 6 (page 608).

d. niche (paragraph 4)

_____

_____

e. renewed (paragraph 8)

_____

3. Define the word *dashed* (paragraph 2) and underline the word or phrase that provides a context clue for its meaning.

_____

_____

4. Define the word *hospitable* (paragraphs 7 and 9) and underline the word or phrase that provides a context clue for its meaning.

_____

_____

_____

_____

5. Determine the meanings of the following words by using word parts:
   a. planetary (paragraph 2)

   _____

   b. uninhabitable (paragraph 3)

   _____

   c. microorganisms (paragraph 3)

   _____

   d. terrestrial (paragraph 4)

   _____

   e. nonbiological (paragraph 8)

   _____

Checking Your Comprehension

1. Why does the author believe that life may have once existed on Mars?

   _____

   _____

2. How does the new view of terrestrial biology support the possibility of life elsewhere in the universe?

   _____

   _____

   _____

   _____

   _____

   _____

3. Describe the evolution of thought regarding the belief in life elsewhere in our solar system.

   _____

   _____

   _____

   _____

   _____

   _____

   _____

   _____

   _____

   _____

4. What chemical in the atmosphere of a planet implies life?

   _____

5. What indirect evidence of past life was found in the Martian meteorite found in Antarctica in 1984?

   _____

   _____

Thinking Critically

1. Describe the authors' purpose.

   _____

   _____

   _____

2. What assumptions do the writers of this selection make about life on other planets?

   _____

   _____

   _____

3. Based on the information presented in this selection, what type of studies could scientists undertake to try to prove or disprove that life exists elsewhere besides Earth?

   _____

   _____

   _____

   _____

   _____

   _____

_____

_____

_____

Questions for Discussion

1. Are you convinced by the author's arguments that life exists elsewhere in the universe? Give supporting evidence to support your position.

2. If you were an explorer on Mars, where would you begin with your search for life on the planet?

Selection 18:		1209 words	
Finishing Time:	_____	_____	_____
	HR.	MIN.	SEC.
Starting Time:	_____	_____	_____
	HR.	MIN.	SEC.
Reading Time:		_____	_____
		MIN.	SEC.
WPM Score:		_____	
Comprehension Score:		_____	%

Go Electronic

For additional readings, exercises, and Internet activities, visit this book's Web site at:

http://www.ablongman.com/mcwhorter

For even more activities, visit the Longman English pages at:

http://www.ablongman.com/englishpages

If you need a user name and password, please see your instructor.

Take a Road Trip to Spring Break! (Florida)
Be sure to visit the Outlining, Summarizing, Mapping, and Paraphrasing module on your Reading Road Trip CD-ROM for multimedia tutorials, exercises, and tests.

PART 3
Academic Scenario

The following scenario is designed to assess your ability to use and apply the skills taught in this part of the book.

THE SITUATION

Assume you are taking a course in geography. You have been directed to read a geography textbook chapter titled *Landforms.* Your instructor gives tests each month on the assigned chapters. The tests include both multiple-choice and essay questions. Assume that Reading Selection #14, page 327, is from the assigned chapter. Read this selection completely before beginning any of the following tasks. Reread the selection as often as necessary.

THE TASKS

1. Highlight and annotate the reading.
2. Write a one-paragraph summary of this reading.
3. Draw a map that shows the relationship of ideas presented in the reading.

CHAPTER 5

Drawing Inferences and Understanding Implied Main Ideas

In this chapter you will learn:

- How to draw inferences

- To recognize connotation and figurative language

- To distinguish between appropriate and inappropriate inferences

- To state main ideas that are implied

■ PREPARE TO READ

Read and reflect on the chapter's title and objectives. Glance through the chapter, observing headings to see what is covered. Now answer these questions:

1. What do you expect to learn from this chapter?

_____

_____

2. What do you already know about the chapter's topic?

_____

_____

3. What two or three questions do you want answered from reading this chapter?

_____

_____

_____

_____

Drawing inferences is an essential part of interacting with the world around us. It is also an essential part of the reading process. The cartoon in Figure 11.1 will get you started thinking about the process of drawing inferences. Study the cartoon and then answer the following questions.

■ FIGURE 11.1

Laugh Parade, by Bunny Hoest and John Reiner

"I'll get it!"

© 1999. Reprinted courtesy of Bunny Hoest and *Parade*.

1. Who are the men in the cartoon? _____

2. Where are they? _____

   How do you know the answer to this question?

   _____

   _____

3. What has just happened?

   _____

   _____

4. Why does one of the men say "I'll get it!"?

   _____

   _____

5. Which of these questions are you answering with facts?

   _____

   Which ones are you answering based on conclusions you are drawing
   from the details in the cartoon?

   _____

■ WHAT ARE INFERENCES?

When you look at the cartoon, you see men playing baseball, and you can
see that one of them has just hit the ball over the wall. So, your answer to
question 3 is a fact, a specific detail that we can see in the cartoon. Your answers to the other questions, though, are inferences. An **inference** is a conclusion based on evidence. An inference is an assumption about something
that is *unknown* based on something that is *known*. Nowhere in the cartoon
are the words *prison* or *prisoners*. You have inferred this condition based on
the details in the drawing. How many details did you list in answer to

question 2? If you did not observe the barbed wire around the wall, the watch tower, and the numbers on the prisoner's shirt, you would not be able to draw the inference that this game is being played in prison.

Drawing Inferences from Life Experiences

Every day you draw inferences about the people and the situations around you. You decide how people are feeling based on their actions and body language in a particular situation. (Remember that 90 percent of communication is *nonverbal*. Often behavior is a better clue to how someone is feeling than what the person actually tells you.) Use the following exercise to increase your awareness of the inferences you regularly draw.

EXERCISE 11-1 Workshop on Drawing Inferences from Life Situations

With your class partner or in small groups, answer the questions following each situation.

1. Walking down the street, you pass a young boy peering down a grate. One pocket of his pants is pulled out; it has a hole in it. As he leans over the grate, his lower lip begins to tremble.

   a. What has happened?

   _____

   _____

   b. How does the boy feel?

   _____

2. As you jog the bike path along the river, you pass a man carrying a metal case and a long pole. He is whistling.

   a. What is the man about to do? _____

   b. Is he looking forward to the activity? _____

3. You move into the left lane to pass a truck. Suddenly a car is on your rear bumper, with lights flashing and horn sounding. As you move

quickly around the truck and back into the right lane, the driver of the car behind you goes by, yelling and gesturing in your direction.

a. What did the driver want to do? _____

b. What is his attitude toward you? _____

c. What can you infer about the driver's emotions?

_____

_____

4. You overhear the following dialogue at work.

Barry, stopping by Joan's desk, says, "Let's have lunch today."
Joan, "I'm sorry. I'm too busy to stop for lunch today."
Barry, "This is the second day this week that I've suggested lunch and you have been too busy."
Joan, "I'm sorry, Barry. This McGarvey project is driving me crazy."
Barry, "You just don't want to have lunch with me."

a. What can you infer about Barry's feelings?

_____

b. What inference has Barry made?

_____

c. If Joan really is busy but wants to keep Barry as a lunch partner, what should she say after Barry's last remark?

_____

_____

■ DRAWING INFERENCES FROM READING

We also need to draw inferences to construct meaning out of the words on the page. We construct meaning from both what those words say and what they suggest or imply. Sometimes we need to "fill in" information or ideas that are suggested but not stated outright. Other times we need to draw a conclusion from the specifics that have been presented, to infer a main idea that has been implied but not directly stated. Always, as active readers, we need to work with the author to understand what we are reading.

Why Writers Suggest Rather Than State

Why can't they just write what they mean? I get tired of "reading between the lines" and looking for "hidden meanings," some readers complain. There are good responses to these complaints. First, remember the cartoon at the beginning of the chapter. Reread your answers to the questions about the cartoon. Those answers aren't funny, are they? Humor is almost always suggestive. Second, language that suggests can be more powerful. It draws us in and makes us participants in the construction of meaning. We don't really read "between the lines." Rather, we are actively engaged in getting the point *of* the lines.

The Role of Knowledge

How well we read is also connected to the knowledge we bring to the reading. Writers assume their readers have certain information. Those lacking the assumed knowledge may have trouble drawing appropriate inferences from their reading. For example, think back to the previous exercise. If you have never seen a fishing pole or tackle box, you will not know what the man is about to do in the second situation. You will be puzzled, or perhaps not take much notice of the man, because the details of the situation do not offer you any clues on which to draw an inference. See what inferences you can draw in the following exercise.

EXERCISE 11-2 Recognizing the Role of Knowledge in Drawing Inferences

Read each of the brief selections and then answer the questions that follow.

1. In addition to saying no to drugs, teenagers today need to spit in Joe Camel's eye.

   a. What does the writer actually want teens to do?

   _____

   _____

b. To answer (a), what information do you need to have, or what do you need to infer from the statement?

_____

_____

2. Pete Townshend of The Who has severely damaged hearing and, in addition, is plagued by tinnitus, an annoying condition in which there is a continuous ringing in the ears.

Wood and Wood, *The World of Psychology*, 2nd ed.

a. How did Pete Townshend damage his hearing?

_____

b. To answer (a), what information do you need to have, or what do you need to infer from the statement?

_____

_____

c. From the reference to Townshend, what point do you infer the authors want to make?

_____

_____

3. The skeleton of an elephant lies out in the grasses near a baobab tree and a scattering of black volcanic stones. The thick-trunked, gnarled baobab gesticulates with its branches, as if trying to summon help. There are no tusks lying among the bones, of course; ivory vanishes quickly in East Africa.

Lance Morrow, "Africa," *Time*

a. From the passage, what do you infer about the elephant's probable cause of death?

_____

b. To understand the last statement, what do you need to know—or infer—about ivory?

_____

_____

c. How does the author want readers to feel about the elephant's death?

_____

_____

4. In the Royal Free Hospital was my mother, Sister McVeagh. He married his nurse which, as they both said often enough (though in different tones of voice), was just as well. That was 1919.

Doris Lessing, "My Father" (a biographical essay)

a. Why was it "just as well" that Lessing's father married her mother? What are readers to infer from this passage?

_____

_____

b. What do you infer to be her father's tone of voice?

_____

c. What do you infer to be her mother's tone of voice? (Consider the time period when reflecting on her tone.)

_____

5. They ate economically, but when he got diabetes in his forties and subsisted on lean meat and lettuce leaves, he remembered suet puddings, treacle puddings, raisin and currant puddings, steak and kidney puddings, bread and butter pudding, "batter cooked in the gravy with the meat," potato cake, plum cake, butter cake, porridge with treacle, fruit tarts and pies, brawn, pig's trotters and pig's cheek and home-smoked ham and sausages. And "lashings of fresh butter and cream and eggs." He wondered if this diet had produced the diabetes, but said it was worth it.

Doris Lessing, "My Father"

a. What are readers to infer about the cause of Lessing's father's diabetes?

_____

_____

b. For the details in the paragraph to provide clues to answer the question, what information do readers need to have?

---

6. Susan Smith came to national fame as a distraught mother, a self-described victim of carjacking and kidnapping. When it all unraveled, and she was taken to court for arraignment, many people lined the streets shouting epithets at her. One woman said it all: "We believed you!" It was strikingly easy to play upon the fear of the stranger.

Ellen Goodman, "Stranger-Danger"

a. What did Susan Smith *say* had happened to her?

---

b. Why was she taken to court? What actually happened?

---

c. Did you answer (b) from inference or knowledge of the Susan Smith case?

---

d. Were you unable to answer (b) because of lack of information?

---

e. Do you think the author expects readers to have knowledge of Susan Smith or to infer from the passage?

On what is your answer based?

■ CONNOTATION

Connotation is one strategy writers use to develop implied ideas. A word's *connotation* is what the word suggests, what we associate the word with. For example, the words *house* and *home* both refer to a structure in which people live. These words have a similar denotation. But the word *home* suggests or is associated with ideas and feelings of family and security and comfort. So, the word *home* has a strong positive connotation. By contrast, the word *house* does not carry any "emotional baggage." Many words do not have connotations, but those that do often carry powerful associations. Studying a writer's use of emotionally charged words is an important way to understand a writer's attitude toward his or her subject.

Because we are familiar with the connotations of many common words, we may read "right over" key words without being aware of the writer's choice of language to direct our attitudes and affect our feelings. As you read, try to be especially sensitive to a writer's choice of words.

EXERCISE 11-3 Becoming Alert to Connotation

I. For each of the following pairs of words, check the one that has the more positive connotation. The first has been done for you.

1. ✔ quiet   _____ withdrawn

2. _____ miserly   _____ economical

3. _____ stubborn   _____ persistent

4. _____ naive   _____ trusting

5. _____ child   _____ brat

6. _____ hard   _____ brittle

7. _____ laid back   _____ lazy

8. _____ female parent   _____ mom

9. _____ pushy   _____ assertive

10. _____ neat   _____ neat freak

II. Select one of the two words provided to complete each of the following sentences. Briefly explain why you did not select the other word.

1. Some events in my brother's life have been quite _____.
   (amazing/bizarre)

   _____

2. Madonna has become _____ for her sexual openness.
   (notorious/famous)

   _____

3. Mary buys her clothes at sales because she is _____.
   (smart/cheap)

   _____

4. Tony's plan to buy out his chief competition showed a _____
   business sense. (shrewd/cunning)

   _____

5. Helena studies hard all the time; she must be a _____.
   (nerd/serious student)

   _____

■ FIGURATIVE LANGUAGE

Sometimes the most effective way to express an idea and create a feeling is to take ordinary words but put them together in ways that do not make sense *literally*. When you read an expression that seems to make no sense, you may be reading a *figure of speech*. Figurative language isn't found only in poetry; it is actually quite common. For example, we say we are on pins and needles over a test grade and complain about the rat race. Now these examples are called *clichés*, because they are worn out from overuse. Understanding figurative language can be difficult at first because the figures of speech are new. The first step to understanding is to recognize that the language is figurative and not take the statement literally. Momma's son in Figure 11.2 below has some trouble with figurative language. Look at the cartoon and then answer the following questions.

■ FIGURE 11.2

Momma, by Mell Lazarus

Reprinted by permission of Mell Lazarus and Creators Syndicate.

1. Why has Momma's son been fired?

_____

2. Why is he confused by the boss's statement?

_____

_____

Metaphors

A *metaphor* is a comparison of two things that are not alike but seem alike in some significant way. The boss in the comic strip has used a metaphor to describe his problem with the young man. The young man is not *really* a rotten apple; he is *like* a rotten apple.

There are several ways to express a metaphor, and some of these ways have their own names, but they all fit the basic definition. Here are the most common.

Simile: A leader is like a mirror.

Think of the expression as having two terms, one literal and one figurative, as if it were an equation: X (leader) = Y (mirror). (Because a leader is a person, not an object with a reflective surface, the expression is figurative, not literal.) In a simile the "equals" sign is spelled out with "like" or "as."

Metaphor: A leader mirrors the desires of his or her followers.

This metaphor makes the same point as the simile does; it just doesn't spell out the comparison with "like." In some metaphors, only one of the terms is stated. The other part of the comparison is implied.

Metaphor (figurative term implied): A leader reflects the desires of his or her followers.

Even though the term "mirror" is not stated, the *idea* of a mirror is there in the word "reflects."

Personification: The daffodils tossed their heads in sprightly dance.

Personification is a metaphor in which the Y term is always a person. When an idea, animal, or object is personified, it is given human qualities. In the example above, the daffodils are compared to humans who can toss their heads and dance. Actually, the daffodils are being blown by the wind but appear to the poet to be dancing.

To respond to metaphors, follow these steps:

1. Recognize that you are reading a metaphor.
2. Recognize the two terms being compared. Know what is the X and what is the Y of the comparison.
3. Reflect on the point of the comparison and the emotional impact of the comparison. How are we to take the metaphor? (Would you want to be called a "rotten apple"?)

EXERCISE 11-4 Understanding Metaphors

I. Read the following passage and then answer the questions below.

> About a mile farther, on a road I had never travelled, we came to an orchard of starved appletrees writhing over a hillside among outcroppings of slate that nuzzled up through the snow like animals pushing out their noses to breathe. Beyond the orchard lay a field or two, their boundaries lost under drifts.
>
> Edith Wharton, Ethan Frome

1. What metaphor is used to describe the orchard of apple trees?

   _____

2. What *type* of metaphor has Wharton used? _____

3. What metaphor is used to describe the outcroppings of slate?

   _____

4. What *type* of metaphor has Wharton used? _____

5. How do Wharton's metaphors make us feel? What do they add to the passage?

_____

II. *Read the following poem by Langston Hughes and then answer the questions that follow.*

Dreams

Hold fast to dreams
For if dreams die
Life is a broken-winged bird
That cannot fly.

5   Hold fast to dreams
For when dreams go
Life is a barren field
Frozen with snow.

1. Explain the metaphor in lines 3 and 4. What is being compared? What point is made?

_____

_____

2. Explain the metaphor in lines 7 and 8. What is being compared? What point is made?

_____

_____

3. Is it good or bad if dreams die? _____

4. What is the idea of the poem? What does the poet want us to understand about dreams?

_____

_____

Irony

Irony is a difference between what we expect to happen and what actually happens, or what a writer says and what the writer means. In narratives (stories, plays, narrative poems), the characters and action may lead us to expect events to end in a particular way. Sometimes the author surprises us with events that are quite different from what we expected. This is irony of situation.

Verbal irony occurs when writers write the opposite of what they mean. Somewhere in the context of the work are clues to help us understand the use of irony. We also use verbal irony in speech. For example, if you see a friend dashing into an early class with clothes that don't match and hair uncombed, you might say, "You're looking great this morning." Of course you—and your friend—understand that you are really commenting on how awful she looks.

Metaphors and irony are two effective figures of speech. Using them, a writer can play with words or move us with a powerful picture or lead us to reflect on the surprises in life.

 EXERCISE 11-5 Understanding Figures of Speech

Read and reflect on the following passage and then answer the questions that follow.

> We set out for the gallows. Two warders marched on either side of the prisoner, with their rifles at the slope; two others marched close against him, gripping him by arm and shoulder, as though at once pushing and supporting him. The rest of us, magistrates and the like, followed behind. Suddenly, when we had gone ten yards, the procession stopped short without any order or warning. A dreadful thing had happened—a dog, come goodness knows whence [from where], had appeared in the yard. It came bounding among us with a loud volley of barks and leapt round us wagging its whole body wild with glee at finding so many human beings together. It was a large wooly dog, half Airedale, half pariah [social outcast]. For a moment it pranced around us, and then, before anyone could stop it, it had made a dash for the prisoner, and jumping up tried to lick his face. Everybody stood aghast, too taken aback even to grab the dog.
>
> George Orwell, "A Hanging"

1. What is about to take place? _____

2. Is the narrator a part of the scene or not? _____

How do you know?

_____

3. Why is it important that the dog is half pariah?

_____

4. Why does the narrator say that the dog's appearance was "a dreadful thing"? Why was everybody "aghast"?

_____

_____

_____

5. What type of figurative language does Orwell use in this passage? (Hint: Is the dog's appearance in this particular scene unexpected and out of place?)

_____

_____

6. What does the passage comment on? What does Orwell want us to understand about hangings?

_____

_____

■ CHARACTERISTICS OF APPROPRIATE INFERENCES

An inference, we have noted, is a conclusion based on *evidence*. It is not an idea we make up rather than doing the hard work of studying the evidence. It is not *our* idea on the subject instead of the author's. Once you are clear about the writer's ideas, you may disagree if you wish. But do not let your views on the subject distort what you are reading. What are appropriate inferences? Appropriate inferences are based on all the details of a passage, do not contradict any of the details, and are not distorted by the reader's views on the subject.

Let's apply these ideas about inferences to the following paragraph.

When a colonial housewife went to the village well to draw water for her family, she saw friends, gathered gossip, shared the laughs and laments of her neighbors. When her great-great-granddaughter was blessed with running water, and no longer had to go to the well, this made life easier, but also less interesting. Electricity, mail delivery and the telephone removed more reasons for leaving the house. And now the climax of it all is Television.

Boorstin, "Television: More Deeply Than We Suspect, It Has Changed All of Us"

Boorstin's paragraph contains specific details but no stated main idea. What main idea are we to infer from the details? Here are three possibilities. Circle the one you think is best.

1. Modern conveniences developed over time.
2. Television is a great modern technological achievement.
3. Some technological advances, especially television, separate us from others.

Which one did you circle? If you focus on the paragraph's listing of new conveniences developed over time, you might select the first statement. But the first statement does not "cover" or take account of the paragraph's discussion of the colonial housewife's lifestyle.

If you focus on the word *climax* in the last sentence, you might select the second inference. But the second statement seems to contradict Boorstin's idea that life, with modern conveniences, requires less mingling with neighbors and is "less interesting." You may think that television is a great achievement, but Boorstin does not appear to agree with you. The best inference is the third sentence because it captures Boorstin's idea that when information comes directly into our homes we become isolated from our community, and this isolation is not a good thing.

◼ UNDERSTANDING IMPLIED MAIN IDEAS

You have practiced generalizing from specifics in Chapter 5 and reading for main ideas in Chapter 6. In this chapter you have practiced drawing inferences about experience and from reading. To read for implied main ideas, you need to make these skills work together. You may find that stating the paragraph's topic will guide you to an appropriate main idea.

Here is another practice paragraph. Circle the best statement of topic and then write a main-idea statement for the paragraph. (Remember: A main idea must be stated as a complete sentence.)

The corner of the office where I work has no windows. The climate is what they call controlled. I can be there all day without knowing if it's hot or cold outside. I commute in a machine on pavement, following the directions of red and green lights. My work day is determined by a clock that remains the same through all tides, moons, and seasons.

Ellen Goodman, "Content to Be in My Place"

Possible Topics:

    a. my workday
    b. modern life's lack of connection to nature
    c. the conveniences of modern life

Main idea: _____

_____

    Which topic did you select? Is the intent of the specific details to recount the writer's workday? If so, she has a rather strange way of describing her day. Is the paragraph about modern conveniences? Is Goodman praising air conditioning when she writes that "the climate is what they call controlled"? Does that sound like a statement of praise? No. The best topic is (b). All of the specifics are parts of the workday that disconnect the writer from the "tides, moons, and seasons"—from the rhythms or patterns of nature. Now, ask yourself: How does the writer feel about the topic? Are we lucky to be sealed off from nature during the workday? If you answer the question with a "No," then you can write a main-idea statement for Goodman's paragraph.

    The following exercises will give you practice in drawing inferences to determine the implied main idea in paragraphs. But first, review the guidelines for appropriate inferences.

Characteristics of Appropriate Inferences

They cover all the details in the passage.
They do not contradict any of the details in the passage.
They explain the writer's ideas, not the reader's ideas, about the topic.

EXERCISE 11-6 Identifying the Best Main-Idea Statement

After reading each paragraph, circle the best main-idea statement.

1. A student of botany and geology, John Muir traveled through much of the Midwest and Plains states on foot. He also traveled through

Nevada, Utah, and the Northwest to study forests and glaciers. After discovering many glaciers in the Sierra Mountains, Muir explored Alaska, where he also discovered glaciers, one of which was named after him. Throughout his travels he wrote and published his observations, and he called for forest conservation and establishing national parks. He helped with the campaign to create Yosemite National Park and later camped there with then President Theodore Roosevelt. Roosevelt set aside public lands as forest preserves and named a redwood forest in California after Muir shortly before Muir's death in 1908.

Adapted from *American Heritage History of the United States*

   a. Muir explored the United States and discovered many glaciers.

   b. Muir was an important geologist and conservationist who contributed to the development of our national parks.

2. The Nile was responsible for creating an area several miles wide on both banks of the river that was fertile and capable of producing abundant harvests. . . . The river . . . was seen as life enhancing, not life threatening. Although a system of organized irrigation was still necessary, the small villages along the Nile could make the effort. . . . In addition to providing food, it [the Nile] promoted easy transportation and encouraged communication.

Jackson J. Spielvogel, *Western Civilization*, 2nd ed., Vol. 1

   a. The Nile River was central to the development of Egyptian civilization.

   b. The Nile was a means of transportation from one part of Egypt to another.

3. Young males and females are equally likely to try alcohol, tobacco or illegal drugs. But males, particularly young men 18 to 21 years old, do so more often and in larger quantities.

   a. There are some gender differences among young people in behavior that threatens health.

   b. Young men are more foolish than young women.

4. H. M. Skeels and H. B. Dye . . . placed thirteen infants whose mental retardation was so obvious that no one wanted to adopt them, in Glenwood State School, an institution for the mentally retarded. Each infant, then about 19 months old, was assigned to a separate ward of women ranging in mental age from 5 to 12 and in chronological age from 18 to 50. The women were pleased with this arrangement. . . . The researchers left a control group of twelve infants, also retarded but higher in intelligence, at the orphanage, where they received the usual care. Two and

a half years later, Skeels and Dye tested all the children's intelligence. Their findings were startling: Those assigned to the retarded women had gained an average of twenty-eight IQ points while those who remained in the orphanage had lost thirty points.

James M. Henslin, *Sociology*, 2nd ed.

a. Orphanages should be done away with.
b. Intelligence is at least partly learned through stimulating social interaction.

5. In 1982, scientists in Antarctica discovered that the ozone layer above them was getting thinner. The cause is a buildup in the atmosphere of chemicals called chlorofluorocarbons (CFCs). These are used in aerosol spray cans, foam plastics, refrigerators, and air-conditioning systems. When these products are dumped, the CFCs slowly rise into the atmosphere, and, in the Antarctic winter, they go through complex chemical reactions that destroy the ozone.

Michael Scott, *Ecology*

a. Discarded products containing CFCs are causing serious damage to the ozone layer in the atmosphere above Antarctica.
b. Winter in Antarctica is difficult.

EXERCISE 11-7 Recognizing Topics and Inferring Main Ideas

After reading each paragraph, circle the best statement of the paragraph's topic. Briefly explain your choice. Then write a main-idea statement for the paragraph.

1. [Elephant] babies are eagerly accepted not only by the members of their own groups but by all other elephants as well, including strange bulls—a phenomenon almost unique in animal behavior. There are many well-documented stories about unrelated bulls rescuing young calves in swamps, for example, and under all manner of other circumstances. Moreover, orphans are readily adopted by new families, even for nursing. Unrelated or only distantly related herds will intermingle and mix freely at waterholes, the adults greeting one another with quiet dignity and the youngsters frolicking together.

P. Jay Fetner, *The African Safari*

Topics:

a. acceptance of baby elephants
b. social nature of elephants

Explain your choice: _____

_____

_____

Main idea: _____

_____

2. In the Medicare program for Americans over 65, for example, women outnumber men 19 million to 13 million. They depend on Medicare longer, using the program for about 15 years compared on average with 7 years for men. They also outnumber men in the Social Security program; nearly 60 percent of beneficiaries are female.

Abigail Trafford, "Growing Old Is Largely a Job for Women"

Topics:

    a. women's dependency on government services for the elderly
    b. women's longevity

Explain your choice: _____

_____

_____

Main idea: _____

_____

3. As far back as 500 B.C., when the Nok culture flourished in Nigeria, furnaces were being used to smelt iron. The Nigerian state of Benin exchanged ambassadors with Portugal in 1486. At that time Timbuktu in Mali was a major trading center of international fame. The splendors of the Songhai Empire, which stretched from Mali to Kano, Nigeria, in the fifteenth and sixteenth centuries, were compared by early travelers with those of contemporary Europe. . . . Iron-Age Africans started building stone structures in the area we call Zimbabwe as early as A.D. 1100, and sixteenth-century Portuguese maritime traders found that some West African textiles were superior to anything then being made in Europe.

David Lamb, *The Africans*

Topics:

    a. African buildings
    b. early cultures in Africa

Explain your choice: _____

_____

_____

Main idea: _____

_____

4. The Black Death of the mid-fourteenth century . . . ravaged Europe, wiping out 25 to 50 percent of the population and causing economic, social, political, and cultural upheaval. A Sienese chronicler wrote that "father abandoned child, wife husband, one brother another, for the plague seemed to strike through breath and sight. And so they died. And no one could be found to bury the dead, for money or friendship." People were horrified by an evil force they could not understand and by the subsequent breakdown of all normal human relations.

Jackson J. Spielvogel, *Western Civilization*, 2nd ed., Vol. 1

Topics:

    a. the Black Death in the fourteenth century
    b. the devastation of the Black Death

Explain your choice: _____

_____

_____

Main idea: _____

_____

5. In the past ten years, Miami's population grew only 3.4 percent, but its Spanish-speaking population grew 15 percent, making the city 62 percent Hispanic. Throughout the United States, 83 percent of residents speak English at home, but only 25 percent of Miami residents do so.

Topics:

    a. Hispanic growth in Miami
    b. Hispanic growth in the United States

Explain your choice: _____

_____

_____

Main idea: _____

_____

■ DRAWING INFERENCES AND UNDERSTANDING IMPLIED MAIN IDEAS IN LONGER PASSAGES

The tasks of drawing inferences and understanding implied main ideas are much the same for longer passages as for sentences or paragraphs. The only difference is that you have to keep working for a longer period of time. If you stop concentrating before finishing the section or article, you may not "fill in" information that is needed for clarity. Or, you may not keep track of all the specifics needed to recognize the implied main idea. As you work with longer passages, keep these guidelines in mind.

Guidelines for Understanding Implied Meanings

1. Annotate carefully as you read.
2. Think about levels of specificity. Focus on major details.
3. Ask yourself, "What does the author want me to learn or understand from this passage?" "What is the author's purpose in writing in this manner about this subject?"
4. State the passage's topic.
5. State the passage's main idea.
6. Check your main idea statement against the details. Have you covered all details? Have you avoided contradicting any details?

EXERCISE 11-8 Recognizing Implied Meanings in Longer Passages

Read and annotate each passage. After reading a passage, complete the exercise that follows.

I. Exactly what are they teaching in our schools these days? . . . A new national survey suggests that, on average, college graduates today know fewer selected basic facts about government and politics than college graduates did in 1947.

Likewise, today's high school grads appear to know less about government and politics than their educational equals of five decades ago.

For example, a Gallup survey in 1947 found that 77 percent of all Americans surveyed who had graduated from high school but not gone on to college knew which party controlled the U.S. House of Representatives.

Today, barely half—54 percent—of all high school graduates know that the Republicans control the House. . . . [in 1996]

Political knowledge also has slipped among college graduates: 90 percent knew which party controlled the House in 1947, compared to 80 percent in the latest survey.

Richard Morin, "Dumbing Down Democracy"

1. What is the passage's topic?

_____

2. What is implied in the opening question?

_____

_____

3. What are we to infer about the cause or causes for the decline in knowledge about government and politics?

_____

_____

4. What is the author's attitude toward the decline in knowledge?

_____

II. All the hours in class tend to blend into one long, vague stretch of time. What I remember best, strangely enough, are two things I couldn't understand and over the years grew to hate: grammar lessons and mathematics. I would sit there watching a teacher draw her long horizontal line and her short, oblique lines and break up sentences and put adjectives here and adverbs there and just not get it, couldn't see the reason for it, turned off to it. I would hide by slumping down in my seat and page through my reader, carried along by the flow of sentences in a story. She would test us, and I would dread that, for I always got Cs and Ds. Mathematics was a bit different. For whatever reasons, I didn't learn early math very well, so when it came time for more complicated operations, I couldn't keep up and started daydreaming to avoid my inadequacy. This was a strategy I would rely on as I grew older. I fell further and further behind. A memory: The teacher is faceless and seems very far away. The voice is faint and is discussing an equation written on the board. It is raining, and I am watching the streams of water form patterns on the windows.

Mike Rose, *Lives on the Boundary*

1. What is the passage's topic?

2. Why did the writer turn to daydreaming?

3. What is important about the memory Rose recounts at the end?

4. What can you conclude about the writer's attitudes toward school when he was in class?

5. Why is Rose telling about his school experiences? What is his purpose?

Amelia Earhart

by **Vincent Wilson, Jr.**

A former college instructor, Vincent Wilson has also served as a writer, editor, and historian with the U.S. government. The following one-page article on Amelia Earhart is part of *The Book of Distinguished American Women* (2nd ed., 1992).

Prepare

1. Identify the author and the work. What do you expect the author's purpose to be?

   _____

   _____

   _____

2. Preread to identify the subject and make predictions. What do you expect to read about?

   _____

   _____

   _____

3. What do you already know about the subject?

   _____

   _____

   _____

4. Raise two questions that you expect the article to answer.

   _____

   _____

   _____

Amelia Earhart

1   Amelia Earhart was the first woman of flight—with an array of first's unmatched in the world. Her daring flights in the 1920s and 1930s captured the imagination of the American public and signaled that women could participate fully in pioneering this new frontier.

2   As a child, Amelia Earhart liked to ride horseback and a miniature homemade roller coaster. After high school, she tried nursing and pre-medical studies before she first flew—with barnstormer[1] Frank Hawks in Glendale, California, in 1920. Two years later she was flying her own Kinner Canary in California air shows.

3   Amelia Earhart was working in a settlement house in Boston and flying in her free time when publisher George Putnam chose her to fly as a passenger on a transatlantic flight a year after Lindberg's historic crossing. Wilmer Stultz piloted the Fokker trimotor from Newfoundland to Wales; Amelia Earhart kept the flight log. She was the first woman to cross the Atlantic by air, and suddenly she was famous. New York gave "Lady Lindy" a ticker-tape parade. In 1931 Miss Earhart married George Putnam—with an agreement that she have complete freedom to travel. Putnam managed her affairs.

4   On May 21–22, 1932, Amelia Earhart flew solo from Newfoundland to Ireland. In a Lockheed monoplane she flew the 2026 miles in 14 hours,

[1]One who tours as a stunt pilot.

56 minutes, much of it through storms and fog—the first woman to fly the Atlantic alone. She was smothered with honors—among others, the cross of the French Legion of Honor and the U.S. Distinguished Flying Cross. Other first's followed: two transcontinental records and the first non-stop flight from Mexico City to New York.

5   In 1937 a round-the-world flight (another first) was planned, to test long-range performance of crew and aircraft. After an unsuccessful attempt, on June 1st Amelia Earhart and navigator Fred Noonan left Miami, Florida, flying east on an equatorial route that took them across the Atlantic Ocean, Africa, and the Indian Ocean. At Lae, New Guinea, on July 2, they took off to fly 2570 miles to Howland Island, a spot in the Pacific scarcely longer than its runway. They never reached it. Hours after they were due, the Coast Guard cutter *Itaska*, near Howland, received their last voice messages: "... gas is running low ..." and "We are on a line of position. ..." Sea and air searches found nothing.

6   For years rumors persisted that Miss Earhart had been on an espionage mission and might have been captured by the Japanese. But the facts—including recent (1992) discoveries of possible plane parts in the Howland area—strongly suggest that the plane simply missed Howland and crashed into the sea.

7   Amelia Earhart had a passion for flying—she even wrote verse about it—but she was also deeply committed to the cause of feminism: both as a woman and a flyer, she was a pioneer. She once confided to her husband that, for her, the ideal way to die would be swiftly to go down with her plane.

496 words

Comprehension Check

Answer the following with a, b, or c to indicate the phrase that best completes each statement.

_____ 1. Amelia Earhart was married to

a. Lindberg.
b. Frank Hawks.
c. George Putnam.

_____ 2. Amelia Earhart was

a. the first woman to fly alone across the Atlantic.
b. the first person to fly alone across the Atlantic.
c. the first female spy.

_____ 3. A Kinner Canary is

      a. a settlement house in Boston.
      b. a type of plane.
      c. the name of an award Earhart won.

_____ 4. On a transcontinental flight, Amelia Earhart

      a. died in New Guinea.
      b. died on the Coast Guard ship _Itaska_.
      c. died at sea when her plane crashed.

_____ 5. Amelia Earhart was given many awards including

      a. the Legion of Honor.
      b. the distinguished Flying Cross.
      c. both (a) and (b).

_____ 6. Amelia Earhart

      a. wanted freedom to travel.
      b. was daring from childhood on.
      c. both (a) and (b).

Expanding Vocabulary

After using context clues and a study of word parts, write a brief definition or synonym for each of the following words or phrases.

smothered (4) _____

equatorial route (5)_____

espionage (6) _____

feminism (7)_____

Analysis of Main Ideas

1. State the article's topic:

    _____

2. Circle the best main-idea statement:

    a. Amelia Earhart made history in the 1920s and 1930s.
    b. Amelia Earhart was a pioneer for women and in the history of flight.

3. Briefly explain your selection of a main idea.

_____

_____

4. What main idea are we to infer from reading paragraph 2?

_____

_____

5. Why was Earhart called "Lady Lindy" in paragraph 3?

_____

6. Why does the author conclude with Earhart's statement to her husband? What are we to infer from the conclusion?

_____

_____

For Discussion and Reflection

1. If you had a chance to go back in time and meet Earhart, what would you talk with her about? Why?
2. Wilson's article about Earhart is one of 50 in his book on distinguished American women. If you were to make such a book for women worldwide, what women would you include? See how long a list of important American women you can make. Remember to consider various fields of endeavor from colonial times to the present.

Your Reading Assessment

1. How accurately did you predict what you would read about?

_____

2. Did the selection answer your questions? _____

If not, why do you think that it did not?

_____

Early Autumn

by **Langston Hughes**

Langston Hughes was a journalist, fiction writer, and poet, the author of more than sixty books. Known as "the bard of Harlem," Hughes became an important public figure and voice for black writers. "Early Autumn" comes from his short fiction collection *Something in Common* (1963).

Prepare

1. Identify the author and work. What do you expect the author's purpose to be?

   _____

2. Preread to identify the subject and make predictions. What do you expect to read about?

   _____

When Bill was very young, they had been in love. Many nights they had spent walking, talking together. Then something not very important had come between them, and they didn't speak. Impulsively, she had married a man she thought she loved. Bill went away, bitter about women.

Yesterday, walking across Washington Square, she saw him for the first time in years.

"Bill Walker," she said.

He stopped. At first he did not recognize her, to him she looked so old.

"Mary! Where did you come from?"

Unconsciously, she lifted her face as though wanting a kiss, but he held out his hand. She took it.

"I live in New York now," she said.

"Oh"—smiling politely. Then a little frown came quickly between his eyes.

"Always wondered what happened to you, Bill."

"I'm a lawyer. Nice firm, way downtown."

"Married yet?"

"Sure. Two kids."

"Oh," she said.

A great many people went past them through the park. People they didn't know. It was late afternoon. Nearly sunset. Cold.

"And your husband?" he asked her.

"We have three children. I work in the bursar's office at Columbia."

"You're looking very . . ." (he wanted to say *old*) ". . . well," he said.

She understood. Under the trees in Washington Square, she found herself desperately reaching back into the past. She had been older than he then in Ohio. Now she was not young at all. Bill was still young.

"We live on Central Park West," she said. "Come and see us sometime."

"Sure," he replied. "You and your husband must have dinner with my family some night. Any night. Lucille and I'd love to have you."

The leaves fell slowly from the trees in the Square. Fell without wind. Autumn dusk. She felt a little sick.

"We'd love it," she answered.

"You ought to see my kids." He grinned.

Suddenly the lights came on up the whole length of Fifth Avenue, chains of misty brilliance in the blue air.

"There's my bus," she said. He held out his hand, "Good-by."

"When . . ." she wanted to say, but the bus was ready to pull off. The lights on the avenue blurred, twinkled, blurred. And she was afraid to open her mouth as she entered the bus. Afraid it would be impossible to utter a word.

Suddenly she shrieked very loudly, "Good-by!" But the bus door had closed.

The bus started. People came between them outside, people crossing the street, people they didn't know. Space and people. She lost sight of Bill. Then she remembered she had forgotten to give him her address—or to ask him for his—or tell him that her youngest boy was named Bill, too.

420 words

Comprehension Check

Fill in the blank with the word or phrase that best completes each sentence, or select either T (true) or F (false).

1. When Mary and Bill were young, they were _____.

2. Both characters now live in _____;

   both are _____ and have _____.

3. Bill thinks that Mary looks _____.

4. Mary gets on her bus without getting Bill's _____.

	T	F
5. Mary is upset when she gets on the bus.	___	___
6. Bill is upset when he parts from Mary.	___	___
7. Mary still loves Bill.	___	___

Analysis of Strategies and Structures

1. What is Bill's reaction to seeing Mary?

   _____

   What specific details support your inference?

   _____

   _____

2. What can we infer from Mary's response to the question: "And your husband?"

   _____

3. What is happening to Mary when the "lights . . . blurred, twinkled, blurred"?

   _____

4. Why did the author call the story "Early Autumn"? (Look at the details of the scene—the time of year, the time of day, the activity around Mary and Bill.)

   _____

   _____

5. Briefly state the story's theme.

   _____

   _____

   _____

For Discussion and Reflection

1. Have you done anything impulsively that you ended up regretting? If so, is there anything you can do now to undo what you did? If not, what is probably one thing you can gain from the experience?

Chapter Review Quiz

Complete each of the following statements.

1. An *inference* is

   _____.

2. We draw inferences from both _____

   and _____.

3. To draw many inferences we need to "fill in" from our

   _____.

4. A *metaphor* compares two _____.

   _____

5. Read the following poem and then complete the questions that follow.

Taxi

by **Amy Lowell**

When I go away from you
The world beats dead
Like a slackened drum.
I call out for you against the jutted stars

5   And shout into the ridges of the wind.
Streets coming fast,
One after the other,
Wedge you away from me,
And the lamps of the city prick my eyes

10   So that I can no longer see your face.

Why should I leave you,
To wound myself upon the sharp edges of the night?

a. What is the "situation" in the poem? What event or activity does the speaker in the poem describe? (Don't overlook the title.)

_____

_____

b. Explain the metaphor in the first three lines. What are the two items being compared?

_____

_____

Is the speaker happy? _____

Why or why not?

_____

c. Explain the metaphor in the last line. What are the two items being compared?

_____

Is the metaphor positive or negative? _____

d. List some words in the poem that have a negative connotation in this context.

_____

e. State briefly the main idea and feelings of the poem.

_____

_____

_____

Chapter 6
CRITICAL READING STRATEGIES

LEARNING OBJECTIVES

- **To make inferences and understand implied meanings**
- **To assess an author's ideas**
- **To react to ideas presented**
- **To synthesize and compare sources**

In college you will be reading many new kinds of material: research articles, essays, critiques, reports, and analyses. Your instructors expect you to be able to do much more than understand and remember the basic content. They often demand that you read critically—interpreting, evaluating, and reacting to assigned readings. To meet these expectations, you'll need to make solid inferences, annotate as you read, analyze and evaluate what you have read, and draw comparisons among several works.

INTERPRET IMPLIED MEANING

So far, we have been concerned primarily with the literal meanings of writing. You have been shown techniques to help you to understand what the author says and retain the literal, factual content. However, you often need to go beyond what authors *say* and to be concerned with what they *mean*. Look at the photograph on page 93, which appeared in a psychology textbook. What do you think is happening here? Where is it happening? What are the feelings of the participants?

To answer these questions, you had to use any information you could get from the photo and make guesses based on it. The facial expressions, body language, clothing, and other objects present in this photo implied or hinted at the emotions of those involved, the event that is occurring, and the locale of that event. This process of drawing conclusions, as you did, from these implied meanings is called "making an inference."

Make Inferences from the Given Facts

An inference is a reasoned guess about what you don't know made on the basis of what you do know. Inferences are common in our everyday lives.

When you enter an expressway and see a long, slow-moving line of traffic, you might predict that there is an accident or roadwork ahead. When you see a puddle of water under the kitchen sink, you can infer that you have a plumbing problem. The inferences you make may not always be correct, even though you based them on the available information. The water under the sink might have been the result of a spill. The traffic you encountered on the expressway might be normal for that time of day, but you didn't know it because you aren't normally on the road then. An inference is only the best guess you can make in a situation, given the information you have.

Inferences from Written Material

When you read the material associated with your college courses, you need to make inferences frequently. Writers do not always present their ideas directly. Instead, they often leave it to you to add up and think beyond the facts they present. You are expected to reason out, or infer, the meaning an author intended (but did not say) on the basis of what he or she did say. In a sense, the inferences you make act as bridges between what is said and what is not said but is meant.

There are several reasons why textbook authors and other writers require you to make inferences. Often, information is left out because it would make the message too long or would divert you from the central point. Sometimes an author assumes the readers know enough to fill in the omitted ideas. Other times, the writer believes that you will get more meaning or enjoyment from engaging in the thought process required in making an inference. Finally, some writers leave out pertinent information in order to make it easier to influence you to draw a desired conclusion, especially if you might have challenged the details had they been included. You can see, then, that making solid inferences is an important first step toward reading critically.

How to Make Inferences

Each inference you make depends on the situation, the facts provided, and your own knowledge and experience. Here are a few guidelines to help you see beyond the factual level and make solid inferences.

Know the Literal Meaning Be sure you have a firm grasp of the literal meaning. You must understand the stated ideas and facts before you can move to higher levels of thinking, which include inference making. You should recognize the topic, main idea, key details, and organizational pattern of each paragraph you have read.

Notice Details As you are reading, pay particular attention to details that are unusual or stand out. Often, such details will offer you clues to help you make inferences. Ask yourself

- What is unusual or striking about this piece of information?
- Why is it included here?

Read the following excerpt, which is taken from a business marketing textbook, and try to mark details that are unusual or striking.

MARKETING IN ACTION

Dressing Up the Basics in Idaho

In almost any grocery store across the United States, consumers can purchase ten pounds of Idaho-grown potatoes for less than $2.00. Despite this fact, Rolland Jones Potatoes, Incorporated, has been extremely successful selling a "baker's dozen" of Idaho potatoes for $18.95. The potatoes are wrapped in a decorative box that uses Easter grass.

The Baker's Dozen of Idaho potatoes is only one example of a growing phenomenon. Laura Hobbs, marketing specialist for the Idaho Department of Agriculture, reports that more than 200 Idaho farms produce specialty or value-added products. These goods typically consist of basic farm commodities that have been "dressed-up" with packaging. Consumers can choose from these products: microwave popcorn that comes on the cob and pops right off the cob, a bag of complete chili ingredients that makers claim won't cause embarrassing side-effects, and chocolate-covered "Couch Potato Chips."

Idaho farmers are supported by two groups, the Idaho Specialty Foods Association and Buy Idaho, whose goals are to help producers market and promote unique items. With the help of the groups, Idaho farmers are getting quite savvy. The marketers have discovered, for example, that packaging certain items together can increase their attractiveness. Hagerman's Rose Creek Winery found that sales of its wines soared when they were packaged in gift baskets with jars of Sun Valley brand mustard.

According to Hobbs, consumers attracted to the unique packaging provide a market for an endless variety of products, all of which are standard commodities transformed into new products through packaging. The value added through the unique packaging also provides opportunities to charge prices in ranges far above the prices of standard products—like $18.95 for 12 potatoes!

—Kinnear et al., *Principles of Marketing*, p. 301

Did you mark details such as the price of $18.95 for potatoes, corn that pops right off the cob, and chocolate-covered potato chips?

Add Up the Facts   Consider all of the facts taken together. To help you do this, ask yourself such questions as the following:

- What is the writer trying to suggest from this set of facts?
- What do all these facts and ideas seem to point toward or add up to?
- Why did the author include these facts and details?

Making an inference is somewhat like assembling a complicated jigsaw puzzle, in which you try to make all the pieces fit together to form a recognizable picture. Answering these questions will require you to add together all the individual pieces of information, which will enable you to arrive at an inference.

When you add up the facts in the article "Dressing Up the Basics in Idaho," you realize that the writer is suggesting that people are willing to pay much more than a product is worth if it is specially packaged.

Be Alert to Clues   Writers often provide you with numerous hints that can point you toward accurate inferences. An awareness of word choices, details included (and omitted), ideas emphasized, and direct commentary can help you determine a textbook author's attitude toward the topic at hand. In the foregoing excerpt, the authors offer clues that reveal their attitude toward increased prices for special packaging. Terms such as *dressed-up* and the exclamation point at the end of the last sentence suggest that the authors realize that the products mentioned are not worth their price.

In addition to these clues, writers of fiction also provide hints in their descriptions of characters and actions and through the conversations of their characters.

Consider the Author's Purpose   Also study the author's purpose for writing. If an author's purpose is to convince you to purchase a particular product, as in an advertisement, as you begin reading you already have a clear idea of the types of inferences the writer hopes you will make. For instance, here is a magazine ad for a stereo system.

> If you're in the market for true surround sound, a prematched system is a good way to get it. The components in our system are built for each other by our audio engineers. You can be assured of high performance and sound quality.

Verify Your Inference   Once you have made an inference, check that it is accurate. Look back at the stated facts to be sure that you have sufficient evidence to support the inference. Also, be certain that you have not overlooked other equally plausible or more plausible inferences that could be drawn from the same set of facts.

EXERCISE 4–1

Read each of the following statements. Place a checkmark in front of each of the sentences that follow that is a reasonable inference that can be made from the statement.

1. Political candidates must now include the Internet in their campaign plans.

   _____ a. Political candidates may host online chats to assess voter opinion.

   _____ b. Informal debates between candidates may be conducted online.

   _____ c. Internet campaigning will drastically increase overall campaign expenditures.

   _____ d. Television campaigning is likely to remain the same.

2. Half of the public education classrooms in the United States are now hooked up to the Internet.

   _____ a. Children are more computer literate than their parents.

   _____ b. Students now have access to current world news and happenings.

   _____ c. Books are no longer considered the sole source of information on a subject.

   _____ d. Teachers have become better teachers now that they have Internet access.

3. The Internet can make doctors more efficient through the use of new software and databases that make patient diagnosis more accurate.

_____ a. The cost of in-person medical care is likely to decrease.

_____ b. Doctors may be able to identify patients with serious illness sooner.

_____ c. Doctors are likely to pay less attention to their patients' descriptions of symptoms.

_____ d. Information on the symptoms and treatment of rare illnesses is more readily available.

EXERCISE 4-2

Read the following paragraph. A number of statements follow it; each statement is an inference. Label each inference as either

PA—Probably accurate—there is substantial evidence in the paragraph to support the statement.

IE—Insufficient evidence—there is little or no evidence in the paragraph to support the statement.

While working for a wholesale firm, traveling to country stores by horse and buggy, Aaron Montgomery Ward conceived the idea of selling directly to country people by mail. He opened his business in 1872 with a one-page list of items that cost one dollar each. People could later order goods through a distributed catalog and the store would ship the merchandise cash on delivery (COD). The idea was slow to catch on because people were suspicious of a strange name. However, in 1875 Ward announced the startling policy of "satisfaction guaranteed or your money back." Contrasting with the former retailing principle of caveat emptor (Latin for "buyer beware"), this policy set off a boom in Ward's business.

—Frings, *Fashion: From Concepts to Consumer,* p. 11

_____ 1. Aaron Ward had experience in sales before he began his own business.

_____ 2. Country people were targeted because they do not have access to stores in cities.

_____ 3. Ward's mistake was to give every item on the list the same price.

_____ 4. Other stores in operation at the time did not offer money back guarantees.

_____ 5. Other mail order business quickly followed Ward's success.

EXERCISE 4–3

Read the following passages, and then answer the questions. The answers are not directly stated in the passage; you will have to make inferences in order to answer them.

Passage A "Is Laughter the Best Medicine?"

Lucy went to the hospital to visit Emma, a neighbor who had broken her hip. The first thing Lucy saw when the elevator door opened at the third floor was a clown, with an enormous orange nose, dancing down the hall, pushing a colorfully decorated cart. The clown stopped in front of Lucy, bowed, and then somersaulted to the nurses' station. A cluster of patients cheered. Most of them were in wheelchairs or on crutches. Upon asking for directions, Lucy learned that Emma was in the "humor room," where the film *Blazing Saddles* was about to start.

Since writer Norman Cousins's widely publicized recovery from a debilitating and usually incurable disease of the connective tissue, humor has gained new respectability in hospital wards around the country. Cousins, the long-time editor of the *Saturday Review,* with the cooperation of his physician, supplemented his regular medical therapy with a steady diet of Marx brothers movies and *Candid Camera* film clips. Although he never claimed that laughter alone effected his cure, Cousins is best remembered for his passionate support of the notion that, if negative emotions can cause distress, then humor and positive emotions can enhance the healing process (Cousins, 1979, 1989).

—Zimbardo and Gerrig, *Psychology and Life,* p. 501

1. What is the purpose of the story about Lucy and Emma?
2. What is a "humor room"?
3. What type of movie is *Blazing Saddles?*
4. Answer the question asked in the title.

Passage B "Oprah Winfrey—A Woman for All Seasons"

Oprah Winfrey—actress, talk-show host, and businesswoman—epitomizes the opportunities for America's women entrepreneurs. From welfare child to multimillionaire, Ms. Winfrey—resourceful, assertive, always self-assured, and yet unpretentious—has climbed the socioeconomic ladder by turning apparent failure into opportunities and then capitalizing on them.

With no playmates, Oprah entertained herself by "playacting" with objects such as corncob dolls, chickens, and cows. Her grandmother, a harsh disciplinarian, taught Oprah to read by age 2-1/2, and as a result of speaking at a rural church, her oratory talents began to emerge.

At age 6, Winfrey was sent to live with her mother and two half-brothers in a Milwaukee ghetto. While in Milwaukee, Winfrey, known as "the Little Speaker," was often invited to recite poetry at social gatherings, and her speaking skills continued to develop. At age 12, during a visit to her father in Nashville, she was paid $500 for a speech she gave to a church. It was then that she prophetically announced what she wanted to do for a living: "get paid to talk."

Her mother, working as a maid and drawing available welfare to make ends meet, left Oprah with little or no parental supervision and eventually sent her to live with her father in Nashville. There Oprah found the stability and discipline she so desperately needed. "My father saved my life," Winfrey reminisces. Her father—like her grandmother—a strict disciplinarian, obsessed with properly educating his daughter, forced her to memorize 20 new vocabulary words a week and turn in a weekly book report. His guidance and her hard work soon paid off, as she began to excel in school and other areas.

—Mosely et al., *Management: Leadership in Action*, p. 555

1. What is the author's attitude toward Winfrey?
2. What is the author's attitude toward strict discipline for children?
3. Is the author optimistic about business opportunities for women? How do you know?
4. What factors contributed to Winfrey's success?

ASSESS THE AUTHOR'S IDEAS

When you read actively and critically, you take very little for granted. You carefully evaluate what you are reading by asking the following questions.

Is the Author a Qualified Expert?

Not everything that appears in print is accurate and competently reported. Also, there are varying levels of expertise within a field. Consequently, you must assess whether the material you are reading is written by an expert in the field who can knowledgeably and accurately discuss the topic. For example, a sociologist who has studied the criminal justice system is not necessarily an expert on problems of immigrant populations. A scientist who specializes in genetics cannot write authoritatively about the greenhouse effect. In some materials, the author's credentials are footnoted or summarized at the end of the work. In journal articles, the author's college or university affiliation is often included. Authors also may establish their expertise or experience in the field within the material itself.

EXERCISE 4-4

Working together with a classmate, discuss and identify who (title or job description) would be considered a qualified expert on each of the following topics.

a. the side effects of a prescription drug
b. building code laws for an apartment building
c. controlling test anxiety

d. immigration laws

e. influence of television violence on children

What Are the Facts, and What Are the Opinions?

Facts are statements that can be tested as true or false—they are verifiable pieces of information. *Opinions* are statements that express feelings, attitudes, or beliefs that are neither true nor false. Here are a few examples of each.

Facts

Birth rates declined from 1960 to 1979.

The proportion of married women in the work force has steadily increased in the past 40 years.

Opinions

A drastic change is soon to occur in family structure.

Parenthood is the most rewarding human experience.

There is also what is known as informed opinion or testimony—the opinion of an expert or authority. Ralph Nader represents expert opinion on consumer rights, for example. Textbook authors, too, offer informed opinions, especially when they interpret events, summarize research, or evaluate trends. In the following paragraph, the author of a sociology textbook on marriage and the family interprets recent studies on sexuality.

> Recent studies of the history of sexuality in Western society have revealed that dramatic changes have taken place in beliefs and behavior. Among the most striking contrasts with our own times are the acceptance of bisexuality among men in ancient times and the disapproval of sexual pleasure in marriage for many centuries of the Christian era. The new studies also reveal that the sexual culture of any particular place and time is a complex mixture of expressive and repressive codes.
>
> —Skolnick, *The Intimate Environment*, p. 224

As you read a work, it is essential to distinguish between fact and opinion. Factual statements from reliable sources can be accepted and used in drawing conclusions, building arguments, and supporting ideas. Opinions, however, are one person's point of view that you are free to accept or reject.

EXERCISE 4–5

Read each of the following statements and identify whether it sounds like fact (F), opinion (O), or informed opinion (IO).

_____ 1. Most Americans feel strongly about the gun control issue.

_____ 2. Mosquitoes can transmit a disease known as encephalitis.

_____ 3. By 2005, more than 500 million people will use the Internet.

_____ 4. Marine biologists use the Internet in researching and identifying plant and animal species.

_____ 5. Computer users often feel guilty and blame themselves when their computer fails or performs an illegal operation.

_____ 6. Borders is the biggest music retailer on the Internet.

_____ 7. James Gleick, a well-known author who writes about technology, notes that networked digital devices set the pace of change in the computer field.

_____ 8. An increasing number of private citizens have their own web sites.

_____ 9. Personal web sites give people a sense of power and importance.

_____ 10. Capron, an author of a textbook on computers, says Internet traffic jams can be expected, creating slow response times in sending and receiving messages.

What Is the Author's Purpose?

As you read an article, ask yourself, "Why did the author write this?" In academic reading, you will most often find that the author's purpose is either to inform (present information) or to persuade. For example, an essay on state aid to private colleges may present information on current levels of funding, it may argue for an increased or decreased level of funding, or it may address both topics. You need to know which is the author's primary purpose because that information will determine how you read and what critical questions you ask.

EXERCISE 4–6

Based on the title of each of the following essays, predict whether the author's purpose is to inform or persuade.

1. Changing Habits: How shopping online is different.
2. I got straight A's, but I wasn't happy.
3. Animals can't speak: We must speak for them!
4. Guns don't kill people; people kill people.
5. What the Bible says about the end of the world.

Does the Author Support His or Her Generalizations?

A generalization is a reasoned statement about an entire group based on known information about part of the group. It requires a leap from what is known to a conclusion about the unknown. The key to evaluating generalizations is to evaluate the type, quality, and amount of evidence given to support them. Each of the following statements is a generalization.

Most college students are undecided about future career goals.

Fast food lacks nutritional value.

Foreign cars outperform similar American models.

EXERCISE 4–7

Read each of the following statements and place a check mark before each generalization.

_____ 1. The Internet is changing America.

_____ 2. Influenza causes severe epidemics every two years.

_____ 3. Most drug cases start with busts of small, local dealers and move to a search of their suppliers.

_____ 4. Attending college is essential for economic success and advancement.

_____ 5. Colds are caused by viruses, not bacteria, not cold weather, and not improper diet.

EXERCISE 4–8

Review "Psychology And Sport," which appears on page 48 in Chapter 2. Working with a classmate, locate and underline generalizations the author makes. For each generalization, discuss whether the author provides adequate evidence to support the generalization.

What Assumptions Is the Author Making?

An assumption is an idea or principle the writer accepts as true and makes no effort to prove or substantiate. Usually, it is a beginning or premise on which he or she bases the remainder of the work. For example, an author may assume that television encourages violent behavior in children and proceed to argue for restrictions on TV watching. Or a writer may assume that abortion is morally wrong and suggest legal restrictions on how and when abortions are performed.

EXERCISE 4-9	*Read each of the following statements and then place a checkmark before those choices that are assumptions made by the writer of the statement.*

1. Cosmetics should not be tested on animals, since they may cause pain, injury, or even death.

   _____ a. Animals have the right to avoid pain and suffering.

   _____ b. Cosmetics should be tested on people.

   _____ c. Animals should be anesthetized before research is conducted.

2. Teachers aides lack advanced college degrees: therefore, they are unable to teach children effectively.

   _____ a. Teachers aides should obtain advanced degrees.

   _____ b. Advanced college degrees are needed in order to teach effectively.

   _____ c. Teachers who hold advanced degrees are not necessarily effective teachers.

3. Border states in the U.S. must take action to curb illegal immigration; otherwise, state funds will be quickly exhausted.

   _____ a. The writer opposes using state funds to help illegal immigrants.

   _____ b. Illegal immigrants must enter the U.S. legally to receive state aid.

   _____ c. State funding guidelines should be revised.

Is the Author Biased?

If an author is biased, he or she is partial to one point of view or one side of a controversial issue. The author's language and selection of facts provide clues about his or her bias.

In the following excerpt from a biology text, the author's choice of words (see underlining) and sarcastic comment in parentheses reveal his attitude toward seal hunters.

> Greenpeace is an organization dedicated to the preservation of the sea and its great mammals, notably whales, dolphins, and seals. Its ethic is <u>nonviolent</u> but its <u>aggressiveness</u> in protecting our oceans and the life in them is becoming legendary.
>
> Greenpeace volunteers routinely place their lives in <u>danger</u> in many ways, such as by riding along the backs of whales in inflatable zodiacs, keeping themselves between the animal and the harpoons of ships giving <u>chase</u>. They have pulled

alongside Dutch ships to stop the <u>dumping</u> of <u>dangerous toxins</u> into the sea. They have placed their zodiacs directly in the paths of ships <u>disrupting delicate</u> breeding grounds of the sea with soundings and have forced some to turn away or even abandon their efforts. They have confronted hostile sealers on northern ice floes to try to stop them from <u>bludgeoning</u> the baby seals in the birthing grounds, skinning them on the spot, and leaving the mother sniffing at the <u>glistening red corpse</u> of her baby as its skin is <u>stacked</u> aboard the ship on the way to warm the <u>backs of very fashionable people</u> who gather where the bartender knows their favorite drink. (The mother seal would be <u>proud</u> to know that her dead baby had nearly impressed some bartender.) They have petitioned the International Whaling Commission to establish rules and enact bans.

—Wallace, *Biology: The World of Life*, p. 754

EXERCISE 4–10

Read each of the following statements, and place a checkmark in front of each that reveals bias.

_____ 1. The feminist movement is no longer oppressed by men; it is oppressed by feminism itself.

_____ 2. Approximately 60% of men feel they are above average in their level of self-confidence.

_____ 3. Racist and sexist speech on the Internet should be prohibited.

_____ 4. There is a marked increase in volunteerism among college students.

_____ 5. Women's fashion magazines portray an ideal woman and create guilt and anxiety for those who cannot measure up to the ideal.

How Strong Are the Data and Evidence?

Many writers who express their opinions, state viewpoints, or make generalizations provide data or evidence to support their ideas. Your task as a critical reader is to weigh and evaluate the quality of this evidence. You must examine the evidence and assess its adequacy. You should be concerned with two factors: the type of evidence being presented and the relevance of that evidence. Various types of evidence include

- Personal experience or observation
- Statistical data
- Examples, descriptions of particular events, or illustrative situations
- Analogies (comparisons with similar situations)

- Historical documentation
- Experimental evidence

Each type of evidence must be weighed in relation to the statement it supports. Acceptable evidence should directly, clearly, and indisputably support the case or issue in question.

EXERCISE 4–11

For each of the following statements, discuss the type or types of evidence that you would need in order to support and evaluate the statement.

1. Individuals must accept primary responsibility for the health and safety of their babies.
2. Apologizing is often seen as a sign of weakness, especially among men.
3. There has been a steady increase in illegal immigration over the past 50 years.
4. More college women than college men agree that abortions should be legal.
5. Car advertisements sell fantasy experiences, not means of transportation.

EXERCISE 4–12

The following brief excerpt is taken from an article titled "Trash Troubles" that appeared in the periodical World and I, in November 1998. Using the guidelines for evaluating writing, answer the questions that follow.

TRASH TROUBLES

Our accumulating piles of solid waste threaten to ruin our environment, pointing to the urgent need for not only better disposal methods but also strategies to lower the rate of waste generation.

As our ship surges forward, we notice a mound jutting up ahead, directly in our path. Like an iceberg, a much larger mass is hidden beneath the surface. If we keep running the vessel at current speed, we may have a major problem on our hands.

No, this not the Titanic. The ship we're on is our consumer-goods-dependent lifestyle that creates as much as a ton of solid waste per person each year. And the peak ahead is but the tip of a massive "wasteberg" that is 95 percent hidden from view: For every ton of trash we generate, there is an underlying loss of another 19 tons of industrial, agricultural, mining, and transportation wastes, building up into a mound that threatens to shatter our future.

The wasteberg entails a formidable economic and environmental challenge. For most local governments, solid waste management ranks behind only schools and highways as the major budget item. Improperly managed solid waste eats up dollars while polluting water supplies, threatening neighborhoods, and squandering natural resources.

So how is this odyssey progressing? Are we about to capsize on the wasteberg and drown, or can we successfully circumnavigate the threat? Better yet, can we shrink the wasteberg?

Circumnavigating the Wasteberg

The simplest way to steer around the wasteberg is to try to isolate wastes from their surrounding environment. This has been the major approach worldwide—solid waste management has usually meant solid waste disposal. Around the world, many nations have chosen incineration as the preferred way to dispose of solid waste. This is particularly the case where landfill sites are scarce. Japan, for example, has around 2,800 municipal incinerators that reduce solid wastes to ashes. In the United States, though, incineration has fallen strongly out of favor. Despite significant improvements in the technology, concerns that the incineration process may release toxic pollutants such as dioxins have brought this once-popular technology to near-obsolescence.

Shrinking the Wasteberg

For every pound of trash that goes into the waste basket, another 19 are released elsewhere in the environment—in forms ranging from industrial byproducts to fertilizer runoff to wasted energy. Thus if we reduce our generation of solid waste, the "leverage effect" is enormous: Each ton of trash kept out of the dump means that 19 tons of waste, along with related environmental impacts and the dollar cost of producing it, are avoided.

There are three major approaches to narrowing the waste stream: reducing, redesigning, and recycling. All require vigorous participation by both producers and consumers.

Reducing. Producers reduce waste through offering products that are less wasteful. Consumers reduce waste by using less of the product and using materials longer.

Redesigning. Producers offer alternative products that have a lower environmental impact than traditional ones, while continuing to meet given needs.

Recycling. Producers make reusable products, utilizing waste materials in manufacturing these goods. Consumers reuse the products and collect the materials to recycle out of the waste stream and back to the producers.

—Purcell, "Trash Troubles" in *The World and I*, p. 190

1. The author, Arthur H. Purcell, is the founder and director of the Resource Policy Institute, the author of *The Waste Watchers*, and a commentator for America Public Radio's "Marketplace." Evaluate his authority to discuss this topic.

2. Is the article primarily fact, opinion, or expert opinion? Support your answer with examples.
3. What is the author's purpose?
4. Does the author make generalizations? If so, underline several examples. Are the generalizations supported by evidence?
5. What assumptions does the author make?
6. Is the author biased?
7. Evaluate the types and adequacy of the evidence the author provides.

EXERCISE 4–13

Working with another classmate as a team, review the reading "Factors Affecting Interpersonal Attraction," which appears on page 34 in Chapter 1, and answer questions 2 through 7 in Exercise 4–12.

REACT TO THE IDEAS PRESENTED

An important part of reading critically is to react to the author's ideas. You may agree, disagree, question, challenge, or seek further information, for example. To do so, begin by writing down your reactions while and after you read. Then, once you have finished, review your notes and evaluate the writer's ideas.

Annotate As You Read

If you were reading the classified ads in a newspaper in search of an apartment to rent, you probably would mark certain ads. Then, when you phoned for more information, you might make notes about each apartment. These notes would be useful when you decided which apartments were worth visiting.

Similarly, in other types of reading, making notes—*annotating*—is a useful strategy. Annotating is a means of keeping track of your impressions, ideas, reactions, and questions as you read. Reviewing your annotations will help you form a final impression of the work. If a writing assignment accompanies the reading, your annotations will serve as an excellent source of ideas for a paper. This reading strategy is discussed in more detail in Chapter 10.

There are no fixed rules about how or what to annotate. In general, try to mark or note any ideas about the work that come to mind as you read or reread. Underline or highlight within the work and use the margins to write your notes. Your annotations might include

- Questions
- Generalizations, assumptions, and other features listed above
- Key points
- Ideas with which you disagree
- Good or poor supporting data or examples
- Inconsistencies
- Key terms or definitions
- Contrasting points of view
- Key arguments
- Words with strong connotations
- Figures of speech (images that reveal the writer's feelings)

A sample annotation is shown in the following passage on the meaning of color. Read it carefully, noticing the types of markings and annotations that were made.

COLOR AND EMOTIONS

the issue or question

would like reference to these studies

does not state nature and strength of evidence

What evidence? describe?

The research in color preference led to a spin-off area of research, that of color and emotional response or moods. Researchers asked whether a reliable mood-color association exists and <u>whether color could influence one's emotional state</u>. Well-controlled research studies have shown that a definite color-mood tone association exists, although the color-mood association differed widely among people participating in the study. In fact, the studies showed all colors to be associated with all moods in varying degrees of strength. Although certain colors are more strongly associated with a given mood or emotion, there was evidence to suggest a <u>one-to-one relationship between a given color and a given emotion</u>. What seemed to make the difference was how strongly a person associated a particular color with a particular mood or emotion.

Colors have been stereotyped by the public when it comes to emotions. In spite of <u>physical evidence</u> to the contrary, most people continue to equate red tones with excitement and activity and blue tones with passivity and tranquillity in color-mood association research. This is a learned behavior. From the time we are very young we learn to associate red with fire engines, stop lights, and danger signals that cause us to form an alert or danger association with red. Further, the red, orange, and yellow tones in fire further cause association between those colors and heat and kinetic energy. We have seen how cultural biases that are a part of our language further support the red equals excitement myth. These subconscious messages clearly affect the response to red. Blue tones, being associated with cool streams, the sky, and the ocean, continue to be equated with calm and tranquillity. This, too, is a learned response with which we are subtly surrounded from early childhood. <u>In understanding color, it is important to differentiate between these culturally learned color associations and true biological responses.</u>

What are the biological ones

Research on the emotional aspects of color <u>has for the most part resulted in a gross oversimplification</u> of a very involved process. Unfortunately, this oversimplification has been promoted heavily in the popular press. The design community too has jumped on the bandwagon, often making sweeping statements about color that are totally unsupported by anything but myth or personal belief. For example, one book refers to blue as "communicating cool, comfort, protective, calming, although may be slightly depressing if other colors are dark; associated with bad taste." There is of course no basis for these statements except as the personal opinion of the author, but too often these <u>personal opinions</u> become accepted as fact.

How

Clothing design? interior design? building design? —which one?

Could be expert opinion, depending on qualifications of author

Summary

Colors do not contain any inherent emotional triggers. Rather, it is more likely that our changing moods and emotions caused by our own physiological and psychological makeup at the moment interact with color to create preferences and associations that we then link to the color-emotion response itself.

—Fehrman and Fehrman, *Color: The Secret Influence*, p. 83–84

Analyze and Evaluate Ideas

After you have read (and perhaps reread) the work and made annotations, the final step is to review your annotations and, thereby, to arrive at some conclusions and final impressions of the work. This is a creative as well as a logical process that involves looking for patterns and trends, noticing contrasts, thinking about the author's intentions, analyzing the effects of stylistic features, and determining the significance of the work. You might think of it as a process similar to evaluating a film after you have seen it or discussing a controversial television documentary. Your overall purpose is analysis: to arrive at an overall interpretation and evaluation of the work.

When analyzing a work, it may be helpful to write lists of words, issues, problems, and questions to discover patterns and evaluate the author's bias. Use the following questions to guide your analysis.

- What did the author intend to accomplish?
- How effectively did he or she accomplish this?
- What questions does the work raise and answer?
- What questions are ignored or left unanswered?
- What contributions to your course content and objectives does this work make?
- How does this work fit with your course textbook?
- How worthwhile is the material? What are its strengths and weaknesses?

**EXERCISE
4–14**

*Preview, read, and annotate the following essay titled "The Barbarity of Meat."
Assume it is one of several articles your health and nutrition instructor assigned
for a class discussion on vegetarianism. Pose several guide questions to focus your
reading. Annotate as you read. Then analyze and evaluate the reading using the
questions listed on p. 111.*

THE BARBARITY OF MEAT

The food industry downplays the connection between steak and cows

If, as some authors suggest, eating meat is indeed an important statement of
human power, it might seem strange that we are apparently becoming progres-
sively more uncomfortable with reminders of its animal origins. Consumer attitudes today are in a state of flux, not least for this reason. Whereas once it was
sufficient simply to display whole animals and pieces of meat, the packing of the
product is now a more delicate task. Most of us prefer not to think too directly
about where our meat has come from, and unwelcome reminders can be distinctly off-putting. As one consumer put it, "I don't like it when you see . . . veins
and things coming out of the meat . . . because it always reminds me of my own
insides in a funny sort of a way. I suppose it's the idea of, like, blood flowing [that]
makes you realize that this slab of meat was once a bit of functioning body, a bit
like your own."

Meat marketing has responded accordingly, to assuage customers' sensitivity to
the nature of the product. Nowadays, the consumer need never encounter animal
flesh in its vulgar, undressed state. Instead it will come cooked and reshaped, in a
sesame bun or an exotically flavored sauce, as a turkey roll or as chicken nuggets,
in a crumb coating or a vacuum package, with not a hint of blood in sight. More and
more butchers' windows sport fresh green vegetables, fragrant herbs, and perhaps
a stir-fry mixture. A deliberate process of disguising the source of animal foods has
gained momentum in the 20th century, reacting to our evident unease with the
idea of eating dead animals: Said one butcher, "I deplore deliveries being carried
into the front of my shop on the neck of a van driver—especially if they are not
wrapped. . . . I can think of little more guaranteed to turn pedestrians off buying
meat than the sight of pigs' heads flopping about as he struggles past them with the
carcass."

The number of independent butchers' shops has declined considerably in
recent years. Supermarkets have clearly derived particular competitive advantage
from presenting meat in conspicuously hygienic conditions with all preparation
completed out of sight. Often only the best cuts are displayed; bones, guts, and skin
are nowhere to be seen. The hermetically sealed package is effectively dissociated
from the animal to which its contents once belonged, a service that is clearly winning customers.

The names we give to the flesh of the main meat animals are another device whereby we reduce the unpleasant impact of having to acknowledge their identity. We do not eat cow, we eat beef; we do not eat pig, we eat pork; we do not eat deer, we eat venison. It is as if we cannot bear to utter the name of the beast whose death we have ordained.

To some, our willingness to consume meat as well as the many other assorted products of the animal industry, but apparent unwillingness to slaughter the beasts for ourselves or even to acknowledge our complicity in that process, is a matter for moral reproof. Said one critic, "I think the meat industry is very dishonest. The people are not allowed to be aware of what's going on. To them meat is wrapped up in cellophane in supermarkets; it's very divorced from the animal that it's coming from. . . . People don't go down on the factory farm to see what's really going on down there. I think if a lot of people did do that or [went] to the slaughterhouse to see how the meat is produced, then a lot of them would become vegetarians."

There is some evidence to support this belief. Many first-generation vegetarians and semivegetarians directly trace their abstinence to occasions when, for one reason or another, they were brought face to face with the connection between the meat on their plate and once-living animals. The particular incident related by any individual—be it the sight of carcasses being carried into a butcher's shop, or an encounter with vegetarian polemicism, or a visit to a slaughterhouse on daily business, or merely an unusually vivid flight of imagination—is of minor importance. What matters is that many people, when confronted with this ethical perplexity, seemingly prefer to forgo meat altogether rather than to condone the treatment of animals on their path from birth to plate. And equally important, perhaps, is how new this rebellion is, or rather how rapid its development has been in recent history.

—Fiddes, *Meat: A Natural Symbol*, p. 100–101

1. Does the author establish his authority on the subject of vegetarianism?
2. Is the article primarily fact or opinion? Justify your answer.
3. What is the author's purpose? How effectively does he accomplish it?
4. What generalizations does the author make?
5. What assumptions about people and human behavior does the author make?
6. Summarize the evidence the author offers in support of his main points.
7. Does the author anticipate and address objections to his argument? If so, what are the objections and how does he refute them?
8. What questions might be raised during a class discussion of this essay?

EXERCISE 4–15

Use the reading "An Open Letter to the Nation's Drug Czar" at the end of this chapter to complete this exercise. Work with a classmate to answer the following questions.

1. Identify the author's thesis or main point.
2. Is the authority of the author evident? Why?
3. Is the article primarily fact or opinion?
4. Does the author make any assumptions? What are they?
5. How does the author support his main points?

SYNTHESIZE AND COMPARE SOURCES

The first step in making a comparison of several works or different sections within the same work is to read, annotate, and analyze each text. Once you have studied each carefully, you are ready to discover the similarities and differences among them. Compare the works on the basis of such factors as

- Overall theme or position
- Types and quality of supporting evidence
- Degree of bias shown in each work
- Authority of each author
- Author's purpose
- Points of agreement and disagreement
- How each work approached the subject
- Effectiveness of each work in persuading or educating you
- Types of arguments used
- Style
- Intended audience

Make notes as you study each work, both in the margins of the works themselves and on separate pieces of paper. Then study your annotations and notes, looking for similarities and differences. Try to put into your own words what you discover. When you write about the two works, rather than just thinking about them, it forces you to clarify your ideas.

Ask questions such as these.

- On what do the sources agree?
- On what do the sources disagree?
- How do they differ?
- Are the viewpoints toward the subject similar or different?
- Does each source provide supporting evidence for major points?

To initiate a discussion on the issue of computer privacy, a business professor distributed two excerpts from articles on the topic. In preparation for the discussion, the instructor asked the class to read both accounts and be prepared to discuss them in class. One student read and annotated each selection as shown below.

Account 1

The advent of e-commerce is, however inadvertently, endangering privacy. Companies have long boasted about the efficiency, convenience and personalized service that distinguish commerce online. But that promise hinges on the merchants' intimate knowledge of their customers' tastes and behavior. For starters, they know who their customers are, where they live and their credit-card numbers. And the more someone buys, the more the seller finds out about him: likes bourbon and trash novels; sends someone not his wife flowers every Wednesday.

types of information collected

Any web-site operator can reconstruct a visitor's every move on his site: what pages he viewed, what information he entered and the Internet service he uses. Privacy advocates warn that most online companies won't fight subpoenas seeking access to those logs. Security guru Richard Smith, founder of Phar Lap Software, likens Web sites to VCRs "constantly recording when you come in, who you talked to and maybe what you talked about."

does not tell us what to do about the problem

—Sandberg, "Losing Your Good Name Online," *Newsweek*, September 20, 1999, p. 57

Account 2

We live in an information age, and data is one of the currencies of our time. Businesses and government agencies spend billions of dollars every year to collect and exchange information about you and me. More than 15,000 specialized marketing databases contain 2 billion consumer names, along with a surprising amount of personal information. The typical American consumer is on 25 marketing lists. Many of these lists are organized by characteristics like age, income, religion, political affiliation, and even sexual preference—and they're bought and sold every day.

exchange of personal information

marketing databases

organization

Marketing databases are only the tip of the iceberg. Credit and banking information, tax records, health data, insurance records, political contributions, voter registration, credit card purchases, warranty registrations, magazine and newsletter subscriptions, phone calls, passport registration, airline reservations, automobile registrations, arrests, Internet explorations—they're all recorded in computers, and we have little or no control over what happens to most of these records once they're collected.

businesses and agencies that collect information

—Beekman, *Computer Confleunce: Exploring Tomorrow's Technology*, p. 204

Then the student made notes and wrote the following paragraph.

Paragraph

Sandberg discusses the types of information that can be collected from e-commerce and focuses on personal data collected by online merchants and from Web sites. Beekman states that information that is collected becomes part of a database and explains that other businesses and agencies collect information, as well. Both emphasize that privacy may be endangered.

EXERCISE 4–16

Assume you are taking a business retailing course. Your instructor has asked you to read each of the following brief descriptions of how Jeff Bezos, founder of Amazon.com, an online bookstore, founded his business. Using information from both articles, write a paragraph summarizing how Bezos began his company.

Statement 1

A leading contender [in online retailing] is the 35-year old son of a Cuban immigrant, Jeffrey P. Bezos, founder and CEO of Amazon.com Inc.—the upstart Internet company that boasts 4.5 million customers in 160 countries. Bezos stands alone against his prime adversary, the very well financed Barnes & Noble Corporation, a behemoth on the brutish playing fields of bookselling. The media have often made comparisons to David and Goliath. But in this showdown, it's no longer easy to tell who is David and who is Goliath.

Bezos concocted the right formula for on-line selling when he chose books as the product to move. In less than four years, he has risen from Wall Street wunderkind to become one of cyberdom's kings of the world. In 1994, Bezos quit his job as a hedge fund manager to stake a claim on the wild frontier of Internet retailing, or "e-tailing." He moved to Seattle and started his business in a rented garage with loans from investment bankers, family, friends, and venture capitalists.

Since its debut on the World Wide Web in July 1995, Amazon.com has become the model to watch—and to envy. Soon after the site appeared, chat group participants praised its availability of product and user-friendly style. Paradoxically, in the nonhuman realm of cyberspace, it is the very pedestrian experience of word of mouth that Amazon executives regard as a major reason for its success.

What Amazon also did early on was spend millions of dollars on advertising in such publications as *The New York Times Review of Books*. It also invested in banner links that touted the site in the "hot corner" of browsers. The huge amounts of money spent—$6.1 million in 1996—stirred excitement in the business world and evoked highly positive press. The advertising blitz helped the company reap $16 million in revenue, much of which went into refining the site.

—Martinez, "Lord of the Jungle," *Hispanic Magazine*, January/February 1999

Statement 2

Bezos's idea was simple: as the Internet extended its reach, an efficient retailer could do away with the bricks and mortar (hereafter referred to as B&M) of physical stores and serve customers better because the Net allows sellers direct contact with buyers. All at a potential profit margin the B&M guys can't match. If a chain of 1,000 stores wants to double sales, Bezos says, it has to open *another* thousand stores, with all the land and manpower costs that that entails. But once an online operation gets past the fixed cost of its Web site and distribution channel, it can handle bigger sales with very few extra expenses. "You can offer both the lowest prices and the highest service level," he says, "which is impossible in the physical-world environment."

These concepts came together in 1994 after the Florida-born Bezos left a job as a financial strategist and flew to Ft. Worth, Texas, to pick up his father's 1988 Blazer. As his wife, MacKenzie, drove, Bezos hammered out his business plan on a laptop. The destination was Seattle, which offered an ideal employment pool of overeducated slackers.

Bezos's business plan originally met with skepticism, and even its author had doubts. "The big problem was not whether the technology would work," he says, "but whether customers would want to shop this way." He spent a year of planning before he opened the site, figuring out what would push book buyers into the digital age. His prime goals: providng a wide selection, good prices and an effortless experience.

Fortunately, Internet users then were early-adopter types, ready to take the virtual bungee jump into the new world of e-commerce. And as the Internet population grew, and increasingly resembled the country's overall demographic, word-of-mouth spread. In the last two years Amazon's customer list has grown from 2 million to 11 million.

—Levy, "Wired for the Bottom Line," *Newsweek*, September 20, 1999, p. 44

Managing Your Study Time

As college students, many of you struggle to divide your time among classes, study, job responsibilities, and friends and family. Effective planning and time management are essential for you to maintain a workable balance. Here are a few suggestions for managing your study time effectively.

1. *Develop a weekly study plan.* Allocate time for reading, reviewing, doing homework, and studying for exams. Select several specific times each week for working on each of your courses.

2. *As a rule of thumb, reserve two study hours for each hour you spend in class.*

3. *Use peak periods of concentration.* Everyone has high and low periods of concentration and attention. First, determine when these occur for you; then reserve peak times for intensive study and use less efficient times for more routine tasks such as recopying

an assignment or collecting information in the library.

4. *Study difficult subjects first.* While it is tempting to get easy tasks and short little assignments out of the way first, do not give in to this approach. When you start studying, your mind is fresh and alert and you are at your peak of concentration. This is the time you are best equipped to handle difficult subjects.

5. *Schedule study for a particular course close to the time when you attend class.* Plan to study the evening before the class meets and soon after the class meeting. For example, if a class meets on Tuesday morning, plan to study Monday evening and Tuesday afternoon or evening. By studying close to class time, you will find it easier to relate class lectures and discussions to what you are reading and studying, to see connections, and to reinforce your learning.

(continued)

6. *Include short breaks in your study time.* Take a break before you begin studying each new subject. Your mind needs time to refocus so that you can switch from one set of facts, problems, and issues to another. You should also take short breaks when you are working on just one assignment for a long period of time. A 10-minute break after 50 to 60 minutes of study is reasonable.

SUMMARY

Critical reading involves interpreting, evaluating, and reacting to ideas.

An inference is a reasoned guess about what you do not know on the basis of what you do know. To make inferences as you read,

- know the literal meaning
- notice details
- add up the facts
- be alert for clues
- verify your inference

To assess an author's ideas, ask the following questions.

- Is the author a qualified expert?
- What are the facts and what are the opinions?
- What is the author's purpose?
- Does the author support his or her generalizations?
- What assumptions is the author making?
- Is the author biased?
- How strong are the data and evidence?

To react to an author's ideas, annotate during and after reading, and analyze the ideas using the following questions.

- What did the author intend to accomplish?
- How effectively did he or she accomplish this?
- What questions does the work raise and answer?
- What questions are ignored or left unanswered?
- What contributions to your course content and objectives does this work make?
- How does this work fit with your course textbook?
- How worthwhile is the material? What are its strengths and weaknesses?

To compare and synthesize several works, focus on similarities and differences among them.

INTEGRATING
PAIRED READINGS
IDEAS

Sociology/Contemporary Issues

PREREADING QUESTIONS

1. Can you predict two arguments the author might use to support his view that drugs should not be legalized?
2. What kinds of questions might the author reasonably pose regarding drug legalization?
3. Do you believe drugs should be legalized?

Why Drug Legalization Should Be Opposed

Representative Charles B. Rangel

1   In my view, the very idea of legalizing drugs in this country is counterproductive. Many well-meaning drug legalization advocates disagree with me, but their arguments are not convincing. The questions that I asked them twenty years ago remain unanswered. Would all drugs be legalized? If not, why? Would consumers be allowed to purchase an unlimited supply? Are we prepared to pay the medical costs for illnesses that are spawned by excessive drug use? Who would be allowed to sell drugs? Would an illegal market still exist? Would surgeons, bus drivers, teachers, military personnel, engineers, and airline pilots be allowed to use drugs?

2   Drug legalization threatens to undermine our society. The argument about the economic costs associated with the drug war is a selfish argument that coincides with the short-sighted planning that we have been using with other social policies. With any legalization of drugs, related problems would not go away; they would only intensify. If we legalize, we will be paying much more than the $30 billion per year we now spend on direct health care costs associated with illegal drug use.

3   Drug legalization is not as simple as opening a chain of friendly neighborhood "drug" stores. While I agree that some drugs might be beneficial for medicinal purposes, this value should not be exploited to suggest that drugs should be legalized. Great Britain's experience with prescription heroin should provide a warning. Until 1968, British doctors were freely allowed to prescribe

drugs to addicts for medicinal purposes. Due to the lack of rigorous controls, some serious problems became associated with this policy. Doctors supplied drugs to non-addicts, and addicts supplied legally obtained drugs to the general population resulting in an increased rate of addiction. There is plenty of evidence to show that drug legalization has not worked in other countries that have tried it. The United States cannot afford such experiments when the data shows that drug legalization policies are failing in other countries.

4   In minority communities, legalization of drugs would be a nightmare. It would be a clear signal that America has no interest in removing the root causes of drug abuse: a sense of hopelessness that stems from poverty, unemployment, inadequate training, and blight. Legalization of drugs would officially sanction the total annihilation of communities already at risk. Instead of advocating drug legalization, we should focus our efforts on rebuilding schools, strengthening our teachers, improving housing, and providing job skills to young people.

5   The issue should not be whether or not drugs should be legalized. Rather, we need to focus on changing the way the war on drugs is being fought. The real problems are our emphasis on incarceration, including mandatory minimum sentences, the unfair application of drug laws, the disparity in sentencing between crack cocaine and powder cocaine, and the failure to concentrate on the root causes of drug abuse. These shortcomings in our drug policy should not become a license for legalization. Many critics of the drug war have the knowledge and skills to improve our national drug control policy. Instead of supporting the Drug Czar, they use their resources to blast all efforts to eradicate drugs in this country. It is a shame that many educated and prominent people suggest that the only dangerous thing about drugs is that they are illegal.

6   If we are truly honest, we must confess that we have never fought the war on drugs as we have fought other adversaries. The promotion of drug legalization further complicates the issue. We must continue our efforts to stop the flow of illegal drugs into our country. Most importantly, we need to remove the root causes of drug abuse and increase our focus in the areas of prevention and treatment through education. Rather than holding up the white flag and allowing drugs to take over our country, we must continue to focus on drug demand as well as supply if we are to remain a free and productive society.

—Rangel, *Criminal Justice Ethics*, Vol. 17, No. 2., Summer/Fall 1998, p. 2

VOCABULARY REVIEW

1. For each of the words listed below, use context; prefixes, roots, and suffixes; and/or a dictionary to write a brief definition or synonym of the word as it is used in the reading.

    a. advocates (para. 1) _____

b. spawned (para. 1) _____

c. undermine (para. 2) _____

d. exploited (para. 3)_____

e. blight (para. 4)_____

f. sanction (para. 4) _____

g. annihilation (para. 4)_____

h. incarceration (para. 5) _____

i. disparity (para. 5) _____

j. eradicate (para. 5) _____

2. Underline new specialized terms introduced in the reading.

COMPREHENSION QUESTIONS

1. Identify three reasons why the author is opposed to legalizing drugs.
2. What effect does the author believe drug legalization would have?
3. What cue words in the first paragraph suggest the author may have a bias?
4. Does the author propose an alternate solution for the drug problem? If so, what is that solution?
5. What does the author imply when he states that "[drug] legalization is not as simple as opening a chain of friendly neighborhood 'drug' stores?"
6. According to the author, why did legalizing heroin in Great Britain by making it a prescription drug fail?

THINKING CRITICALLY

1. What is the author's purpose in writing this essay?
2. What do you believe is the strongest argument the author uses to support his position? Why is this a strong argument?
3. The author states that there is "plenty of evidence to show that drug legalization has not worked in other countries . . ." Other than with information about Great Britain, does the author support this statement? How does this weaken or strengthen the author's argument?
4. The author believes that we will be paying much more money in health care costs if we legalize drugs. Do you agree or disagree? Why?

5. The author states that legalizing drugs "will undermine our society." Does he support this with generalizations or specific facts? Explain.

6. In general, do you think the author is essentially biased or essentially objective in presenting his arguments? On what do you base your assessment?

LEARNING/STUDY STRATEGY

Annotate the reading by highlighting why the author is opposed to legalizing drugs. Then record your ideas and reactions to these arguments.

Sociology/Contemporary Issues

Prereading Questions

1. Has the current drug policy failed? Why do you think so?
2. Can you speculate on why the author believes it has failed?
3. Can you predict what the author will suggest the Office of Drug Policy do instead?

An Open Letter to the Nation's Drug Czar

Judge James P. Gray

General Barry McCaffrey
Director, Office of Drug Policy
The White House

Dear Gen. McCaffrey:

1   Our great country is reeling from wounds which we have been inflicting upon ourselves because of our current failed drug policy. It is clear that we are not in better shape today than we were five years ago regarding drug use and abuse and all of the crime and misery which accompany them, and, unless we change our approach, we can have no legitimate expectation that we will be in better shape next year than we are today. However, we will not pursue change until we realize, as a country, that it is all right to talk about this issue—and that just because we talk about the possibility of changing our drug policy does not mean that we condone drug use or abuse.

2   Change for the better starts with a leader who has a proven record of honesty, dedication, experience, and results—one who will be able to discuss realities without effectively being labeled as 'soft' on crime or criminals. Our country desperately needs a person in authority who will not be afraid to take a fresh and objective look at our most basic assumptions and recommend changes based upon the evidence. Our country needs you.

3   You are known to be an intelligent, non-political, dedicated public servant who is in that position of authority and respect. If you would speak about our country's futile efforts to eradicate the growing of these dangerous drugs in, and the shipping of them from, various foreign countries, people in and out of our government will listen.

4   If you would quote the Rand Corporation study of June, 1994, which concluded that drug treatment is seven times more effective than drug prosecution

even for heavy drug users and 11 times more effective than interdiction at our country's borders, people will begin to realize why we are going broke trying to incarcerate our way out of this pervasive and multi-faceted problem.

5   If you would acknowledge that no one in law enforcement will even tell us with a straight face that we seize more than 10 percent of the illegal drugs in our society and that the more candid estimate is that we seize only about five percent, our people will begin to understand that each seizure of a ton of cocaine in not a victory, but is instead merely a symptom of the depth of the problem.

6   Our citizens and taxpayers will then realize that for every ton of cocaine we seize, we easily fail to seize between nine and 19 tons. In the War on Drugs, victory is now literally being viewed as slowing down the pace of defeat.

7   Our present policy has made cocaine the most lucrative crop in the history of mankind. It has made marijuana the most lucrative crop in my home state of California, easily outdistancing the second leading crop, which is corn.

8   Our present policy is directly responsible for the material and demonstrable reduction of our cherished liberties under the Bill of Rights.

9   Our present policy is directly funneling tens of billions of dollars per year into organized crime, with all of its accompanying violence and corruption, both in our country and around the world.

10   Our present policy is directly causing our children in the inner cities and virtually everywhere else to have drug dealers as their role models, instead of people like you who have gotten their education and who have worked hard to be successful.

11   Our present policy has directly spawned a cycle of hostility by the incarceration of vastly disproportionate numbers of our minority groups.

12   And our present policy is directly responsible for medical doctors being unable to prescribe appropriate medications for their patients who are either in pain or are suffering from a number of devastating diseases. We all understand the necessity of holding people accountable for their actions. However, our citizens recognize that what we are doing in the critical area of drug policy is not working. They are frustrated because their ostensible leaders are afraid to discuss the subject openly.

13   As a result, thousands of Americans such as Dr. Milton Friedman, former Secretary of State George Shultz, Mayor Kurt Schmoke of Baltimore, and former San Jose Chief of Police Joseph McNamara have signed a resolution calling for the investigation of change by a neutral commission. This resolution actually was passed by Congress and signed into law by President Clinton as a part of the recent crime bill; however, it has been widely ignored since that time. The signatories include a formidable list of judges; civic, business, and religious leaders; probation officers and prison officials; medical doctors; teachers; and

counselors. There is wide support for the investigation of change—our present policy simply will not stand scrutiny. However, our country needs a credible person in government like you to step forward and legitimize the discussion.

14   We do not ask you to support any particular method or approach for addressing the drug problem. We simply ask you to agree that there are fundamental problems with our current policy and that both our government and our citizens need better to understand the history and social forces which drive this problem, and our options for the future. We need to investigate the possibility of change. Education and the honest exchange of information are the only ways we will begin to reduce the continuing harm wrought by these dangerous drugs in our country. Accordingly, we ask you publicly to join us in a non-partisan and non-political search for the truth. If you would do this, you simply could not provide our country and all of its people with a greater or more lasting service.

Sincerely,
Judge James P. Gray*
*Judge Gray is a judge in the Superior Court of California in Orange County.

—Gray, In *The Orange County Register*, August 12, 1996

VOCABULARY REVIEW

1.   For each of the words listed below, use context; prefixes, roots, and suffixes; and/or a dictionary to write a brief definition or synonym of the word as it is used in the reading.

   a. condone (para. 1) _____

   b. interdiction (para. 4) _____

   c. pervasive (para. 4) _____

   d. demonstrable (para. 7) _____

   e. disproportionate (para. 7) _____

   f. ostensible (para. 12) _____

   g. signatories (para. 13) _____

   h. scrutiny (para. 13) _____

   i. wrought (para. 14) _____

   j. non-partisan (para. 14) _____

2.   Underline new specialized terms introduced in the reading.

COMPREHENSION QUESTIONS

1. Is the author in favor of legalizing drugs as a solution to the problem? How can you tell?
2. What were the implications of the Rand Corporation study of June 1994?
3. What is the author's purpose in telling General McCaffrey that he is "known to be an intelligent, non-political, dedicated public servant?"
4. What is it that the author really wants General McCaffrey to do? What in the reading leads you to believe this?
5. What does the author believe will cause the government to listen to McCaffrey? (See paragraph 3.)

THINKING CRITICALLY

1. At the end of the first paragraph, the author makes it clear that he does not necessarily "condone drug use." What evidence in the selection indicates that he does or does not condone drug use?
2. What is the author implying when he says that we are trying to "incarcerate our way out of this pervasive and multi-faceted problem?"
3. Why is seizing 5–10% of the illegal drugs in this country not perceived as a victory by the author?
4. What is the first indication the reader has that the author believes Americans' civil rights have been violated?
5. The author states that the present drug policy "has made cocaine the most lucrative crop in the history of mankind." Is this a statement of fact or opinion? How can you tell?
6. The author blames the current drug policy for the country's drug problem. How does the author support this statement?

LEARNING/STUDY STRATEGY

Annotate the reading by listing the author's beliefs about what he wants the office of Drug Policy to do to try to solve the current drug problem. Then record your reactions to these ideas.

THINKING ABOUT THE PAIRED READINGS

INTEGRATING IDEAS

1. How do the authors' purposes differ in these two readings?
2. Which reading is more objective? Why? (What about this reading makes it more objective?)

3. In which selection does the author better support his ideas? Give an example of this.
4. Do you think both sources are equally credible? Why or why not?
5. Apart from the fact that one reading is written in letter form, what is the major difference in style between these two readings? How does this difference affect the reader in assessing which reading is more persuasive?
6. Is there a common overall theme in each of the two readings? If so, what is that theme and who expresses it more clearly?

GENERATING NEW IDEAS

1. Using one quote from each source, write a 1–2 page paper stating whether you believe drugs should be legalized.
2. Make a list of the strengths and weaknesses of each selection.

Section II

Academic Reading 024

CHAPTER 7

RECOGNIZE THE AUTHOR'S STANCE

One reason to *plan* before you read is to prime your brain. Planning helps you to start thinking, not just about the tasks you have to do, but about ideas. It gives you the chance to make connections between what you know and what you are going to read.

As you prepare to read this chapter, think about your stance, or position, on an issue—for example, "getting older." Consider what kind of words and actions you use when you want to let others know how you feel about your coming birthday. How do you communicate that you're delighted about finally getting older or, on the other hand, that you're feeling ancient and need some quiet understanding?

Could you write an essay that equally presents the positive and negative aspects of getting older even if you have strong feelings about the issue? What precautions would you take if you wanted to make sure you were presenting both sides of the issue? Do you think it would be wrong if you wrote only your feelings? Do you think it would be important for someone reading your essay to know if you had personal feelings about aging that influenced what you wrote?

WHAT IS MY BASIC STRATEGY FOR RECOGNIZING THE AUTHOR'S STANCE?

As You Plan:

1. Understand the vocabulary.
2. Predict the thesis and/or main idea.
3. Determine how much detail you need to know.
4. Review the sources of the author's information.
5. Try to determine if the author is reliable as well as knowledgeable.

As You Read:

6. Actively search for information that helps to clarify and refine your prediction about the thesis and/or main idea.
7. Identify words with connotative meanings.
8. Identify the author's point of view.
9. Determine which information is fact, which is opinion, and which is reasoned judgment.
10. Determine the author's tone.

As You Review:

11. Revise and restate the thesis/main idea.
12. Confirm the author's reliability and the source of the information.
13. Compare the author's point of view with your own.
14. Review the facts, opinions, and reasoned judgments given to support the thesis/main idea.
15. Based on your purpose, and considering the author's stance, organize the thesis, main ideas, and supporting details.

WHAT IS THE AUTHOR'S STANCE?

You discovered early on that all writing is purposeful; an author wants to communicate information and ideas to you for a reason. In addition, you found it is important to look at the author's knowledge of the subject and the sources of information.

Now you must build on what you know about the author's expertise and basic reason for writing and determine the author's stance, or position, on the subject. In modern terms, you want to find out where the author is "coming from."

Much of the time an author does not directly state his or her stance. So, as you have done when you have made other inferences, you must carefully combine what the author says directly, with clues the author provides, and your own knowledge to infer the stance. Uncovering the author's motivation and point of view gives you additional perspective on the author's message. It enables you to go beyond what the author says to what the author means.

IS THE AUTHOR RELIABLE?

By reliable, I mean you can trust the author to give you a fair analysis of the topic without undue influence from others.

For example, a professional athlete and a sports medicine doctor could both write knowledgeably on the topic of athletic footwear—from different perspectives—but with knowledge about the topic. It would be difficult, however, to know whether their writing would be reliable—giving a fair analysis of the footwear without undue influence from a sponsor or manufacturer.

It is difficult to find out an author's motivation for writing, so it is often hard to know whether he or she is reliable. To investigate an author's reliability, read other pieces the author has written, read what others have to say about him or her, and ask teachers and librarians for information.

WHAT IS POINT OF VIEW?

Another element of the author's stance is point of view—his or her position or opinion. Two broad categories of writing are (1) objective, meaning without the author's point of view, or neutral and impartial, and (2) biased, reflecting the author's point of view about the topic.

Writing that reflects the author's point of view is not necessarily bad. Although the connotations of the word "objective" make it seem positive and those of the word "biased" make it seem negative, do not assume that objective writing is good writing or that biased writing is bad writing. *Writing is not good or bad as long as you identify the author's bias and factor that into your comprehension of the information.*

Readers expect expository pieces such as encyclopedia entries and scientific reports to be objective, and persuasive works like political brochures and editorials to be biased. However, all writers are human; even texts and journal articles can reflect the author's bias. What you, as a careful, critical reader must watch for is a biased point of view, even when the primary purpose is exposition.

HOW CAN I IDENTIFY POINT OF VIEW?

To identify point of view in writing, you must use clues such as author background information, the title, and the sources of quotations, references, and illustrations. In addition, watch for words and phrases that have special connotations and a preponderance, or majority, of one-sided information.

The following is the first three paragraphs from "Computers Can't Teach Awareness" by political and environmental columnist Liz Caile. She wrote this column for *The Mountain-Ear*, a small Colorado mountain-town weekly newspaper. Read to discover her point of view about computers and humans.

In a recent discussion of careers, young people were told to master computer skills and math if they wanted to "work for the environment." That stuck in my mind the way the limited concept of outdoor education sometimes sticks. It's OK as far as it goes, but are we going to solve global warming or ozone holes with computers, or just diagnose them that way? Are we going to reverse population growth through mathematical models, or just extrapolate the possibilities?

The key to solutions is awareness of what constitutes a healthy environment. You can't get that awareness staring into a glass tube lit by electricity generated someplace out of sight, out of mind (in our neighborhood by burning coal). You can't feel the complex relationships of air, water, plants and animals. No matter how sophisticated our technology gets, it will never be as intricate as the real thing. Would you like to make love to your computer? They're making great strides in "virtual reality," but....

Holly Near has a line in one of her songs, a song both political and environmental, "love disarms." Being disarmed is part of being aware. Disarmed, we become observers. We enlarge our receptiveness to the planet's needs to balance out our active manipulations of it. Awareness requires that we love wild ecosystems as much as ourselves—that we give them life and soul. That kind of awareness can't be taught by a computer.

Based on the questions Caile asks and the words and phrases she uses, we can infer Caile's point of view is that it's up to people, not computers, to help the environment. She appears to view the computer's role as very limited. Do you think Caile is reliable? Why or why not?

Professors Fuori and Gioia in their text *Computers and Information Processing*, 3rd ed., conclude their final chapter, "Computers Down the Road," with the following paragraphs. Read to find their point of view about computers and humans.

Whereas some computer experts believe that computers hold the key to great progress for the human race, others feel that computers will eventually lead to depersonalization, unemployment, an invasion of our privacy, and the nuclear destruction of our planet. While some are moving with the flow and striving to acquire computer knowledge and skills, others are laying back and hoping computer technology will not disrupt their lives too much.

As with any powerful scientific advancement, the computer can be a curse or a blessing. Historically, human beings have never reached a new level of technological advancement and deemed it too dangerous to use. Despite its destructive capabilities, there is little chance that we will ever ban the use of nuclear energy; similarly, it looks as though computers are here to stay. But is it the computer we should fear? Or is it the nature of those who would harness its power for good or evil? As always, it is not the tool but the tool user that must be monitored.

One of the goals of artificial intelligence research is to help us determine how we think, why we interpret as we do, and ultimately, who we are. We humans have been perplexed by our existence since earliest history. By providing us with a clearer understanding of the human mental process, perhaps AI research may eventually lead us to a better understanding of self. As was once said many years ago, "The answer lies within."

Fuori and Gioia present two sides of the controversial technology issue: Computers provide the key to success for humanity, versus computers provide the key to destruction of humanity. But because of the questions they ask in paragraph 2, and the words and phrases they use—it's not the tool (computer) but the tool user (human) that needs watching, and that possibly computer research will provide insight to a better humanity—we can infer their point of view is that computers do have a vital role. Do you think Fuori and Gioia are reliable? Why or why not?

PRACTICE: IDENTIFYING POINT OF VIEW

1. Cigarette smoking accelerates artery clogging and greatly increases the risk of death from coronary artery disease, heart attack, and stroke in the adult years. The incidence of cancer, chronic bronchitis, and emphysema also increases. (Greenberg and Dintiman, *Exploring Health*)

   a. What is Greenberg and Dintiman's point of view on smoking?

   b. Do you think they are reliable? Why or why not?

   c. What point of view might a representative of the tobacco industry have?

   d. Assume that you have to write a research paper on the effects of smoking. Why would it be necessary to read more than one source for your research?

2. We are tempted to say that [Elvis] Presley did not evolve with the times, but a careful listening to his recordings from the end of his career would suggest the opposite. Retained in his music were country and blues roots, but the instrumental backing was constantly updated. He used contemporary music where it fit, and his performances made use of modern technology—additional musical resources and contemporary subjects. Although Presley was tied to his background, he changed as his background changed. His last performance in Las Vegas was exciting and filled with energy. (Brown, *The Art of Rock and Roll*)

    a. What is Brown's point of view on Elvis Presley's music in his last years?

    b. Who might have a different point of view about Elvis Presley's music in his last years?

3. As long as Americans spend more time watching [TV] than reading, educators must address the need for critical viewing as well as critical reading. If readers are trained to read interpretively, so too must viewers be taught to look critically at TV. And if we succeed with this teaching, we'll have changed the present pattern in which 70 percent of what Americans hear in a political campaign consists of thirty- and sixty-second commercials consisting of half-truths and innuendo....

    As E. B. White noted a half century ago, television is "the test of the modern world." Used correctly, it can inform, entertain and inspire. Used incorrectly, television will control families and communities, limiting our language, dreams, and achievements. It is our "test" to pass or fail. (Trelease, "Television")

    a. What is Trelease's point of view on current television viewing habits?

    b. Who might have a different point of view about the effects of television?

    c. What is your point of view about the effects of television?

4. WYSIWYG. Say it again: What you see is what you get. When we looked at Dreamweaver 1.0 (May/98), we affirmed its reputation as the first respectable WYSIWYG Web-authoring package because it got the "what you get" part—the HTML source code. Dreamweaver 2.0's HTML tools are even more powerful, offering precise control over HTML formatting and grep find-and-replace functions that make the bundled BBEdit nearly redundant. In visual mode Dreamweaver 2.0 makes it easier than ever to arrange "what you see" while building interactive Web sites with all the latest Dynamic HTML tricks, like the proverbial bells and whistles of JavaScript and Cascading Style Sheets. (Coucouvanis, "Reviews: Dreamweaver 2.0," *MAC Addict*)

    a. What is Coucouvanis's point of view on Dreamweaver 2.0 Web-authoring software?

    b. Do you think he is reliable? Why or why not?

    c. Who might have a different point of view?

5. New scientific advances promise to multiply future food yields. Biotechnology offers genetically altered crops that can be custom designed to fit the environment, produce bountiful harvests, and resist plant diseases. One bacterial gene eliminates the need for chemicals to kill worms by producing a natural protein that disintegrates the worms' digestive system. Genetically engineered viruses can be used as pesticides. In 1988 scientists mapped the genome of rice—the set of 12 chromosomes that carries all the genetic characteristics of rice. This development could enable geneticists to produce improved strains of rice. Biotechnology can replace chemical pesticides and fertilizers, whose biological or even genetic impact on our own bodies is not fully understood. (Bergman and McKnight, *Introduction to Geography*)

    a. What is Bergman and McKnight's point of view about the impact of biotechnology?

    b. What point of view might a person who prefers health foods or natural foods have about the impact of biotechnology?

    c. What point of view might a representative of a pesticide company have?

How Can I Differentiate among Facts, Opinions, and Reasoned Judgments?

An author can use facts, opinions, or a combination of facts, opinions, and reasoned judgments to support his or her point of view.

A fact is an objective statement that can be proved true or false. A fact can be verified—no matter where you look or whom you ask, the information is the same. Examples of facts include the following:

> In the mid-1800s the work of Louis Pasteur and others revealed that epidemic diseases were caused by microorganisms.

> A lobbyist is a person hired by an individual, interest group, company, or industry to represent its interests with government officials.

An opinion is a subjective statement that cannot be proved true or false. An opinion cannot be verified; the information can change depending on where you look or whom you ask. Examples of opinions include the following:

> Louis Pasteur made the most significant contributions to the world of medicine of any scientist in history.

> Lobbyists are the primary cause of problems in the government today.

An opinion is not right or wrong, or good or bad. However, depending on the amount and type of evidence the author considered before forming the opinion, it can be valid or invalid. You should be skeptical of invalid opinions.

Reasoned judgments are my label for thoughtful, coherent evaluations that informed individuals make from the available evidence. Articles, essays, and even textbooks rarely use only verifiable facts, and most of the time we're grateful because it's the author's insight, wisdom, and conclusions—their reasoned judgments—that help our understanding of the topic.

Practice: Distinguishing between Fact and Opinion

Indicate whether a sentence is primarily fact, opinion, or reasoned judgment—or a combination of facts, opinions, and/or reasoned judgments.

1. [1]In managing the planning process, more and more firms have adopted a management by objectives (MBO) approach. [2]MBO is a system of collaborative goal setting that extends from the top of the organization to the bottom. [3]Under this system, managers meet with each of their subordinates individually to discuss goals. [4]This meeting usually occurs annually and focuses on the coming year. [5]The manager and the subordinate agree on a set of goals for the subordinate. [6]The goals are stated in quantitative terms (for example, "I will decrease turnover in my division by 3 percent") and written down. [7]A year later, the subordinate's performance is evaluated in terms of the extent to which the goals were met. [8]MBO has been shown to be quite effective when applied at all levels of the company. [9]Tenneco, Black & Decker, General Motors, General Foods, and Alcoa have all reported success using MBO. [10]However, MBO involves quite a bit of paperwork and is sometimes used too rigidly. (Griffin and Ebert, *Business*)

2. [1]A major federal program aimed at identifying and cleaning up existing waste sites was initiated by the Comprehensive Environmental Response, Compensation, and Liability Act of 1980, popularly known as Superfund. [2]Through a tax on chemical raw materials, this legislation provided a fund of 1.6 billion over the period 1980–85 to identify and clean up sites that posed a threat to groundwater. [3]However, the

Environmental Protection Agency's (EPA's) record in administering this program over the first five years was disgraceful. (Nebel, *Environmental Science*)

3. [1]American adults consume an average of 32.0 gallons of beer, 2.5 gallons of wine, and 1.8 gallons of distilled spirits a year (*Statistical Abstract*, 1996). [2]Despite these high rates of consumption, the problems associated with alcohol abuse—chronic inebriation, vagrancy, drunken driving—arouse less interest and concern than the abuse, or even the use, of other drugs. [3]In contrast to other drugs, alcohol is thoroughly integrated into Western culture. [4]It may also be better adapted to our complex lifestyle because, in addition to relieving tension and reducing sexual and aggressive inhibitions, alcohol seems to facilitate interpersonal relations, at least superficially, whereas other drug experiences, even in groups, are often highly private. (Kornblum and Julian, *Social Problems*)

4. [1]Inflation is a perennial problem. [2]We are not likely to repeat in the near future the double-digit inflation numbers of the 1970s and early 1980s, but more modest amounts are very possible. [3]Recent annual rates have been between 2 and 4 percent, a range that is likely to continue. [4]Although these numbers suggest a tame inflationary environment, over long periods of time they can seriously erode the value of your savings. [5]Your investments must earn more than the inflation rate if you hope to grow your wealth in real terms. [6]Unfortunately, many people have been content to leave too much of their money in low-yielding savings accounts that often only match, or fall short of, inflation rates. [7]We hope you won't make that mistake. (Winger and Frasca, *Personal Finance*)

WHAT IS TONE?

Tone is the emotional feeling or attitude we create with our words. As illustrated in Chapter 3, words by themselves don't have much meaning. For example, the words "I don't care" can be a simple phrase meaning "I just don't have a preference," or a complex of emotions meaning "you've made me so angry it doesn't matter." If you misunderstand the meaning, you can be in big trouble. But how do you know which meaning to select?

When you're talking with someone you identify tone by listening to the pitch and volume of his or her voice, and watching gestures and facial expressions. Using these clues, you determine if someone is being serious, humorous, straightforward, or ironic. And knowing that helps you understand their meaning.

HOW CAN I IDENTIFY AN AUTHOR'S TONE?

Although you don't have a speaker's verbal or visual clues available when you are reading, you can understand the author's tone by paying attention to the words and details the author chooses to use or chooses to leave out. Using these clues, along with what the author says directly and your own knowledge, will help you correctly infer the author's tone.

Read to determine the author's tone in these paragraphs. How does the author want you to feel about the person being described? What elements contribute to the differences?

Description A: He had apparently not shaved for several days and his face and hands were covered with dirt. His shoes were torn and his coat, which was several sizes too small for him, was spotted with dried mud.

Description B: Although his face was bearded and neglected, his eyes were clear and he looked straight ahead as he walked rapidly down the road. He looked very tall; perhaps the fact that his coat was too small for him emphasized that impression. He was carrying two books snugly under his left arm and a small terrier puppy ran at his heels.

Both paragraphs could be describing the same man but the words and details the author has chosen present two very different impressions of the man. Notice how the negatives in Description A (unshaven, coat too small) have been reworded and turned into assets in Description B. Also, leaving out details (like torn shoes) and adding details like the books and the puppy in Description B contributes to the different tone.

WHAT KINDS OF TONE DO AUTHORS USE?

Like a speaker, a writer can create any emotion. In some of your reading assignments you may need to narrowly define the author's tone—e.g., decide whether the tone is funny, witty, whimsical, or comical. However, most of the time you can place the tone of the writing into one of eight general groupings.

General Types of Tone

	General Description of Tone	Similar Types of Tone
straightforward	objective; without bias	honest, objective, fair
ironic	means opposite of what it says	contradictory, paradoxical
serious	very thoughtful and sincere	solemn, dignified
humorous	intended to be enjoyable	funny, joking, amusing, comical
emotional	subjective; with strong feeling	passionate, sympathetic, fervent
positive	confident and up-beat attitude	optimistic, enthusiastic, hopeful
negative	skeptical and gloomy attitude	cynical, angry, grim, pessimistic
sarcastic	witty, biting humor	satire, mockery, acerbic

WHAT IS AN IRONIC TONE?

Recognizing tone is especially important when an author doesn't intend for the reader to take his or her words literally. If you don't realize that the author is being ironic—saying the opposite of what he or she means—you misinterpret the message.

For example, consider this portion of a scientist's presentation to his colleagues. If they take his words literally and follow his principles of good writing, will they be good writers?

The Principles of Good Writing

Write hurriedly, preferably when tired. Have no plans; write down items as they occur to you. The article will thus be spontaneous and poor. Hand in your manuscript the moment it is finished. Rereading a few days later might lead to revision—which seldom, if ever, makes the writing worse. If you submit your manuscript to colleagues (a bad practice), pay no attention to their criticisms or comments. Later, resist any editorial suggestions. Be strong and infallible; don't let anyone break down your personality. The critic may be trying to help you or he may have an ulterior motive, but the chance of his causing improvement in your writing is so great that you must be on guard.

The scientist's title tells us that his purpose is to give information on techniques for good writing. But when his first details—e.g., writing hurriedly, when tired, and without plans—seem to contradict what you know about good writing practices, you begin to question his real meaning. Then, in his third sentence when he actually says his advice will lead to a poor article—the opposite of his stated purpose—you know that he's being ironic. Rather than just listing the practices of good writing, he used a bit of ironic humor to make his point.

WHAT KIND OF TONE ARE SATIRE AND SARCASM?

Satire and the more caustic sarcasm often use ironic statements to poke fun at people and deride foolish or dishonest human behaviors. Satire and sarcasm make use of ridicule, mockery, exaggeration, and understatement.

This type of biting humor is used by cartoonists like *Doonesbury*'s Gary Trudeau and comedians on shows like *Saturday Night Live*. When you're reading a cartoon or watching one of these comedy shows and you understand the words but don't understand that they are making fun of the politician or the movie star, you miss the point and the humor. You also miss the point when you don't understand that an author is using satire or sarcasm.

Veteran Chicago columnist Mike Royko was known for his biting, sarcastic style. He begins his jab at trendy public television viewing habits this way in his syndicated column. Look for words and details Royko uses as clues to his sarcasm.

Work the Bugs Out, Channel 11

Mike Royko

A friend of mine asked if I had seen some wonderful television show recently presented on the public channel. When I told him that I hardly ever watch that channel, he looked amazed.

"You don't watch public TV?" he said, "But that's the only station that shows anything of quality."

That's what everybody always says. If you want to see thoughtful drama or fine music shows with deep social significance, you are supposed to watch public TV.

Well, maybe they have such shows, but they're never on there when I turn my set on. No matter when I turn my set on, all I ever see is one of four shows:

1. Insects making love. Or maybe they are murdering each other. With insects it's hard to tell the difference. But after a day's work, my idea of fun isn't watching a couple of bugs with six furry legs and one eye trying to give each other hickies.

2. A lion walking along with a dead antelope in its jaws. I don't know how many times I've seen that same mangy lion dragging that poor antelope into a bush. The tourist bureau in Africa must bring him out every time a TV crew shows up. But the question is, why do they keep showing it? Does somebody at the channel think that we must be taught that lions don't eat pizza?

3. Some spiffily dressed, elderly Englishman sitting in a tall-backed chair in a room that is paneled in dark wood. He is speaking to a younger Englishman who wears a WWI uniform and stands before a crackling fire. The older bloke says things like: "Well Ralph, see you're back from the front. Jolly good you weren't killed. Sorry to hear about your brother. Bloody bad luck, that. Shell took his head clean off. Oh, well, we must go on. Will you be joining us for dinner?" And the younger man says: "Thank you, Father."

4. The station announcer, talking about what great shows they have on Channel 11. The last time I tuned in, he talked about it for so long that I dozed off. When I awoke, he was talking about how great the show had been. Before I could get to the dial, two insects started making love again.

That's it. That's all I ever see on public TV.

Wait, I forgot. There are a couple of others. Some skinny, bearded, squeaky-voiced, wimpy guy from Seattle does a cooking show....

If you read only the words written by Royko, you miss the message; you must infer—read between the lines—to determine what he means by what he says. For any form of wit or humor like irony, satire, or sarcasm to be effective, the reader must clearly understand the author's intended message, not just the words he or she uses.

PRACTICE: IDENTIFYING TONE

1. There are those who believe that a rapidly advancing computer technology exhibits little regard for the future of the human race. They contend that computers are overused, misused, and generally detrimental to society. This group argues that the computer is dehumanizing and is slowly forcing society into a pattern of mass conformity. To be sure, the computer revolution is presenting society with complex problems, but they can be overcome. (Long, *Introduction to Computers and Information Systems*)

   a. What is Dr. Long's point of view about computers?

   b. Would you describe Dr. Long's tone as optimistic or cynical? Why?

2. Donald Trump had not granted an interview or smirked into a camera in nearly a month. It was his longest media dry spell since 1986—when he started taking reporters on grand tours aboard his black Puma helicopter, laying claim to the Manhattan-to-Atlantic City landscape with a lordly wave of his hand. At forty-four, despite almost daily, banner-headlined catastrophes since the beginning of 1990, he was still willing to play posterboy, and a birthday was a great photo opportunity. So, after weeks of hiding from a suddenly carnivorous press, he decided to surface at a birthday blast organized by his casino dependents. With his golden hair backing up beneath his starched collar, a wounded half smile on his silent lips, and perfectly protected by his ever-present blue pinstriped suit, the icon of the eighties—slowed in the first six months of the new decade to an uncertain pace—worked his way out onto a Boardwalk blanketed by a mid-June haze. (Barrett, *Trump: The Deals and the Downfall*)

   a. What is Barrett's point of view about Trump?

   b. How would you describe Barrett's tone? Why?

3. One of the strongest barriers to good thinking, then, is fear. Fear may show itself as anger, envy, selfishness, or hatred, but these are just expressions of our fear. And don't underrate the power of such emotions. History has shown what devastation fear and hatred among nations can wreak. Our personal fears can be just as damaging to our inner world, blinding our critical faculties with their dark energies. When we argue, then, we must be aware of what we feel as well as what we think. A good critical thinker may have to scrutinize not only the intellectual character of an argument, but its emotional temperature as well. (White, *Discovering Philosophy*)

   a. What is White's point of view about the impact of fear?

   b. How would you describe White's tone? Why?

4. Two new books—*Built from Scratch* by founders Bernie Marcus and Arthur Blank (Times Business, 332 pages, $24.95) and *Inside Home Depot* by journalist Chris Roush (McGraw-Hill, 266 pages, $24.95)—tell the story of how Home Depot succeeded beyond anyone's dreams.

   Alas, much of *Inside Home Depot* smacks of old interview notes, faded newspaper clippings and public-relations puff. The dust jacket for Mr. Roush's book proclaims: "Unauthorized! Not sponsored or approved by The Home Depot." If Home Depot executives were nervous about what Mr. Roush would build from scratch, they can relax. (Hagerty, "Bookshelf: Do-It-Yourself Dreams" *Wall Street Journal*)

    a. What is Hagerty's point of view about *Inside Home Depot*?

    b. How would you describe Hagerty's tone? Why?

REVIEW QUESTIONS

1. What is the author's stance?
2. What does the word reliable mean? Why is it difficult to determine if an author is reliable?
3. What is point of view? How can you recognize an author's point of view?
4. Define fact, opinion, and reasoned judgment.
5. What is tone?
6. What are strategies for recognizing tone?

THINK AND CONNECT QUESTIONS

7. Reread "The Benefits of the Sociological Perspective" Exercise 4, Chapter 5, page 112.

    a. Do you consider Macionis to be knowledgeable and reliable? Why or why not?

    b. What is Macionis's point of view on the benefits of the sociological perspective and tone?

    c. Does Macionis use primarily facts, opinions, or reasoned judgments? Give examples to support your answer.

8. Make a list of the following:

    things you have bought recently (like shoes, jeans, cereal, a car)

    things you have done recently (such as gone to a movie, drunk a soft drink, voted)

    views you have adopted (such as for or against abortion, for or against nuclear energy, for or against affirmative action)

    Can you identify who or what you saw or read that influenced you to buy, do, or believe? Did you realize you were being influenced? What types of thing will you watch for in the future?

APPLICATION EXERCISES

9. Using the topic "getting older," write a humorous paragraph and then a serious paragraph. Notice how you can make the change easily by the type of words, details, and punctuation you use.
10. Using the primary reading material (texts, journals, etc.) in one of your classes, determine the authors' general tone and point of view. Also, investigate their backgrounds and evaluate their expertise and reliability.

WEB EXERCISE

11. These web sites contain book reviews or links to book reviews. Log onto one of these sites or use a search directory/engine to locate two reviews (of the same book, if possible).

http://www.bookwire.com/bbr/bbr-home.html

http://www.suntimes.com/index/kisor.html

http://www.anatomy.usyd.edu.au/danny/book-reviews/

http://dir.yahoo.com/Arts/Humanities/Literature/Reviews/

a. Print out the two reviews.

b. For each review write:

the reviewer's name and if you believe he or she is reliable, including your reasoning;

the reviewer's point of view;

the reviewer's tone.

c. Attach your answers to the print-outs and turn them in to your professor.

USE YOUR STRATEGIES—EXERCISE #1

E. J. Montini writes on social and political issues and their effect on people. This selection, "Execution Has Benefits—Doesn't It?" is from the *Arizona Republic*.

Define these words or phrases:

a. reap (¶1)

b. abolished (¶11)

c. extremely beneficial (¶13)

d. high-profile proponent (¶15)

e. deterrent (¶15)

f. too barbaric (¶20)

g. less tangible (¶26)

Execution Has Benefits—Doesn't It?

E. J. Montini

[1]Now that Don Harding is dead, now that we've killed him, it's time to reap the rewards, to count up the ways we're benefiting from his death. There must be plenty.

[2]Two days ago, the convicted murderer was alive and in prison. Today, he's dead. He was killed at our expense. In our name. By us. Which means we must have thought it was important to kill him. We must have believed there were benefits in it for us.

[3]Like, for instance, safety.

[4]Maybe we're safer today than we were Sunday, when Harding was still alive.

[5]No, that's not it.

[6]Harding was in a maximum-security prison cell Sunday, as he had been every day for the past 10 years. We were as safe from him then, while he was alive, as we are from him now.

[7]It must be something else. There must be some other benefit to having strapped Harding into a chair in a tiny room and filled the space with poison gas. It took him about 10 minutes to die.

$16,000 TO KEEP HIM ALIVE

[8]How about money?

[9]Some people say that killing Harding saved us a lot of money. It was costing us $16,000 a year to keep him alive, and we no longer have to spend the cash. That's the benefit, right?

[10]Wrong.

[11]Our efforts to kill Harding (and anyone else on death row) probably cost us more than it would have cost to keep him in prison for life. In fact, several states have abolished the death penalty partly because it costs so much.

[12]It must be something else.

[13]There must be some other extremely beneficial reason for standing by calmly as the tiny capillaries in Harding's lungs were exploded by the cyanide gas, filling his chest with blood. Drowning him from the inside.

[14]Maybe we figured that, if we execute Harding, others will think twice before killing. That would be nice.

[15]Too bad it's not true. Not even those who foam at the mouth at the thought of executing people, like high-profile proponent Arizona Attorney General Grant Woods, believe the death penalty is a deterrent. Studies in states that execute people—as we now do—show that it's not, that murder rates don't go down.

[16]It must be something else.

WE DON'T KILL ALL MURDERERS

[17]I know. Everyone says there's a benefit to the families of the victims. We kill people like Harding for them. So the families can get revenge.

[18]What about other cases, though?

[19]There are hundreds of inmates in Arizona prisons who have killed people. Yet there are only 99 on death row. We don't kill all murderers, even though the families of all victims suffer the same loss.

[20]We're willing to kill 100 but not 1,000. Killing 1,000 would be considered too barbaric, wouldn't it? A little death goes a long way.

[21]Still, the fact that we don't kill all murderers proves we're really not interested in satisfying the revenge of all victims' families.

[22]If there's a benefit to having killed Harding, it must be something else.

[23]Like the fact that it freed up a prison cell. That's something. We might say there's now room for one more criminal in Arizona prisons.

[24]Except, unfortunately, there isn't. The prisons already contain about 1,000 more inmates than they're designed to handle. Killing one or two people won't help. We'd have to kill a thousand or so, and, like I said, we don't have the stomach for that.

[25]So, it must be something else.

[26]Maybe the benefit we got from killing Harding is less tangible. Maybe we killed him only to prove, as Attorney General Woods likes to say, that "justice is being served."

[27]In other words, to send a message. To teach a lesson.

[28]That must be it. The execution was a lesson. Our children, I figure, will learn something by it. They'll find out we're willing to strap a man down, poison him, then stand around and watch him slowly and painfully die.

[29]That's the benefit.

[30]The boys and girls we sent to bed Sunday night, before the killing, eventually will learn something very important from what we did. They'll learn what type of people their parents really are.

EXERCISE #1 QUESTIONS

1. What is Montini's purpose?
2. What is his thesis?
3. What is Montini's point of view on the death penalty?
4. What is his tone?
5. How does his tone relate to his point of view?
6. Do you think he has the knowledge to write this article? Why or why not?
7. Do you think he is reliable? Why or why not?
8. Do you think anything could cause him to change his point of view?
9. What event happened to make Montini write this column?
10. How and where was Harding killed?
11. Montini lists and discounts five "benefits" of Harding's execution. Name them.
12. What is the "benefit" that Montini decides "must be it"? Does he really think it is a benefit?
13. Montini says that children will "learn what type of people their parents really are." What does he mean?
14. Do you agree or disagree with Montini? Why or why not?
15. If you wanted to get more information on the death penalty, list three places you would likely find more information.

USE YOUR STRATEGIES—EXERCISE #2

Roger Rosenblatt is an essayist for *Time, The New Republic*, and the *NewsHour with Jim Lehrer* on PBS. This essay, "Why I Don't Compute," is from *Modern Maturity* where he is a contributing editor.

Define these words or phrases:

a. forbearing editors (¶1)

b. bamboozled (¶2)

c. allure (¶8)

Why I Don't Compute

Roger Rosenblatt

---

[1]It says something that I have been able to survive the past 15 years without using a word processor. Forbearing editors have been willing to enter my typewritten pieces into systems for me. Other than that kind accommodation, I have had no contact with that so-called invention for which people like Steve Jobs and Bill Gates have claimed evangelical powers. In my line of "work," I could not get along for a day without the telephone, TV, radio, automobile, and fax. But I shall happily live out my days computer-free.

[2]Fact is, I think that Jobs, Gates, and all the other cyberspace billionaires have bamboozled the world. Not only is a computer slower than a typewriter in the long run, its research function is also faulty; and worst of all, it encourages a society of increasing isolation (though it claims the opposite). What the computer has done is to make a few clever fellows rich.

[3]Slower than a typewriter? Yes, even slower than a Bic ballpoint pen, my principal machine, because a word processor (what a name!) facilitates bad writing by way of fast and easy corrections. When something is wrong with a piece, it is usually all wrong. A writer needs to start from scratch, not to transpose paragraph 19 for 36. Writers need writing to be difficult. An honest writer, looking at a screen full of patched copy, will begin again. He would've gone faster if he'd gone slower.

[4]The research function faulty and inadequate? Of course it is. People use NEXIS, LEXIS, and "SEXIS" to look up all sorts of things, and they think they're doing research. But real research requires happy accidents. A computer offers nowhere near the same capacity for serendipity that a stroll through the stacks of a library offers. It also suggests that we always know what we want to learn. What happens to the meandering dream state necessary for learning? Computers turn dream states into theme parks.

[5]As for encouraging increasing isolations, that's self-evident. I grew up in a world in which the declared enemy of the human mind was mechanization. Science fiction would routinely scare you silly by presenting people becoming machines. (Read *R.U.R.*) Or people would be warned of losing control to machines. (See *2001*.) Computer salesmen want us to join machines, not to beat 'em.

[6]But the deeper isolations occur within those very functions of computer life that hackers praise most lavishly. Take a trip on the Internet and link up with people exactly like yourself. The emerging technologies are simply imposing a new class system on the existing ones. Their overarching context is the ability to use computers at all; if everyone has one, everyone belongs to the same class. But within that class lie thousands of subclasses—from chess players to militia members to nuts of every stripe. What is gained if everybody still hangs out with his or her own kind?

[7]Information, the god of these gizmos, is not only a poor form of learning, it's the dumbest form of communication. Give me a good face-to-face conversation any time, or a bad one. And even good communication should not be confused with sympathetic social existence. There's still a difference between talking and living.

[8]A magazine once gave me a PC to try to allure me into modern America. I used it as a planter. Don't compare these things with real inventions. A stick with a small ball at one end that dispenses ink from a plastic tube: That's an invention.

EXERCISE #2 QUESTIONS

1. What is Rosenblatt's purpose?
2. What is his thesis?
3. How does he support and develop his thesis?
4. What is Rosenblatt's point of view on computers?
5. What is his tone?
6. Do you feel Rosenblatt has the knowledge to write this article? Why or why not?
7. Do you feel he is reliable? Why or why not?
8. Has Rosenblatt used word processing or a computer?
9. What are three reasons Rosenblatt won't use computers?
10. What does he believe is the "worst" thing about computers?
11. Generally the word "isolation" means to be alone. What does Rosenblatt mean by the "deeper isolations" in paragraph 6?

USE YOUR STRATEGIES—EXERCISE #3

International Paper Company asked author Kurt Vonnegut to help college students understand "How To Write With Style." His critically acclaimed novels include *Slaughterhouse-Five, Jailbird*, and *Cat's Cradle*.

Define these words and phrases:

a. ink-stained wretches (¶1)

b. damning revelation (¶4)

c. piquant (¶9)

d. locutions (¶10)

How To Write with Style

Kurt Vonnegut

Main idea: A writers style can influence reader.

[1] Newspaper reporters and technical writers are trained to reveal almost nothing about themselves in their writings. This makes them freaks in the world of writers, since almost all of the other ink-stained wretches in that world reveal a lot about themselves to readers. We call these revelations, accidental and intentional, elements of style.

[2] They tell us as readers what sort of person it is with whom we are spending time. Does the writer sound ignorant or informed, crooked or honest, humorless or playful? And on and on.

[3] Why should you examine your writing style with the idea of improving it? Do so as a mark of respect for your readers, whatever you're writing. If you scribble your thoughts any which way, your readers will surely feel that you care nothing about them. They will mark you down as an egomaniac or a chowderhead or worse, they will stop reading you.

[4] The most damning revelation you can make about yourself is that you do not know what is interesting and what is not. Don't you yourself like or dislike writers mainly for what they choose to show you or make you think about? Did you ever admire an empty-headed writer for his or her mastery of the language? No.

[5] So your own winning style must begin with ideas in your head.

FIND A SUBJECT YOU CARE ABOUT

[6] Find a subject you care about and which you feel others should care about. It is this genuine caring, and not your games with the language, which will be the most compelling and seductive element in your style.

[7] I am not urging you to write a novel—although I would not be sorry if you wrote one, provided you genuinely cared about something. A petition to the mayor about a pothole in front of your house or a love letter to the girl next door will do.

KEEP IT SIMPLE

[8] As for your use of language: Remember that two great masters, William Shakespeare and James Joyce, wrote sentences which seemed almost childlike when their subjects were most profound. "To be or not to be?" asks Shakespeare's Hamlet. The longest word is three letters long. Joyce, when he was frisky could put together a sentence as intricate and as glittering as a necklace for Cleopatra, but my favorite sentence in his short story "Eveline" is this one: "She was tired." At that point in the story, no other words could break the heart of a reader as those three words do. Simplicity of language is not only reputable, but perhaps even sacred. Your rule might be this: If a sentence, no matter how excellent, does not illuminate your subject in some new and useful way, scratch it out.

SOUND LIKE YOURSELF

[9] The writing style which is most natural for you is bound to echo the speech you heard when a child. English was the novelist Joseph Conrad's third language, and much that seems piquant in his use of English was no doubt colored by his first language, which was Polish. And lucky indeed is the writer who has grown up in Ireland, for the English spoken there is so amusing and musical. I myself grew up in Indianapolis, where common speech sounds like a band saw cutting galvanized tin, and employs a vocabulary as unornamental as a monkey wrench.

[10] In some of the more remote hollows of Appalachia, children still grow up hearing songs and locutions of Elizabethan times. Yes, and many Americans grow up hearing a language other than English, or an English dialect a majority of Americans cannot understand.

[11] All these varieties of speech are beautiful, just as the varieties of butterflies are beautiful. No matter what your first language, you should treasure it all

your life. If it happens not to be standard English, and if it shows itself when you write standard English, the result is usually delightful, like a very pretty girl with one eye that is green and one that is blue.

¹²I myself find that I trust my own writing most, and others seem to trust it most, too, when I sound most like a person from Indianapolis, which is what I am. What alternatives do I have? The one most vehemently recommended by teachers has no doubt been pressed on you as well: to write like cultivated Englishmen of a century or more ago.

SAY WHAT YOU MEAN TO SAY

¹³I used to be exasperated by such teachers, but am no more. I understand now that all those antique essays and stories with which I was to compare my own work were not magnificent for their datedness or foreignness, but for saying precisely what their authors meant them to say. My teachers wished me to write accurately, always selecting the most effective words, and relating the words to one another unambiguously, rigidly, like parts of a machine. The teachers did not want to turn me into an Englishman after all. They hoped that I would become understandable—

and therefore understood. And there went my dream of doing with words what Pablo Picasso did with paint or what any number of jazz idols did with music.

¹⁴If I broke all the rules of punctuation, had words mean whatever I wanted them to mean, and strung them together higgledy-piggledy, I would simply not be understood. So you, too, had better avoid Picasso-style or jazz-style writing, if you have something worth saying and wish to be understood.

¹⁵Readers want our pages to look very much like pages they have seen before. Why? This is because they themselves have a tough job to do, and they need all the help they can get from us.

FOR REALLY DETAILED ADVICE

¹⁶For a discussion of literary style in a narrower sense, in a more technical sense, I commend to your attention *The Elements of Style*, by William Strunk Jr. and E. B. White (Macmillan, 1979). E. B. White is, of course, one of the most admirable literary stylists this country has so far produced.

¹⁷You should realize, too, that no one would care how well or badly Mr. White expressed himself, if he did not have perfectly enchanting things to say.

EXERCISE #3 QUESTIONS

1. What is Vonnegut's purpose?
2. What is his thesis?
3. How does he develop and support his thesis?
4. What is his point of view on writing style?
5. What is Vonnegut's tone?
6. In paragraph 11, Vonnegut uses two figurative expressions (similes) to support his main idea. What are they? How do they add to the paragraph?
7. Why does he think his teachers, and your teachers, require students to read all those "antique essays and stories"?
8. What does he believe would happen if authors had words mean whatever they wanted and broke the rules of punctuation and grammar?
9. According to Vonnegut, readers "have a tough job to do." Explain what he means.

USE YOUR STRATEGIES—EXERCISE #4

The funny, acerbic syndicated columnist Mike Royko took on any and all social and political issues in his column that appeared in hundreds of newspapers daily. This selection, "Endorsements Just a Shell Game," is from *Dr. Kookie You're Right*.

Explain these phrases or figures of speech:

a. cameo appearance (¶3)

b. king's ransom (¶15)

c. walking-around money (¶15)

d. that kind of scratch (¶24)

e. a sham (¶41)

Endorsements Just a Shell Game

Mike Royko

¹The man from an advertising agency had an unusual proposition.

²His agency does the TV commercials for a well-known chain of Mexican restaurants in Chicago.

³"You may have seen our commercials," he said. "They include a cameo appearance by Lee Smith and Leon Durham of the Cubs. It shows them crunching into a tortilla."

⁴No, I somehow missed seeing that.

⁵"Well, anyway, we'd like to have you in a commercial."

⁶Doing what?

⁷"Crunching into a tortilla."

⁸I thought tortillas were soft. I may be wrong, but I don't think you can crunch into a tortilla. Maybe you mean a taco.

⁹"Well, you'd be biting into some kind of Mexican food."

¹⁰What else would I have to do?

¹¹"That's it. It would be a cameo appearance. You'd be seen for about four seconds. You wouldn't have to say anything."

¹²I'd just bite into a piece of Mexican food?

¹³"Right. For a fee, of course."

¹⁴How big a fee?

¹⁵He named a figure. It was not a king's ransom, but it was more than walking-around money.

¹⁶"It would take about forty-five minutes to film," he said.

¹⁷Amazing. In my first newspaper job almost thirty years ago, I had to work twelve weeks to earn the figure he had mentioned.

¹⁸It was a small, twice-a-week paper, and I was the only police reporter, the only sports reporter, the only investigative reporter and the assistant political writer, and on Saturday I would edit the stories going into the entertainment page. The publisher believed in a day's work for an hour's pay.

¹⁹Now I could make the same amount just for spending forty-five minutes biting into a taco in front of a TV camera.

²⁰And when I was in the military, it would have taken eight monthly paychecks to equal this one taco-crunching fee. Of course, I also got a bunk and meals and could attend free VD lectures.

²¹"Well, what do you think?" he asked.

²²I told him I would think about it and get back to him.

²³So I asked Slats Grobnik, who has sound judgment, what he thought of the deal.

²⁴"That's a lot of money just to bite a taco on TV. For that kind of scratch, I'd bite a dog. Grab the deal."

²⁵But there is a question of ethics.

²⁶"Ethics? What's the ethics in biting a taco? Millions of people bite tacos every day. Mexicans have been biting them for hundreds of years. Are you saying that Mexicans are unethical? Careful, some of my best friends are Mexicans."

²⁷No, I'm not saying that at all. I like Mexicans, though I'm opposed to bullfighting.

²⁸"Then what's unethical?"

²⁹The truth is, I can't stand tacos.

³⁰"What has that got to do with it? I can't stand work, but I do it for the money."

³¹It has everything to do with it. If I go on TV and bite into a taco, won't I be endorsing that taco?

³²"So what? You've endorsed politicians and I've never met a politician that I liked better than a taco."

³³But endorsing a taco I didn't like would be dishonest.

³⁴"Hey, that's the American way. Turn on your TV

and look at all the people who endorse junk. Do you think they really believe what they're saying?"

³⁵Then it's wrong. Nobody should endorse a taco if they don't like a taco.

³⁶"Then tell them you'll bite something else. A tortilla or an enchilada."

³⁷But I don't like them either. The truth is, I can't stand most Mexican food. The only thing I really like is the salt on the edge of a margarita glass. Oh, and I do like tamales.

³⁸"Good, then bite a tamale."

³⁹No, because the only tamales I like are the kind that used to be sold by the little Greeks who had hot dog pushcarts on the streets. They were factory-produced tamales about the size and weight of a lead pipe. But I don't think anybody would want me to do a TV commercial for hot dog stand tamales.

⁴⁰"Can't you just bite the taco and spit it out when the camera is turned off?"

⁴¹That would be a sham. Besides, even if I liked tacos or tortillas, what does it matter? Why should somebody eat in a restaurant because they see me biting into that restaurant's taco? Am I a taco expert? What are my credentials to tell millions of people what taco they should eat? I'm not even Mexican.

⁴²"Well, you're a sucker to turn it down. Why, it's almost un-American. Do you think that in Russia any newsman would ever have an opportunity to make that much money by biting into a pirogi?"

⁴³That may be so. But maybe someday a food product will come along that I can lend my name to, something I can truly believe in.

⁴⁴"I doubt it. Not unless they start letting taverns advertise shots and beers on TV."

EXERCISE #4 QUESTIONS

1. What is Royko's purpose?
2. What is his thesis?
3. What is Royko's point of view on endorsements?
4. What is his tone?
5. How does his tone relate to his point of view?
6. Do you think he has the knowledge to write this article? Why or why not?
7. Do you think he is reliable? Why or why not?
8. Do you think anything could cause him to change his point of view?
9. What did the advertising agency want Royko to do?
10. Do you think Royko made the commercial? Why or why not?
11. How much of a factor do you think money was in Royko's decision?
12. How does Royko's thesis match or contradict your concept of reliability? Explain.
13. If you were in Royko's position, what would you have decided to do? Why?
14. This type of situation is often referred to as a moral dilemma. Have you ever had a moral dilemma? How did you resolve the dilemma?

Use Your Strategies—Exercise #5

Dr. Bergman is chairman of the geography department at Lehman College of the City University of New York. He has taught in Europe and written about New York City, U.S. history, political geography, and international affairs. Dr. McKnight teaches geography at the University of California, Los Angeles. Most of his professional life has been based at UCLA, but he has also taught at other schools in the United States, Canada, and Australia. This selection, "The Future," is from their text *Introduction to Geography*.

Explain these words or phrases:

a. specter of worldwide starvation (¶1)
b. newly emerging technology (¶2)
c. per hectare (¶3)
d. genetically altered crops (¶5)
e. halophytes (¶6).

The Future

Edward F. Bergman and Tom L. McKnight

¹Until now all the factors just discussed have held off the specter of worldwide starvation. Is it possible that humankind is now, at last, at the end of its ability to increase food supplies?

²The answer to this question is no. There is no reason to fear that humankind is, technologically, in danger. If demographers are correct in their projections of the Earth's future population, the population can be fed. Although farmers now utilize almost all potential cropland, and the amount of cropland per capita is declining, humankind has scarcely begun to maximize productivity even with present-day technology. The leading contemporary technology has been applied to only a small portion of the Earth, and newly emerging technology offers still greater possibilities.

³A 1983 study by the Food and Agriculture Organization (FAO, a UN agency) of the world's soil and climate determined that with basic fertilizers and pesticides, all cultivable land under food crops, and the most productive crops grown on at least half the land, the world in the year 2000 could feed four times its projected 2000 population. (That study discounted any possible technological breakthroughs between 1983 and 2000.) If average farm yields rose just from the present 2 tons of grain equivalent per hectare (2.47 acres) to 5 tons, the world could support about 11.5 billion people. Each person could enjoy "Plant energy"—food, seed, and animal feed—of 6,000 calories per day, the current global average. (North America currently uses about 15,000 calories per person per day, but most of that is consumed by animals, which are then eaten by people.)

⁴In addition, humankind could improve its diet by concentrating on raising those domesticated animals that most efficiently transform grain into meat. Chickens are the most efficient. They yield 1 pound (0.46 kg) of edible meat for every 4 pounds (1.8 kg) of grain they consume. Pigs produce 1 pound for every 7 pounds of grain, and beef cattle 1 pound for every 15 pounds (6.8 kg) of grain. In addition, chickens reach maturity—and therefore can be consumed—much faster than do pigs and cattle. Therefore, a greater emphasis placed on raising chickens could immensely improve the human diet. China is widely replacing swine with chicken farming, and several other countries have established programs to multiply their chicken populations. In many societies, however, cattle are viewed as a status symbol, and this preference delays the switch into more productive livestock.

Biotechnology in Agriculture

⁵New scientific advances promise to multiply future food yields. Biotechnology offers genetically altered crops that can be custom designed to fit the environment, produce bountiful harvests, and resist plant diseases. One bacterial gene eliminates the need for chemicals to kill worms by producing a natural protein that disintegrates the worms' digestive system. Genetically engineered viruses can be used as pesticides. In 1988 scientists mapped the genome of rice—the set of 12 chromosomes that carries all the genetic characteristics of rice. This development could enable geneticists to produce improved strains of rice. Biotechnology can replace chemical pesticides and fertilizers, whose biological or even genetic impact on our own bodies is not fully understood.

[6]Scientists have also conducted research on halophytes, plants that thrive in salt water. Interbreeding halophytes with conventional crops has made these crops more salt-resistant, which means that they can grow in more diverse environments. Farmers are today harvesting lands in Egypt, Israel, India, and Pakistan once thought too salt-soaked to support crops. Conventional crops may someday be grown in salt water.

[7]Mechanized fishing on technologically advanced ships has already multiplied yields from the sea, but humankind has scarcely begun the shift from hunting and gathering seafood (fishing and gathering a few aquatic plants) to aquaculture, which involves herding or domesticating aquatic animals and farming aquatic plants. Humankind took this step with agriculture and livestock herding on land thousands of years ago. Presumably this food frontier will be expanded.

[8]All these possibilities justify optimism. The economist Henry George (1839–97) succinctly contrasted the rules of nature with the multiplication of resources through the application of human ingenuity. He said, "Both the jayhawk and the man eat chickens, but the more jayhawks, the fewer chickens, while the more men, the more chickens."

[9]This principle is key to understanding and counting all resources, but technological solutions to problems can still trigger unexpected new problems. Over reliance on insecticides, for example, can lead to the poisoning of farm workers or the contamination of water supplies. The debate between the optimists and the pessimists continues.

EXERCISE #5 QUESTIONS

1. What is Bergman and McKnight's purpose?
2. What is their thesis?
3. What is their point of view on the ability of the world to provide food for its population in the future?
4. What is their point of view on the promise of genetically altered crops?
5. What is their general tone?
6. How does their tone relate to their point of view?
7. Do you think Bergman and McKnight have the knowledge to write this article? Why or why not?
8. Do you think they are reliable? Why or why not?
9. What, if anything, do you think could cause them to change their point of view?
10. If farmers are currently using almost all available cropland and the amount of available cropland is diminishing, how do Bergman and McKnight suggest food yields can be increased to meet future demands?
11. Why do the authors suggest that raising a greater percentage of chickens could improve the human diet?
12. Name the three advantages of genetically altered crops.
13. Why do Bergman and McKnight compare aquaculture to agriculture and livestock herding? Do you think it is a useful comparison? Explain.
14. Explain, in your own words, the meaning of economist Henry George's quote in paragraph 8, "Both the jayhawk and the man eat chickens, but the more jayhawks, the fewer chickens, while the more men, the more chickens." Do you agree or disagree with George? Why?

CHAPTER 6 CONNECTIONS

A. Reread the paragraphs on pages 119–20 by Caile and those by Fuori and Gioia about computers. Which piece most closely matches your point of view about the use and impact of computers? Why? Did either Caile or Fuori and Gioia spark an idea you hadn't thought about? Did either author change your mind?

B. In paragraphs 1 and 2 of "The Future," the excerpt from Bergman and McKnight's *Introduction to Geography* text (page 137), they ask the question: "Is it possible that humankind is now, at last, at the end of its ability to increase food supplies?" They then answer the question: "no." Do you think it is acceptable for textbook authors to include their point of view in the text? Why or why not?

CHAPTER 8
Evaluating Arguments and Persuasive Writing

IN THIS CHAPTER YOU WILL LEARN:

1. To evaluate source and authority.
2. To understand and evaluate arguments.
3. To identify reasoning errors.

An education professor opens a class discussion on the issue of coeducation by distributing the following statement:

BOYS AND GIRLS HAVE DIFFERENT EDUCATIONAL NEEDS

There are many reasons to think that boys and girls may need different kinds of schooling. First, some have observed that males and females appear to have different aptitudes, or at least different average mixes of aptitudes. Whether these differences are inborn, or a result of family childhood socialization, or both, is hard to say. But it has often been noted that females are less likely to study mathematics, science, or computers at any level of the co-ed school system.

What is also known from research is that females do better in these subjects—show more interest and achieve higher grades, for example—in all-girl schools, particularly where teachers strongly encourage such achievement by girls. Also, some research suggest that a key method of getting girls interested in these subjects is by emphasizing communication and creative problem solving, rather than the theoretical or technical aspects of the topic. Treating girls as if they had the same interests as boys doesn't work.

Tepperman and Blain, *Think Twice!*

She then asks the class to analyze and respond to the statement. An impulsive student responded immediately, saying "The writers oppose coeducation, but I disagree with them." The instructor seems dissatisfied with this response, suggesting she wants more detailed and carefully reasoned responses.

How would you analyze the statement? If you agreed with the writer's position, how would you defend it? If you disagreed, how would you dispute it?

To analyze the statement, you must study the writer's line of reasoning and thought process. You must also evaluate how the writer presents ideas, and evaluate their worth. This chapter focuses on techniques to evaluate persuasive writing. Specifically, you will learn to evaluate source and authority, recognize the structure of and evaluate arguments, identify reasoning errors, and evaluate illogical appeals.

EVALUATING SOURCE AND AUTHORITY

Two very important considerations in evaluating any written material are the source in which it was printed and the authority, or qualifications, of the author.

Considering the Source

Your reaction to and evaluation of printed or electronic material should take into account its source. Obviously, a reader cannot check or verify each fact that a writer provides, but you must assess whether or not the writer has carefully researched and accurately reported the subject. Although many writers are careful and accurate, some are not. Often the source of a piece of writing can indicate how accurate, detailed, and well documented the article is. For example, in which of the following sources would you expect to find the most accurate, up-to-date information on the gas mileage of various cars?

- an advertisement in *Time*
- a research report in *Car and Driver*
- an article in *Reader's Digest* on buying an economical car

The report in *Car and Driver* would be the most likely source for information that is detailed and up-to-date, because it is a magazine devoted to the subject of cars and their performance. *Reader's Digest*, on the other hand, publishes selected articles and condensed writing from other periodicals and may not provide such timely information on a subject. A paid advertisement in *Time*, a weekly news magazine, most likely would not provide completely objective information.

Let's consider another example. Suppose you are in the library trying to find information on sleepwalking for a term paper. You locate the following sources, each of which contains an article on sleepwalking. Which would you expect to be the most factual, detailed, and scientific?

- an encyclopedia entry on sleepwalking
- an article titled "Strange Things Happen While You Are Sleeping," in *Woman's Day*
- an article titled *"An Examination of Research on Sleepwalking"* in the *Psychological Review*

Again you can see that from the source alone you can make predictions about the content and approach used. You would expect the encyclopedia entry to provide only a general overview of the topic. You might expect the article in *Woman's Day* to discuss various abnormalities that occur during sleep; sleepwalking might be only one of the topics discussed. Also, you might expect the article to relate several unusual or extreme cases of sleepwalking, rather than to present a factual analysis of the topic. The article in *Psychological Review,* a journal that reports research in psychology, would be the one that contains a factual, authoritative discussion of sleepwalking.

In evaluating a source you might ask the following questions:

1. **What reputation does the source have?**
2. **What is the audience for whom the source is intended?**
3. **Are documentation or references provided?**

Considering the Authority of the Author

To evaluate printed or electronic material, the competency of the author also must be considered. If the author lacks expertise in or experience with the subject, the material he or she produces may not meet an acceptable level of scholarship and accuracy.

Depending on the type of material you are using, you have several means of checking the qualifications of an author. In textbooks, the author's credentials may be described in one of two places. The author's college or university affiliation, and possibly his or her title, may appear on the title page beneath the author's name. Second, in the preface of the book, the author may indicate or summarize his or her qualifications for writing the text. In nonfiction books and general market paperbacks, a synopsis of the author's credentials and experiences may be included on the book jacket or the back cover. However, in other types of material, little effort is made to identify the author or his or her qualifications. In newspapers, magazines, and reference books, the reader is given little or no information about the writer. You are forced to rely on the judgment of the editors or publishers to assess an author's authority.

DIRECTIONS: Predict and discuss how useful and appropriate each of the following sources will be for the situation described.

1. Using an article from *Working Women* on family aggression for a term paper for your sociology class.

---

2. Quoting an article in *The New York Times* on recent events in China for a speech titled "Innovation and Change in China."

---

3. Reading an article titled "Bilingual Education in the Twenty-First Century" printed in the *Educational Research Quarterly* for a paper arguing for increased federal aid for bilingual education.

---

4. Using an article in *TV Guide* on television's coverage of crime and violence for a term paper on the effects of television on society.

---

5. Using information from a book written by former First Lady Nancy Reagan in a class discussion on use and abuse of presidential power.

READING ARGUMENTS

Argument is a common mode of presenting and evaluating information. It is also used to establish and evaluate positions on controversial issues. In a philosophy course you might read arguments on individual rights, the rights of the majority, or the existence of God. For a literature class you may read a piece of literary criticism that argues for or against the value of a particular work, debates its significance, or rejects an interpretation.

An argument generally refers to a piece of writing that makes an assertion and provides supporting evidence to support that assertion. Two types of arguments are common: inductive and deductive. An inductive argument reaches a general conclusion from observed specifics. For example, by observing the performance of a large number of athletes, you could conclude that athletes possess physical stamina.

A deductive argument, on the other hand, begins with a general conclusion and moves to specifics. For example, from the general conclusion that "Athletes possess physical stamina," you can reason that because Anthony is an athlete, he must possess physical stamina.

Both types of arguments begin with statements that are assumed to be correct. Basically, both follow a general pattern of "If that is so, then this is so. . . ." At times, an argument may be more complex, involving several steps—"If that is so, and this happens, then this should be done." Here are a few examples of arguments:

- Many students have part-time jobs that require them to work late afternoons and evenings during the week. These students are unable to use the library during the week. Therefore, library hours should be extended to weekends.

- Because parents have the right to determine their children's sexual attitudes, sex education should take place in the home, not at school.

- No one should be forced to inhale unpleasant or harmful substances. That's why the ban on cigarette smoking in public places was put into effect in our state. Why shouldn't there be a law to prevent people from wearing strong colognes or perfumes, especially in restaurants, since sense of smell is important to taste?

When reading arguments, use the following steps:

1. **Identify the assertion—what is being argued for.** Determine what position, idea, or action the writer is trying to convince you to accept. Often, a concise statement of this key point appears early in the argument or in the introduction of a formal essay. This point is often restated.

2. **Read the entire article or essay.** Underline important parts of the argument.

3. **Watch for conclusions.** Words and phrases like "since," "thus," "therefore," "accordingly," "it can be concluded," "it is clear that," and "it follows that" are signals that a conclusion is about to be given.

4. **Notice the types of evidence the author provides.**

5. **Identify the specific action or position the writer is arguing for.**

6. **Reread the argument and examine its content and structure.** What is stated? What is implied or suggested? What assertions are made?

7. **Write a brief outline of the argument and list its key points.** Pragmatic learners may find this step especially helpful.

8. **Discuss the argument with a friend or classmate.** Especially if you are a social or auditory learner, you may "hear" yourself summarizing the assertion or evaluating the evidence supplied.

Now, read the following brief article and apply the previous steps.

EQUALITY ISN'T SAMENESS

Soldiers guilty of misconduct must be punished, but let's not sacrifice common sense and our national defense on the altar of feminism and political correctness.

It's unconscionable that military supervisors would take advantage of female subordinates. These officers have violated a special trust. But the Army's scandal raises a very serious question: Does placing men and women in forced intimate settings for extended periods promote or detract from military effectiveness?

Desert Storm commander Gen. Norman Schwarzkopf testified to Congress, "Decisions on what roles women should play in war must be based on military standards, not women's rights."

On the modern battlefield, every soldier is a potential combatant, and all should have equal opportunity to survive. Women don't. That doesn't mean women and men aren't equal. They are, but equality is not sameness. Women are not equally equipped to survive in the violent and physically difficult environment of combat because they have 50% less upper body strength and 70% of a man's aerobic fitness.

The Clinton administration removed many exemptions for women in the military. Congress helped by rescinding laws that precluded their combat service. All without considering the findings of the 1992 President's Commission of the Assignment of Women in the Armed Forces.

Integrating the sexes has become a difficult challenge for commanders. Merely raising the women-in-the-military issue is to jeopardize one's career.

Commanders have the nearly impossible task of fighting the enemy while minimizing the impact of sexual tensions, which creates readiness problems, such as increased fraternization, sex-based rivalries and many unwanted pregnancies. Readiness also suffers because many pregnant soldiers can no longer perform their mission and often must be replaced on short notice with less experienced personnel.

The goal of the military is to protect and defend the United States, but social experiments are weakening the armed forces. Those who engage in sexual improprieties must be prosecuted, but the status of women in the armed services must be reviewed in light of reality instead of some mystical feminist agenda. We have a duty to support those who volunteer to serve us.

Maginnis, "Equality Isn't Sameness."

This article is arguing for reconsidering the place of women in the armed forces. The author makes a four-part argument, offering four reasons why we should rethink women's military roles. The argument can be outlined as follows:

REASONS

1. Women are not equally equipped to survive in combat.
2. Commanders face the added task of controlling sexual tensions and at the same time fighting the enemy.
3. Military readiness suffers because of pregnancies.
4. The armed forces are being weakened by "social experiments" such as placing women in combat roles.

CONCLUSION

Therefore, the current role of women in the military should be reconsidered.

EXERCISE 11–2

DIRECTIONS: Read the following argument and answer the questions that follow.

"The life of each man should be sacred to each other man," the ancients tell us. They unflinchingly executed murderers. They realized it is not enough to proclaim the sacredness and inviolability of human life. It must be secured as well, by threatening with the loss of their own life those who violate what has been proclaimed as inviolable—the right of innocents to live. Else the inviolability of human life is neither credibly proclaimed nor actually protected. No society can profess that the lives of its members are secure if those who did not allow innocent others to continue living are themselves allowed to continue living—at the expense of the community. To punish a murderer by incarcerating him as one does a pickpocket cannot but cheapen human life. Murder differs in quality from other crimes and deserves, therefore, a punishment that differs in quality from other punishments. There is a discontinuity. It should be underlined, not blurred.

Van Den Haag, "Capital Punishment."

1. What is the author's position on the death penalty?

   _____

2. Summarize the argument.

   _____

   _____

   _____

   _____

   _____

EVALUATING ARGUMENTS

Once you have understood the article by identifying what is asserted and how it is asserted, the next step is to evaluate the soundness, correctness, and worth of the argument. Specifically, you must evaluate evidence, both type and relevancy, definition of terms, cause-effect relationships, value systems, and recognition of counterarguments.

Types of Evidence

The validity of an inductive argument rests, in part, on the soundness and correctness of the evidence provided to draw the conclusion. The validity of a deductive argument, on the other hand, rests on the accuracy and correctness of the premises on which the argument is based. Evaluating each type of argument involves assessing the accuracy and correctness of statements on which the argument is based. Writers often provide evidence to substantiate their observations or premises. As a critical reader, your task is to assess whether or not the evidence is sufficient to support the claim. Here are a few types of evidence often used:

Personal Experience

Writers often substantiate their ideas through experience and observation. Although a writer's personal account of a situation may provide an interesting perspective on an issue, personal experience should not be accepted as proof. The observer may be biased or may have exaggerated or incorrectly perceived a situation.

Examples

Examples are descriptions of particular situations that are used to illustrate or explain a principle, concept, or idea. To explain what aggressive behavior is, your psychology instructor may offer several examples: fighting, punching, and kicking. Examples should *not* be used by themselves to prove the concept or idea they illustrate, as is done in the following sample:

> The American judicial system treats those who are called for jury duty unfairly. It is clear from my sister's experience that the system has little regard for the needs of those called as jurors. My sister was required to report for jury duty the week she was on vacation. She spent the entire week in a crowded, stuffy room waiting to be called to sit on a jury and never was called.

Statistics

Many people are impressed by statistics—the reporting of figures, percentages, averages, and so forth—and assume they are irrefutable proof. Actually, statistics can be misused, misinterpreted, or used selectively to give other than the most objective, accurate picture of a situation. Suppose you read that magazine X has increased its readership by 50 percent while magazine Y made only a 10 percent increase. From this statistic some readers might assume that magazine X has a wider readership than magazine Y. However, if provided with complete information, you can see that this is not true. The missing, but crucial, statistic is the total readership of each magazine before the increase. If magazine X had a readership of 20,000, and increased it by 50 percent, its readership would total 30,000. However, if magazine Y's readership was already 50,000, a 10 percent increase (bringing the new total to 55,000) would still give it the larger readership despite the fact that it made the smaller increase. Approach statistical evidence with a critical, questioning attitude. (See Critical Reading Tip #6, p. 275.)

Comparisons and Analogies

Comparisons or analogies (extended comparisons) serve as illustrations and are often used in argument. Their reliability depends on how closely the comparison corresponds or how similar it is to the situation to which it is being compared. For example, Martin Luther King Jr., in his famous letter from the Birmingham jail, compared nonviolent protesters to a robbed man. To evaluate this comparison you would need to consider how the two are similar and how they are different.

EXERCISE 11–3

DIRECTIONS: For the article "Equality Isn't Sameness" on page 450, evaluate whether the author uses adequate evidence to support his claim. ■

Relevancy and Sufficiency of Evidence

Once you have identified the evidence used to support an argument, the next step is to decide if there is enough of the right kind of evidence to lead you to accept the writer's claim. This is always a matter of judgment; there are no easy rules to follow. You must determine whether the evidence provided directly supports the statement, and whether sufficient evidence has been provided.

Suppose you are reading an article in your campus newspaper that states that Freshman Composition 101 should not be required of all students at your college. As evidence, the writer provides the following:

Composition does not prepare us for the job market. Besides, the reading assignments have no relevancy to modern times.

This argument provides neither adequate nor sufficient evidence. The writer does nothing to substantiate his claims of irrelevancy of the course to the job market or modern times. For the argument to be regarded seriously, the writer needs to provide facts, statistics, expert opinion, or other forms of documentation.

EXERCISE 11–4

DIRECTIONS: Read the following argument, and pay particular attention to the type(s) of evidence used. Then answer the questions that follow.

It is predictable. At Halloween, thousands of children trick-or-treat in Indian costumes. At Thanksgiving, thousands of children parade in school pageants wearing plastic headdresses and pseudo-buckskin clothing. Thousands of card shops stock Thanksgiving greeting cards with images of cartoon animals wearing feathered headbands. Thousands of teachers and librarians trim bulletin boards with Anglo-featured, feathered Indian boys and girls. Thousands of gift shops load their shelves with Indian figurines and jewelry.

Fall and winter are also the seasons when hundreds of thousands of sports fans root for professional, college and public school teams with names that summon up Indians—"Braves," "Redskins," "Chiefs." (In New York State, one out of eight junior and senior high school teams call themselves "Indians," "Tomahawks" and the like.) War-whooping team mascots are imprinted on school uniforms, postcards, notebooks, tote bags and car floor mats.

All of this seems innocuous; why make a fuss about it? Because these trappings and holiday symbols offend tens of thousands of other Americans—the Native American people. Because these invented images prevent millions of us from understanding the authentic Indian America, both long ago and today. Because this image-making prevents Indians from being a relevant part of the nation's social fabric.

Hirschfelder, "It's Time to Stop Playing Indians."

1. What type(s) of evidence is used?

_____

2. Is the evidence convincing?

_____

_____

3. Is there sufficient evidence?

_____

4. What other types of evidence could have been used to strengthen the argument?

_____ ▬

Definition of Terms

A clear and effective argument carefully defines key terms and uses them consistently. For example, an essay arguing for or against animal rights should state what is meant by the term, describe or define those rights, and use that definition through the entire argument.

The following two paragraphs are taken from two different argumentative essays on pornography. Notice how in the first paragraph the author carefully defines what he means by pornography before proceeding with his argument, while in the second the term is not clearly defined.

PARAGRAPH 1: CAREFUL DEFINITION

There is unquestionably more pornography available today than 15 years ago. However, is it legitimate to assume that more is worse? Pornography is speech, words, and pictures about sexuality. No one would consider an increase in the level of speech about religion or politics to be a completely negative development. What makes speech about sexuality different?

Lynn, "Pornography's Many Different Forms: Not All Bad."

PARAGRAPH 2: VAGUE DEFINITION

If we are not talking about writing laws, defining pornography doesn't pose as serious a problem. We do have different tastes. Maybe some of mine come from my middle-class background (my mother wouldn't think so!). I don't like bodies presented without heads, particularly female bodies. The motive may sometimes be the protection of the individual, but the impression is decapitation, and I also happen to be someone who is attracted to people's faces. This is a matter of taste.

Rule, "Pornography Is a Social Disease."

Cause-Effect Relationships

Arguments are often built around the assumption of a cause-effect relationship. For example, an argument supporting gun control legislation may claim that ready availability of guns contributes to an increased number of shootings. This argument implies that availability of guns causes increased use. If the writer provides no evidence that this cause-effect relationship exists, you should question the accuracy of the statement. (See Critical Reading Tip #5, p. 229.)

Implied or Stated Value System

An argument often implies or rests on a value system (a structure of what the writer feels is right, wrong, worthwhile, and important). However, everyone possesses a personal value system, and although our culture promotes many major points of agreement (murder is wrong, human life is worthwhile, and so forth), it also allows points of departure. One person may think that telling lies is always wrong; another person may say it depends on the circumstance. Some people have a value system based on religious beliefs; others may not share those beliefs.

In evaluating an argument, look for value judgments and then decide if the judgments are consistent with and acceptable to your personal value system. Here are a few examples of value judgment statements:

1. Abortion is wrong.
2. Financial aid for college should be available to everyone regardless of income.
3. Capital punishment violates human rights.

Recognition of Counterarguments

An effective argument often includes a refutation of counterarguments—a line of reasoning that can be used to deny or refute what the writer is arguing for. For example, if a writer is arguing against gun control, he or she may recognize the counterargument that availability of guns causes shootings and refute it by saying "Guns don't kill people, people kill people."

Notice how in the excerpt from an essay advocating capital punishment, the author recognizes the counterargument that everyone has a right to live and argues against it.

> Abolitionists [of the death penalty] insist that we all have an imprescriptible right to live to our natural term: if the innocent victim had a right to live, so does the murderer. That takes egalitarianism too far for my taste. The crime sets victim and murderer apart; if the victim died, the murderer does not deserve to live. If innocents are to be secure in their lives murderers cannot be. The thought that murderers are to be given as much right to live as their victims oppresses me. So does the thought that a Stalin, Hitler, an Idi Amin should have as much right to live as their victims did.
>
> Van Den Haag, "Capital Punishment."

Identifying Assumptions

Many writers begin an argument assuming that a particular set of facts or principles is true. Then they develop their argument based on that assumption. Of course, if the assumption is not correct or if it cannot be proven, the arguments that depend on that assumption may be incorrect. For instance, the following passage begins with an assumption (*underlined*) that the writer makes no attempt to prove or justify. Rather, he uses it as a starting point to develop his ideas on the function of cities.

> <u>Given that the older central cities have lost their capacity to serve as effective staging areas for newcomers</u>, the question inevitably poses itself: What is the function of these cities? Permit me to suggest that it has become essentially that of a sandbox.
>
> A sandbox is a place where adults park their children in order to converse, play, or work with a minimum of interference. The adults, having found a distraction for the children, can get on with the serious things of life. There is some reward for the children in all this. The sandbox is given to them as their turf. . . .
>
> Palen, *City Scenes.*

The author offers no reasons or evidence in support of the opening statement: it is assumed to be true. This assumption is the base on which the author builds his argument that the city is a sandbox.

As you read arguments, always begin by examining the author's initial assumptions. Decide whether you agree or disagree with them as a check to see whether the author provides any evidence that his or her assumptions are accurate. Once you have identified an assumption, consider this question: If the assumption were untrue, how would it affect the argument?

EXERCISE 11–5

DIRECTIONS: Read the following argument by Luis Rodriguez, and answer the questions that follow.

REKINDLING THE WARRIOR

Over the past year and a half, I have spoken to thousands of young people at schools, jails, bookstores, colleges, and community centers about the experiences addressed in my book *Always Running: La Vida Loca, Gang Days in L.A.*

What stays with me is the vitality and clarity of the young people I met, many of them labeled "at risk." They saw in my experiences and my book both a reflection of their lives and the possibility of transcendence, of change, which otherwise appears elusive. In those faces I saw the most viable social energy for rebuilding the country and realigning its resources. They are the future, but this society has no clear pathway to take them there.

For one thing, today's youth are under intense scrutiny and attack. Schools, for the most part, fail to engage their creativity and intellect. As a result, young people find their own means of expression—music being the most obvious example, but also the formation of gangs.

Despite conventional thinking, gangs are not anarchies. They can be highly structured, with codes of honor and discipline. For many members, the gang serves as family, as the only place where they can find fellowship, respect, a place to belong. You often hear the word love among gang members. Sometimes the gang is the only place where they can find it.

Gabriel Rivera, director of the Transitional Intervention Experience of Bend, Oregon, and a former East Los Angeles gang member, came up with a concept he calls "character in motion" to describe the essence, not the form, of gang participation.

"[Character in motion] is marked by the advertent or inadvertent beginnings of physical, psychological, and spiritual struggle that happens for every young person," writes Rivera. "[It] is what happens when a young person responds to the inevitable inner call to embrace 'the journey,' and chooses to honor that journey above all else with a courage that relies upon connecting with one's 'warrior energy.'"

The warrior needs to be nurtured, directed, and guided—not smothered, crushed, or corralled. This energy needs to be taken to its next highest level of development, where one matures into self-control, self-study, and self-actualization. Most anti-gang measures have nothing to do with any of this. A serious effort would address the burning issue of adolescent rage. It would address a basic need for food, shelter, and clothing, but also needs for expressive creativity and community.

Sociopathic behavior exists within the framework of a sociopathic society. Under these circumstances, gangs are not a problem; they are a solution, particularly for communities lacking economic, social, and political options.

Two examples: Two years ago, I did a poetry reading in a part of eastern Ohio that was once alive with coal mines and industry but now has 50 to 70 percent unemployment in some areas. Many of the young people are selling drugs to survive. In this sense, they could be from the South Bronx or the Pine Ridge Reservation. They are, however, "white." They are listening to their own music ("Wherever kids find obstacles, I find music," an independent record producer recently told *Rolling Stone* magazine), and establishing ganglike structures to survive.

Soon after the 1992 Los Angeles rebellion, members of the Crips and the Bloods, two of the city's most notorious gangs, circulated a plan. They included proposals to repair the schools and streets and get rid of drugs and violence. At the end of the plan, they wrote: "Give us the hammers and the nails, and we will rebuild the city."

It was a demand to take responsibility, which rose from the inner purpose of Crip and Blood warrior consciousness, and a demand for the authority to carry out the plan. Unfortunately, no one took them up on it.

These young people face great barriers to educational advancement, economic stability, and social mobility—but little or none to criminal activity or violence (as everyone knows, prison is no deterrence; for some youth it is a rite of passage).

Power is the issue here. Without autonomy to make decisions that affect their lives, these young people can only attempt to approximate it, too often with disastrous results.

You want to stop the body count? Empower the youth.

1. Summarize the author's position on gangs.

_____

_____

2. What assumptions does Rodriguez make?

_____

_____

3. What type(s) of evidence is offered?

_____

_____

4. Do you feel the evidence is adequate and convincing?

_____

5. What values does the author hold?

_____

_____

6. Does the author refute counterarguments? If so, describe how he does this.

_____

_____

ERRORS IN LOGICAL REASONING

Errors in reasoning, often called logical fallacies, are common in arguments. These errors invalidate the argument or render it flawed. Several common errors in logic are described below.

Circular Reasoning

Also known as begging the question, this error involves using part of the conclusion as evidence to support it. Here are a few examples:

Cruel medical experimentation on defenseless animals is inhumane.

Female soldiers should not be placed in battle situations because combat is a man's job.

In circular reasoning, because no evidence is given to support the claim, there is no reason to accept the conclusion.

Hasty Generalization

This fallacy means that the conclusion has been derived from insufficient evidence. Here is one example: You taste three tangerines and each is sour, so you conclude that all tangerines are sour. Here is another: By observing one performance of a musical group, you conclude that the group is unfit to perform.

Non Sequitur ("It Does Not Follow")

The false establishment of cause-effect is known as a non sequitur. To say, for example, that "Because my instructor is young, I'm sure she'll be a good teacher" is a non sequitur because youth does not cause good teaching. Here is another example: "Sam Goodwin is the best choice for state senator because he understands the people." Understanding the people will not necessarily make someone an effective state senator.

False Cause

The false cause fallacy is the incorrect assumption that two events that follow each other in time are causally related. Suppose you walked under a ladder and then tripped on an uneven sidewalk. If you said you tripped because you walked under the ladder, you would be assuming false cause.

Either-Or Fallacy

This fallacy assumes that an issue is only two sided, or that there are only two choices or alternatives for a particular situation. In other words, there is no middle ground. Consider the issue of censorship of violence on television. An either-or fallacy is to assume that violence on TV must either be allowed or banned. This fallacy does not recognize other alternatives such as limiting access through viewing hours, restricting the showing of certain types of violence, and so forth.

Emotional Appeal

Also called *ad populum* (to the people), this logical fallacy appeals to the prejudices and emotions of people. For example, an advertisement for a new clothing line may appeal to a reader's sense of patriotism by suggesting that a product is American made using fabrics manufactured made in the U.S. and sewn only by American workers. A writer may use this appeal as a means of omitting evidence that readers need to properly evaluate the writer's claim.

False Analogy

An analogy is an extended comparison between two otherwise unlike things. A sound analogy assumes that two things are alike in some ways. A false analogy compares two things that do not share a likeness. A writer arguing against gun control may say, "Guns are not a major problem in this country. Fatal accidents on the road, in the workplace, and at home kill many more people than do guns." Here the writer is suggesting that death by guns is similar to fatal accidents in the car, on the job, or at home. Yet, accidents and murder are not similar.

Bandwagon Appeal

The bandwagon appeal suggests that readers should accept an idea or take a particular action because everyone else believes or does it. In arguing that an idea or action is popular, and therefore, right or just, allows the writer to evade discussing the issue itself and avoid presenting evidence to support the claim. Here is an example of a bandwagon appeal. "Eighty-five percent of women say they prefer gas ovens and stovetops. Women in the know use gas—so should you."

Ad hominem

An *ad hominem* (against the man) is an attack on a person rather than on the issue or argument at hand. An *ad hominem* argument may attack the speaker or author of a statement, rather than the statement itself. For example, a bulimic teenager may reject the medical advice of her physician by arguing that her physician knows nothing about bulimia since the physician has never experienced it. Or a politician may attack an opponent's personal characteristics or lifestyle rather than his or her political platform.

Abstract Concepts as Reality

Writers occasionally treat abstract concepts as real things that hold a single opinion. For example, a writer may say, "Research proves that divorce is harmful to children." Actually, there are hundred of pieces of research on the effects of divorce and they offer diverse findings and conclusions. Some but not all research reports harmful effects. Here is another example: "Criminology shows us that prisons are seldom effective in controlling crime." Writers tend to use this device to make it seem as if all authorities are in agreement with their positions. This device also allows writers to ignore contrary or contradictory opinion.

Red Herring

A red herring is something that is added to an argument to divert attention from the issue at hand. It is introduced into an argument to throw readers off track. Think of a red herring as an argumentative tactic, rather than an error in reasoning. Suppose you are reading an essay that argues for the death penalty. If the author suddenly starts reporting about the horrific living conditions of death row prisons and the unjust treatment of prisoners, the writer is introducing a red herring. The living conditions and treatment of prisoners on death row are not relevant to whether the death penalty is just.

EXERCISE 11–6

DIRECTIONS: Identify the logical fallacy in each of the following statements; write your answer in the space provided.

1. All Native American students in my accounting class earned A grades, so Native Americans must excel with numerical tasks.

   _____

2. If you are not in favor of nuclear arms control, then you're against protecting our future.

   _____

3. Linguistics proves that the immersion approach is the only way to learn a second language.

   _____

4. My sister cannot compose business letters or memos because she has writer's block.

   _____

5. People who smoke have a higher mortality rate than nonsmokers. Urban dwellers have a higher mortality rate than suburban dwellers. Now, since we do not urge urban dwellers to move to the suburbs, why should we urge smokers to quit smoking?

---

6. A well-known senator, noting a decline in the crime rate in the four largest cities in his state, quickly announced that his new "get-tough on criminals" publicity campaign was successful and took credit for the decline.

---

7. I always order cheesecake for dessert because I am allergic to chocolate.

---

8. Stricter driving while intoxicated laws are needed in this country. It is a real shame that some adults allow preschool age children to drink sips of wine and to taste beer long before they reach the age of reason. If stricter driving laws were in place, many lives would be saved.

---

9. Did you know that Dr. Smith is single? How could she possibly be a good marriage counselor?

---

10. Two million pet owners feed their pets VitaBrite Tabs to keep their dogs healthy and increase longevity. Buy some today for your best friend.

EXERCISE 11-7

DIRECTIONS: The following two essays were written in response to the question "Should animals be used in research?" Read each essay and answer the questions that follow.

DIALOGUE

ARGUMENT 1: SHOULD ANIMALS BE USED IN RESEARCH?

The use of animals in research has become an extremely emotional as well as legal issue. Very strict federal regulations on the care, maintenance, and use of animals in research now exist. But even though research using animals is closely monitored to identify and eliminate any potential source of pain or abuse of experimental animals, activists still object to the use of animal species, particularly the vertebrates, for research.

Those who oppose the use of animals have become caught up in the developments of the "high tech" world and frequently propose the use of simulators and computer modeling to replace biological research with live animals. Unfortunately, simulators and computer modeling cannot generate valid biological data on their own. Scientific data obtained from experiments using live animals must first provide base data before modelers can extrapolate results under similar conditions.

Simulators and computer modeling do have their place in teaching and research, but they will not and cannot replace the use of animals in many kinds of critical medical research. For example, consider modern surgical procedures in human organ repair and transplanting. The techniques in use today were developed and perfected through the use of laboratory animals. Would you want a delicate operation to be performed by a physician trained only on simulators?

Laboratory animal research is fundamental to medical progress in many other areas as well. Vaccines for devastating human diseases like polio and smallpox and equally serious animal diseases like rabies, feline leukemia, and distemper were all developed through the use of research animals.

The discovery, development, and refinement of drugs that could arrest, control, or eliminate such human diseases as AIDS, cancer, and heart disease all require the use of laboratory animals whose physiological mechanisms are similar to humans.

I have only noted above a few of the many examples where animals have been used in human and veterinary medical research. It's also important to note that studies in behavior, ecology, physiology, and genetics all require the use of animals, in some capacity, to produce valid and meaningful knowledge about life on this planet.

Donald W. Tuff

ARGUMENT 2: SHOULD ANIMALS BE USED IN RESEARCH?

I cannot accept the argument that research on animals is necessary to discover "cures" for humans. Many diseases and medications react very differently in animals than they do in humans. Aspirin, for example, is toxic to cats, and there are few diseases directly transmittable from cats to humans.

I particularly abhor the "research" conducted for cosmetic purposes. The Draise test—where substances are introduced into the eyes of rabbits and then examined to see if ulcers, lesions or other observable reactions take place—is archaic and inefficient. Other alternatives exist that are more accurate and do not cause unnecessary suffering to our fellow creatures.

Household products such as the LD–50 test are also tested needlessly on animals. This test is routinely used in substances like bleach. Animals, in many cases puppies, are force-fed these toxic chemicals to determine the dosage at which exactly 50 percent of them die. These tests are not necessary and do not give very useful information.

Many top medical schools no longer use animals for teaching purposes, but have their medical students practice on models, computer simulations, and then observe techniques on human patients. A medical doctor is expected to honor and revere life, and this approach emphasizes that idea.

If medical students are deliberately taught that animal life is not important, then the next step to devaluing human life is made that much easier. Anatomy and biology classes do not need to use cats for all their students, either. A video of a dissection that is shown to the entire class or a model or computer simulation would be just as effective.

If an experiment using animals is deemed absolutely necessary, then that claim should be fully documented and all previous research should be examined thoroughly to avoid needless replication. In addition, the facility should not be exempt from cruelty laws and should be open to inspection by animal rights advocates not affiliated with the research institution.

Humans have a duty to take care of the earth and to respect all life, for if we poison the earth and annihilate other life on the planet, we are poisoning and annihilating ourselves. We were put on this earth to take care of our earth and the creatures upon it.

Angela Molina

ARGUMENT 1

1. Summarize Tuff's position on the use of laboratory animals.

   _____

   _____

2. Outline the main points of his argument.

   _____

   _____

   _____

   _____

3. What types of evidence does he offer?

   _____

   _____

   _____

4. Evaluate the adequacy and sufficiency of the evidence provided.

   _____

5. Does the author recognize or refute counterarguments?

   _____

   _____

ARGUMENT 2

1. Summarize Molina's position.

    _____

2. Outline the main points of her argument.

    _____

    _____

    _____

    _____

    _____

    _____

3. What types of evidence does she offer?

    _____

    _____

    _____

4. Evaluate the adequacy and sufficiency of the evidence provided.

    _____

    _____

    _____

    _____

5. Does the author recognize or refute counterarguments?

    _____

BOTH ARGUMENTS

1. Which argument do you feel is stronger? Why?

    _____

2. Compare the types of evidence each uses.

    _____

    _____

Critical Thinking Tip #11

Evaluating Emotional Appeals

Emotional appeals attempt to involve or excite readers by appealing to their emotions, thereby controlling the reader's attitude toward the subject. Several types of emotional appeals are described here.

1. **Emotionally Charged or Biased Language** By using words that create an emotional response, writers establish positive or negative feelings. For example, an advertisement for a new line of fragrances promises to "indulge," "refresh," "nourish," and "pamper" the user. An ad for an automobile uses phrases such as "limousine comfort," "European styling," and "animal sleekness" to interest and excite readers.

2. **Testimonials** A testimonial involves using the opinion or action of a well-known or famous person. We have all seen athletes endorsing underwear or movie stars selling shampoo. This type of appeal works on the notion that people admire celebrities and strive to be like them, respect their opinions, and are willing to accept their viewpoints.

3. **Association** An emotional appeal also is made by associating a product, idea, or position with others that are already accepted or highly regarded. Patriotism is already valued, so to call a product "All American" in an advertisement is an appeal to the emotions. A car being named a Cougar to remind you of a fast, sleek animal, a cigarette ad picturing a scenic waterfall, or a speaker standing in front of an American flag are other examples of association.

4. **Appeal to "Common Folk"** Some people distrust those who are well educated, wealthy, highly artistic, or in other ways distinctly different from the average person. An emotional appeal to this group is made by selling a product or idea by indicating that it is originated from, held by, or bought by ordinary citizens. A commercial may advertise a product by showing its use in an average household. A politician may describe her background and education to suggest that she is like everyone else; a salesperson may dress in styles similar to his clients.

5. **"Join the Crowd" Appeal** The appeal to do, believe, or buy what everyone else is doing, believing, or buying is known as crowd appeal. Commercials that proclaim their product as the "Number one best-selling car in America" are appealing to this motive. Essays that cite opinion polls on a controversial issue in support of a position—"sixty-eight percent of Americans favor capital punishment"—are also using this appeal.

**EXERCISE
11–8**

*Academic
Application*

DIRECTIONS: From among the reading assignments you have completed this semester, choose one that involved persuasive or argumentative writing. Review this piece of writing and then complete the following.

1. Summarize what is being argued for.
2. List the key points of the argument.
3. Indicate what type of evidence the writer uses.
4. Determine if the evidence is adequate and sufficient to support the author's point.
5. Identify any counterarguments the author recognizes or refutes.

**EXERCISE
11–9**

*Electronic
Application*

DIRECTIONS: Visit a newsgroup that focuses on a controversial issue and either observe or participate in the discussion. What persuasive techniques or emotional appeals (see Critical Thinking Tip #11) did you observe? ▬

SUMMARY

1. What is involved in evaluating arguments and persuasive writing?

Persuasive and argumentative writing urges the reader to take action or accept a particular point of view. To evaluate this type of writing readers must learn to evaluate source and authority, recognize the structure of arguments, and identify logical fallacies in arguments.

2. Why should you consider the source of the material and the author's authority when reading this type of writing?

Evaluating both the source in which material was printed and the competency of its author are essential in evaluating any argument or piece of persuasive writing. Where a piece of writing came from can be an indication of the type of information that will be presented as well as its accuracy and value. The author's qualifications and level of expertise with the subject provide a further indication of the reliability of this information.

3. How can you read arguments more effectively?

Since both inductive and deductive arguments make assertions and give evidence to support them, when reading them it is important to
- identify what is being argued for
- read very closely and carefully
- watch for conclusions
- be alert to the types of evidence given
- reread to examine both content and structure
- underline or outline the key parts

4. How should you evaluate an argument?

Critical readers evaluate the soundness, correctness, and worth of an argument. To do so,
- determine the type of evidence used
- decide if there is enough and the right kind of evidence
- notice if key terms are defined and used properly
- be alert to value judgments, assumptions, or cause-effect connections
- look for counterarguments and whether they are adequately refuted

5. What are the common errors in logical reasoning?

Eleven common logical fallacies that can weaken or destroy an argument are:
- circular reasoning
- hasty generalization
- non sequitur
- false cause
- either-or fallacy
- emotional appeal
- false analogy
- bandwagon appeal
- *ad hominem*
- abstract concepts as reality
- red herring

READING SELECTION 21

FROM A VEGETARIAN: LOOKING AT HUNTING FROM BOTH SIDES NOW

Timothy Denesha
From *The Buffalo News*

This editorial, originally published in The Buffalo News, *explores the issue of sports hunting. Read the essay to answer the following questions:*

1. What was Denesha's original position on sports hunting?

2. How has his position changed?

— · —

1   Deer hunting season opened Nov. 18, and as the gunfire resumes in our woodlands and fields so will the perennial sniping between hunters and animal rights supporters. I always feel caught in the cross-fire on this matter, because I have been a vegetarian and animal rights advocate for over 25 years, but I also have friends I respect who are hunters. I've learned the issue is not as black-and-white as I once believed.

2   Growing up with many beloved pets and no hunters in my life, I assumed these people were bloodthirsty animal haters. When, in my 20s, I read the great humanitarian Albert Schweitzer's writings on reverence for life, I became a vegetarian and even more contemptuous of hunters.

3   But I had to revise my opinion after seeing the classic 1981 African film, "The Gods Must Be Crazy." The hero, a good-hearted bushman slays a small gazelle, then tenderly strokes her, apologizing for taking her life. He explains his family is hungry and thanks her for providing food. I was stunned: a hunter practicing reverence for life! Later, I learned that Native American tradition has the same compassionate awareness about life lost so another life may be sustained.

4   My position softened further several years ago when Alex Pacheco, a leading animals-rights activist, spoke here. Detailing inhumane prac-

tices at meat-packing plants and factory farms, he said the most important thing anyone could do to lessen animal suffering was to stop eating meat. I decided to work toward being vegan (eating no animal products) and reluctantly admitted that hunters were not the animal kingdom's worst enemies. However, I still disliked them.

5   What really changed my perspective was getting to know some hunters personally, through my job at a Red Cross blood-donation center. Some of my co-workers and a number of our donors are civic-minded people who donate blood (which most people don't) but also shed animal blood with their guns and arrows. Confronting this paradox brought me some realizations.

6   First, hunters are like any group that differs from me: lacking personal experience of them made it easier to demonize them. They aren't monsters. I don't know if any of them apologizes to or thanks his kill as the hungry bushman did, but I do know they aren't cruel, sadistic or bloodthirsty—quite the opposite, as I later discovered.

7   Second, these people aren't just amusing themselves by ending a life; they are acquiring food. This death that sustains another life has a meaning that, for example, fox hunting does not. To the animal, this distinction may mean little. But it is significant when considering a person's intentions.

8   Also, I was informed that hunters don't "like to kill." They enjoy the outdoors, the camaraderie and the various skills involved. (One of these skills, the "clean kill," is prized precisely because it minimizes suffering.) Like vegetable gardeners,

they enjoy providing food [for] themselves and their families with their own hands. Like those who fish, they enjoy a process of food acquisition that involves an animal's death, but not because it does. Again, this may seem a small point (especially to the prey), but I feel it is meaningful from the standpoint of the hunter's humanity.

9   In addition, I've come to see a certain integrity in hunters as meat-eaters who "do their own dirty work." Packaged cold-cuts and fast-food burgers mask the fact of lives bled out on the killing floor. Hunters never forget this, for they accept personal responsibility for it.

10   Furthermore, were I an animal that had to die to feed a human, I'd rather it happen one-on-one, at the hands of that person in the woods that were my home, than amidst the impersonal mass-production machinery of a meat factory. Either way is death, but one way had more dignity, less fear and less suffering.

11   There are bad hunters who trespass, shoot domestic animals, hunt intoxicated or disregard

that cardinal rule of hunting's unwritten code of ethics: wounded prey must not be allowed to suffer. Last Thanksgiving morning in Chestnut Ridge Park, I found a fresh trail of deer tracks in the snow, heavily splashed with blood. It was horrible.

12   One of my hunter co-workers was also upset when I told him about it, and had this story. He himself was able to hunt only one day last season and sighted a small, wounded doe. As a student on a tight budget with a family, he hunts for food and would have preferred to ignore the doe's plight and meet his license limit with a large buck. Instead, he devoted a long, difficult day to trailing her until he was close enough to end her suffering. This was an act of mercy and even self-sacrifice, not the action of a heartless person insensitive to animals. It was reverence for life. He claims many hunters would do and have done the same.

13   And I realized that compassion has many faces, some of the truest the most unexpected.

EXAMINING READING SELECTION 21

Checking Your Vocabulary

Directions: Using context, word parts, or a dictionary if necessary, circle the letter of the meaning for each word as it is used in the reading.

1. contemptuous (paragraph 2)
   a. hateful
   b. suspicious
   c. disrespectful
   d. patronizing

2. reverence (paragraph 3)
   a. tenderness
   b. disbelief
   c. respect
   d. honesty

3. inhumane (paragraph 4)
   a. lacking pity or compassion
   b. not respectful
   c. not purposeful
   d. lacking self-awareness

4. paradox (paragraph 5)
   a. evidence
   b. variation
   c. behavior
   d. contradiction

5. camaraderie (paragraph 8)
   a. risk
   b. thrill
   c. companionship
   d. self-sufficiency

Checking Your Comprehension

Directions: Circle the letter of the best answer.

1. This reading is primarily concerned with
   a. the barbarism of hunting.
   b. the reverence hunters have for human life.
   c. the defensibility of hunting.
   d. why people become vegetarians.

2. The main point in this reading is
   a. it is unethical to hunt.
   b. animals suffer as a result of hunting.
   c. hunters have as much integrity and compassion as nonhunters.
   d. most hunters are only interested in killing helpless creatures for sport.

3. It is clear from the article that the author is *not*
   a. a vegetarian.
   b. a health care worker.
   c. a hunter.
   d. an animal rights advocate.

4. According to the article, hunters
   a. have little respect for animal life.
   b. don't eat processed meat.
   c. hunt only to acquire food.
   d. don't enjoy killing.

5. Initially, what made the author begin to change his mind about hunters?
   a. a speech by Alex Pacheco.
   b. the African film "The Gods Must Be Crazy."
   c. the Red Cross blood donation center.
   d. the writings of Albert Schweitzer.

6. The author discusses the issue of sports hunting primarily by
   a. comparing hunters and non-hunters.
   b. classifying types of hunters.
   c. examining his own changing beliefs.
   d. defining sports hunting.

Thinking Critically

7. As used in the first paragraph, a synonym for "sniping" is
   a. shooting.
   b. cutting.
   c. killing.
   d. arguing.

8. Which of the following statements best describes the author's attitude about hunting?
   a. Hunters are aggressive and blood thirsty.
   b. Hunters often take animals' lives with respect and compassion.
   c. Hunting should not be allowed under any circumstances.
   d. Hunting is just a sport like any other sport.

9. From this reading, we can infer that deer hunters' licenses allow them to
   a. kill as many deer as they choose.
   b. hunt on any property where deer can be found.
   c. hunt only one day per season.
   d. kill only a limited number of deer.

10. Which of the following is an example of a deer hunter abiding by hunting's unwritten code of ethics?
    a. He hunts with a bow and arrow instead of a rifle.
    b. He kills a deer that is already wounded.
    c. He brings a wounded deer to the vet for treatment.
    d. He kills only to supply his family with food.

Questions for Discussion

1. Do you think hunting is moral or immoral? Justify your position.

2. Discuss the ways in which hunters prevent animals from suffering.

3. What lessons can be learned from the author's statement that "Hunters are like any group that differs from me: lacking personal experience of them made it easier to demonize them"?

4. When the author refers to hunting he states that "compassion has many faces." What does he mean? Give an example to support your point.

Selection 21:			822 words
Finishing Time:			
	HR.	MIN.	SEC.
Starting Time:			
	HR.	MIN.	SEC.
Reading Time:			
		MIN.	SEC.
WPM Score:			
Comprehension Score:			_____%

READING SELECTION 22

SOCIOLOGY

OUT OF TIME

Alan Weisman and Sandy Tolan
From *Societies: A Multicultural Reader*

Taken from a collection of multicultural readings that accompany a sociology textbook, this essay focuses on the destruction of lands and cultures of primitive societies. Read it to discover what effects such destruction has had and may have in the future.

— · —

1   An old Indian stands in the rain in northern Argentina, amid the charred ruins of his village. His name is Pa'i Antonio Moreira. Over his thin sweater two strings of black beads crisscross his chest like bandoliers, signifying that he is a ñanderú, a shaman[1] of his people. They are among the last few Guaraní Indians in this country, part of a cultural group that once inhabited a forest stretching from Argentina to the Amazon. Now only remnants of that forest and its creatures and people are left.

2   The night before, government men in forest-service uniforms torched the community's village. The 1,500-acre tract of semitropical wood-

land where they lived is only a few miles from Iguazú Falls, the biggest waterfall in South America. Once sacred to the Guaraní, Iguazú is now overwhelmed by tourists. Moreira's village was burned to make way for yet another hotel. The next Indian village to the south is also gone, swallowed by the waters of a new reservoir. The villages beyond that are no longer surrounded by black laurel and ceiba trees, which sheltered the deer and tapir the Guaraní once hunted, but by silent forests of Monterey pine, imported from California and planted by a nearby paper company for its superior fiber content.

3   The old shaman's kinsmen huddle around a fire, while the embers of their homes hiss and sizzle in the rain. The people descend from a stubborn band of Guaraní who refused to be evangelized when Jesuits arrived here 400 years ago. Moreira tells us that these ills curse the Guaraní's world because white men ignore the true way of God. Only the Indian, he says, remembers how God intended the world to be.

4   Then why, we ask, has God allowed the white man to triumph, and the Indian to suffer?

---
[1] Spiritual leader.

5 He gazes at us from beneath heavy-lidded eyes filled with loss and compassion. "The white man hasn't triumphed," he says softly. "When the Indians vanish, the rest will follow."

6 Throughout the Americas, great changes fueled by visions of progress have swept away the habitats of countless plants and animals. But entire human cultures are also becoming endangered. During the past two years, we traveled to 15 countries, from the United States to Chile, to document this swift, often irreversible destruction.

7 Nations with growing, impoverished populations strike a Faustian[2] bargain with the developed world: to create jobs and electricity for industry, they borrow hundreds of millions of dollars from foreign banks. They build huge dams that flood their richest lands and displace thousands of rural poor. To repay the massive debt, they invite foreign companies to mine their timber, gold, oil, and coal, or convert their farmlands to produce luxury crops for consumers in North America, Europe and Japan. To ease pressures on overcrowded lands, they allow poor settlers to slash and burn their way into virgin forests, where they clash with the indigenous people already living there—including some of the last uncontacted tribes in the hemisphere.

8 For centuries the Yuguí Indians of the Bolivian Amazon roamed naked through jungles so remote they thought no one else existed. Their word for *world* translates simply as *leaves*.

9 "When we first saw the white people, we thought they were the spirits of our dead ancestors," recalled Ataiba, the last of the Yuguí chiefs. He recalled how his people had begun to encounter strange things in the jungle—fresh fish hung from trees, sacks of sugar, cooking pots, machetes—all laid beside new trails. One day, at the end of one of these gift trails, Ataiba saw light-skinned people watching him. After many months, the pale strangers, evangelicals from the Florida-based New Tribes Mission, convinced

Ataiba that they could offer safe haven from the growing violence of confrontations with loggers and settlers. One morning late in 1989, Ataiba led his people out of the forest forever, to become permanent wards of the mission village.

10 Often, on the heels of the missionaries, come the forces of development. In Ecuador during the early 1970s, the government contracted with Texaco to build an oil industry in the Ecuadorian Amazon and help bring the country into the global economy. Until then, many natives there had never even heard of a nation called Ecuador, let alone petroleum.

11 "We didn't know the sound of a motor," explained Toribe, a young Cofán leader. The Cofán, who live along Ecuador's Tío Aguarico, were still hunting peccaries and monkeys with blowguns. "We couldn't figure out what animal could be making those noises." The sounds were Texaco's helicopters. Soon settlers streamed down the oil-company roads, changing life irrevocably for the Cofán.

12 "With the petroleum companies came epidemics," recalled Toribe. "We didn't know flu, measles, and these other illnesses. Many fled from here. Those that stayed were finished. It was all contaminated. There were fifteen thousand of us on this side of the Río Aguarico. Now we are only four hundred."

13 Oil from Ecuador, hardwoods from Bolivia, and from Honduras to Costa Rica to Brazil, beef cattle raised for export where forests once stood; we had stumbled onto another kind of gift trail, this one leading back to the United States. The savanna surrounding Bogotá, Colombia, with some of the finest soil in Latin America, produces not food but bargain-priced roses, chrysanthemums, and carnations to sell on street corners and in supermarkets in the United States and beyond. In Honduras, mangrove forests lining the Gulf of Fonseca's estuaries are threatened by modern mariculture. Huge shrimp farms resist local fishermen's access to the crabs, mollusks, and small fish they have netted for generations.

[2]Faust is a legendary figure who sold his soul to the devil in return for power and knowledge.

14   In Brazil, the biggest dam in the Amazon, Tucurui, has displaced thousands of people and created such mosquito infestations that thousands more are leaving. Tucurui was built to power aluminum smelters owned by U.S., European, and Japanese companies. The ore comes from the Amazon's largest mine, which strips away hundreds of acres of jungle each year to provide foil and cans.

15   On South America's second-biggest river, the Parana, we watched men building the longest dam in the world: Yacyreta, along the Argentina-Paraguay border. More than $1 billion in World Bank and Inter-American Development Bank loans was allegedly diverted from the dam project to finance things like Argentina's Falklands war. Now there's not enough money to relocate the 40,000 people whose cities and farms will be flooded. As much as $30 million was spent, however, on an elevator to carry fish like dorado, a prized local species, upstream to spawn. Unfortunately, the elevator, built by North American dam contractors, was designed for salmon, which go upstream, spawn, and die. Dorado need to return. And there's no down elevator.

16   Our travels did reveal a few signs of hope: a land-recovery program run by villagers in southern Honduras, a proposal to put Kuna Indians in charge of protecting the watershed of Panama's Bayano Dam. But these projects are exceptions. Alone, they are not enough to half the momentous effects of uncontrolled development. Sustainable development must be contoured to local needs rather than imposed from afar by economic forces.

17   When we reached the Strait of Magellan, residents of southern Chile showed us great inland sounds that soon will be dammed to power yet more aluminum smelters—this time Australian. On Tierra del Fuego, they took us to ancient hardwood rainforests, scheduled to be turned into fax paper by Canadian and Japanese companies.

18   Finally, we stood with Professor Bedrich Magas of Chile's Magellan University at the tip of the Americas, looking out toward the growing polar ozone hole. Magas reminded us that the National Aeronautics and Space Administration had recently discovered destructive chlorine over the northern United States—just like that which was found over Antarctica only a few years earlier. It was a disturbing reminder of the warning of the Guaraní shaman: what we do to the lives and lands of others may ultimately determine the fate of our own.

EXAMINING READING SELECTION 22*

Checking Your Vocabulary

Directions: Complete each of the following items; refer to a dictionary if necessary.

1. Discuss the connotative meanings of the word *endangered* (paragraph 6).

2. Define each of the following words:
   a. evangelized (paragraph 3)

   _____

   b. habitats (paragraph 6)

   _____

   c. wards (paragraph 9)

   _____

   _____

   d. allegedly (paragraph 15)

   _____

   e. epidemics (paragraph 12)

   _____

   _____

_____
*Multiple-choice questions are contained in Part 6 (page 611).

3. Define the word *indigenous* (paragraph 7) and underline the word or phrase that provides a context clue for its meaning.

_____

_____

4. Define the word *contoured* (paragraph 16) and underline the word or phrase that provides a context clue for its meaning.

_____

_____

5. Determine the meanings of the following words by using word parts:
   a. semitropical (paragraph 2)

   _____

   b. displace (paragraph 7)

   _____

   c. irrevocably (paragraph 11)

   _____

   d. mariculture (paragraph 13)

   _____

   e. diverted (paragraph 15)

   _____

Checking Your Comprehension

1. Why is Iguazú no longer sacred to the Guaraní?

   _____

   _____

2. Why were the black laurel and ceiba trees in the Indian villages of Argentina replaced by Monterey pine?

   _____

   _____

   _____

3. Explain why the Yuguí Indians of the Bolivian Amazon referred to "world" as "leaves."

   _____

   _____

   _____

   _____

4. Why were many people from the Cofán in Ecuador forced to leave after the petroleum companies came?

   _____

   _____

   _____

   _____

Thinking Critically

1. What did the authors mean when they said that impoverished populations struck a "Faustian bargain with the developed world. . . ."?

   _____

   _____

   _____

   _____

   _____

   _____

   _____

2. Why did Ataiba, a Yuguí chief, lead his people from the forest to the mission village? Was this decision in the best interest of his people? Why or why not?

   _____

   _____

Chapter 9
Critical Reading

QUESTIONING, COMPARING, AND EVALUATING

In preceding chapters you have learned how to read in order to obtain literal comprehension of what an author actually states on the printed page. You have also learned that after you comprehend what is stated, you need to read "between the lines" to get a clearer meaning by understanding the author's implied meanings. To be a truly successful reader, you must now read beyond what is stated and implied so that you can analyze the material according to your purpose for reading. Critical reading is an active, creative skill that requires you to *question, compare,* and *evaluate.* Critical-reading skills are necessary in order to determine the value of reading material, to detect faulty logic and information, to separate facts from opinions, and then to determine whether you need to accept or reject the information.

If you never questioned what you read, you would accept every bit of information as fact and every author's opinions as your own. Simply because material is published does not make it relevant to your needs.

If you never compared what you read, you would have no standard by which to judge and would not be able to select the best information for your needs. Comparison is essential, especially when you read conflicting information and interpretations.

If you never evaluated, you would never know whether what you read or hear is valuable or whether it is worthless. In other words, you would not know whether the reading material was worth your valuable time needed to read it.

Critical reading could be considered a form of critical thinking. You think critically each day in everything you do. It is the means by which you make each decision, purchase any product, and decide what to say or do in any situation. Critical thinking also guides you in developing opinions of major and minor happenings in your life. For example, you use critical thinking (and reading) when you decide which brand of jeans to buy. First you *question* the cost, shrinkage, durability, and appearance. Next, you *compare* the brand you are considering with other brands you have worn, heard about from friends, or seen advertised. Finally, you *evaluate* on the basis of your own needs, budget, and personal taste. Then, and only then, are you ready to make the purchase that is best suited for you. This same process can, and indeed should, be applied to everything you read. At first the process of critical reasoning sounds long and tiresome. Instead, it actually saves you time by guiding you in selecting only the material relevant to your needs and personal taste. The process also increases your total comprehension because the analysis aids you in understanding what the author actually intended.

When you read critically, the following questions will help to guide you in questioning, comparing, and evaluating what you read.

1. **What is the purpose of the material?** The material could be intended to inform, explain, define, compare, contrast, illustrate, persuade, or simply to entertain. Determining the author's purpose will aid you in setting your own purpose for reading.

2. **When was the material written?** Whether you need the latest in print or something printed years earlier will depend on what type of information you need at the time. When you need recent developments, for example, the latest-dated material you can find would be best. In our fast-changing society, ideas that were valid years ago might no longer be in use. On the other hand, just because material is not current does not mean it is useless. Much of our best information, ideas, and recreational reading was written years ago.

3. **If the material is in a periodical (a newspaper or magazine), what is the type and reputation of the publication?** When you desire movie gossip, you go to a magazine that specializes in this type of news. On the other

hand, if you need factual information about a current event, a reputable news magazine would be best.

4. **Is the author qualified to write about the subject?** Inaccurate information could be more harmful than no information. The only way to be sure you are receiving accurate information is to select books and articles by qualified authors. Often there is information about the author in front of the book. If not, the library reference section carries several books that will give you information about authors.

5. **Does the author omit or suppress information needed about the subject?** This question is appropriate to ask whenever you need to know all sides of a situation before making a decision or forming an opinion. Whenever the material is intended to persuade you to believe or act in a certain way, it is imperative that you ask this question.

6. **Does the author use emotional words and pictures to persuade you to believe as he or she believes?** Authors choose words that convey the message that they intend the reader to receive; for example, if you were reading an article that was designed to make you want to join the armed forces, the author would use such words as *patriotism, liberty, free, oppressed, brave,* and *freedom.*

7. **Is the information fact or opinion?** A fact is something that has actually happened or is true and that can be proved. An opinion is a belief that is based on a personal evaluation. Needless to say, opinions can be true and worthy of acceptance, but you, the reader, should be able to recognize the difference between a fact and an opinion and then, through critical reading, to decide your own course of action or thinking.

8. **Does the information meet a need for you?** With the wealth of informational and recreational materials available today, this is an important question. Our fast-paced lifestyle demands that we be selective. If one piece of information or book does not meet your needs, there are many others that will.

Read the following sentences and the explanation of each to help you understand how to distinguish between fact and opinion.

1. **Susie is the most beautiful girl in the class.** This statement is an opinion because "beautiful" can mean something different to each individual. Indeed, you may agree that Susie *is*, without doubt, the most beautiful girl; however, this merely means that your opinion is the same as that of the person who made the statement. Remember, an opinion is not necessarily incorrect, but it has not been proved.

2. **Susie was elected by her classmates as the most beautiful girl in the class.** Susie now has been *voted* the most beautiful girl in the class. You can prove that according to a vote, Susie is considered the most beautiful.

Therefore, a statement is an opinion when it is a belief that is based on what seems true instead of what can be proved. A fact, on the other hand, states something that has actually happened or is true.

Read the following passage. Study the questions and answers carefully to help you better understand how to read a passage critically.

Fur Coats: Where Do They Come From?

Millions of coyote, bobcat, raccoon, muskrat, and other wild animals are caught in the steel jaw leghold trap every year. The trap shuts tight on the animal's leg, like a car door slamming on your finger. The animal may be left for hours or days in panic and pain. Some chew off their own legs to escape.

Some fur animals, like mink or fox, are bred in captivity. They are often raised in small cages that are crowded together. Controlled breeding for new pelt colors sometimes causes blindness or deformities. These animals are killed by clubbing, poisoning, electrocution—methods chosen because they do not harm the pelt.

Most seal furs are obtained by clubbing the seals into unconsciousness, then stabbing and skinning them. In some hunts, the seals are harassed and driven some distance over rocks before being clubbed.

EVERY FUR COAT HURTS—DON'T BUY FUR!

1. What is the purpose of this article?

   To convince the reader that it is wrong to buy a fur coat.

2. Does the author use emotional language to persuade the reader? Give examples.

   Yes. Words and phrases such as "caught in the steel jaw leghold trap," "animal may be left for hours or days in panic and pain," "causes blindness or deformities," "killed by clubbing," and "stabbing and skinning them."

3. This article was published by the Humane Society of the United States. What is the purpose of this organization?

   To protect and ensure the rights of animals.

4. Does this article reflect that purpose?

   Yes.

5. After evaluating the information according to the purpose, what conclusion did you draw?

   That a fur coat is made at the expense of innocent and helpless animals.

List some words and phrases that a person who manufactures or sells fur coats would use to convince you to buy a fur coat. Then use these words and phrases in a short paragraph written in favor of purchasing a fur coat.

_____

_____

_____

_____

_____

_____

_____

_____

_____

_____

_____

_____

_____

_____

_____

_____

_____

EXERCISE 17: Fact and Opinion

NAME _____ **DATE** _____

Read the following sentences, and decide which are facts and which are opinions. Indicate your choice by writing O or F on the lines provided.

_____ 1. The best advice to follow when choosing a career is to choose the one that promises the highest income.

_____ 2. Books are more expensive today than they were ten years ago.

_____ 3. The sun rises in the east and sets in the west.

_____ 4. Most people look forward to summer because there are so many more fun activities available than during the winter.

_____ 5. Statistics support the claim that seat belts reduce accident fatalities.

_____ 6. Every city needs at least two modern, well-staffed hospitals.

_____ 7. Current best-selling novels are far superior to the best-sellers of past years and cover a much wider range of interests.

_____ 8. When juveniles commit serious crimes, they should be tried as adults.

_____ 9. Hurricanes are one of nature's most powerful and destructive forces.

_____ 10. Mount McKinley in Alaska, at an impressive height of over 20,000 feet, is the highest mountain in North America.

_____ 11. Alcoholism, the uncontrollable need for alcohol, is a serious disease that affects millions of people in our country.

_____ 12. Hans Christian Andersen, who published over 150 fairy tales, is considered one of the outstanding storytellers of all time.

_____ 13. Every young child enjoys fairy tales, especially the ones written by Hans Christian Andersen.

_____ 14. Your purpose for reading should determine your reading rate.

_____ 15. Since speed is a major factor in the severity of automobile accidents, everyone understands the need for a controlled speed limit on our highways.

_____ 16. With all its vibrant colors, pleasant weather, and fun festivals, fall is the most favored of the four seasons.

_____ 17. Light travels faster than sound.

_____ 18. It is easy to understand why everyone would support strict laws that would curb smoking among young people.

_____ 19. All intelligent people recognize the need for a college education.

_____ 20. George Washington was inaugurated as the first president of the United States on April 30, 1789.

_____ 21. Washington, D.C., is located in a federal zone known as the District of Columbia.

_____ 22. Although there were a token number of women in combat during the Gulf War, the practice of using women in combat will never be fully accepted in our country.

_____ 23. The telephone was invented by Alexander Graham Bell. The first message, "Mr. Watson, come here, I want you," was transmitted on March 10, 1876.

_____ 24. The sun is our primary source of light, heat, and energy.

_____ 25. When the sun is high in the sky, it should never be viewed with the naked eye because light from the sun's rays can cause blindness.

_____ 26. At 105 degrees, Tuesday was the hottest day on record for Danville.

_____ 27. There has never been a truer statement than "a picture is worth a thousand words."

_____ 28. Figures from the police department records show a slight decrease in violent crime in our city.

_____ 29. Alaska is the largest state in the United States.

_____ 30. The State Department of Education issued a report that described the condition of schools in the state and outlined plans for improvements.

_____ 31. The polio vaccine developed by Dr. Jonas Salk has practically eradicated polio throughout the world.

_____ 32. Establishing an independent political party would guarantee each individual an opportunity to make better decisions about issues.

_____ 33. Reading enriches our lives and is fun!

EXERCISE 18: Critical Evaluation

NAME _____ **DATE** _____

Read the following passages, and then answer the questions that follow each passage.

Public Apathy— Highway Killer

This passage is a reprint of a leaflet published and distributed by the Public Affairs Division of the Motor Vehicle Manufacturing Association of the United States.

More than 46,000 people die on the nation's highways every year. More than 38,000 of them die in motor vehicles—nearly 25,000 in passenger cars.

And, almost 4,000,000 are injured—3,766,000 of whom are occupants of motor vehicles. Many of those injured suffer permanent disability or are scarred for life.

Yet, car occupants have available the most effective life-saving and injury-reducing device for all types of vehicle accidents—the safety belt.

The 25,000 fatalities in passenger cars is a huge decrease from the 37,000 passenger car fatalities in 1969, but this number could be reduced by one-half if all occupants wore safety belts.

The carnage of America's highways continues year after year because the majority of drivers and passengers—58 percent—do not buckle the safety belts installed in all domestic passenger cars built since 1964.

And, it continues despite conclusive evidence that the chances of death and injury are reduced by 50 percent with the use of safety belts.

Safety belt use is not the panacea that will eliminate all highway death and injury. But, when used, safety belts are effective in reducing deaths . . . and they do make a difference in the types and severity of injuries suffered.

Many drivers and passengers who don't use safety belts simply don't believe they will be involved in an accident.

Believing that motor vehicle accidents "happen to someone else" can kill, injure and destroy lives and families.

According to a study done by the University of Michigan's Transportation Research Institute, a typical American is almost certain to be involved in a traffic crash during his or her lifetime and faces a 1-in-50 chance of becoming a fatality and a 50 percent probability of suffering a disabling injury.

BEING FREE IS COSTLY

"It's a free country."

Sure it is. But that's an expression used to justify doing—or not doing—almost anything.

For many people, it's a costly expression, particularly for those not using the safety belt system installed in virtually every car on the highway.

The cost of highway accidents in dollars and human suffering is far from free.

In 1986, the latest year for which complete government fatality and injury data are available, over 46,000 persons were killed in accidents on our nation's highways. Nearly 4 million were injured, about 162,000 of them seriously.

Economic losses to society from motor vehicle accidents in 1986, the last year for available data, are estimated at $27.3 billion from property damage, $16.3 billion due to lost productivity, $4.1 billion from medical treatment and $26.3 billion from emergency services, insurance administration, legal fees, medical examiner services, administration of public assistance programs and other costs.

Dr. B. J. Campbell of the Highway Safety Research Center of the University of North Carolina finds that in a survey of 24 states plus the District of Columbia with belt use laws, traffic fatalities were reduced by nearly 7 percent—some 1,300 lives.

SAFETY BELTS RESTRAIN FOR LIFE . . .

Many non-belt users feel they can brace themselves to prevent injury in an accident. But they don't realize the forces involved until an accident happens. Some live to consider the error in their thinking. Many don't.

In a 30-mile-per-hour collision with a solid object, an unbelted driver or passenger slams into the windshield, the instrument panel or the steering wheel and column at a force more than 100 times the force of gravity.

This is the g force discussed in rocket launches. A 30-mph vehicle crash exerts g forces more than 20 times stronger than those an astronaut experiences at blastoff!

Put another way, the unbelted occupant of a 30-mph vehicle crash hits the windshield or other interior surface of the vehicle with the same impact as a fall from a three-story building. Even the impact of a slower 10-mph crash is roughly equivalent to catching a 100-pound weight dropped from about six feet.

Unbelted adults holding a child on their laps in a 30-mph crash are thrown forward with the force of one and one-half tons.

The child would be crushed to death.

Safety belts help vehicle occupants "ride down" the force of the crash (the first collision) by holding them in place and preventing contact with either the interior of the vehicle or other occupants (the so-called second collision).

Belts also keep occupants inside the vehicle. Studies reveal ejection as a major factor in fatalities and severe injuries. Being thrown out of a vehicle is 40 times more lethal. Belts can prevent you from being crushed by your own car.

According to a study covering 28,000 traffic accidents in Sweden, no fatalities involving safety belt users were found at crash speeds of under 60 mph. But speeds as low as 12 mph resulted in deaths among unbelted occupants.

The evidence is clear and dramatic . . . when used, safety belts reduce death and reduce the severity and frequency of injury in vehicle crashes. In two common accidents—head-on and rollover—belt use has a dramatic effect in reducing fatalities by body area. Safety belt users, for example, experienced 80 percent fewer deaths from head injuries—and no deaths from neck injuries.

The reduction in serious injuries by body area in both types of crashes also shows a dramatic difference between use and non-use.

1. What is the purpose of the article?

   _____

   _____

2. To whom is it directed?

   _____

3. Note the source of the article. Would this association benefit financially from the extended use of safety belts?

   _____

4. Consider your answer to the preceding question. In light of your answer, would you consider the information biased or unbiased?

   _____

5. Is the information mostly facts or opinions?

   _____

291

6. What claim does the passage make about highway deaths regarding the use of seat belts?

_____

_____

_____

7. In what ways would the source be able to support its claims and statistics?

_____

_____

8. Are the claims and statistics presented and explained in such a way that the reader can totally comprehend them?

_____

9. Is the information realistic and in accord with information on the subject that you have read from other sources?

_____

10. Is there enough clear, conclusive information on which to base a decision?

_____

11. How do you feel about using safety belts? Give reasons for your answer.

_____

_____

_____

_____

_____

_____

_____

_____

Quality of Life Is Much
More Than a Job

LARRY FENNELLY

Larry Fennelly is Chairman of the Developmental Studies Department at Macon State College, a reviewer for the Macon Telegraph and News, and an enthusiastic observer of the arts in Middle Georgia. His arts column is designed to inform the public of behind-the-scenes activities and special achievements of individuals and groups.

It has often been remarked that the saddest thing about youth is that it is wasted on the young.

Reading a recent newspaper report on a survey conducted among college freshmen, I recalled the lament, "If only I knew then what I know now."

The survey disclosed what I had already suspected from informal polls of students both in Macon and at the Robins Resident Center: If it (whatever it may be) won't compute, and you can't drink it, smoke it or spend it, then "it" holds little value.

According to the survey, which was based on the responses of over 188,000 students, today's traditional-age college freshmen are "more materialistic and less altruistic" than at any time in the 17 years of the poll.

Not surprising in these hard times, the student's major objective "is to be financially well off. Less important than ever is developing a meaningful philosophy of life." It follows then that today the most popular course is not literature or history but accounting.

Interest in teaching, social service and the "altruistic" fields is at a low, along with ethnic and women's studies. On the other hand, enrollment in business programs, engineering and computer science is way up.

That's no surprise either. A friend of mine (a sales representative for a chemical company) was making twice the salary of her college instructors her first year on the job—even before she completed her two-year associate degree.

"I'll tell 'em what they can do with their (music, history, literature, etc.)" she was fond of saying. And that was four years ago; I shudder to think what she's earning now.

Frankly, I'm proud of the young lady (not her attitude but her success). But why can't we have it both ways? Can't we educate people for life as well as for a career? I believe we can.

If we're not, then that is an indictment of our educational system—elementary, secondary and higher. In a time of increasing specialization, a time when 90 percent of all the scientists who have ever lived are currently alive, more than ever we need to know what is truly important in life.

This is where age and maturity come in. Most people, somewhere between the ages of 30 and 50, finally arrive at the inevitable conclusion that they were ordained to do more than serve a corporation, a government agency, or whatever.

Most of us finally have the revelation that quality of life is not entirely determined by a balance sheet. Sure, everyone wants to be financially comfortable, but we also want to feel that we have a perspective on the world beyond the confines of our occupation; we want to be able to render service to our fellow man and to our God.

If it is a fact that these four realizations do not dawn until mid-life, is it then not incumbent upon educational institutions to prepare the way for the revelation? Most people, in their youth, resent the Social Security deductions from their paychecks, yet a seemingly few short years later find themselves standing anxiously by the mailbox.

While it's true that we all need a career, preferably a lucrative one, it is equally true that our civilization has amassed an incredible amount of knowledge in fields far removed from our own and that we are better for our understanding of these other contributions—be they scientific or artistic. It is equally true that, in studying the diverse wisdom of others, we learn how to think. More important, perhaps, education teaches us to see the connections between things, as well as to see beyond our immediate needs.

Weekly we read of unions who went on strike for higher wages, only to drive their employer out of business. No company; no job. How shortsighted in the long run.

But the most important argument for a broad eduction is that in studying the accumulated wisdom of the ages, we improve our moral sense. I saw a cartoon recently which depicts a group of businessmen looking puzzled as they sit around a conference table; one of them is talking on the intercom: "Miss Baxter," he says, "could you please send in someone who can distinguish right from wrong?"

In the long run that's what education really ought to be about. And I think it can be. My college roommate, now head of a large shipping company in New York, not surprisingly was a business major. But he also hosted a classical music show on the college's FM station and listened to Wagner as he studied his accounting.

That's the way it should be. Oscar Wilde had it right when he said that we ought to give our ability to our work but our genius to our lives.

Let's hope our educators answer the students' cries for career education, but at the same time let's ensure that the students are prepared for the day when they realize their folly. There's a lot more to life than a job.

1. What is the author's purpose?

   _____

2. How is the author qualified to write about the subject?

   _____

   _____

3. To whom is this information directed?

   _____

4. Does the author present both sides of the question?

   _____

5. Can the facts stated in the article be verified? How?

   _____

   _____

6. Are the opinions that are given realistic and in accord with what you know to be true?

   _____

7. Does the author give enough evidence for you to draw a conclusion? If so, what is your conclusion?

   _____

8. What is the author's conclusion?

   _____

   _____

   _____

   _____

9. Compare your conclusion with the conclusion of the author.

   _____

   _____

EXERCISE 19: Questioning, Comparing, and Evaluating

NAME _____ **DATE** _____

The following two articles are concerned with using the Scholastic Aptitude Test (SAT) as a measure of academic potential. The first article supports using the SAT, and the second opposes using the test for this purpose. Read each article carefully, and then answer the questions that follow.

SAT Is the Best Way to Test Reasoning Skill

GEORGE H. HANFORD

George H. Hanford wrote this article while serving as president of the College Board.

Since its introduction in the mid-1920s, the Scholastic Aptitude Test has become the most widely used measure of individual, developed verbal and mathematical reasoning skills.

The SAT's purpose has been to provide a uniform, objective measure of academic readiness for college-level work.

Because it is relatively independent of any curriculum, it helps to compensate for differences in grading and curriculum among the nation's more than 27,000 secondary schools.

Students and their parents often see the SAT as a barrier to be overcome in reaching the goal of higher education.

The truth is that the SAT is more often a stepping stone than an obstacle.

By helping colleges to consider all students equally, the SAT has provided more opportunity to get an education, not less. It ensures that the true abilities of any student are not masked by subjective notions about group differences.

What is the SAT *not?*

First, it is not a measure of the creativity, motivation, or special talents of students—things that may very well help them succeed in college.

Second, the SAT is not a measure of the nation's "gross educational product."

Still, many people have mistakenly come to view the SAT as a reliable report card on the nation's schools.

Most students, after all, do not take the SAT. Thus there is an urgent need to give colleges a more realistic portrait of what incoming high school students actually have learned.

There is also an urgent need to help non-collegiate students figure out what they should do. It's ironic that students who need the most advice often get the least. Those not going on to college get only snippets of information about jobs from family or friends.

It is unacceptable to focus our elaborate evaluation program on those moving on to college, while neglecting the other half who urgently need guidance.

That is why we have recommended that a new test be developed to serve all students. Its goal would be to evaluate a student's academic achievement by linking testing to the core curriculum in the school—and to help all students make academic and vocational decisions.

The aim of a standardized test should not be to screen students out of options, but to help them move on with confidence to college—and to jobs.

1. List four reasons stated in the article that oppose using the test.

    (1) _____

    (2) _____

    (3) _____

    (4) _____

2. Does the article state any support for using the test? If so, what?

    _____

    _____

    _____

3. Is the information presented mostly facts or opinions? List examples of each.

    _____

    _____

    _____

    _____

4. Is the author qualified to write on the subject? On the basis of his qualifications, would you expect him to support or oppose the test? (One of the functions of the College Board, an educational organization, is to sponsor tests, such as the SAT, to aid colleges in the placement and guidance of students.)

Why We Need a Test to Replace the SAT

Ernest L. Boyer

Ernest L. Boyer is a past president of the Carnegie Foundation for the Advancement of Teaching.

Every year, about a million high school students sit for $2\frac{1}{2}$ hours with soft pencils in their hands, marking up SAT score sheets. For many, it's a dramatic and frightening rite of passage.

However, I believe that the Scholastic Aptitude Test will come to play a decreasingly important role.

The SAT score is not very helpful in predicting how a student will perform in college—though when the score is combined with high school grades, the prediction rate improves.

I am troubled by the inflated attention given the SAT at a time when the majority of the nation's colleges are not highly selective and when few use the test as the primary yardstick for admission.

The Scholastic Aptitude Test was created at a time when high school standards were extremely uneven and when racial intolerance in college admissions was a harsh reality.

The SAT sought to overcome these barriers by measuring the "intellectual aptitude" of students.

Today, it's generally agreed that measuring what's sometimes called innate ability is difficult, if not impossible, to accomplish. It's also agreed that the SAT does not adequately measure what students are learning in the classroom.

Still, many people have mistakenly come to view the SAT as a reliable report card on the nation's schools.

Most students, after all, do not take the SAT. Thus there is an urgent need to give colleges a more realistic portrait of what incoming high school students actually have learned.

There is also an urgent need to help non-collegiate students figure out what they should do. It's ironic that students who need the most advice often get the least. Those not going on to college get only snippets of information about jobs from family or friends.

It is unacceptable to focus our elaborate evaluation program on those moving on to college, while neglecting the other half who urgently need guidance.

That is why we have recommended that a new test be developed to serve all students. Its goal would be to evaluate a student's academic achievement by linking testing to the core curriculum in the school—and to help all students make academic and vocational decisions.

The aim of a standardized test should not be to screen students out of options, but to help them move on with confidence to college—and to jobs.

1. List four reasons stated in the article that oppose using the test.

   (1) _____

   (2) _____

   (3) _____

   (4) _____

2. Does the article state any support for using the test? If so, what?

   _____

   _____

   _____

3. Is the information presented mostly facts or opinions? List examples of each.

   _____

   _____

   _____

   _____

_____

_____

4. Is the author qualified to write on the subject? On the basis of his qualifications, would you expect him to support or oppose using the test? (One of the functions of the Carnegie Foundation for the Advancement of Teaching is to conduct and publish educational studies.)

_____

_____

Now that you have *questioned* the information in each article, you are ready to compare and then to evaluate.

Compare your answers on each article. Do you find that one author uses more facts and better logic and reasoning than the other? Is the information presented complete and objective so that you are able to draw a conclusion? Are the arguments used reasonable? Do you detect personal bias in either article? Asking yourself these kinds of questions when dealing with conflicting information will help you to detect any inconsistencies, faulty logic, and flaws in reasoning.

Evaluate by writing a short paragraph in support of or opposition to the SAT, using the information in the two articles.

_____

_____

_____

_____

_____

_____

_____

_____

_____

_____

_____

_____

_____

_____

NAME _____ **DATE** _____

Although women have served in the military for many years, they have not been allowed in combat. However, their more active role in the Persian Gulf War has raised the question of allowing women to fight alongside men. The following passages present both sides of the issue. Read the passages, answer the questions that follow, and then cirtically analyze your own ideas concerning women in combat.

Should Women Be Allowed in Combat?
Yes

Becky Constantino

Becky Constantino is a former chairwoman of the Defense Advisory Committee on Women in the Services. The passage is from testimony before the Senate Arms Services Subcommittee on Manpower and Personnel, June 18, 1991.

The performance of American servicewomen in the Persian Gulf War calls into question existing combat restrictions for women—and highlights the benefits of fully using the capabilities of all personnel to further enhance combat readiness and to optimize the quality of the military. The time has come to give the chain of command the flexibility to use their best people to accomplish the tasks which our country asks of them. . . .

Physical gender differences, which could negatively impact combat readiness, would be valid reasons for closing positions for women. But limitations based on substantiated rationales would be more acceptable than the current limitations, which are strictly gender-related with an assumed intent of protecting the military women's exposure to hostile fire.

Servicewomen go through the same training, make the same sacrifices and sign the same contract as servicemen. They want an opportunity to fulfill their commitments and serve their country to the best of their abilities. They do not expect special treatment or want standards to be reduced to assure their success. . . . They know that equal opportunity means equal responsibility, and they are willing to accept the responsibility and corresponding risks.

Sometimes those who fight in opposition to women being in the military and in combat roles forget the reason these women join. They join for the same reasons the men join—to be full-fledged defenders of our country and our military.

The spirit of the U.S. servicewoman was captured when Major Marie Rossi said: "I think if you talk to the women who are professionals in the military, we see ourselves as soldiers. We do not really see it as man versus woman."

As a nation, we now know what we will do if women become prisoners of war. We will wear yellow ribbons for them and pray for their early return. We now know what we will do if women die for their country. We will grieve for them and bury them beside their brothers in Arlington Cemetery.

The lesson of the Gulf War is that those who support a strong defense and those who want to expand opportunities for women in the military are on the same team. In spite of the inequities servicewomen face, they set aside personal frustrations and become part of a team whose objective is to protect and defend the United States.

Should Women Be Allowed in Combat? No

General Robert H. Barrow

General Robert Barrow is a former commandant of the United States Marine Corps. The passage is from testimony before the Senate Armed Services Subcommittee on Manpower and Personnel, June 18, 1991.

The issue of women in combat is not about women's rights, equal opportunity or career assignments for enhancement purposes for selection to higher rank. It is most assuredly about combat effectiveness, combat readiness, winning the next conflict, and so we are talking about national security.

Those who advocate change have some strange arguments, one of which is that there is a de facto women-in-combat situation already, that women have been shot at, that they have heard gunfire, that they have been in areas where they could have been hit with missiles. But exposure to danger is not combat; combat is a lot more than that. It is a lot more than getting shot at or even getting killed by being shot at. Combat is finding and killing or capturing the enemy. It is killing, that is what it is.

And it is done in an environment that is often as difficult as you can possibly imagine—extremes of climate, brutality, deaths, dying. It is uncivilized, and women cannot do it. Nor should they be even thought of as doing it. And I may be old-fashioned, but I think the very nature of women disqualifies them from doing it. Women give life, sustain life, nurture life, they do not take it.

I just cannot imagine why we are engaged in this debate about even the possibility of pushing women into the combat part of our profession. The most harm that could come would probably come to what it would do to the men in that kind of situation. I know in some circles it is very popular to ridicule something called male bonding, but it is real, and one has to have experienced it to understand it. . . . It is cohesiveness. It is mutual respect and admiration. It is one for all and all for one. . . .

The other attendant problems to being in a combat situation—sexual harrassment, fraternization, favoritism, resentment, male backlash—would be insurmountable for anyone to deal with. Who would deal with it? Not some faceless political appointee over there in the Pentagon, but the corporals and sergeants and the lieutenants and the captains would have to maintain good order and discipline and also fight the war. . . .

If you want to make a combat unit ineffective, assign some women to it. It is a destructive proposition, and the thing that puzzles me about this, there is no military requirement for it. . . . We have all the men we need for those requirements. . . .

I. 1. In the first passage, what is the stated reason that women join the military?

   _____

   _____

   2. What does Ms. Constantino state as the only valid reason for not allowing women in combat?

   _____

   _____

   3. What is the reason currently used for not allowing women in combat?

   _____

   _____

4. What does Ms. Constantino state as the major benefits of allowing women in combat?

_____

_____

_____

_____

5. List three arguments stated in support of this issue.

_____

_____

_____

_____

_____

6. How does Ms. Constantino foresee the reaction of the nation when women become prisoners of war or are killed in combat?

_____

_____

_____

_____

_____

7. According to General Barrow in the second passage, the issue of women in combat is not about women's rights. What does he say it is about?

_____

_____

_____

8. Contrast _exposure to danger_ and _combat_ as discussed in the passage.

_____

_____

_____

9. What argument does General Barrow use in regard to the nature of a woman to support not allowing women in combat?

_____

_____

10. According to the second passage, how would women in combat harm the men who serve in combat?

_____

_____

11. List three broad arguments in opposition to allowing women in combat as discussed in the second passage.

_____

_____

_____

_____

_____

12. In addition to the broad arguments you listed in question 11, what other problems does General Barrow consider insurmountable? Why does he consider these problems insurmountable?

_____

_____

_____

_____

_____

II. Now that you have *questioned* the information in each passage, you are ready to *compare* and then to *evaluate*. Compare your answers on each passage, question what you have learned about each side of the issue, and then evaluate. Write a short essay <u>in support of</u> or <u>opposition to</u> allowing women in combat. (Use this space and a sheet of your own paper—if needed—to answer.)

_____

_____

_____

_____

_____

_____

_____

_____

_____

_____

_____

_____

_____

_____

_____

_____

_____

_____

SUGGESTIONS FOR FURTHER STUDY

- Select a current controversial topic, and read information for and against the controversy. Question each side, compare the information, and then evaluate.
- Read editorials in the local newspaper, determine whether each is in favor of or is opposed to the topic being discussed, and then write an essay taking the side not favored in the editorial.

CHAPTER 10

Reading Essays and Articles

IN THIS CHAPTER YOU WILL LEARN:

1. To recognize the parts of formal essays.
2. To read narrative, descriptive, and expository essays.
3. To read popular press articles.
4. To read scholarly journal articles.
5. To critically analyze essays and articles.

While textbooks are your primary source of information in a college course, they are by no means your only source. Many instructors assign supplemental readings, often in the form of essays and articles. They may be from current popular magazines and may illustrate concepts, principles, or issues you are studying. They may be readings from scholarly journals assigned to update you on new research or to acquaint you with current issues. You also need to read essays and articles when you research a topic for a research paper, prepare for a panel discussion, or provide support for your own ideas in your essays. In English and literature classes you will read a wide variety of essays and be expected to respond to them in discussions and to react to them in writing.

This chapter discusses various types of essays and articles and offers approaches for reading each. The information you learn in this chapter will also be helpful to you in your own writing. For example, as you learn the structure of an essay, you can use that structure to write more effective essays. As you learn the characteristics of each essay type, you will be better prepared to write them. Likewise, as you learn the structures of various types of articles, you will enhance your ability to write them.

Comparing Essays and Articles

Both essays and articles will be part of the reading assignments in many of your courses. You will encounter them in your textbooks as special features within chapters, or in scholarly journals, newspapers, and magazines, as outside reading assignments, or as part of researching a topic for a paper.

Essays differ from articles in that essays present the personal views of an author on a subject. They are more subjective than articles because they frequently emphasize the author's individual feelings and perceptions about a particular topic. Articles, on the other hand, are generally more objective. When writing an article the author assumes the role of a reporter. He or she avoids expressing personal feelings or viewpoints and concentrates on directly stating the facts. This does not mean that essays are not factual or accurate. Essays simply provide a personal approach to the information presented. Essays allow a writer to describe things as he or she pictures them, to tell a story as if he or she were there, or to present information as he or she understands it. In short, essays and articles differ mainly in their viewpoints.

READING ESSAYS

Essays usually have a different structure than articles. Understanding how they are organized will help you read them more effectively and efficiently. This section will examine how essays are organized and will help you become aware of their common parts and what is contained in each part. We will then look at three types of essays and how to read them.

Examining the Structure of Essays

Essays are short pieces of writing that examine a single topic and focus on a single idea about that topic. They may be encountered in anthologies, newspapers, and magazines of all types. Essays follow a standard organization and have the following parts:

- title
- introduction
- thesis statement
- supporting information
- summary or conclusion

The structure of an essay is similar to that of a paragraph. Like a paragraph, an essay has a topic. It also explores a single idea about the topic; in an essay this is called the thesis statement. Like a paragraph, an essay provides ideas and details that support the thesis statement. However, unlike a paragraph, an essay deals with a broader topic and the idea that it explores is often more complex. You can visualize the structure of an essay as follows:

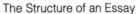

The Structure of an Essay

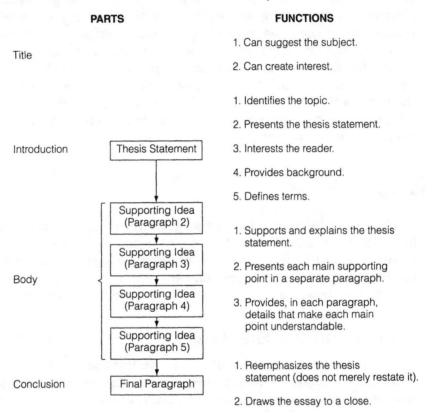

PARTS		FUNCTIONS
Title		1. Can suggest the subject.
		2. Can create interest.
Introduction	Thesis Statement	1. Identifies the topic.
		2. Presents the thesis statement.
		3. Interests the reader.
		4. Provides background.
		5. Defines terms.
Body	Supporting Idea (Paragraph 2)	1. Supports and explains the thesis statement.
	Supporting Idea (Paragraph 3)	2. Presents each main supporting point in a separate paragraph.
	Supporting Idea (Paragraph 4)	3. Provides, in each paragraph, details that make each main point understandable.
	Supporting Idea (Paragraph 5)	
Conclusion	Final Paragraph	1. Reemphasizes the thesis statement (does not merely restate it).
		2. Draws the essay to a close.

Note: There is no set number of paragraphs that an essay contains. This model shows six paragraphs, but in actual essays, the number will vary greatly.

Let's examine the function of each of these parts of an essay in greater detail by referring to an essay titled "Citizenship or Slavery? How schools take the volunteer out of volunteering." It was written by Andrea Martin and first appeared in the *Utne Reader*.

Citizenship or Slavery?

How schools take the volunteer out of volunteering

Introduction

"Service-learning" is a new buzzword for sending high school students into the community to do volunteer work. Service-learning isn't really volunteering, though, when it is required for high school graduation—and there's the rub. Americans generally applaud community service, but make that service mandatory and sizzling controversy erupts. George Bush promoted the notion of mandatory youth services as a means of reinvigorating responsible citizenship. The hotly debated issue of a national community service draft was finally settled in 1993 with the creation of the voluntary AmeriCorps. Locally, though, requirements for mandatory community service are on the increase, and they're being met with sturdy opposition.

Community service as an adjunct to classroom education is not new. Elective programs began to draw attention about 10 years ago, and both educators and students are generally pleased with them. Students develop new skills, greater self-esteem, and more enthusiasm for school. Communities benefit as energetic young people help in nursing homes and day care centers, lend a hand in nonprofits, and plant trees and pick up roadside trash. Noting these benefits, some enthusiasts began to make the case for required service.

body

The National Service-Learning Cooperative Clearinghouse estimates that more than a million high school students did community work through their schools in 1993, reports Suzanne Goldsmith in the liberal political journal *The American Prospect* (Summer 1995). Some of that is voluntary, but one quarter of America's public schools now impose a service requirement, according to Educational Research Service findings cited by Eric Felten in a critical article in the conservative newsweekly *Insight on the News* (Aug. 15, 1994). Washington, D.C., for example, requires 100 hours of service for high school graduation.

Before service-learning entered the schools, community service was an individual undertaking or was organized by scouts, churches, and other groups for their members. Many question the intrusion of education into what should be a private matter. Amitai Etzioni, a noted communitarian and a vocal advocate of volunteerism, argues in *Insight on the News* that the "public schools have moved beyond their mission by requiring community service." Politics becomes entangled in the educational process when schools encourage lobbying for specific causes or approve some forms of service and exclude others. (For example, in one community, service to Planned Parenthood was approved but service to an anti-abortion group was not.) As Goldsmith notes, opposition to an educational system perceived as setting a social agenda may ultimately be the most serious threat to service-learning.

There are also legal objections to mandatory service. Three high school students in Bethlehem, Pennsylvania, sued the school board on the grounds that the service requirement violated the constitutional prohibition of slavery. The students were represented by the Institute for Justice, a libertarian group that also represented students in similar cases in Mamaroneck, New York, and Chapel Hill, North Carolina. All three cases have failed in the courts. In denying the North Carolina slavery case, U.S. District Judge Frank W. Bullock cited the argument made by the American Alliance for Rights and Responsibilities that service-learning is an educational initiative that prepares students for participation in society.

Whether or not mandatory service is moral or legal, some educators question its merit. In the short run, it diverts diminishing resources from teaching basic skills to covering the costs of administering programs and transporting students to their work sites. When they work after the school day is over, students who live in far-flung rural areas are at a disadvantage, as are those who have after-school jobs or whose parents can't provide transportation. In the long run, making volunteer work just one more demand imposed on students may create a backlash, prejudicing them against future volunteer work. Critics of education often point out that schools diminish the joy of learning. Now they run the risk of diminishing the joy of community service too.

Writing in the National Civic Review (Summer/Fall 1995), Matthew Moseley describes the enormous resurgence of volunteerism among American youth—a movement that, as witnessed and supported by magazines such as *Who Cares* is proving to be a major social force. And Goldsmith, in *The American Prospect,* holds up as models schools that have made community service an appealing elective course; these programs usually generate enthusiasm and plenty of participation. It all suggests that communities should urge their schools to stimulate young people's natural urge to be useful by ensuring that service remains a genuine choice.

The Title

The title usually suggests the subject of the essay and is intended to capture the reader's interest. Some titles are highly descriptive and announce exactly what the essay will be about. For example, an essay titled "Television Addiction" announces the subject of the essay. Other titles are less directly informative. The title "It Begins at the Beginning" reveals little about the subject matter and only becomes meaningful within the context of the essay itself. (It is an article about differences in how males and females communicate and how those differences begin in childhood years.)

Some essays have both a title and a subtitle. In these essays, the subtitle usually suggests the subject matter more directly. In the sample essay, the title "Citizenship or Slavery?" is mainly intended to capture your interest rather than to directly announce the subject. The subtitle "How schools take the volunteer out of volunteering" focuses you more clearly on what the essay will be about.

EXERCISE 6–1

DIRECTIONS: What would you expect to be discussed in essays with each of the following titles?

1. Animal Rights: Right or Wrong

   _____

2. Firearms, Violence, and Public Policy

   _____

3. The Price of Power: Living in the Nuclear Age

   _____

4. The Nature and Significance of Play

   _____

5. Uncivil Rights—The Cultural Rules of Anger

   _____

   _____

EXERCISE 6–2

DIRECTIONS: Read the following title and subtitle of an essay. Predict what you think the essay will discuss.

"Attention Must Be Paid—New Evidence for an Old Truth: Babies need love that money can't buy"

_____

_____

The Introduction

The introduction, usually one or two paragraphs long, sets the scene for the essay and places the subject within a framework or context. The introduction may

- present the thesis statement of the essay
- offer background information (explain television addiction as an issue, for example)
- define technical or unfamiliar terms (define addiction, for example)
- build your interest (give an instance of an extreme case of television addiction)

Notice how the sample essay "Citizenship or Slavery?" accomplishes these goals in its first two paragraphs. It opens by defining "service learning," the topic of the essay, and then in the second sentence states its thesis—that service learning isn't true volunteerism when it is required. The remainder of the first two paragraphs provides background for the controversy over mandatory community service programs.

EXERCISE 6–3

DIRECTIONS: Read only the first two paragraphs of the essay "Attention Must Be Paid" by Mortimer Zuckerman. What types of information do they provide?

_____

_____

_____ ■

Attention Must Be Paid

Later than I might have expected, I have begun learning about parenthood first-hand. On July 7, Abigail Jane Zuckerman was born. Now I understand what all the excitement has been about.

Looking at a newborn in her crib, anyone must have a sense of the many things that have been determined about her life, by genes and circumstances, but also of the countless decisions and shaping experiences that lie ahead. Parents of every era have worried about making these choices in the right way. Recent scientific findings give new reason for concern—in particular, about whether children can thrive under the modern belief that parents can contract out their basic responsibilities for care.

Every day a newborn baby's brain is developing with phenomenal speed. Billions of nerve cells—neurons—are growing and specializing. By age 2, the number of synapses, or connections among the neurons, approaches adult levels, and by age 3 a child's brain has 1 quadrillion such connections. The synapses are the basic tools of processing within the brain.

Is inherited ability the main factor in establishing these connections? Apparently not. Interactions with an attentive adult—in most cases, a mother—matter most. The sight, sound, touch, smell, and especially, the intense involvement, through language and eye contact, of parent and child affect the number and sophistication of links within the brain. These neural patterns—again, set by age 3—seem to be more important than factors we usually emphasize, such as gender and race. In their book *Meaningful Difference in the Everyday Experience of Young American Children,* professors Todd Risley and Betty Hart say that the number of words an infant hears each day may be the single most important predictor of later intelligence and economic and social success.

This should be hopeful news, for it suggests that rich possibilities are open to every child. But the same research shows that verbal stimulation differs by income and education. On average, the child of professional parents hears about 2,100 words an hour; of working-class parents, 1,200 words. Parents on welfare speak about 600 words an hour. Professional parents give their children emotional encouragement 30 times an hour—twice as often as the working-class baby and five times as often as the welfare baby. This word play is so important that those left behind at age 2 may never catch up.

These findings come when many subscribe to the notion that there is no harm in a mother's leaving her baby in someone else's care and returning to work. More than half of all mothers are back at work before their baby is 1. The working mother is a fundamental feature of this era. But what will parents do when they learn that absence in the first three years may have a significant effect on their baby's future? Most working parents know in their hearts that "quality time" is no substitute for quantity time—the time that a child requires for emotional and, it now seems, intellectual development.

What children need is the touching, holding, cooing, rocking, and stimulation that come traditionally from a mother. In some households a stay-at-home father will fill the role of the absentee mother, but that is rare. In most families, if it is not the mother spending those three years with an infant, it will be a baby sitter or day-care worker. Often there are class, educational, and—increasingly—language differences between the parents and the hired caretaker. Parents are therefore going to be challenged to find a better balance between raising their children and working, especially parents who are too tired and emotionally drained to give children the *stimulus* and engagement they need. When babies are cared for by caring adults, they become much better learners and are much more confident to take over the world. Attention is the greatest gift that parents can bestow.

The Thesis Statement

The thesis statement of an essay is its main point. All other ideas and paragraphs in the essay support this idea. Once you identify an essay's thesis, you have discovered the key to its meaning. The thesis is usually stated in a single sentence and this sentence appears in the introductory paragraphs. It often follows the background information and the attention-getter. In our sample essay "Citizenship or Slavery?" the thesis is stated early in the first paragraph and is followed by background information.

Occasionally, an author will first present evidence in support of the thesis and finally state the thesis at the end of the essay. This organization is most common in argumentative essays (see Chapter 12). You may also find, on occasion, that an author implies rather than directly states the thesis; the thesis is revealed through the supporting paragraphs. When you cannot find a clear statement of the thesis, ask yourself this question: "What is the one main point the author is making?" Your answer is the implied thesis statement.

Here are a few sample thesis statements.

- Due to its negative health effects, cigarette smoking is once again being regarded as a form of deviant behavior.

- Career choice is influenced by numerous factors including skills and abilities, attitudes, and life goals.

- Year-round school will provide children with a better education that is more cost effective.

DIRECTIONS: Read the entire essay "Attention Must Be Paid" (pp. 248–249) and identify its thesis statement.

Body

The body of the essay contains sentences and paragraphs that explain or support the thesis statement. This support may be in the form of

- examples
- descriptions
- facts
- statistics
- reasons
- anecdotes (stories that illustrate a point)
- personal experiences and observations
- quotations from or references to authorities and experts
- comparisons

Most writers use various types of supporting information. In the sample essay "Citizenship or Slavery?" (pp. 245–246) the author uses several types of information in her supporting paragraphs. Notice how she uses *facts* and *statistics* in the third paragraph to show how widespread community service requirements are. Her fourth paragraph refers to *authorities* and *quotes* them directly and indirectly. She also includes an *example* of politics at work in these programs. The fifth paragraph concentrates on *descriptions* of and facts about legal cases on required community service programs and the results of these cases. The final paragraph of the body of this essay provides *reasons* against mandatory service.

EXERCISE 6–5

DIRECTIONS: Review the essay "Attention Must Be Paid" and mark where the body begins and ends. Then, in the margin beside each supporting paragraph, label the type(s) of supporting information the author used. ▬

Conclusion

An essay is brought to a close with a brief conclusion, not a summary. (A summary provides a review of the key ideas presented in an article. Think of a summary as an outline in paragraph form. The order in which the information appears in the summary reflects the order in which it appears in the article itself.) A **conclusion** is a final statement about the subject of the essay. A conclusion does not review content as a summary does. Instead, a conclusion often refers back to, but does not repeat, the thesis statement. It may also suggest a direction of further thought or introduce a new way of looking at what has already been said. The sample essay "Citizenship or Slavery?" (pp. 245–246) ends with a conclusion that strengthens the case in favor of volunteerism and elective courses rather than required community service courses. It refers back to the thesis statement by encouraging communities to allow service learning to be a matter of choice.

EXERCISE 6–6

DIRECTIONS: Explain how the conclusion of "Attention Must Be Paid" draws this essay to a close.

_____

_____

_____

_____

_____ ▬

Reading Various Types of Essays

There are four common types of essays: narrative, descriptive, expository, and argumentative. Each has a distinct purpose and unique characteristics. This section will discuss only narrative, descriptive, and expository essays. Argumentative essays are discussed in detail in Chapter 11, "Evaluating Arguments and Persuasive Writing."

Narrative Essays

Narrative essays relate a sequence of events, often in the form of a story. They review events that have happened, usually in the order in which they occurred. A narrative uses the time order thought pattern discussed in Chapter 5 as a means of organization. A narrative, however, goes beyond an ordering or listing of events. A narrative makes a point, communicates an attitude or feeling, or explains an idea. It has a thesis—a central idea that grows out of the story. Narrative essays often use vivid descriptions to bring to life the story being told and the point being made. In this sense, the categories of narrative and descriptive essays may often seem to overlap.

If you write an essay describing an important event or telling how someone influenced your life, you may use the narrative form. You describe events as they happened, showing how or why they were important or meaningful. Follow these steps when reading narratives:

1. **Establish the setting.** Determine when and where the events are taking place.

2. **Notice how the story is told and who is telling it.** The perspective or point of view of the person relating the events is often important.

3. **Look beyond the specific events to discover their overall meaning.** Ask yourself why the writer is telling the story. What point is the author trying to make? What is his or her thesis?

4. **Watch for the writer's commentary as he or she tells the story.** This commentary provides clues about the author's overall message or purpose for writing.

The following narrative essay is taken from a book titled *Mortal Lessons,* written by Richard Selzer, a medical doctor. This essay tells the story of a patient who is recovering from surgery that left her face deformed.

I stand by the bed where a young woman lies, her face postoperative, her mouth twisted in palsy, clownish. A tiny twig of the facial nerve, the one to the muscles of her mouth, has been severed. She will be thus from now on. The surgeon had followed with religious fervor the curve of her flesh; I promise you that. Nevertheless, to remove the tumor in her cheek, I had cut the little nerve.

Her young husband is in the room. He stands on the opposite side of the bed, and together they seem to dwell in the evening lamplight, isolated from me, private. Who are they, I ask myself, he and this wry-mouth I have made, who gaze at and touch each other so generously, greedily? The young woman speaks.

"Will my mouth always be like this?" she asks.

"Yes," I say, "it will. It is because the nerve was cut."

She nods, and is silent. But the young man smiles.

"I like it," he says. "It is kind of cute."

All at once I *know* who he is. I understand, and I lower my gaze. One is not bold in an encounter with a god. Unmindful, he bends to kiss her crooked mouth, and I so close I can see how he twists his own lips to accommodate to hers, to show her that their kiss still works. I remember that the gods appeared in ancient Greece as mortals, and I hold my breath and let the wonder in.

The incident takes place in a hospital where a woman is recovering from surgery to remove a tumor on her cheek. The author, who is the surgeon, is relating the events. Imagine how differently the events might have been told by the woman herself or by her husband. The article describes the occasion when the woman learns her mouth will be permanently twisted. The surgeon's purpose in writing becomes clear in the last paragraph. His main point is that the husband's kiss is godlike—it determines the woman's response to and acceptance of her deformity. Through his narrative of these events, the surgeon is making a comment on life: A person's limitations and handicaps are not as important as how they are perceived by and reacted to by others.

EXERCISE 6–7

DIRECTIONS: Read the following narrative essay by Lucinda Franks and answer the questions that follow.

THE STORY OF "JAMES B"

The gentleman in the corner had been regarded as a true American success, lanky and deep-voiced, brilliant and beloved, the master of all he surveyed. Now, he gazed out defiantly, as if still on the summit, too high to see the cat feces at his feet or the unopened mail or the mirror that would have told him he was master of nothing but his own delusions.

Those who were to thrust the mirror in front of the 62-year-old man, whom I will call James B, were his daughter Isabel, myself and three of the friends who loved him best. Isabel and I had been inseparable summertime friends, and James B, through an enormous white telescope in his backyard, had first introduced me to the stars in their firmament. His whimsies about what lay beyond them still quickened the heart of the child in me. Now, I was sitting impertinently in his living room, preparing to tell him that it didn't matter if he could no longer ponder eternity—he would soon be part of it.

If James B had denied his problem, so had we. He had been depressed over the death of his wife and the loss of his architectural business. He had been presenting different excuses to each of us for his growing isolation. He had kept us at bay by clever use of the telephone, until it was cut off for nonpayment of a bill he had never opened.

Yet at last we had gathered into a crisis intervention team and surprised him, hung-over, before he could perfect his alibis. Dr. Nicholas Pace, of New York's Pace Health Services, who helped refine the crisis intervention technique, had advised us to use reason, histrionics and even threats to strip James B of his defenses and deliver him to a treatment center. We were not to leave without him. The effectiveness with which we played our parts might mean the difference between his life and death.

"Daddy, we are here because we love you." Isabel's voice wavered, but the 9-month-old baby on her knee stared at her grandfather unblinkingly. James B, very gingerly, poured out coffee. "I can understand your concern," he said. He had thrown on a shirt—even a tie—but below his bathrobe, his thin, red legs had the look of arms flung down in defeat. "I've had this local flu. I've been going to my doctor for shots every day."

"I checked with your doctor, Daddy, and he hasn't seen you for two years. We think your disease is alcoholism."

All of James B's roles now seemed to collide and fall away, revealing the obsession which shone in his eyes like unrequited love. "That's preposterous! My problems have nothing to do with alcohol."

Mel, his former business partner, said he had watched the most brilliant man he had ever known become addled into dull predictability. George, his former chess opponent, blushed and said that James B had begun to cheat at the game. Lisa, his former lover, tremulously said she was going to marry a man she didn't love because the one she did had not preferred her to the bottle. I reminded him of the stars, and of all the people, including my baby and Isabel's who could still learn from him.

Coached about the new science of alcohol and the liver, we tried to convince James B that there was no shame in being an alcoholic.

"Look, can't you understand?" James B said. "I'm sick, yes; depressed, yes; getting old, yes. But that's all."

"Jim," Mel said, in a voice that resonated with the tension we all felt, "it sounds like you would rather be anything at all than an alcoholic."

After 14 hours of this scenario, some of us began to question whether he really *was* an alcoholic. Maybe it was some other illness. Then he let spill a few words. "Geez, if I couldn't go down to the pub for a few, I think I'd go nuts!"

"Aaah," Isabel said. "You just admitted it." She put the baby on her father's knee. "Look at your granddaughter. This is your immortality, Daddy, and she needs you. Please don't die. Please choose life, for us."

James B put his face, the color of gravel, in his hands. No one spoke. When he looked up, he said he would go to a local hospital.

At the emergency room, the doctor couldn't feel James B's liver and doubted whether the blood test, which could only measure severe damage, would show anything. "You're wasting time. An alcoholic won't stop drinking unless he wants to, and I've got dying patients here."

"But if we don't get him help, my father *is* going to die," Isabel said. "You can always bring him back when he starts hemorrhaging," the doctor said. Nevertheless, he agreed to do a blood test. Three hours later, the doctor came over to us with a sheepish look. Over the cries of James B's overtired granddaughter, he told us the test showed extensive liver damage. James B, who had been sitting stonily, swallowed hard. It was probably his diet, he argued at first, but finally he said he would enter a treatment center. We all cheered and shook his hand; he could have been a POW come home.

That very night, we drove him to the Edgehill treatment center in Newport, R.I. After 28 days, he emerged looking considerably changed. Over the next few months, he managed to restore order to his house. Though not yet emotionally able to handle frequent family meetings, he sent his granddaughter a toy a week.

Isabel, having learned that alcoholism is a family disease, afflicting each member to some degree, attended Al-Anon meetings, for the family and friends of alcoholics, where she was told that to cover up for her father was to destroy him. At Adult Children of Alcoholics, she got help in dealing with the deep scars of having grown up with an alcoholic parent.

"My father was so strong a figure and my identification with him was so intense that I always accepted his masks and his manipulations," Isabel said. "But I was suffering inside my own mask, and the games we played were killing us both."

James B, now about half-way through the long recovery process, looks back at the crisis intervention with bitter gratitude. "They stripped me of my skin and I'm still bleeding, but they saved my life," he says. "A person I haven't known for years is taking the place of alcohol. I like and respect him, and I never want to lose him, or my family, again."

1. What sequence of events does this article recount?

   _____

   _____

2. Who is recounting the story?

   _____

3. How does the writer feel about the events she describes? Substantiate your answer with references to the essay.

   _____

   _____

4. Why do you think the author wrote the essay?

_____

_____

5. What did you learn about the disease of alcoholism from reading the essay?

_____

Descriptive Essays

Descriptive writing appeals to the senses—to your sense of touch, taste, smell, sight, and sound. Descriptive essays provide extensive sensory details about the characteristics of people, objects, events, or places. The details are intended to appeal to your senses and to help you create a mental picture. The writer usually provides the sensory details to create a single impression that becomes the author's thesis. Descriptive writing is used in many forms of writing, including advertising. In the following travel advertisement, notice how the writer helps you form a visual image and impression of Bermuda.

> For more than a century, people who value relaxation have been returning to Bermuda year after year. They appreciate the pink-tinted beaches, the flower-laden garden paths, the cozy pubs, and the clear, turquoise waters.

Do the phrases "pink-tinted beaches," "flower-laden garden paths," and "clear, turquoise waters" help you picture a beach in Bermuda? Do you have an impression of Bermuda as a beautiful tropical paradise?

In reading descriptive writing, be sure to follow these steps:

1. **Identify the subject of the essay.** Ask yourself: "Who or what is being described?"

2. **Pay close attention to the writer's choice of words.** Notice sensory details; the writer often paints a picture with words. Through word choice, a writer tries to create an attitude or feeling. Try to identify that feeling.

3. **Establish the overall impression the writer is trying to create.** Ask yourself these questions: What do all these details, taken together, suggest about the subject? What is the writer trying to say? How am I supposed to feel about the subject?

4. **Pay particular attention to the first and last paragraphs.** They will probably provide the most clues about the writer's main points and purpose for writing.

Now read the following excerpt from an essay titled "Aging in the Land of the Young" by Sharon Curtin, and apply the steps listed. As you read, mark words that are particularly descriptive.

Old men, old women, almost 20 million of them. They constitute 10 percent of the total population, and the percentage is steadily growing. Some of them, like conspirators, walk all bent over, as if hiding some precious secret, filled with self-protection. The body seems to gather itself around those vital parts, folding shoulders, arms, pelvis like a fading rose. Watch and you see how fragile old people come to think they are.

Aging paints every action gray, lies heavy on every movement, imprisons every thought. It governs each decision with a ruthless and single-minded perversity. To age is to learn the feeling of no longer growing, of struggling to do old tasks, to remember familiar actions. The cells of the brain are destroyed with thousands of unfelt tiny strokes, little pockets of clotted blood wiping out memories and abilities without warning. The body seems slowly to give up, randomly stopping, sometimes starting again as if to torture and tease with the memory of lost strength. Hands become clumsy, frail transparencies, held together with knotted blue veins.

This essay discusses the process of aging. Words and phrases such as "fading rose," "filled with self-protection," "paints every action gray," "ruthless," and "torture" create a feeling of depression, dread, and despair. The overall impression is that aging is something to dread. This author shows us nothing positive about aging—no reference to a golden age, to inner peace, to depth or wisdom.

EXERCISE 6–8

DIRECTIONS: Read the following descriptive essay by Brenda Peterson and answer the questions that follow.

SEAGULL SONG

"Seagulls memorize your face," the old man called out to me as he strode past on his daily walk. I stood on the seawall feeding the flock of gray-and-white gulls who also make this Puget Sound beach their home. "They know their neighbors." He tipped his rather rakish tweed motoring cap and kept walking fast. "Can't let the heartbeat stop," he explained.

I met this man many days on the beach. We rarely talk; we perform our simple chores; I feed the seagulls and say prayers, he keeps his legs and his heart moving. But between us there is an understanding that these tasks are as important as anything else in our lives; maybe they even keep us alive. Certainly our relationship with each other and with this windswept Northwest beach is more than a habit. It is a bond, an unspoken treaty we've made with the territory we call home.

For twelve years I have migrated from beach shack to cabin, moving along the shore like the Native tribes that once encircled all of Puget Sound. But unlike the first people who loved this wild, serpentine body of cold water, my encampments have changed with the whim of my landlords rather than with the seasons. Somehow mixed up in my half-breed blood is a belief that I may never own land even if one day I might be able to afford it. Ownership implies possession; as much as I revere this inland sea, she will never belong to me. Why not, then, belong to her?

Belong. As a child the word mesmerized me. Because my father's forestry work moved us every other year, the landscape itself seemed in motion. To *belong* in one place was to take deep root like other settled folk, or like the trees themselves. After I have lived a long life on this beach, I hope that someone might someday say, "She belonged here," as much as the purple starfish that cling to rock crevices covered in algae fur.

The Hopi Indians of Arizona believe that our daily rituals and prayers literally keep this world spinning on its axis. For me, feeding the seagulls is one of those everyday prayers. When I walk out of my front door and cross the street to the seawall, they caw-welcome, their wings almost touching me as they sail low over my shoulders, then hover overhead, midair. Sometimes if it's been raining, their feathers flick water droplets onto my face like sprinklings of holy water. The brave fliers swoop over the sea and back to catch the bread in their beaks inches above my hand. Then the cacophonic choir—gulls crying and crow *kak-kak*-ing as my special sidearm pitch sends tortillas whizzing through the air, a few of them skipping across the waves like flour Frisbees.

I am not the only neighbor who feeds these gulls. For the past three years, two afternoons a week, a green taxi pulled alongside the beach. From inside, an ancient woman, her back bent like the taut arch of a crossbow, leaned out of the car window and called in a clear, tremulous soprano. The seagulls recognized the sun-wrinkled, almost blind face she raised to them. She smiled and said to the taxi driver, "They *know* I'm here."

It was always the same drive, the same ritual—a shopping bag full of day-old bread donated by a local baker. "She told me she used to live by the sea," the driver explained to me once. "She don't remember much else about her life . . . not her children, not her husband." Carefully the driver tore each bread slice into four squares the way the woman requested. "Now she can't hardly see these birds. But she hears them and she smells the sea. Calls this taking her medicine."

Strong medicine, the healing salt and mineral sea this old woman took into her body and soul twice a week. She lived in the nursing home at the top of our hill, and every time I saw the familiar ambulance go by I prayed it was not for Our Lady of the Gulls.

Several years ago, when wild hurricanes shook the South and drought seized the Northwest, the old woman stopped coming to our beach. I waited for her all autumn, but the green taxi with its delighted passenger never came. I took to adding two weekly afternoon feedings to my own morning schedule. These beach meetings are more mournful, in memory of the old woman who didn't remember her name, whose name I never knew, who remembered only the gulls.

Not long afterward my landlady called with the dreaded refrain: "House sold, must move on." I walked down to the beach and opened my arms to the gulls.

With each bread slice I said a prayer that Puget Sound would keep me near her. One afternoon I got the sudden notion to drive down the sound. There I found a cozy cottage for rent, a little beach house that belongs to an old man who's lived on this promontory since the 1940s. A stroke had sent him to a nursing home, and the rent from the cottage would pay for his care.

Before I moved one stick of furniture into the house, I stood on the beach and fed the gulls in thanksgiving. They floated above my head; I felt surrounded by little angels. Then I realized that these were the very same gulls from two miles down the beach near my old home—there was a bit of fishline wrapped around a familiar webbed foot, that wounded wing, the distinct markings of a young gray gull, one of my favorite high fliers.

Who knows whether the old man was right? The seagulls may have memorized my face and followed me—but I had also, quite without realizing it, memorized them. And I knew then that I was no newcomer here, not a nomad blown by changeable autumn winds. It is not to any house, but to this beach I have bonded. I belong alongside this rocky inlet with its salt tides, its pine-tiered, green islands, its gulls who remember us even when we've forgotten ourselves.

1. In the fifth paragraph the author describes her daily ritual of feeding the seagulls. Underline words or phrases that you think are especially descriptive.

2. What is the main point the author is making in this essay?

   _____

   _____

   _____

3. How does the author use the last paragraph to conclude this essay? What does she do to tie this essay all together?

   _____

   _____

   _____

   _____

   _____

   _____

   _____

   _____

_____

_____

_____

4. This essay conveys a feeling of reverence for the Puget Sound. Which words and phrases does the author use to achieve this feeling of almost religious awe?

_____

_____

_____

_____

_____

_____

EXERCISE 6–9

DIRECTIONS: Brent Staples in his essay "Just Walk On By: A Black Man Ponders His Power to Alter Public Space" (Reading Selection #4, pp. 100–103), uses descriptive detail to effectively convey his message. Read or review the essay and highlight sentences or paragraphs that are particularly descriptive. ◼

Expository Essays

An **expository essay** presents information on a specific topic from a particular writer's point of view. Its purpose is to present the facts as the author understands them on a given topic and to explain them to the reader. For example, a story in *Time* magazine that reports a new method of gene therapy is expository. It is written to explain the new method. An essay titled "What Causes Earthquakes?" is written to explain the changes in the earth that produce earthquakes.

The essay "Attention Must Be Paid" is also an example of an expository essay. Its purpose is to present and explain new findings about the effects of hired child care on the development of young children. The author accomplishes this by giving facts and statistics and by referring to authorities on the subject. This essay does reflect the author's individual interpretation of recent findings on the topic, but its central purpose is to inform the reader about the importance of more direct care of young children by parents rather than by babysitters or day care workers.

Expository essays are often organized using one or more of the thought patterns described in Chapter 5, "Patterns: Relationships Among Ideas." Depending on a writer's purpose, he or she may choose a specific pattern, as shown here.

If a Writer's Purpose Is To	The Pattern Used Is
Trace the history or sequence of events	Chronological order
Explain how something works	Chronological order
Explain a subject by describing types or parts	Classification
Explain why something happened	Cause-Effect
Explain what something is	Definition
Emphasize similarities or differences between two or more things	Comparison-Contrast

When reading expository essays, use the following guidelines.

1. **Establish the authority of the author whenever possible.** In order to trust that the author presented accurate, reliable information, make sure he or she is knowledgeable about or experienced with the subject.

2. **Pay attention to background information the author provides.** Especially if the subject is one with which you are unfamiliar, you must fill in gaps in your knowledge. If the background supplied is insufficient, consult other sources to get the information you need.

3. **Identify the author's thesis.** Determine exactly what information the author is presenting about the subject. Test your understanding by expressing it in your own words.

4. **Pay attention to new terminology.** Mark or underline new terms as you read them. If some are not defined and you cannot determine their meaning from context, be sure to look them up.

5. **Highlight as you read.** Mark the thesis statement and each major supporting detail.

6. **Outline, map, or summarize the essay.** To ensure recall of the information, as well as to test your understanding of it, use some form of writing.

EXERCISE 6–10

DIRECTIONS: Read the following expository essay by Andrea Martin and highlight it as suggested in the guidelines above. Circle any new terminology you encounter, then either outline, map, or summarize the essay. ■

WHY GET MARRIED?

MORE COUPLES FIND "LIVING IN SIN" A GOOD FAMILY VALUE

About 3.5 million unmarried opposite-sex couples are living together in the United States today, up from 2 million a decade ago. If you think this is merely an explosion of passionate anti-authoritarianism, guess again: Many of the couples who are joining the boom may simply be making a sound fiscal decision.

Some observers link the widespread acceptance of cohabitation with recognition that the economics of marriage are often unfavorable. To begin with, there's a 50 percent chance that a marriage will fail, and divorce is expensive. Beyond that, tax laws and other governmental policies—in a country that says it wants strong families—may actually be discouraging marriage.

It's well known that the poor are often victims of tax and government-benefit marriage penalties. When marriage reduces welfare eligibility, many decide against it. In addition, as Joseph Spiers noted in *Fortune* (July 11, 1994), married low-wage workers may be at an income-tax disadvantage. For example, the standard deduction and Earned Income Credit are often lower for working couples than for two singles. Spiers concludes that "the task of welfare reform might get easier if government first removes this disincentive to build stable families."

The problem persists higher up on the economic ladder, too. In *Forbes* (May 22, 1995), Janet Novack describes tax penalties that affect well-to-do couples, including income taxes higher than singles pay and business expense ceilings that don't double for marrieds. "[Had] Congress set about to create a tax code to encourage people to avoid marriage, it could scarcely have done a better job," says Novack. She concludes: "We hate to say it, but if you are a prosperous person contemplating marriage with a well-heeled partner, maybe you should forget the ceremony and just move in together."

Middle-aged couples of more modest means face another hurdle if either partner is divorced or widowed and has college-age children. Colleges routinely include stepparents' income in calculating whether a student will receive financial aid and, if so, how much. This forces potential stepparents to take on burdensome responsibilities for children who are not their own, and it may result in the denial of aid. Divorced parents have to decide between remarriage and their children's education.

In the American Association of Retired Persons magazine *Modern Maturity* (May/June 1995), Linda Stern describes the various marriage and remarriage penalties that threaten older people: Social Security earnings limits, capital gains exclusions on home sales, and Medicaid eligibility limits, for example. As a result, unmarried couples quietly move in together and enjoy companionship, while long-married couples sometimes divorce in order to avoid financial disaster.

Are these penalties causing cohabitation? It's impossible to say for sure, but the fact that older couples are an important part of the boom suggests a connection. "The Census Bureau estimates that the percentage of cohabiting unmarried couples has doubled since 1980, and older couples are keeping pace," writes Stern. "In 1993 some 416,000 couples reported that they were unmarried, living together,

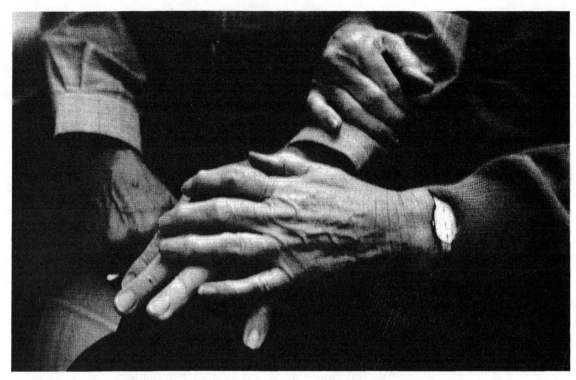

An elderly couple.

and over 45. That compares with 228,000 who fit the description in 1980." And in the *New York Times* (July 6, 1995), Jennifer Steinhauer reports on the research of Professor Larry Bumpass of the University of Wisconsin, who found that the biggest increase in couples choosing to live together was not among twenty-somethings, but among people over 35. Bumpass found that 49 percent of his subjects between 35 and 39 are living with someone, up from 34 percent in the late 1980s. Among people 50 to 54, the practice has doubled. Using data from his survey, Bumpass showed that only a small segment of people disapprove of cohabitation and sex outside marriage. He concluded that "the trends we have been observing are very likely to continue, with a declining emphasis on marriage."

Of course, marriage still has its advantages, beyond obvious ones like greater emotional security and social and religious approval. It can be a social welfare system, providing health insurance and retirement security to a spouse who otherwise would have none. For couples in which one person earns most of the family income, tax laws are favorable to marriage.

But overall, official economic policy makes marriage a bad option for too many people. Those who determine our income taxes, government benefits, and institutional practices must remember that marriage is an economic as well as a social arrangement. In a society in which many marriages have failed, financial security is tenuous, and living together is acceptable, we can no longer assume that the institution of marriage will survive the burdens it has carried in the past. Moving toward marriage-neutral tax and benefit policies would, in the long run, lay a better foundation for true family values.

EXERCISE 6–11

DIRECTIONS: The essay "How to Brag About Yourself to Win and Hold a New Job" (Reading Selection #1, pp. 55–56) is an example of an expository essay. Read or review the essay and answer the following questions.

1. Why is the essay an example of an expository essay?

   _____

2. To what extent does the essay include the author's opinions and interpretations?

   _____

3. Do you feel Challenger is qualified to write an essay on the subject? Why?

   _____

   _____

4. Write a list of job-seeking and job-holding advice that summarizes Challenger's suggestions.

   _____

READING ARTICLES

Articles, like essays, can tell a story, describe, or inform. Unlike essays, they do this with little personal involvement of the author. Also, they have structures that are somewhat different from that of an essay. Three types of articles are discussed in this section: popular press articles, feature articles, and scholarly articles. The structure of an article depends upon its type. Each has special features that will help you to locate the information you want more efficiently.

Reading Popular Press Articles

Articles that appear primarily in magazines and newspapers assume a different style and format from most essays. While popular press articles examine a topic and focus on an aspect of a topic, they tend to be more loosely or informally structured than most essays and scholarly journal articles. The title is usually eye catching and descriptive. The introductory section may be less fully developed and a formal paragraph conclusion may not be used.

The two most common types of popular press articles found in both newspapers and magazines are hard news articles and feature articles. They have essentially the same form, consisting of a beginning, called the *lead,* the story itself, called the *body or development,* and sometimes a formal *conclusion* as an ending.

Hard News Articles

Articles that directly report the serious news are known as hard news articles. They are stories about conflict, death, and destruction as well as items of interest and importance in government, politics, science, medicine, business, and the economy. Articles of this type may be organized in one of two ways.

Inverted Structure   The traditional structure used in newspaper articles is known as the *inverted pyramid,* because the article moves from general to more specific information. It contains the following parts:

- *Title.* Titles, or headlines, used in hard news stories are brief and directly informative about the article's content. They are usually expressed in active language, somewhat in the form of a telegraph message: "President Threatens Veto Over Budget" or "Diet Drug Thought to Be Health Risk." Reading the title is usually sufficient to help you decide whether or not to read the article.

- *Datelines, Credit Lines,* **and** *Bylines.* These follow the title and come just before the *summary lead. Datelines* appear on all but local news stories and generally only give the place where the story came from; occasionally the date will be given. *Credit lines* may also appear before the lead and supplement datelines. They give the name of the wire service or newspaper from which the story was taken, such as "Associated Press" or *Washington Post. Bylines* name the writer of the article and are sometimes also included between the title and the lead.

- *Summary Lead.* This opening paragraph contains a summary of the most essential information in the story. It is similar to the *thesis statement* in an essay and the *abstract* in a scholarly article. Reading this lead alone may provide you with all the information you need from the article and will help you to determine if you need to read further to get the information you want.

• **Body or Development.** The supporting facts are presented here—arranged in descending order of importance or interest. The most important details are placed first, followed by those second in importance or interest, and so on, until those facts most easily dispensed with are placed at the end of the story. If the lead paragraph doesn't contain the information you need, this type of organization will permit you to locate it easily. Since the *inverted pyramid* structure contains no conclusion there is no need to skip to the end of the article when pre-reading it.

Look at the following news article and note where its parts are located.

Title or Headline —————

LAWSUITS SEEK HEART MONITORING FOR USERS OF WITHDRAWN DIET DRUGS

Byline ————— By Beth Powell

Credit line ————— *Associated Press*

Dateline

Summary lead

WASHINGTON—Class-action suits demanding payment for heart monitoring for former diet drug users have been filed in five states against the makers of prescription drugs pulled off the market a week ago.

Body

The suits were filed last week in New York, Utah, Colorado and Hawaii and earlier in California on behalf of patients who might have been injured by using fen-phen, the popular name for a combination of prescription diet drugs, attorney Gary Mason said.

After studies linked the diet pills to serious heart damage, drug makers withdrew from the market fenfluramine and dexfenluramine, sold under the brand names Pondimin and Redux, respectively.

The Food and Drug Administration urged millions of dieters to stop taking both drugs immediately.

The FDA said phentermine, which combined with fenfluramine made the once-popular fen-phen combination, appears safe when used by itself. But doctors said phentermine has only mixed results when taken alone.

The lawsuits seek medical monitoring, emergency notification and updated patient warnings for class members, Mason said. Some suits seek specific monetary damages for individuals.

Mason, whose law firm Cohen, Milstein, Hausfeld & Toll is coordinating the class-action suits, said similar actions would be filed in all 50 states within the next few weeks.

The nine defendants in the suits are Wyeth-Ayerst Laboratories Co., division of American Home Products Corp.; Interneuron Pharmaceuticals; Gate Pharmaceuticals, a division of Teva Pharmaceuticals, USA; Smithkline Beecham Corp.; Abana Pharmaceuticals; Richwood Pharmaceutical Co.; Ion Laboratories; Medeva Pharmaceuticals; and A. H. Robins Co.

Body

Action Story   A second common format for hard news articles is the *action story*. It contains all the parts of the inverted pyramid with a few variations. It also begins with a telegraphic title that can be followed by a byline, credit line, and dateline. Its opening paragraph is also in the form of a summary lead. However, its body presents the events in chronological order of their occurrence, rather than in order of importance or interest. Furthermore, this format includes a conclusion that contains additional information that does not fit within the chronology used in the body.

EXERCISE 6–12

DIRECTIONS: Locate a hard news article from a newspaper or magazine. Determine which format is used, the inverted pyramid or the action story. Then label the article's parts. ▬

Feature Articles

A second type of popular press article is the feature article. Found in both newspapers and magazines, the feature article is longer and goes into greater depth than the usual hard news article. It usually deals with larger issues and subjects. Because of its length, this type of article requires a different structure than hard news articles.

It also begins with a *title* that is often in the form of a complete sentence and may contain a byline, credit line, and dateline. Its other parts may differ, though.

- *Feature Lead.* The lead in a feature article does not usually summarize its contents. Instead, it is intended to spark your interest in the topic being presented. It may begin with an interesting anecdote, present some highlight of the article, or offer an example of something you will learn more about later. Since the feature lead is primarily an interest builder, you may be able to skim through it quickly when reading the article.

- *Nut Graph.* The nut graph explains the nature and scope of the article. Depending upon the length of the article it may be one paragraph, or it may run to several paragraphs. When reading feature articles, read this section carefully. It will offer clues to the organization and content of the article and help you to grasp its main points.

- *Body or Development.* This is where the detailed information of the article is presented. Unlike hard new stories, the information can be organized in more than one way. Each paragraph or section may use a different thought pattern to develop its ideas, much like the expository essay. Mark and annotate this section as you read it, sifting through the main and secondary points.

- *Conclusion.* Feature articles often end with a conclusion, which, like the conclusion of a formal essay, makes a final statement about the subject of the article. Rather than summarizing the information presented, it may refer back to the nut graph, introduce a new way of looking at it, or suggest a direction for further thought.

Refer to the following feature article to see an example of this structure.

Title ——————————— **WHY DO DOGS BARK?**

Byline ——————— By Richard Folkers

Feature lead

Dogs can be pretty good communicators. A yelp is easy to recognize as a sound of distress. Growls are obvious. A whine, coupled with a scratch at the door, may just keep the carpet clean and dry.

Nut Graph

But what about barking? Is a dog sounding an alarm? Defining its territory? Just playing? The principles of evolution dictate that animals retain traits through natural selection. They hang on to functions that contribute to their survival, and that applies to making sounds no less than anything else. Scientists believe male birds sing, for example, to mark their territory, to attract mates, to maintain pair relationships, and to warn of impending predatory doom. But barking seems to defy all the rules of biological necessity.

Body or Development

Biologists Raymond Coppinger and Mark Feinstein, who have studied this puzzle, say dogs often seem to bark extravagantly and for no apparent reason at all. The two Hampshire College scientists once spent the night in a Minnesota field listening to a guard dog bark continuously for seven hours. There were no other dogs around, no humans responding, no predators lurking. It just barked. Feinstein recently came upon two dogs in a hot car. "One was barking like crazy, the other staring out the window. They were under the same conditions," he says. "They've got this capacity which doesn't play any necessary function in their lives."

Those dogs, like all domestic dogs, are descended from the wolf, and wolves don't bark much. But their puppies do, and Coppinger and Feinstein believe that may help explain the mystery of barking. Early dogs (wolves really) were scavengers, hanging around human habitations—and their plentiful heaps of garbage. Humans, in turn, tended to tolerate the tamer ones; it was they that became the sires of what would become the domestic dog. Experiments in a number of animals have shown that breeding for tameness breeds animals that are, in effect, perpetual adolescents, displaying many youthful traits into adulthood. "You get an animal more like a juvenile wolf," says Feinstein.

Body or Development

So why do juveniles bark? Feinstein and Coppinger believe

Body or Development

wolf pups are in a transition period; a bark is acoustically halfway between an infantile attention-seeking whine and an adult, hostile growl.

Adult dogs do find ways to use their barks to communicate; they might be asking to go in or out, defending territory, or just playing. But

as Feinstein notes, precisely because barking has no biological necessity for dogs, "they can adapt it to use under almost any circumstance."

Ultimately, science's best answer may be the punch line of the old joke about why dogs chase their tails and lick themselves: because they can.

Body or Development

Conclusion

EXERCISE 6–13

DIRECTIONS: Select a feature article from the periodicals available to you. Label its parts, then mark and annotate it.

Reading Articles from Scholarly Journals

Scholarly journals are publications by professional societies or college and university presses that report developments and research in a particular academic discipline. For example, in the field of psychology, scholarly journals include *American Journal of Psychology, Journal of Abnormal Psychology,* and *Psychological Bulletin.* Articles published in scholarly journals are usually peer reviewed. That is, before an article is published, other professionals in the field read the article and confirm that it is legitimate, accurate, and worthwhile.

You need to read articles from scholarly journals when you research a topic for a paper or write a research paper. Some professors distribute a reading list each semester, of which scholarly articles are a part. Others supplement text assignments by assigning articles and placing copies of them on reserve in the library. Many scholarly articles, especially those that report research conducted by the author, follow a similar format and often include the following parts, although different journals use different headings to organize their articles, or may not label all sections with headings.

- **Abstract.** An abstract is a brief summary of the article and its findings and is sometimes labeled as "Summary." It usually appears at the beginning of the article following the title and author. Read the abstract to get an overview of the article, and when doing research, to determine if the study or report contains the information you need.

- **Summary of Related Research.** Many research articles begin by summarizing research that has already been done on the topic. Here authors will cite other studies and briefly report their findings. This summary brings you up to date on the most current research as well as suggests a rationale for why the author's study or research is necessary and appropriate. In some journals, this rationale may appear in a section called *Statement of the Problem*.

- **Description of Research.** In this section, which may also be labeled "Method," the author describes his or her research or explains his or her ideas. For experimental research, you can expect the author to present the research design, including the purpose of the research, description of the population involved, sample size, methodology, and statistical tests applied.

- **Results.** Results of the research are presented in this section.

- **Implications, Discussion, and Conclusions.** Here the author explains what the results mean and draws possible implications and conclusions.

- **Further Research.** Based on his or her findings, some authors end the article by suggesting additional research that is needed to further explain the problem or issue being studied.

Here is a sample scholarly article from *Psychological Reports*. Read the article and study the annotations.*

Sex Differences in Humor[1]

Scott A. Myers

Barbara Lorene Ropog,
R. Pierre Rodgers

*Department of Speech and Theatre Arts
McNesse State University*

*School of Communication Studies
Kent State University*

Abstract

Summary—This study examined how 48 men and 88 women at a small southern university differed in their orientation toward and their uses of humor. They completed two self-report scales with reference to their general use of humor. Analysis indicated that the men reported a greater frequency of attempts at humor than women; men perceived these attempts as more effective than did the women; and the men reported using humor for negative affect more often than women.

} What studied

} Results

Summary
of related
research

Humor provides utility of communication in every day interactions (Graham, Papa, & Brooks, 1992), in part because everyday conversation thrives on wordplay, sarcasm, anecdotes, and jokes (Norrick, 1993). And as noted by Booth-Butterfield and Booth-Butterfield (1991), a sense of humor is highly valued in American society; however, some research suggests that men and women differ in their approach to the

* Reproduced with permission of authors and publishers from Myers, S.A., Ropog, B.L., and Rodgers, R.P., "Sex Differences in Humor." *Psychological Reports*, 1997, 81, 221–222. © Psychological Reports 1997.

[1] An earlier version of this paper was presented at the 1997 Central States Communication Association meeting in St. Louis, Missouri. Address enquires to S. A. Myers, Ph.D., Department of Speech and Theatre Arts, POB 90420, McNesse State University, Lake Charles, LA 70609–0420 or e-mail (symers@acc.mcnesse.edu).

use of humor. In general communicative interactions, men's humor is characterized by aggression, hostility, and competition (Palmer, 1994; Walker & Dresner, 1988) that often targets women for disparagement (Cantor, 1976, Crawford & Gressley, 1991; Palmer, 1994). Women, on the other hand, are more inclined to use understatement, irony, and self-deprecation (Walker & Dresner, 1988) as forms of humor.

Studies of humor in general and men's humor in particular have provided a large body of data regarding how and why humor is used (e.g., Morris, 1994; Walker & Dresner, 1988) but is incomplete regarding the humor used by women and the difference in use of humor by men and women (e.g., Crawford & Gressley, 1991). Therefore, we were interested in whether men and women differ in their frequency and effectiveness of attempted humor and in their uses of humor for positive affect, expressiveness, and negative affect.

Method.—Participants were 136 undergraduate students (48 men and 88 women) from a small southern university. The ages of the respondents ranged from 17 to 43 years ($M = 20.7$, $SD = 4.4$). Participants were asked to complete two self-report scales in reference to their general use of humor, the Humor Orientation Scale (Booth-Butterfield & Booth-Butterfield, 1991) and the Uses of Humor Index (Graham, *et al.*, 1992). Responses for all items were solicited using a 5-point rating scale anchored by strongly agree (5) and strongly disagree (1).

The Humor Orientation Scale is a 17-item measure that asks respondents to assess both the perceived frequency , i.e., the rate at which humor attempts are made—"I regularly tell jokes and funny stories when I am with a group," and the perceived effectiveness, i.e., whether the actor believes the attempt was perceived as humorous—"People usually laugh when I tell a joke or story," of the attempts. A coefficient alpha of .80 ($M = 32.0$, $SD = 5.7$) was reported for the frequency dimension and also for the effectiveness dimension ($M = 29.0$, $SD = 4.8$).

The Uses of Humor Index is an 11-item measure on which respondents report their reasons for use of humor across (three) dimensions: (a) positive affect, i.e., prosocial use—"I use humor to make light of a situation," (b) expressiveness, i.e., self-disclosure, emotional expression—"I use humor to let others know my likes and dislikes," and (c) negative affect, i.e., anti-social use—"I use humor to demean and belittle others." A coefficient alpha of .78 was reported for the positive affect dimension ($M = 12.2$, $SD = 2.0$), of 4.7 for the expressiveness dimension ($M = 15.5$, $SD = 3.1$), and .84 for the negative affect dimension ($M = 6.9$, $SD = 3.0$).

Results—Three significant findings emerge from the study. First, men ($M = 33.4$) reported more frequent attempts at humor than women ($M = 31.2$, $F_{1,134} = 5.16$, $p < .05$). Second, men ($M = 30.6$) perceived their humor as more effective than women ($M = 28.1$; $F_{1,134} = 8.86$, $p < .01$). Third, men ($M = 7.7$) reported using humor for negative affect more often than women ($M = 6.5$; $F_{1,134} = 5.45$, $P < .05$).

Margin annotations:

Summary of related research

Purpose of study

Sample population & size

How data was obtained

Description of research

Description of scales used

Data reliability

Data reliability

Results

Moderately significant

Highly significant

No significant sex difference was evident for either positive affect ($F_{1,134} = 1.39$, ns) or expressiveness ($F_{1,134} = .06$, ns).

Moderately significant

Because the data were gathered using self-report ratings rather than behavioral or objective measures, the results should be interpreted with caution. However, the findings indicate that not only do men engage in more frequent attempts at humor than women, but that they perceive these attempts as more effective and use humor for expression of negative affect. These findings support the notion advanced by Crawford and Gressley (1991) that perhaps women do not incorporate humor into their repertoire of interpersonal communication behaviors as readily as men. White (1988) posited that women do not use humor regularly due to the social norms that govern communication. Because women are conditioned to not complain, to accept existing social norms, and to not express objections to male attitudes (Rowe, 1995), women may be reluctant to violate social norms against being negative, which may naturally contribute toward a reluctance to use humor. In addition, Walker and Dresner (1988) posited that women are conditioned to accept subordinate and passive roles, which subsequently affects the situations in which they use humor.

Conclusions, Implications, Discussion

conclusion

Why this may be so

References

BOOTH-BUTTERFIELD, S., & BOOTH-BUTTERFIELD, M. (1991) Individual differences in the communication of humorous messages. *Southern Communications Journal,* 56, 205–218.

CANTOR, J. R. (1976) What is funny to whom? The role of gender. *Journal of Communication,* 26, 110–118.

CRAWFORD, M., & GRESSLEY, D. (1991) Creativity, caring, and context; women's and men's accounts of humor preferences and practices. *Psychology of Women Quarterly,* 15, 217–231.

GRAHAM, E. E., PAPA, M. J., & BROOKS, G. P. (1992) Functions of humor in conversation: conceptualization and measurement. *Western Journal of Communication,* 56, 161–183.

MORRIS, L. A. (Ed.) (1994) *American women humorists.* New York: Garland.

NORRICK, N. R. (1993) *Conversational joking: humor is everyday talk.* Bloomington, IN: Indiana Univer. Press.

PALMER, J. (1994) *Taking humor seriously.* New York: Routledge.

ROWE, K. (1995) *The unruly woman: gender and the genres of laughter.* Austin, TX: Univer. of Texas Press.

WALKER, N., & DRESNER, Z. (Eds.) (1988) *Redressing the balance: American women's literary humor from colonial time to the 1980s.* Jackson, MS: Univer. Press of Mississippi.

WHITE C. L. (1988) Liberating laughter: an inquiry into the nature, content, and functions of feminist humor. In B. Bate & A. Taylor (Eds.), *Women communicating: studies of women's talk.* Norwood, NJ: Ablex. pp. 75–90.

Accepted June 9, 1997.

When reading scholarly journals, keep the following tips in mind.

1. **Be sure you understand the author's purpose.** Determine why the study was conducted.

2. **Highlight as you read.** You may need to refer back to information presented earlier in the article.

3. **Use index cards.** If you are reading numerous articles keep a 4×6 index card for each. Write a brief summary of the purpose and findings.

4. **Use quotations.** If you take notes from the article, be sure to place in quotations any information you copy directly from the article. If you fail to do so, you may inadvertently plagiarize. Plagiarism is presenting someone else's ideas as your own, and carries stiff academic and legal penalties.

ANALYZING ESSAYS AND ARTICLES

Essays and articles require close analysis and evaluation. While textbooks usually present reliable, unbiased factual information, essays and even some articles often express opinions and represent particular viewpoints; consequently, you must read them critically. Use the following questions to guide your analysis.

1. **Who is the author?** Check to see if it is a name you recognize. Try to discover whether or not the author is qualified to write about the subject.

2. **What is the author's purpose?** Is the writer trying to present information, convince you of something, entertain you, or express a viewpoint?

3. **What does the introduction or lead add to the piece of writing?** Does it interest you or supply background information, for example?

4. **What is the author's thesis?** Try to express it in your own words. By doing so, you may find bias or discover a viewpoint you had not previously recognized.

5. **Does the author adequately support the thesis?** Is a variety of supporting information provided? An article that relies entirely upon the author's personal experiences, for example, to support a thesis may have limited usefulness.

6. **Does the author supply sources, references, or citations for the facts and statistics presented?** You should be able to verify the information presented and turn to those sources should you wish to read more about the subject.

For more information on thinking critically about essays and articles, refer to Chapters 10, 11, and 12 in Part Four, "Reading Critically."

EXERCISE 6–14

DIRECTIONS: Evaluate the expository essay "How to Brag About Yourself to Win and Hold a New Job" (pp. 55–56) by answering each of the questions listed above.

1. _____

_____

2. _____

_____

3. _____

_____

4. _____

_____

5. _____

_____

6. _____

_____

EXERCISE 6–15

Electronic Application

DIRECTIONS: Use an Internet source to locate an article or essay. Try to locate one from an electronic magazine, rather than from an electronic version of a print magazine. Then answer the following questions.

1. Answer questions 1–6 for analyzing essays and articles.

2. In what ways is the article similar to print magazine articles and in what ways is it different?

3. What are the advantages of electronic magazines over print magazines?

EXERCISE 6–16

Academic Application

DIRECTIONS: Compile a list of articles and essays that you have been assigned to read this semester. For each assignment indicate its source: popular press, scholarly journal, or in-text reading. ▬

Critical Thinking Tip #6

Evaluating Research Sources

When you conduct research, you will read a variety of articles and essays, as well as other source material. Not all sources you encounter while preparing a research paper are equally worthwhile or appropriate. Therefore, it is essential to critically evaluate all sources when conducting research. The following suggestions will help you to evaluate reference sources:

1. Check your source's copyright date. Make certain you are using a current source. For many papers such as those exploring controversial issues or scientific or medical advances, only the most up-to-date sources are useful.
2. Be sure to use an authoritative source. The material should be written by a recognized authority or by someone who is working within his or her field.
3. Choose sources that provide the most complete and concrete information.
4. Select first-hand accounts of an event or experience rather than second- or third-hand accounts whenever possible.
5. Avoid using sources that present biased information and be wary of those that include personal opinion and reactions.

SUMMARY

1. How do essays and articles differ?

Essays and articles differ mainly in viewpoint. Essays are written from a personal perspective while articles are more objective in their presentation of information.

2. What are the parts of an essay?

Essays have five essential parts with different functions:
- Title: suggests the subject and attracts the reader.

- Introduction: offers background, builds interest, defines terms, and states the thesis.
- Thesis Statement: clearly and sufficiently expresses the main point of the essay.
- Body: presents, in a number of paragraphs, information that supports or explains the thesis.
- Conclusion: brings the essay to a close by making a final statement of the subject.

3. What should you look for when reading narrative essays?

Narrative essays present a series of events, often in story form and vividly described. When reading them look for

- the time and place of the events
- the point of view from which it is told
- the overall meaning or thesis of the narrative
- any commentary by the author that helps reveal his or her point

4. What should you focus on in descriptive essays?

Descriptive essays emphasize sensory impressions to create a vivid picture of a person, object, event, or place. It is useful to focus on

- who or what is being described
- the writer's choice of words and the feeling they convey
- the overall impression the description leaves you with
- the first and last paragraphs for clues to the writer's purpose or main point

5. What can you do to improve your reading of expository essays?

Expository essays are meant to inform you about a particular viewpoint. When reading such essays you should

- check that the author can be trusted to present the facts fairly and accurately
- be sure the background information given is complete
- get the writer's thesis clearly in mind

- focus on new terminology used
- mark and highlight the thesis statement and important terms
- make an outline, map, or summary to ensure your recall

6. How are popular press articles organized?

Articles found in magazines and newspapers have a different style and format than essays. Hard news stories, action stories, and feature articles have some differences in format but can contain the following parts:

- Title—often eye catching and descriptive.
- Dateline—the location and date of the story.
- Credit Line—the wire service or newspaper the story came from.
- Byline—the name of the writer.
- Lead—an opening paragraph that either summarizes major information (news stories) or sparks interest in the topic (feature stories).
- Nut Graph—one or more paragraphs that define a feature article's nature and scope.
- Body or Development—the section that presents the supporting facts.
- Conclusion—the final statement about the subject of the article.

7. What are the parts of most scholarly journal articles?

Professional societies publish journals that report research and developments in their fields. They often contain the following six parts which may or may not be labeled:

- Abstract or Summary—follows the title and author.
- Summary of Related Research—reviews current research on the topic.
- Description of Research—also called "Method," tells how the research was carried out or explains the author's ideas, including the purpose of the study.
- Results—states the outcomes of the study.

• Implications, Discussion, and Conclusions —explains the meaning and implications of the study's results.
• Further Research—suggestions for additional studies needed.

8. How can you read essays and articles more critically?

To closely analyze and evaluate essays and articles, ask these questions:
• Who is the author?
• What is his or her purpose?
• What does the introduction or lead add to the piece of writing?
• What is the thesis?
• Is it adequately supported?
• Are sources, references, or citations given for the facts and statistics used?

READING SELECTION 11

ECOLOGY

WILL WE CONTROL THE WEATHER?

J. Madeleine Nash
From *Time Magazine*

Can or should we attempt to affect the weather? This article claims that we have already done so and that the results have been damaging to our environment. Read the article to find out what actions have already negatively affected the climate.

— · —

1   A tropical storm quickly takes shape over the Atlantic Ocean, a furiously whirling dervish with a skirt of thunderstorms. But just as quickly the storm is challenged by dozens of National Weather Service planes, which sally forth from East Coast airstrips like fighters on the tail of an enemy bomber. Attacking from above and below, the planes fire off a barrage of esoteric weapons

that sap the strength of the raging winds in the developing eye wall.

2   Ammunition expended, the lead pilot flashes a thumbs-up, confident that once again she and her team of veteran storm chasers have prevented a hurricane from forming.

3   Could something like this really happen? Probably not. Such fanciful scenarios are period pieces. They belong to the 1950s and '60s, when scientists harbored an almost naive faith in the ability of modern technology to end droughts, banish hail and improve meteorological conditions in countless other ways. At one point, pioneering chemist Irving Langmuir suggested that it would prove easier to change the weather to

our liking than to predict its duplicitous twists and turns. The great mathematician John von Neumann even calculated what mounting an effective weather-modification effort would cost the U.S.—about as much as building the railroads, he figured, and worth incalculably more.

4   At the start of the 21st century, alas, all that remains of these happy visions are a few scattered cloud-seeding programs, whose modest successes, while real, have proved less than earthshaking. In fact, yesterday's sunny hopes that we could somehow change the weather for the better have given way to the gloomy knowledge that we are only making things worse. It is now clear that what the world's cleverest scientists could not achieve by design, ordinary people are on the verge of accomplishing by accident. Human beings not only have the ability to alter weather patterns on local, regional and global scales, but they are already doing it—in ways that are potentially catastrophic.

5   Consider the billions of tons of carbon dioxide that are emitted every year in the course of our daily life. Driving a car, switching on a light, working in a factory, fertilizing a field all contribute to the atmosphere's growing burden of heat-trapping gases. Unless we start to control emissions of CO_2 and similar compounds, global mean temperatures will probably rise somewhere between 2°F and 7°F by the end of the next century; even the low end of that spectrum could set the stage for a lot of meteorological mischief. Among other things, the higher the temperature, the more rapidly moisture can evaporate from the earth's surface and condense as rain droplets in clouds, substantially increasing the risk of both drought and torrential rain. There could also be a rise in the number of severe storms, such as the tornado-spawning monsters that hit Texas last week.

6   Human activity is modifying precipitation in other dramatic ways. Satellite images show that industrial aerosols—sulfuric acid and the like—

emitted by steel mills, oil refineries and power plants are suppressing rainfall downwind of major industrial centers. In Australia, Canada and Turkey, according to one study, these pollution patterns perfectly coincide with corridors within which precipitation is virtually nil. Reason: the aerosols interfere with the mechanism by which the water vapor in clouds condenses and grows into raindrops big enough to reach the ground.

7   This creates an additional conundrum. Because a polluted cloud does not rain itself out, notes University of Colorado atmospheric scientist Brian Toon, it tends to grow larger and last longer, providing a shiny white surface that bounces sunlight out to space. Indeed, one reason the earth has not yet warmed up as much as many anticipated may be due to the tug-of-war between industrial aerosols like sulfuric acid (which reflect heat) and greenhouse gases like carbon dioxide (which trap it). Ironically, then, the cost of reducing one kind of pollution may come at the price of intensifying the effects of the other.

8   Deforestation has a similarly broad range of impact. One thing trees do is lock up a lot of carbon in their woody tissues, thereby preventing it from escaping into the atmosphere. Trees are also important recyclers of moisture to the atmosphere. In some parts of the Amazon basin, deforestation has reached the point where it is altering precipitation patterns. This is because so much of the moisture entrained by clouds comes from the canopy of the forest below; as large tracts of trees disappear, so do portions of the aqueous reservoir that feeds the local rainmaking machine.

9   Shrubs, grasses and other vegetative covers act in much the same way, trapping water, feeding moisture into the atmosphere and providing shade that shields the surface of the land from the drying rays of the sun. Large-scale land-clearing efforts under way around the world

wipe all that out. The ongoing development of South Florida, for instance, has filled in and paved over much of the Everglades wetlands, which have long served as an important source of atmospheric moisture. As a consequence, says Colorado State University atmospheric scientist Roger Pielke Sr., South Florida in July and August has become significantly dryer and hotter than it would have been a century ago under the same set of climactic conditions.

10   To complicate matters further, we are changing the landscape in ways that increase our exposure to meteorological extremes, so that even if weather patterns in coming decades were to turn out to be identical to those of the past century, the damage inflicted would be far worse. To appreciate what happens when vegetative cover is removed, one need look no further than the 1930s Dust Bowl in the U.S. and the 1970s famine in Africa's Sahel. In both cases, a meteorological drought was exacerbated by agricultural and pastoral practices that stripped land bare, exposing it to the not so tender mercies of sun and wind.

11   Removal of vegetative cover also worsens the flooding that occurs during periods of torrential rain. Riverine forests serve as sponges that soak up excess water, preventing it from rushing all at once into rivers and tributaries. In similar fashion, estuarine wetlands and mangrove forests help shield human settlements from the storm surges that accompany tropical cyclones and hurricanes. Biologists estimate that 50% of the world's mangrove forests have already been replaced by everything from shantytowns to cement plants and shrimp farms. Stir in the expectation that rising temperatures will trigger a rise in sea level, and you have a recipe for unprecedented disaster.

12   Scientists are just beginning to disentangle the myriad levels on which human beings and the natural climate system interact, which only increases the potential for surprise. For example,

we now realize that not all the aerosols we are pumping into the atmosphere exert a cooling effect. A notable exception is soot, which is produced by wood fires and incomplete industrial combustion. Because of its dark color, soot absorbs solar energy rather than reflecting it. So when a recent scientific excursion to the Indian Ocean established that big soot clouds were circulating through the atmosphere, a number of scientists speculated that their presence might be raising sea-surface temperatures, potentially affecting the strength of the monsoon.

13   The monsoon is not the only climate cycle that human activity could alter. Atmospheric scientist John M. Wallace of the University of Washington believes that rising concentrations of greenhouse gases are already beginning to have an impact on another important cycle, known as the North Atlantic or Arctic Oscillation. In this case it's not the warming these gases create in the lower atmosphere that is key, but the cooling they cause in the stratosphere, where molecules of carbon dioxide and the like emit heat to space rather than trapping it in the upper atmosphere. This stratospheric cooling, Wallace and others speculate, may have biased prevailing wind patterns in ways that favor a wintertime influx of mild marine air into Northern—as opposed to Southern—Europe.

14   Is Wallace right about this? No one yet knows. We are tampering with systems that are so complex that scientists are struggling to understand them. Climatologist Tom Wigley of the National Center for Atmospheric Research, for one, fervently believes the answer to our probelms lies not just in improved knowledge of the climate system but in technological advances that could counter—and perhaps reverse—present trends. In other words, the farfetched dreams that prominent scientists like Von Neumaann once harbored have not died. Rather they have been transformed and, in the process, become more urgent.

EXAMINING READING SELECTION 11

Checking Your Vocabulary

Directions: Using context, word parts, or a dictionary if necessary, circle the letter of the meaning for each word as it is used in the reading.

1. barrage (paragraph 1)
   a. few
   b. rapid discharge
   c. average number
   d. definite count

2. duplicitous (paragraph 3)
   a. deceptive
   b. predictable
   c. certain
   d. general

3. incalculably (paragraph 3)
   a. definitely
   b. suitably
   c. immeasurably
   d. timelessly

4. myriad (paragraph 12)
   a. obvious
   b. important
   c. incomplete
   d. many

5. fervently (paragraph 14)
   a. justifiably
   b. clearly
   c. passionately
   d. partially

Checking Your Comprehension

Directions: Circle the letter of the best answer.

1. This selection is primarily concerned with
   a. the fact that scientists have controlled weather in the past.
   b. the idea that the weather cannot be altered.
   c. the presumption that weather is always unpredictable.
   d. the ways in which our actions can alter the weather.

2. The selection supports which of the following ideas?
   a. We have never been able to control the weather and we never will be able to control it.
   b. We should not want to control the weather.
   c. We have controlled the weather in negative ways, and now we need to control it in positive ways.
   d. We cannot expect meteorologists to ever be able to predict the weather.

3. According to the selection, which of the following is a result of moisture evaporating from the earth's surface and condensing in clouds as rain?
   a. thunderstorms only
   b. light rain only
   c. drought only
   d. both drought and torrential rain

4. One of the major ways in which we have negatively altered the weather is by
   a. creating more rivers and streams.
   b. placing carbon dioxide into the atmosphere.
   c. seeding clouds.
   d. creating landfills.

5. One effect of industrial aerosols is
   a. tornadoes.
   b. hurricanes.
   c. drought.
   d. thunderstorms.

6. This selection focuses on
   a. historical events in weather control.
   b. causes and effects of weather.
   c. comparisons among regional weather systems.
   d. classifications of weather systems.

Thinking Critically

7. Which of the following actions is the writer likely to oppose?
   a. building reservoirs in Africa
   b. creating new resorts in South Florida
   c. mining in Arizona
   d. creating landfills in the Dust Bowl

8. The author's tone is one of
   a. casualness.
   b. anger.
   c. confrontation.
   d. danger.

9. The writer refers to the Everglades wetlands to show that
   a. when we alter an environment which acts as a controller of precipitation, the weather will become hotter and dryer.
   b. if we create an area of wetlands, we may alter the weather conditions in that area.
   c. Florida continues to receive an increased amount of rain over the years.
   d. the Everglades area is a good example of how and why severe thunderstorms, without warning, can become tornadoes and hurricanes.

10. Which of the following is a generalization?
    a. A satellite image can show areas affected by industrial aerosols.
    b. Vegetative removal caused famine in Africa's Sahel.
    c. Ordinary people are on the verge of changing the weather.
    d. Carbon dioxide is emitted into our atmosphere by factories.

Questions for Discussion

1. Do you think greater regulation of activities, such as deforestation, is justifiable? Why?

2. Have you noticed recent climactic changes in the area in which you live? If so, describe them.

3. The author states that "we are only making things worse." In what areas, other than the weather, do you feel humans have made matters worse?

Selection 11:		1419 words
Finishing Time:		
	HR. MIN.	SEC.
Starting Time:		
	HR. MIN.	SEC.
Reading Time:		
	MIN.	SEC.
WPM Score:		
Comprehension Score:		%

READING SELECTION 12

EDUCATION

CHANGING THE PATTERN OF GENDERED DISCUSSION: LESSONS FROM SCIENCE CLASSROOMS*

Barbara J. Guzzetti and Wayne O. Williams

From *Journal of Adolescent and Adult Literacy*

Do girls respond differently in classroom discussions? This scholarly journal article explores the question of how male and female students are influenced by each other in class participation and discussion in a science classroom. Read the article to discover the outcomes of a research study designed to answer these questions.

— · —

1   A plethora of research shows that the true discussion of the concepts in texts facilitates students' learning. True discussion occurs when students' voices dominate, when students interact with each other, and when students talk in phrases and sentences (Alvermann, Dillon & O'Brien, 1987). Discussion is particularly effective in changing students' alternative conceptions (ideas that vary from scientifically accepted concepts) when individuals are asked to provide evidence from the text to support their opinions (Guzzetti, Snyder, Glass, & Gamas, 1993) Hence, discussion that disenfranchises females is especially detrimental in science because it is important to discuss ideas when students' theories are contradicted by scientific thought (Alvermann & Hynd, 1989).

2   Students seem to agree with researchers who find discussion necessary, because they self-report that discussion is one of the most effective ways to learn science material (Tobin & Garnett, 1987). Yet, both true discussion and the more typical recitation-type discussion, where the teacher asks a question and a student provides the answer, (Alvermann et al., 1987), are dominated by males (Tobin & Garnett, 1987). Some researchers believe that the tendency for boys to achieve more than girls in science may be a result of greater opportunities to engage in academic activities, like discussions (Tobin & Garnett, 1987).

3   These insights from research in reading education and science education focused mainly on observations of verbal interactions between teachers and students. Researchers from science education agree that teachers have disparate expectations for students' responses in teacher-led discussion. For example, in teacher-led, whole-class discussion, boys are spoken to and are asked higher level questions more frequently (Becker, 1981; Hall & Sadler, 1982). Science teachers elaborate more on males' responses than females' responses in large-group discussions of scientific concepts (Jones & Wheatley, 1990). Teachers will take a student's argument on a position more seriously when it comes from a male (Lemke, 1990).

4   This research from science education focuses on the teacher's behavior that fosters gender disparity in classroom discussion. But, teachers aren't the only ones whose behaviors constrain girl's contributions to discussions. Students may well constrain or enable each other. Hence, we (the university researcher, Guzzetti, and the participating physics teacher, Williams) decided to examine interactions between students in discussion.

5   Recent research in gender and literacy (conducted in other subject areas) provides evidence that who talks in discussion, how much, and what is said are influenced by changing relationships of power among students (Alvermann &

---

* Due to the length of this reading, timing is inappropriate and word-per-minute conversions are not provided.

Anders, 1994). Researchers from reading education (Alvermann, 1993; Alvermann & Anders, 1994) have directed teachers to examine "the reasons behind the silence," like students' self-confidence and peer relationships.

6   Sociolinguists identify other social norms in classrooms that favor males in instructional conversations. Males are enabled by females to dominate instructional talk because females respond to social pressures that women be good listeners who are valued for their ability to be attentive to others (Lafrance, 1991). Hence, there is a cultural proclivity to see any talk by females as too much talk (Tromel-Plotz, 1985). As a result, language practices have been cited as key influences contributing to the domination and oppression of young women in classrooms (Gilbert, 1989).

Why we did the study

7   Stimulated by our readings from four fields (reading/literacy education, science education, sociolinguistics, and feminist pedagogy) and in response to calls for descriptions of students' interactions that perpetuate gender disparity (Krockover & Shepardson, 1995; Tobin 1988), we conducted this investigation. We wanted to know specifically how students were influenced by each other in their talk about science concepts.

8   In addition to whole-class discussion, we wanted to examine students' interactions in small groups because some researchers recommend this structure to address gender disparity (Tannen, 1992), while others warn that males dominate science talk, whatever the structure or activity (Lemke, 1990; Morse & Handley, 1985).

9   We also decided to explore students' interactions in various types of discussion, as well as various structures. The range of interactions we sought to examine included debate or refutational discussion in whole-class settings and collaborative discussion for team work in small groups. We anticipated making comparisons of verbal interactions between genders from one form and structure to another.

How we did the study

10   This article presents an overview of our findings from a 2-year study and provides recommendations for fostering equitable participation in discussion. In the first year, we identified and described the types of behaviors and language patterns that characterized gender disparity, without changing the normal structure of the class (Guzzetti & Williams, 1996). To accomplish this, we (Guzzetti and two graduate assistants) observed the same two sections of physics (juniors and seniors, 9 females and 15 males) and honors physics (juniors and seniors, 14 females and 17 males) daily for almost the entire school year (commencing in August and ending in March).

11   We also administered a questionnaire that assessed students' preferences for classroom structure, their perceptions of gender differences in talk, and their individual participation. Finally, we conducted informal interviews with those students whose academic performance was affected by their gendered interactions.

12   In the second year of our study, we used the knowledge we had gained from our first year's observations to change the structure of the physics classroom. In response to the gender disparity we described during the first year, we implemented same-sex lab groups and small-group discussions. In doing so, we were influenced by our reading of The American Association of University Women's (AAUW) 1992 report, *How Schools Shortchange Girls*. This synthesis of research states that although girls often perform better in same-sex work groups, researchers have not yet described the dynamics of participants' interactions, or the circumstances under which single-sex groups are most beneficial.

13   Hence, we wanted to identify how same-sex grouping might diminish gender bias in science activity and talk about that activity. We also hoped to change student interaction that impeded female participation. We wondered if

enabling females to participate in small-group, single-sex discussions would have an influence on their participation in whole-class, dual-sex discussions.

14 To accomplish these goals, the second year of our study consisted of daily observation of two related units—gravity and projectile motion. We chose these units because they represent counterintuitive concepts (i.e., contrary to logic and common sense). Students typically have alternative conceptions for these concepts, and are often found discussing their ideas with each other. Hence, we anticipated that we would be able to observe a myriad of discussions forms and participation styles in these units.

What we found

15 Listed and explained below are five findings from our 2-year study. These findings were evidenced in at least three sources—observations of whole-class or small-group discussions, formal or informal interviews, and students' questionnaire responses. Each finding complements or extends other research on gender disparity in discussion and has direct implications for instructional practice.

16 1. *Refutational discussions favor males.* We had frequent opportunities to observe students arguing their ideas because Williams structured a whole-class, refutational discussion (called "inquiry training") during each unit. Williams would choose a counterintuitive concept, formulate a question about it, and, before class started, would secretly select a student to be a "shill" during the discussion. Williams provided this student with a logical but scientifically incorrect idea as a response to the question, and a logical but faulty explanation for that idea. The shill was awarded extra credit points if he or she could convince others of that position.

17 Few females were shills, as Williams selected shills from students' responses to a questionnaire indicating their desire to assume this role. Not many females desired to be shills; large numbers

of boys did, however. Two females we interviewed who had been shills before our observations either thought their assertions were ineffectual or did not remember the details of the discussions.

18 Inquiry training was particularly interesting to us because we knew from past research that written forms of refutation are effective in learning counterintuitive science concepts (Guzzetti et al., 1993). Hence, we anticipated that oral forms of refutation would be potentially powerful in changing students' alternative conceptions. We believed that equal access to this type of discussion would be especially necessary for students to evolve an understanding of these concepts. We also knew however, from past research that whole-class discussion typically favors males (Tannen, 1992).

19 Examination of our observation notes during both years of our study documented that girls spoke only rarely in whole-class, refutational discussions. In these discussions, it was always the same few girls who volunteered to speak. When girls did refute, they tended to pose their refutation as a question, like "Have you thought about this . . ." or "Shouldn't that be . . . ?" Boys, however, would argue directly with each other, making assertions like "That's wrong because . . . ." Males were also most likely to display aggressive language behavior, like interruptions, louder vocalizations, and emphatic intonations.

20 This contrast in language styles was perceived by the males as an indicator that girls didn't understand physics as well as the boys did. Males made this inference because, in the words of one boy in honors physics, "Girls ask a lot of questions, but I think the guys know the basic facts, so they don't need to." Another male in the class, John (pseudonym), volunteered that "Girls don't seem to grasp the concepts as the guys do"; when asked why he thought so, he stated, "Because they're the ones asking most of the questions. . . . Most of the time, when I have something to say, it's usually an argument about air resistance or friction."

21 This perception on the part of the males that the girls' questioning indicated their lack of knowledge was consistent across sections of physics.

22 Girls' explanations for their differential participation in whole class, refutational discussions alluded to issues of self-confidence and social norms. In response to the questionnaire item "How likely are you to argue with a shill in class discussion?" in the first year without intervention, the majority (across sections) of the females (78%) stated that they were not likely to argue. In comparison, less than half (40%) of the males stated they wouldn't debate. Comments from girls included statements like "I'm not confident enough in my knowledge of physics to debate about it," "I don't know enough to argue about it," and "I'm not too sure of the answer." In contrast, comments from boys were typically a remark like "I'll argue with anyone about anything, especially if I disagree with them."

23 In our second year (after the interventions of same-sex lab groups and small group discussions), more females were likely to debate, although refutational discussions still favored males. Less than half of the girls (45%) stated they might or would argue, in contrast to about two thirds of the boys (66%) across sections. Comments from girls still indicated a lack of self-confidence, like "I have doubts about my thoughts" and "I'm not very likely to argue because I probably wouldn't know if they were right or wrong." In response to the query "Do you talk very much in whole-class discussions?" an Asian female in a single-sex lab group replied, "Mostly in small groups I don't have a problem. I talk as much as possible. But, in a bigger class I don't talk as much unless I'm very sure about what I'm saying."

24 These students' remarks that refer to gender differences in self-confidence are consistent with observations by researchers. Writers on gender and language characterize women's speech as insecure or lacking in confidence (Lakoff, 1975). Others argue that questions rather than asser-

tions provide social grace (Dubois & Crouch, 1975; Edelsky, 1979) and typify females' inclusive conversational style (Tromel-Plotz, 1985). Hence, by refuting less often and by posing their refutations as a query, the girls were being consistent with socially learned norms of gender-appropriate language.

25 Females who were inclined to voice their opinions during refutational discussions reported feeling ineffectual and having their opinions dismissed by the boys. One female, Barbara (pseudonym), in honors physics (during year 2) stated:

> It's really hard to get what you think across. [Boys think] "Oh, you're a girl, I'm going to listen to my buddy over here. He knows what he's talking about; I'm going to be cool." It's such a male-dominated class that I definitely notice a difference. I may talk out a lot, but I don't feel like they're even listening to my ideas.

26 Barbara's perception of being ignored in whole-class discussion is consistent with Tromel-Plotz's (1985) observation that women are forced into subservient positions in discussion by males not giving females a chance to talk, disregarding what they say when they do get a chance, and not taking women seriously as equal participants in the discussion. Tannen (1994) explains that women who use conversational strategies (like being indirect) that are designed to take others' feelings into account may perceive that they are not being listened to. They also may be seen by others as less competent and confident than they really are.

27 Comments from females who did not participate in refutational discussions alluded to conversational preferences that reflect social norms, like "I'm not very likely to argue because I don't enjoy trying to prove myself in this class" or "I hate arguing." These remarks about conversational style (proclivity to argue or not argue) are consistent with research citing girls' socialization to avoid arguments. Researchers identify social norms like these as a constraining influence on girls' participation in scholarly debate (Meyer &

Fowler, 1993). Girls feel a social expectation as females to avoid sounding intellectually threatening (equal or superior) around young men (Johnson, 1995). Our findings agree with Tannen's (1992) conclusion that "debate-like formats as learning tools make classrooms more hospitable to men" (p. 4).

28   2. *Females do not participate in whole-class discussions because they are afraid.* In both years of our study, females' reasons for not speaking out were not only because of their lack of self-confidence or fear of violating social conventions, but also because they felt intimidated. Their comments focused on their fears of repercussions from the male students, such as "I like working with all girls because you don't have to worry about your reputation"; "I wouldn't argue in class because they [boys] would probably bite off my head if I did"; and "Guys tend to be hostile—if you're wrong, you're stupid, according to them."

29   Comments like these were more likely to be heard in classes where the proportion of males to females was most asymmetrical, and in classes where there were no groupings by gender.

30   3. *Small groups do not necessarily facilitate females' participation unless grouped by gender.* Observation notes from our first year showed that merely putting students into small groups did not facilitate females' participation in instructional activity or talk about that activity. Most often, the males were the ones in lab groups who were engaged in manipulating the equipment, giving directions, and making verbal inferences about their observations. Females were most likely to be confined to setting up the equipment and passively recording data the boys had actively generated by conducting the experiment. A summary of observation notes by a research assistant reads "Only the boys in each team operate the experiment, whereas the girls just sit there and record the data."

31   Observations and interviews from our second year (when most students were grouped by gender for lab assignments—uneven numbers of males and females prevented total division) showed that females became more active participants when placed in same-sex groups, and they engaged more often in a wider range of verbal interactions. Our observation notes document girls' discussion while setting up the equipment, manipulating the experiment, identifying errors and resolving them, measuring, making observations, recording the data, and negotiating their meaning.

32   Females' talk during these events was characterized by collaborative inquiry and equal participation. In contrast, when only one male was present in a group, that male was most likely to give orders, to ask only assumptive questions (assuming agreement), and to talk to demonstrate or show girls how to proceed. Girls' voices were generally silenced.

33   4. *Males and females display different conversational styles in small groups as well as in large groups.* Female students characterized their discussions with each other as more interactive, more concerned about consensus, more willing to consider others' opinions, more prone to question, and more likely to consult authority to settle disagreements. In response to the questionnaire item "Do you notice any differences in the way boys talk in class versus the way girls talk in class, and, if so, what?" females supported our inferences with statements like "Guys are hostile," "Girls are likely to listen to opinions," and "Guys are more direct and narrow minded." Males made comments like "The boys generate ideas faster than the girls," "Most of the girls seem timid and shy compared to the boys," and "The boys make it sound technical, and the girls say it in words they understand."

34   Females' collaborative discussion style was in sharp contrast to the males' independent discussion style. Even in small-group discussions, we found males more assertive or aggressive in their verbal interaction and less likely to negotiate shared meanings (except when required to find evidence for their opinions from the text). This pattern may be consistent across both large and

small groups because males have been characterized as having more self-confidence and less need for dependence on others (American Association of University Women, 1992). Boys recognized this disparity, as they wrote comments on their questionnaires like "Boys are more opinionated," "Boys are louder and more confident," "Boys are always right," and "Girls ask questions; boys express what they think."

35 We also found males to be competitive and, on the whole, unlikely to incorporate verbal suggestions from females. Guzzetti's observation notes during an experiment on projectile motion read (pseudonyms used):

> I notice that a lab group of boys next to a lab group of girls has marks all over their paper [indicating many trials and errors]. Bryan tells me it's because their steel ramp is "drunk"; it keeps moving [causing error]. I tell them that happened to Janice's group yesterday. Immediately, Bryan asks Janice's group how they fixed that. Amanda tells Bryan that they didn't, they just put a mark on the table to align the ramp each time. Bryan says they'll start to do that. Amanda informs him that they have a patent on it [entitlement to extra credit points if others use their idea]. Upon hearing this, the other two boys in Bryan's group retort "Oh! Never mind!" Bryan tells me that he doesn't care if the girls get extra credit just so long as his group gets the experiment right. Bryan's group, however, does not incorporate the girls' idea.

36 5. *Students are well aware of gender disparity in classroom discussion.* One of the most common findings from prior research is that teachers are usually unaware of gender bias in classroom activity and talk about that activity (Jones & Wheatley, 1990; Tobin, 1988). For example, Williams was not aware of any gender inequities in his classes prior to reading our data and believed he was gender fair in his interactions with students. Our observations confirmed that Williams used the seating chart to call on fairly proportional numbers of males and females. He reported that in his 30 years of teaching, girls and boys achieved equally in his classes, and that some of his best students (selected for honors or awards in science) had

been girls. Prior to our study, Williams was looking for gender bias only in his own attitudes and behaviors.

37 Our investigation provided a plethora of evidence, however, that teachers like Williams may be unaware of gender disparity in their own or their students' actions, students are not unaware. Both males and females consistently reported males' domination of science activity and talk about that activity before we changed the classroom structure. In the first year of our study, 100% of the girls in physics reported gender differences in how often and the ways boys talk in class, and all of the girls nominated a male as the person who talked the most.

38 Although only 50% of the males in the class reported gender differences in classroom talk, 94% of them nominated a boy as the person who talked the most in class. In honors physics that year, 80% of the females and 60% of the males reported that males dominated discussions. (In year 2, after our intervention, these numbers were reduced to about half of the females and a third of the males across sections who noticed gender differences in discussion.) These data also indicate that students who do not notice gender inequities are most likely to be males.

What can be done

39 These data show us that teachers not only need to be concerned with their own language that fosters gender inequity in discussion, but must also monitor their students' ways of talking. Teachers must provide conditions that foster gender equity among students in instructional activity and talk about that activity. In our research, students were the major contributors to gender inequities in discussion. It was their interactions with each other that intimidated and threatened the girls, made them afraid of repercussions, and silenced their voices.

40 The following four suggestions for addressing gender disparity in classroom discussion are based on our experiences during the 2 years of

our study and on our readings in the literature on gender bias.

41 **1. Recognize gender bias in discussion.** Because teachers are generally unaware of gender inequities among students in their verbal interactions, teachers will need to become active observers for gender bias. Teachers must consciously observe to identify students who dominate the discussion and be aware of those who practice covert or overt tactics to gain control. Although awareness is not sufficient for change (Taylor, 1989; Tobin, 1988), teachers must be able to recognize the problem to take steps to alleviate it.

42 Teachers can observe gender bias in discussion by looking for specific behaviors that characterize it. Ploys that indicate gender bias include both verbal and nonverbal behaviors that ultimately inhibit equitable discussion (Tromel-Plotz, 1985). Verbal ploys to gain control include interruptions, call outs, and increased vocal pitch, tone, or loudness. Nonverbal tactics include withholding active feedback, using elaborate gestures (e.g., jumping out of a seat, wildly waving a hand) to gain attention, and body language (e.g., frowns, looks of disapproval, and gaze aversion) to stifle discussion of a verbalized idea.

43 In addition to noticing the quality of verbal interactions, it is also necessary to notice the quantity of talk between genders. Power relationships often depend more on who is doing the talking than on what is actually said. When one gender consistently has the floor over another, power relationships between genders are unbalanced (Edelsky, 1981).

44 **2. Group by gender in small groups for refutational discussion.** Since whole-class and refutational discussions favor males, teachers can encourage females' participation by grouping by gender to debate views. These types of discussions are useful in learning new concepts and should, therefore, be made gender-fair. Conditions that encourage females to participate in discussion can be established by allowing girls to debate with each other and to elect a spokesperson to report their group's view to the total class.

45 We recommend incorporating a Discussion Web (Alvermann, 1991) for these debates. We suggest adapting this procedure by pairing students by gender to reach consensus on a response to a central question. Students may be required to provide evidence from the textbook, trade books, or labs to support their views. After reaching agreement, this group of two then joins another group of two and again attempts to reach consensus through substantiated persuasion. This group of four may join another group of four and repeat the process. Finally, the group of eight students elects a spokesperson who reports the group's view to the whole class, stimulating whole-class discussion and consensus.

46 By using a Discussion Web, females will be given the opportunity to be discussion leaders in smaller groups. They will also gain more confidence in their opinions because they will have textual or external support for their views. Based on our observations, we believe that this type of leadership in small groups may assist females in asserting their opinions more freely in whole-class discussion, give them practice in being leaders in discussion, and make debates less biased toward males.

47 **3. Promote self-confidence by providing an intellectually safe environment.** Teachers can encourage girls' participation in discussion by calling on them more often (prompting), restating or elaborating on their remarks, and by giving positive reinforcement for their comments and questions (Morse & Handley, 1985). By doing so, teachers can demonstrate that they value females' participation and take their comments seriously. If the teacher models these behaviors, students may be inclined to emulate them.

48 Teachers, together with their students, can also establish rules for discussion. In the classes we observed during our second year, Williams monitored interruptions and call outs in whole-class discussion and did not allow them. In a

similar way, teachers and students, by having discussions together, may create a list of unacceptable tactics (like those identified in our first recommendation) and expect that all students, whatever their gender, avoid them.

49   4. *Expand acceptable notions of science and ways of talking about science.* Teachers can present a view of science as active questioning and exploration, dispelling the misconception of science as passive observation and memorization of facts (Carey, Evans, Honda, Jay, & Unger, 1989), while at the same time publicly valuing feminine ways of talking. Teachers can demonstrate that they value females' language strategies by presenting women's tendencies to question as positive rather than negative, and modeling questioning as a legitimate way to "talk science." Teachers can remind students that questions are the first step in scientific inquiry, that scientists frequently form new theories by questioning, and that science is not static and stable, but constantly changing due to questioning and requestioning prior assumptions. Teachers can model this behavior in discussion by sharing with the class questions they and other scientists still have about the concepts under study.

50   Hence, teachers can demonstrate sensitivity to gender by expanding their philosophies of science and what counts as science talk. Discursive practices that emphasize objectivity, logic, and rationality may well disenfranchise women. Rather than creating a dichotomy between objective and subjective, teachers can strive for a holistic way of approaching science inquiry and talk about that inquiry.

51   Teachers can also demonstrate that they value feminine ways of talking about science by modeling and rewarding collaborative (rather than authoritative) discussion styles. We believe that recommendations for addressing gender bias should not simply focus on ways to make women sound more like men in instructional conversations, but should expand the possibilities for each gender. For when males are not

socialized to listen to others, they, too, are disenfranchised, denied a strategy that enables learning through collaboration, by talking with rather than to others.

Reflections

52   These suggestions are only first steps in creating gender-fair discussions. Teachers and their students may together find other more contextually appropriate ways to address gender disparity in their own classroom activity and talk. Whatever teachers choose to do, we agree with Tobin (1988) that students should be involved in creating solutions to a problem that so directly affects their opportunities for learning and their views of each other.

References

Alvermann, D. E. (1991). The discussion web: A graphic aid for learning across the curriculum. *The Reading Teacher, 45,* 92–99.

Alvermann, D. E., & Anders, P. A. (1994, July). *New directions for inquiry and practice: Content area literacy from a feminist/critical perspective.* Paper presented at the International Reading Association's 15th World Congress on Reading, Buenos Aires, Argentina.

Alvermann, D. E., Dillon, D. R., & O'Brien, D. G. (1987). *Using discussion to promote reading comprehension.* Newark, DE: International Reading Association.

Alvermann, D. E., & Hynd, C. R. (1989, November). *The influence of text and discussion on the learning of counter-intuitive science concepts.* Paper presented at the annual meeting of the National Reading Conference, Austin, TX.

American Association of University Women. (1992). *How schools shortchange girls: A study of major findings on girls and education.* Washington DC: Author.

Becker, J. R. (1981). Differential treatment of females and males in mathematics classes.

Journal for research in Mathematics Education, 12, 40–53.

Carey, S., Evans, R., Honda, M., Jay, E., & Unger, C. (1989). An experiment is when you try it and see if it works: A study of grade 7 student's understanding of the construction of scientific knowledge. *International Journal of Science Education,* 11, 514–529.

Dubois, B. L., & Crouch, I. (1975). The question of tag questions in women's speech: They don't really use more of them, do they? *Language in Society,* 4, 289–294.

Edelsky, C. (1979). Question intonation and sex role. *Language in Society,* 8, 15–32.

Edelsky, C. (1981). Who's got the floor? *Language in Society,* 10, 383–421.

Gilbert, P. (1989). Personally (and passively) yours: Girls, literacy and education. *Oxford Review of Education,* 15, 257–265.

Guzzetti, B. J., Snyder, T. E., Glass, G. V. & Gamas, W. S. (1993). Promoting conceptual change in science: A comparative meta-analysis of interventions from reading education and science education. *Reading Research Quarterly,* 28, 116–159.

Guzzetti, B. J., & Williams, W. O. (1996). Gender, text, and discussion: Examining intellectual safety in the science classroom. *Journal of Research in Science Teaching,* 33, 5–20.

Hall, R., & Sadler, B. R. (1982). *The classroom climate: A chilly one for women? Project on the status of women.* Washington, DC: Association of American Colleges. (ERIC ED 215 628)

Jones, M. G., & Wheatley, J. (1990). Gender differences in teacher-student interactions in science classrooms. *Journal of Research in Science Teaching,* 27, 861–874.

Krockover, G. H, & Shepardson, S. D. P. (1995). The missing links in gender equity research. *Journal of Research in Science Teaching,* 32, 223–224.

Lafrance, M. (1991). School for scandal: Different educational experiences for females and males. *Gender and Education.* 3(12), 312.

Lakoff, R. (1975). *Language and women's place.* New York: Harper and Row.

Lemke, J. (1990). *Talking science: Language, learning and values.* Norwood, NJ: Ablex.

Meyer, D. K., & Fowler, L. A. (1993, December). *Is gender related to classroom discourse across content areas?* Paper presented at the annual meeting of the National Reading Conference, Charleston, SC.

Morse, L. W., & Handley, H. M. (1985). Listening to adolescents: Gender differences in science classroom interaction. In L. C. Wilkinson & C. B. Marrett (Eds.), *Gender influences in classroom interaction* (pp. 37–56). New York: Academic Press.

Tannen, D. (1992). How women and men use language differently in their lives and in the classroom. *The Chronicle of Higher Education,* 3–6.

Tannen, D. (1994). *Talking from 9 to 5: How women's and men's conversational styles affect who gets heard, who gets credit, and what gets done at work.* New York: Morrow.

Taylor, S. (1989). Empowering girls and young women: The challenge of the gender-inclusive curriculum. *Journal of Curriculum Studies,* 21, 441–456.

Tobin, K. (1988). Differential engagement of males and females in high school science. *International Journal of Science Education,* 10(3), 239–252.

Tobin, K., & Garnett, P. (1987). Gender related differences in science activities. *Science Education,* 71(1), 91–103.

Tromel-Plotz, S. (1985, September). *Women's conversational culture: Rupturing patriarchal discourse.* Unpublished manuscript. Roskilde Universitetscenter, Roskilde, Denmark.

Examining Reading Selection 12*

Checking Your Vocabulary

Directions: Complete each of the following items; refer to a dictionary if necessary.

1. Discuss the connotative meanings of the phrase *gender bias* (paragraph 36).

2. Define each of the following words:
   a. plethora (paragraph 1, 37)

   _____

   b. disenfranchises (paragraph 1, 51)

   _____

   c. proclivity (paragraph 6, 27)

   _____

   d. emulate (paragraph 47)

   _____

   e. dichotomy (paragraph 50)

   _____

3. Define the word *disparate* (paragraph 3) and underline the word or phrase that provides a context clue for its meaning.

   _____

   _____

4. Define the word *repercussions* (paragraph 28) and underline the word or phrase that provides a context clue for its meaning.

   _____

   _____

   _____

5. Determine the meanings of the following words by using word parts:
   a. sociolinguists (paragraph 6)

   _____

   _____

b. counterintuitive (paragraph 14)

_____

c. refutational (paragraph 16)

_____

d. ineffectual (paragraph 25)

_____

e. subservient (paragraph 26)

_____

Checking Your Comprehension

1. What was the basic purpose of this study?

   _____

   _____

   _____

2. What was the goal of the first year of this study? The second year?

   _____

   _____

   _____

   _____

   _____

   _____

3. What was the purpose of "shills" in the whole class refutational discussions?

   _____

   _____

4. What were the basic findings of this study?

   _____

   _____

   _____

*Multiple-choice questions are contained in Part 6 (page 603).

_____

_____

_____

_____

_____

_____

Thinking Critically

1. In what ways do the authors believe teachers can alter their own behaviors to help eliminate gender bias in science classrooms?

   _____

   _____

   _____

   _____

   _____

   _____

2. Why do the authors favor the "Discussion Web" as a means of involving females in science debates?

   _____

   _____

   _____

3. What do the authors think is the major cause of gender inequality in science discussions? Why?

   _____

   _____

   _____

   _____

   _____

   _____

   _____

   _____

Questions for Discussion

1. It appears that males are given more opportunities to excel in high school science than females. Name and discuss a situation in which the opposite is true—that females are given an advantage over males in other academic areas.

2. If you had to come up with one additional suggestion for science teachers to soothe the gender bias problem, what would it be?

3. Do you agree that separating boys from girls in small groups results in better learning? Why?

Go Electronic

For additional readings, exercises, and Internet activities, visit this book's Web site at:

http://www.ablongman.com/mcwhorter

For even more activities, visit the Longman English pages at:

http://www.ablongman.com/englishpages

If you need a user name and password, please see your instructor.

CHAPTER 11 | READING RESEARCH, REFERENCE, AND COLLATERAL ASSIGNMENTS

LEARNING OBJECTIVES

- ■ To learn a systematic approach for reading research materials
- ■ To develop alternative reading strategies
- ■ To learn note taking
- ■ To develop skills for reading collateral reading assignments
- ■ To learn to evaluate sources

Your political science professor assigns a 20-page research paper. Your psychology professor assigns a text and 30 related readings—research articles from *Science Digest*. Your marketing professor requires that you read and abstract two articles per week on topics related to her weekly lectures. You probably have discovered that your reading assignments are not limited to textbooks; many of your professors require that you locate sources, read research articles, and report their findings. Some professors distribute reading lists and direct you to read or write a specified number of abstracts. Others place materials to be read on reserve in the library. Still others assign a research paper on a related topic of your choice.

Many students make the mistake of reading research and supplementary material in the same way they read their textbook assignments. Consequently, they become frustrated with the assignments, claiming, "I'll never finish the research for this paper" or "These reading assignments are impossible!" This chapter describes new approaches to dealing with research, reference, and collateral reading assignments that are distinct from textbook reading techniques.

READING RESEARCH MATERIALS

Reading research and reference materials is very different from reading textbooks. When reading textbooks, your goal is usually a high level of retention and recall. In reading research papers, however, complete retention is not always necessary. You may be searching for evidence to support an argument, reading widely to gain overall familiarity with a subject, or locating a particular statistic. Also, whereas textbooks have a consistent format and organization, research and reference sources differ widely in these characteristics. Consequently, you must adapt your reading strategy to suit the nature of the material. The following sections present a systematic approach to reading research and reference material when you must prepare a written report or research paper.

Define and Focus Your Topic

The first critical step in doing research for a written assignment is to define and focus your topic. It is a waste of time to begin a full search for information and to read numerous sources until you know exactly what you are looking for. Suppose you begin with a topic, such as "Hypnotism." This subject is much too broad. You couldn't possibly cover everything about hypnotism in one paper in any meaningful way. It may take two or three attempts at narrowing to arrive at a topic you can reasonably handle. For example, "Hypnotism" could be narrowed to "Uses of Hypnotism," then to "Modern Uses of Hypnotism," and finally to "Modern Medical Uses of Hypnotism."

To help narrow your topic, especially if it is one with which you are not familiar, some preliminary research or reading may be helpful. Here are some suggestions.

1. *Consult with your reference librarian to find out whether computerized searches are available.* Many libraries have access to data banks that identify all possible sources on a given topic. (Some libraries charge a fee for this service.)

2. *Read an encyclopedia entry to get an overview of the subject.*

3. *Check the* Reader's Guide to Periodical Literature *for listings on your topic.* Look through the list of articles for ideas on how to narrow your topic.

4. *Check the card catalogue or on-line computer system to see how your topic is subdivided.*

5. Consult your instructor if you're not sure whether your topic is sufficiently narrow.

Once you have narrowed your topic, try to establish a focus or direction for your research. Your paper should focus on, explore, and answer a question; it should take a position. For example, your paper on "Modern Medical Uses of Hypnotism" might discuss the ways hypnotism is useful in modern medicine, or it might take the position that hypnotism is of limited use in modern medical practice, or even that hypnotism is dangerous and that its use should be restricted.

| **EXERCISE 11–1** | *Assume that one of your professors has assigned a research paper on one of the following subjects. Choose one subject, and narrow it to a topic that is manageable in a 10-page paper.* |

1. Environmental problems
2. Pornography
3. Test-tube babies
4. Professional sports

Devise a Search Strategy

In researching a topic, some students begin by gathering all the sources on the topic and then working through them randomly. This approach is time-consuming and often repetitious. Instead, devise and follow a search strategy—an orderly way of sifting through available sources on your topic. A search strategy enables you to select the most suitable materials and to approach the topic in a logical fashion. A search strategy proceeds from general to specific. You begin by reading general materials that provide an overview of your topic. You then move gradually to more detailed sources that address a particular aspect of your topic. Of course, your search strategy depends on your topic, your familiarity with it, and the requirements of your assignments, but a common search strategy is shown in Table 11–1.

As you proceed through the search strategy, you will find additional references. Each source will list its own references; eventually, the sources will converge. That is, you will come on the same sources several times and will begin to recognize authorities in the field. For example, as you research quality control in business and industry, you keep coming across the name of W. Edwards Deming, so you realize you need to know more about him and his ideas. If you have difficulty locating bibliographies or working through the search strategy, reference librarians are ready to offer valuable, time-saving assistance.

TABLE 11–1 A SEARCH STRATEGY

SOURCE	PURPOSE
1. Encyclopedia	Obtain an overview; learn the language of the subject; discover subdivisions.
2. Bibliographies and Indexes (list of sources on a topic)	Locate a list of sources on the subject.
3. Books	Obtain basic information on the topic (or aspects of the topic).
4. Periodicals	Investigate particular aspects of the topic; obtain current or recent information.
5. Special sources (documents, directories, review of the literature, pamphlet files, media resources)	Zero in on specialized information.

Previewing Sources

As you proceed through your search strategy, it is useful to preview sources before delving into them. Previewing is an excellent research strategy; it enables you to select the most useful sources and to select sources of appropriate difficulty and complexity.

Let's assume you have located 15 books for a term paper on the psychological effects of terrorism on its victims. Your next step is to preview those sources to determine which are useful to your paper. If your paper requires current information, check the copyright date and eliminate any sources that are outdated. Next, glance through the table of contents to get an overall idea of the material covered by each source. Check the index to determine how extensively the source treats your specific topic. Select only those sources that provide a comprehensive treatment of your topic. Once you have identified these sources, randomly select a sample page in each and skim it to get a "feel" for the source. Pay particular attention to the level of difficulty. Is the source too basic, containing little more information than is in your course textbook? Or is the source too complicated? Does it assume extensive background knowledge of the subject, such as an extensive knowledge of psychoanalysis, for example? Previewing will enable you to select sources that contain sufficient information and that are of an appropriate degree of difficulty.

Defining Your Purpose

Be sure to have a specific purpose for reading each reference source. Your purpose determines *how* you will read the material, as well as what type of note taking, if any, is necessary. To define your purpose, determine what level of comprehension and retention is expected. Is complete recall necessary, or is familiarity with key concepts sufficient? Your choice will hinge in part on the type of follow-up activity, if any, that will be involved. Will you be expected to write a summary or abstract, discuss the material in class, or use the information to write a term paper? (Refer to "Documentation and Note Taking" later in this chapter for suggestions.)

Comprehension is not an either/or situation. Rather, comprehension is a continuum, and many levels of understanding are possible. In this respect, you might think of comprehension as similar to temperature: There is a wide range of conditions between freezing and boiling. And just as snowball fights go with freezing temperatures and cool drinks in the shade go with high temperatures, so are various levels of comprehension appropriate for various materials and types of assignments. An extremely high level of comprehension is necessary if you are reading a critical interpretation of a poem for an English literature paper. Each detail is important. However, a lower level of comprehension is appropriate for reading excerpts from a biography assigned for an American history course. Here, you would not be expected to recall each descriptive detail or bit of conversation.

The reading strategy you select is also shaped by the tasks that will follow your reading. If, for example, you are reading an encyclopedia article to get an overview of a subject so that you can narrow a topic for a term paper, then complete comprehension is not needed. You require only an understanding of the major aspects or divisions of the subject in order to begin topic selection. Therefore, moderate to low comprehension is appropriate. Suppose, however, you are required to write a critical evaluation of a magazine article arguing against capital punishment. A high or complete level of comprehension is required, because you need to follow the argument carefully, search for points of inconsistency, and so forth.

TABLE 11–2   LEVELS OF COMPREHENSION

LEVEL OF COMPREHENSION	PERCENTAGE OF RECALL	WHEN USED
Complete	100%	Reading critical analysis; reading directions or procedures.
High	90–100%	Reading a primary reference source.
Moderate	70–90%	Reading for an overview of a subject.
Low	50–70%	Reading to obtain background information; reading only for key ideas.
Selective	50% or below	Looking up a statistic in an almanac; checking a date in a biographical dictionary.

Comprehension can, somewhat arbitrarily, be divided into five levels: complete, high, moderate, low, and selective, as described in Table 1–3 on page 15. Study Table 11–2 before continuing to read.

EXERCISE 11–2

Working with a classmate, select a level of comprehension that seems appropriate for each of the following research situations.

1. Reading a biographical entry on Ella Fitzgerald in *The Encyclopedia of Jazz* for a term paper on the history of jazz.
2. Locating names of leaders of Third World countries in the *International Yearbook* and *Statesman's Who's Who.*
3. Reading the directions for using a computerized card catalogue.
4. Reading a source to verify that you have not missed any key information in sources you have already used.
5. Reading a newspaper review of a performance of *Cats* in preparation for a drama class discussion on audience responsiveness.

ALTERNATIVE READING STRATEGIES

Now that you have learned to gauge the level of comprehension appropriate for various reading assignments, the next step is to learn alternative reading strategies to meet these varied comprehension demands.

Most students are accustomed to reading everything completely. They read each word successively, from beginning to end. Few students realize there are other options available. Two alternative reading strategies are presented here: skimming and scanning.

When and How to Skim

Most textbook assignments must be read completely; complete or high comprehension is required. However, for some reading assignments that demand lower levels of comprehension, you can afford to read some parts and skip others. This strategy is known as **skimming.** Skimming is a technique in which you selectively read and skip in order to find only the most important ideas. Here are a few situations in which skimming is appropriate.

1. *Reading a section of a textbook chapter that reviews the metric system.* If you have already learned and used the metric system, you can afford to skip over much of the material.

2. *Reading a section of a reference book that you are using to complete a research paper.* If you have already collected most of your basic

information, you might skim through additional references, looking only for new information not discussed in sources you have used before.

3. *Sampling a two-page, 30-item supplementary reading list for a sociology class.* Your instructor has encouraged you to review as many of the items as possible. You anticipate that the final exam will include one essay question that is related to these readings. Clearly, you cannot read every entry, but you can skim a reasonable number.

4. *Reviewing a textbook chapter you have already read.* To review the chapter for a class discussion, you could skim it.

In skimming, your goal is to identify those parts of any reading material that contain the main ideas. The type of material you are reading will, in part, determine how you should adapt your reading techniques. Authors use different patterns of organization and various formats, and skimming is a highly flexible technique that can be adapted to these varying structures and formats. To acquaint you with the process of skimming, here is the procedure. Generally, read the following items.

1. *The title.* The title announces the subject of the material and provides clues about the author's approach or attitude toward it.

2. *The subtitle or introductory byline.* Some material includes, underneath the title, a statement that further explains the title or is written to catch the reader's interest.

3. *The introductory paragraph.* The first paragraph often provides important background information and introduces the subject. It also may provide a brief overview of the treatment of the subject.

4. *The headings.* A heading announces the topic that will be discussed in the paragraphs that follow it. When read successively, the headings form an outline or a list of topics covered in the material.

5. *The first sentence of each paragraph.* Most paragraphs are built around a topic sentence that states the main idea of the paragraph. The most common position for the main idea is in the first sentence of the paragraph. If you read a first sentence that clearly is not the topic sentence, then you might jump to the end of the paragraph and read the last sentence. Your goal as you skim each paragraph should be to get an overview of its structure and content. The first sentence, if it functions as a topic sentence, usually states the main idea and provides clues about how the rest of the paragraph is organized.

6. *The remainder of the paragraph.* Quickly glance through the remainder of the paragraph. Let your eyes quickly sweep through the paragraph. Try

to pick out words that answer questions such as "who," "what," "when," "where," or "how much" about the main idea of the paragraph. Also, note any words that indicate a continuation or a change in thought pattern as you glance through the paragraph. Try to pick up names, numbers, dates, places, and capitalized or italicized words and phrases. Note any numbered sequences too. This quick glance will add to your overall impression of the paragraph and will confirm that you have identified the main idea of the paragraph.

7. *The title or legend of any maps, graphs, charts, or diagrams.* The title or legend will state what is depicted and suggest what important event, idea, or relationship is emphasized.

8. *The last paragraph.* The last paragraph often provides a conclusion or summary for the article. It might concisely state the main points of the article, or it might suggest new ways to consider the topic.

Now that you are familiar with the procedure for skimming, you are probably wondering how fast to skim, how much to skip, and what level of comprehension to expect. Generally, your reading rate should be about three or four times as fast as you normally read. You should skip more than you read. Although the amount to skip varies according to the type of material, a safe estimate is that you should skip about 70 to 80 percent of the material. Because you are skipping large portions of the material, your comprehension will be limited.

To give you a better idea of what the technique of skimming is like, the following article has been highlighted to indicate the portions of the article that you might read when skimming. Of course, this is not the only effective way to skim this article. Depending on your purpose for reading it, you could identify different parts of the article as important. You also might select different key words and phrases while glancing through each paragraph.

AN OVERVIEW OF LEGAL GAMBLING: THE ISSUE AT A GLANCE

Not so long ago—1977—casino gambling was a crime in 49 states and a Mafia founded enterprise in Nevada. Now gambling (or "gaming," as supporters prefer to call it) is a national pastime, a pastime that many Americans consider simply another form of entertainment. While the expansion of legal gambling seems to have leveled off in recent years, it has become a fact of life in communities around the nation.

Competition for the gambling dollar is so cut-throat that a casino industry group in Nevada distributes anti-gambling literature to discourage other states from legalizing casinos. Many state lotteries are evolving into state casinos as they install video gambling machines in bars, restaurants, gas stations, and convenience stores. And couch potatoes need not leave home, as the Internet provides 24-hour-a-day access to Aruba Palms, Sportz Casino, and 20 other international casinos that provide high-stakes gambling via the family computer. Federal law prohibits the use of telephones for gambling, and American casinos have not yet gone online. If they do, experts say the Internet would revolutionize the gambling industry and present new challenges to families.

Gambling has evolved with dizzying speed. Polling suggests most Americans haven't had time to adjust and still have mixed views about the practice.

Waves of History

Illegal gambling, of course, has always been with us, but even legal gambling is nothing new in American history. Historians say legal gambling has been through several cycles of boom and ban, dating back to the very beginning of the colonial era. The first American settlement in Jamestown, for example, was funded by an English lottery. Then again, the Pilgrims limited gambling to the well-to-do in 1621, just a year after they arrived—they thought it wouldn't be right to entice poor people to gamble in a "shining city on a hill."

In each of the earlier cycles, legal gambling spread because states and communities needed the money; and contracted because somebody stole the money. The early 19th Century saw widespread use of lotteries, till a series of scandals over corruption and mismanagement led to restrictions in the 1840s. After the Civil War, gambling was widely used as a economic-development tool for war-ravaged states, then died out by 1910 as a byproduct of Progressive Era anti-corruption campaigns. Nevada legalized casinos again in 1931 to fight the Great Depression, but the taint of Mafia involvement kept other states from following suit for more than 40 years.

So far, the latest wave of gambling has been driven by the same need for revenue—New Jersey legalized casinos as a tool for urban redevelopment in Atlantic City; Native American tribes have used their status as sovereign nations to open casinos on disadvantaged reservations; and 37 state governments now run lotteries as a relatively painless way to raise tax revenue. The growth of legal gambling has slowed in recent years after the explosion of the 1980s and early 1990s, with voters in seven states rejecting various gambling proposals in 1996.

A new twist on an old concern has come up during the latest expansion: compulsive gambling, formerly considered a character flaw, is now labeled as a mental health problem. Gamblers Anonymous, founded in 1957, now has 2,000 chapters worldwide, and the American Psychiatric Association has added compulsive gambling to its official Diagnostic and Statistical Manual of Mental Disorders. A Harvard Medical School study sponsored by a casino trade group found compulsive gambling among adults increased from 0.84 percent to 1.29 percent over the past 20 years, and among people being treated for some other mental illness or substance abuse the rate was 14.3 percent. Compulsive gambling among adolescents, however, has held relatively steady at 4 percent, the study found.

The Public View

The public is still coming to terms with legal gambling and its financial and moral implications. A substantial number of Americans (44 percent) view gambling as harmless recreation, while 26 percent said it is fundamentally immoral and 25 percent consider it "somewhere in-between." When it comes to the social and economic impact of gambling, 46 percent of Americans said casino gambling is more likely to aid economic growth, while 39 percent said it would more likely cause crime and social problems.

In a 1996 Gallup Organization poll, most Americans cited three major concerns with legalized gambling: it would make compulsive gamblers out of people who would never participate in illegal gambling; it encourages people who can least afford it to squander their money; and it would not deter organized crime. Yet a significant minority of Americans didn't see these problems.

Gallop found that most Americans opposed the legalization of casino gambling in 1993. But three years later, in response to a differently worded question, most Americans said they were resigned to gambling's growth: people will gamble whether it's legal or not, most Americans told Gallup, so the state might as well make it legal to get some of the revenue.

Three Perspectives

The Perspectives section offers three public approaches to legalized gambling:

- Cut the red tape on gaming and treat the industry as a beneficial generator of jobs and entertainment;
- Regulate gambling to make it safer, by treating games of chance like alcohol—a pleasant but potentially dangerous activity that can be abused without government oversight.
- Stop gambling to the extent possible, treating the industry as a predatory business that should be phased out.

—*Public Agenda Online*, October 1999

EXERCISE 11–3

After you have skimmed "An Overview of Legal Gambling: The Issue at a Glance," *p. 329, answer the following questions.*

1. What is the purpose of the article?
2. Name one recent problem created by gambling.
3. Why has legal gambling spread?
4. Name at least one future action that might be taken regarding legalized gambling.

EXERCISE 11–4

Skim "Giving Viruses a Cold Reception," *and answer the following questions.*

1. What is the main point of the article?
2. How are cold viruses transmitted?

3. What should you do to prevent colds?
4. List several symptoms that suggest that an infection may be more serious than a cold.
5. List several things to do to relieve cold symptoms.

GIVING VIRUSES A COLD RECEPTION

The immune system learns to recognize specific disease agents through exposure to them. Antigen exposure can occur through vaccination or by natural means. We acquire immunity to chickenpox, measles, mumps, tetanus, cholera, smallpox, and many other life-threatening diseases. So, one might wonder, if the immune system can do such amazing things, why can't it defend us from the common cold?

We are susceptible to at least 200 different cold-causing viruses. The most common type, rhinoviruses (literally "nose viruses"), cause about 30 to 50 percent of all colds in adults. As soon as the immune system learns to recognize and defend us from one, another comes along, and then another. This antigenic diversity creates quite a challenge for the immune system, so much so that most people succumb to one to six colds per year.

Nonspecific Resistance

Cold symptoms are not produced directly by the cold virus, but by the body's nonspecific immune response as it fights the virus. When viruses invade the cells lining the nasal passages, your body responds with inflammation and the production of extra mucus. This causes nasal congestion, a "stuffy nose." As mucous membranes in the nose accelerate their secretion of antibody-containing mucus, you get a runny nose. Congestion in the middle ear or sinuses can cause dizziness or a headache.

The "swollen glands" sometimes felt during a cold are actually swollen lymph nodes. The nodes swell as immune cells, including macrophages, T-cells, and B cells, work overtime to fight pathogens. A sore throat can result from "postnasal drip" as the sinuses drain mucus into the throat. Throat tissue can also become dry and irritated from breathing through your mouth or coughing.

Like the nasal passages, the trachea and bronchial tubes become inflamed and produce extra secretions if invaded by the cold virus. A wheezing sound indicates airway congestion as mucus accumulates and restricts the flow of air. A "productive" cough assists the respiratory passages in getting rid of the mucus and the virus. A "nonproductive" or dry cough is usually caused by throat irritation. Your body may produce a fever to create an inhospitable climate for the virus. Most cold viruses prefer temperatures of 86 to 96° F (30 to 35.5° C). Since fever is a helpful part of your nonspecific resistance, medication should only be used if the fever exceeds 101.5° F (38.6° C) or is needed to treat accompanying aches and pains.

Cold Prevention

Despite its name, a cold is not caused by cold weather, wet feet, or getting cold, at least according to laboratory studies. Colds do occur more frequently in the winter than in the summer, but no one knows why. The incidence of colds usually rises sharply in the early fall and spring. Some believe that when children go back to school and are exposed to each other's viruses, they bring them home to their families.

Research indicates that most of the time cold viruses are transmitted from the hands of an infected person to the hands of a susceptible person. The virus can survive on the skin for only a few hours and must reach the nose in order to invade the body. On the face near the nose is no good, since the skin provides an effective barrier. The mucous membranes of the mouth are also an inhospitable environment; kissing seldom spreads colds.

If all goes well for the virus, eventually the hand delivers the virus to its new home, the person's respiratory system, by touching the mucous membranes of the nose or the eyes (the virus can travel down the tear duct to the upper nose). One study found that 40 to 90 percent of people with colds had rhinoviruses on their hands. The viruses were also found on about 15 percent of nearby objects, such as door knobs, telephones, and coffee cups.

It is not known what makes some people more susceptible to colds. Small children are the most susceptible, because their immune systems are still immature and haven't learned to recognize as many pathogens. People who are around children a lot also get colds more frequently. Smokers are more likely to catch colds than nonsmokers, partly because smoking inhibits the airway cilia that help move mucus. Some studies have shown that stress can decrease the effectiveness of the immune system, and many people believe that stress and fatigue increase their susceptibility to colds.

Given what we know about the transmission of colds, the single best way to prevent colds is frequent handwashing, especially when you're around people who have colds. Avoid sharing telephones, glasses, towels, and other objects with a person who has a cold. And try not to touch your nose or eyes.

Getting enough rest, eating well, exercising moderately, and managing stress certainly won't hurt and may help keep your resistance up. If you're a smoker, cold prevention is yet another good reason to quit.

What about vitamin C? Studies have failed to show that vitamin C prevents colds, although some research has found that it may lessen the severity of cold symptoms. Vitamin C also increases the intactness of cell membranes, so it may make them harder for viruses to penetrate.

Cold Self-Care

Since a cure for colds continues to elude medical researchers, the best we can do is to treat the symptoms. It's been said that with aggressive medical treatment a cold will disappear in seven days, while if left alone a cold will last a week. Nevertheless, symptom treatment can at least make us feel better until the cold has run its course.

The first step in cold self-care is to decide whether your symptoms are those of a cold or something more serious requiring medical attention. People who have heart disease, emphysema, diabetes, or another health condition should get professional advice before initiating self-care, especially before taking over-the-counter medication. Pregnant and lactating women should also check with their doctors before taking any medication.

Symptoms that indicate your infection may be more than a cold include:

1. Oral temperature over 103° F (39.5° C).
2. Sore throat with temperature above 101° F (38.5° C) for over 24 hours.
3. Temperature over 100° F (37.5° C) for three days.
4. Severe pain in ears, head, chest, or stomach.
5. Symptoms that persist more than a week.
6. Enlarged lymph nodes.
7. In a child, difficulty breathing or greater than normal irritability or lethargy.

Once you decide you have a cold, there are several things you can do to help yourself feel better. They include the following.

1. Chicken soup, broth, or other hot drinks. Your mother was right: hot fluids help relieve congestion by increasing the flow of nasal secretions. They also soothe irritated throats.
2. Gargle with salt water ($1/4$ teaspoon salt in 8 oz. water) to soothe a sore throat.
3. Use a vaporizer or humidifier to increase humidity, especially if the air is very dry. Humid air is gentler on nose and throat.
4. Breathing steam gives your nose a temporary fever, creating an inhospitable environment for the virus. It also helps to thin the mucus causing a stuffy nose, and thus temporarily relieve congestion. The steam may also feel soothing to irritated throats and nasal passages.
5. While rest may not hasten your recovery, it may help you feel better. It's good to stay out of circulation for the first few days of a cold to keep others from getting it.
6. Many over-the-counter cold medications are available. If you decide you need something, avoid combination drugs that contain several active ingredients to treat several symptoms. If, instead, you buy single drugs for the symptoms you wish to treat, you will avoid taking unnecessary drugs and decrease unpleasant side effects.

Should You Exercise When You Have a Cold?

Many people wonder whether they should continue their exercise programs when they have a cold. Some hope that the exertion will create a fever and "burn out the cold," while others believe that the added stress of exercise will only exhaust an already overwhelmed immune system. At this point, there is nothing but anecdotal evidence for these two beliefs. As long as symptoms are mild, exercising doesn't appear to either prolong the cold or hasten recovery.

It is important to recognize, however, that colds can sometimes lead to more serious complications, such as secondary bacterial infection in the middle ear, sinuses, or respiratory system. Medical authorities generally advise rest during the initial days of infection, just to be sure that what you are catching (or that what is catching you) is really just a cold. People who insist on exercising should start slowly. If they begin to feel better after five or ten minutes, then the exercise is probably not harmful.

—Tortora, *Introduction to the Human Body: The Essentials of Anatomy and Physiology*, pp. 407–08

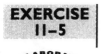

EXERCISE 11–5

Working with another student, select and skim one of the end-of-chapter readings in this text. Then question each other on the main points of the reading by using the comprehension questions as guidelines.

EXERCISE 11–6

Look ahead to the chapter you will study next in one of your textbooks. Skim one or two sections of this chapter and write a brief summary including the main point and most important information. Then check the accuracy of your summary by reading those sections more closely.

When and How to Scan

Have you ever become frustrated when trying to locate a statistic in an almanac or find a reference to a particular research study in a lengthy research review? Have you ever had to read an article completely in order to find a particular fact? These frustrations probably occurred because you were not scanning in the most effective, systematic manner. *Scanning* is a technique for quickly looking through reading material to locate a particular piece of information—a fact, a date, a name, a statistic.

Every time you use a dictionary to find a particular word, you are scanning. When you locate a call number in a card catalogue or find a book on a library shelf, you are scanning. In each case, you are looking for a particular piece of information, and your only purpose in looking through the material is to locate that information. In fact, when you scan you are not at all interested in anything else on the page, and you have no reason to notice or remember any other information.

Many people do not scan as efficiently as possible because they randomly search through the material, hoping to stumble on the information they are seeking. Scanning in this way is time-consuming, is frustrating, and often forces the reader to "give up" and read the entire selection. The key to effective scanning is to approach the material in a systematic manner, as outlined in the following steps.

Know Your Purpose Fix in your mind what you are looking for. Scanning is effective only if you have a very specific purpose. Before you begin to scan, try to form very specific questions that you need to answer. For example, instead of scanning for information on the topic of abortions in New York state, it would be more effective to develop questions such as:

How many abortions were performed in 1999?

What rules and limitations restrict abortions?

Where are the majority of abortions performed?

The more specific your purposes and questions are, the more effectively you will be able to scan.

Check the Organization Before you begin to scan, check to see how the article or material is organized.

For graphics (maps, tables, graphs, charts, and diagrams), this step is especially important. The title of the item you are scanning and other labels, keys, and legends are important. They state what the graphics are intended to describe and tell you how they are presented.

For prose selections, assessing the organization is similar to previewing. Your purpose should be to notice the overall structure of the article so that you will be able to predict where in the article you can expect to find the information you are looking for. Headings are especially important, because they clearly show how a selection is divided into subtopics.

Anticipate Clue Words The next step is to anticipate clues that may help you locate the answer. For example, if you were trying to locate the population of New York City in an article on the populations of cities, you might expect the answer to appear in digits, such as 4,304,710, or in an estimate form using words such as "four million." If you were looking for the name of the researcher in a journal article, you would expect to find the name capitalized. In looking for the definition of a particular term, you might look for italics and you might scan for the word itself or for words or phrases such as "means," "can be defined as," or "refers to." As accurately as possible, then, try to fix the image of your clue words or phrases in your mind before you begin to scan.

Identify Probable Answer Locations Using what you have learned from checking the organization of the material, try to identify places where you are likely to find the information you are looking for. You might be able to identify a column or section that could contain the needed information, you might be able to eliminate certain sections, or you might be able to predict that the information will probably appear in a certain portion of the article.

Use a Systematic Pattern   Once you know what you are looking for and can anticipate the location and form of your answer, you are ready to scan. Scanning should be organized and systematic. Do not randomly skip around, searching for clues. Instead, rhythmically sweep your eyes through the material. The pattern or approach you use will depend on the material. For material printed in narrow six- or seven-word columns (newspaper articles, for example), you might move your eyes straight down the middle, catching the phrases on each half of the line. For wider lines of print, a zigzag or Z pattern might be more effective. Each of these patterns is shown in Figure 11–1. Using this pattern, you move your eyes back and forth, catching several lines in each movement. When you do come to the information you are looking for, it may almost seem as though the clue words "pop out" at you.

Confirm Your Answer   Once you think you have located the answer you have been looking for, read the sentence or two that contain the answer to confirm that it is the information you need. Often, you can be misled by headings and key words that seem to indicate that you have found your answer when in fact you have located related information, opposite information, or information for another year, a different country, or a merely similar situation.

Now try out this procedure. Assume that you are writing a term paper on applications of genetic engineering and need to find out how it is regulated in agricultural production. You have located a reference book on

Figure 11–1   Scanning patterns

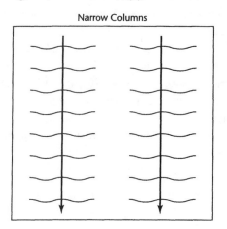
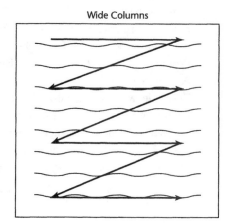

Narrow Columns   Wide Columns

animal science that contains the following section. Scan to find the answer to one of your research questions: What government agency determines the guidelines for genetically engineered foods coming from plants?

REGULATION OF GENETICALLY ENGINEERED PRODUCTS

Three federal agencies currently regulate genetically engineered products: the Environmental Protection Agency (EPA), the Food and Drug Administration (FDA), and the United States Department of Agriculture (USDA). In addition, most states monitor development and testing of genetically monitored products within their borders.

Animal and Plant Health Inspection Service (APHIS), a division of the United States Department of Agriculture, regulates genetically engineered products under several statutes. Genetically engineered crops are regulated under the Federal Plant Pest Act. This legislation enables APHIS to regulate interstate movement, importation into the United States, and field testing of altered crops.

The Food and Drug Administration has broad authority and primary responsibility for regulating the introduction of all new foods, including genetically engineered foods, under the Federal Food, Drug, and Cosmetic Act (FFDCA). Two different sets of provisions in the FFDCA pertain to genetically engineered foods. The first are the "adulteration" provisions, which give the FDA authority to remove unsafe foods from the market. The other pertinent section of the act requires premarket approval of food additives. In 1992, the FDA released guidelines for genetically engineered foods coming from plant sources. These guidelines can be found in the Federal Register, and vol. 57, pages 22984 and 22986–88. Because the FDA has authority over drug approval, it also has authority over drugs produced through biotechnological means. In this case, the fact that a drug is produced through biotechnology is not the issue. The FDA already had authority over drugs.

The Environmental Protection Agency oversees genetically engineered microbial pesticides and certain crops that are genetically engineered to produce their own pesticides under the Federal Insecticide, Fungicide, and Rodenticide Act (FIFRA). The FFDCA authorized the FDA to set tolerances and establish exemptions for pesticide residues on and in food crops. Nonpesticidal, nonfood microbial products are regulated under the Toxic Substances Control Act (TSCA). The regulation under which the TSCA Biotechnology Program functions is titled "Microbial Products of Biotechnology; Final Regulation Under the Toxic Substances Control Act," which can be found in the Federal Register, vol. 62, No. 70, pages 17909–58. This rule was developed under TSCA because intergeneric microorganisms are considered new chemicals under the act.

Animal vaccines are regulated under the Virus, Serum, and Toxin Act; and engineered poultry and livestock fall under various meat inspection statutes. Transgenic animals other than poultry and livestock are not regulated for environmental risks.

—Damron, *Introduction to Animal Science,* pp. 202–03

Scanning Lists and Tables

In scanning information in list form, the most important step is to become familiar with how the writer has arranged the information. Check the overall organization, and then see whether it is divided in any particular way. For instance, a TV program schedule is organized by day of the week, but it is also arranged by time. In scanning a table of metric equivalents, you would see that it is arranged alphabetically but that it is subdivided into measures of volume, length, and so on. Column titles, headings, and any other clues are important to show the organization of the material.

Many reference books that are arranged alphabetically have guide words at the top of each page to indicate the words or entries that are included on each page. For instance, in the upper-right or upper-left corner of a page of a dictionary, you might find the two words *cinder-circle*. These guide words indicate that the first entry on the page is *cinder* and that the last entry on the page is *circle*. Guide words are valuable shortcuts to help you quickly locate the appropriate page to scan. For lengthy alphabetical material that does not include guide words, you should check the first entry and the last entry on a page to determine whether that page contains the item you are looking for.

In scanning columnar material, often you will be able to scan for a specific word, phrase, name, date, or place name, and it may not be necessary to guess at the form of your answer. For example, in scanning an almanac to find the length of Lake Ontario, you are looking for one very specific statistic. Similarly, you can check *Taber's Cyclopedic Medical Dictionary* just for a description of brittle diabetes.

When scanning material that is arranged alphabetically, focus on the first letter of each line until you reach the letter that begins the word you are looking for. Then focus on the first two letters until you reach the two-letter combination you seek. Successively widen your focus until you are looking for whole words.

EXERCISE 11-7

Scan Figure 11–2 (p. 340) from the Reader's Guide to Periodical Literature *to locate the answers to the following questions.*

1. Under what heading can you locate information on voice communications on the Internet?
2. In what periodical did L. Dormen publish an article on the social uses of the Internet?
3. What is the title of the article by N. Weinberg on TV and the Internet?
4. In what periodical was an article published on blocking out pornography on the Internet?
5. Locate an article about using the Internet to learn about taking cruises.

Figure 11–2 Reader's Guide to Periodical Literature

INTERNET— *cont.*
Real estate use
Using a mouse to hunt for a house. T. Gutner. il *Business Week* p162 Je 24, '96
Religious use
See also
Partenia (World Wide Web site)
Free speech or piracy? Copyright ruling favors Scientologists. C. Reid. *Publishers Weekly* v243 p14 Ap 15 '96
The Word and the Web [comparison of biblical cross-references to hyperlinks] E. Mendelson. il *The New York Times Book Review* v101 p35 Je 2 '96
Scientific use
See also
Science on-line (Periodical)
Science journals go wired. G. Taubes. il *Science* v271 p764–6 F 9 '96
Securities
The next Microsoft. M. K. Evans. i. *Gentlemen's Quarterly* v66 p101+ Mr '96
Security measures
Inoculating against invaders. L. Wiener. il *U.S. News & World Report* v120 p78 Ap 29 '96
Privacy and data collection on the Net. A. Eisenberg. il *Scientific American* v274 p120 Mr '96
Stop, thief! J. C. McCune. il *Success* v43 p54 Mr '96
Surveillance in cyberspace [journalists may be ensnared by Usenet spies] W. Andrews. il *American Journalism Review* v18 p13 Mr '96
Self help use
Can going on-line make you healthier? P. Hise. il *Glamour* v94 p46+ F '96
Hope for nail biters [online support groups for nail biters and hair pullers] W. Block. il *American Health* v15 p41 Ap '96
Sexual aspects
See also
Communications Decency Act
Internet dangers. C. Rubenstein. il *Parents* v71 p145–6+ Mr '96
Policing cyberspace [programs to block out pornography] S. Curtis. il *Maclean's* v109 p56–7 F 19 '96
Port central [Microsystems Software] D. Steinberg. il *Gentlemen's Quarterly* v66 p88+ Ap '96
Sex and the single modem. A. Billen. *World Press Review* v43 p15 Je '96
When kids prowl the Net, parents need to be on guard. R. M. Bennefield. il *U.S. News & World Report* v120 p75 Ap 29 '96
Shopping services
See also
Firefly (World Wide Web site)
On-line shoppers: "just looking, thanks". S. J. Vaughan-Nichols. il *Byte* v21 p34 Mr '96
Shopping for electronics [on the Internet] D. Karagiannis. il *Popular Electronics* v13 p28––30 Mr '96
Social use
E-mail romance: can the Internet help your love life? L. Dormen. il *Glamour* v94 p108 F '96
He typed, she typed. M. Greaves ad J. Valentine. il pors *Essence* v26 p77+ F '96
It's a jungle out there. M. Mannix. il *U.S. News & World Report* v120 p73–5 Ap 29 '96
Sports use
Olympic torch burns online. M. Cahlin. il *PC Novice* v7 p78–9 Ap '96
Taxation
Shaking down the Net. J. Simons. il *U.S. News & World Report* v120 p60 Je 10 '96
Television broadcasting
Destination family room: PC-TV [Destination from Gateway 2000] C. O'Malley. il *Popular Science* v248 p74–5 Ap '96
Getting granny to surf the Net. N. Weinberg. il *Forbes* v157 p119+ My 6 '96
I want my Web TV! il *PC Computing* v9 p297 My '96
Television arrives on the Internet. J. Browning. il *Scientific American* v274 p28 My '96
Traffic
Bandwidth blues. M. Hawn. il *Macworld* v13 p145–7 F '96
Circumventing traffic jams on the Internet. I. Peterson. il *Science News* v149 p181 Mr 23 '96
It's the end of the Net as we know it. W. Gurley. il por *Fortune* v133 p181–2+ Ap 29 '96

Stress, strain and growing pains. J. Simons. il *U.S. News & World Report* v120 p59 My 6 '96
Terminal congestion? D. Kelly. il *World Press Review* v43 p37–8 My '96
Travel use
Adventures on-line . . . D. Ruben. il *Working Woman* v21 p60–4+ Ap '96
California dreamin'. B. Foster. il *Home Office Computing* v14 p46–7 Mr '96
Internet address book. P. J. Bell. il *Gourmet* v56 p100 Ap '96
A little plane talk on the Web. K. T. Beddingfield. il *U.S. News & World Report* v120 p64 Je 3 '96
Surfing for safaris—or cruises, beaches, b&bs . . . E. C. Baig. il *Business Week* p106–7 My 20 '96
Traveling by Net and by phone. *Time* v147 p70 Ap 22 '96
Unauthorized use
Free speech or piracy? Copyright, ruling favors Scientologists. C. Reid. *Publishers Weekly* v243 p14 Ap 15 '96
Voice communications
See Internet telephony
Canada
Plugging into the future [cover story; special section] i. *Maclean's* v109 p28–35 Ja 29 '96
INTERNET AND BLACKS
See also
BET Networks (World Wide Web site)
Getting connected: an African-American guide to surfing the Internet. M. C. Brown. *American Visions* v11 p34–5 Ap/My '96
INTERNET AND THE BLIND
A word is worth a thousand pictures. B. Logue. il *Byte* v21 p236 Ap '96
INTERNET AND WOMEN
An insider's guide to the Internet. J. Schwartz. i. *Working Woman* v21 p49–53 Mr '96
INTERNET AND YOUTH
See also
Communications Decency Act
Internet dangers. C. Rubenstein. il *Parents* v71 p145–6+ Mr '96
Media mongrels [sales pitches to children on the Internet] M. Frankel. il *The New York Times Magazine* p20+ Je 2 '96
When kids prowl the Net, parents need to be on guard. R. M. Bennefield. il *U.S. News & World Report* v120 p75 Ap 29 '96
INTERNET APPLIANCES
The $500 PC: dumber is dumb. S. Manes. il *PC World* v14 p39 F '96
Cadillac or Model T? A. J. Kessler. por *Forbes* v157 p286 My 20 '96
First Web Pcs arrive. D. L. Andrews. il *Byte* v21 p24–5 Ap '96
Inside the Web PC [cover story] T. R. Halfhill. il *Byte* v21 p44–8+ Mr '96
Internet appliances. il *PC Computing* v9 p291 Mr '96
The next home computer. G. Smith. il *Popular Science* v248 p32 Ap '96
Rethinking the PC [L. Ellison's network computer] R. Laver. il *Maclean's* v109 p48 Mr 18 '96
The spinal column of civilization. J. Holtzman. *Electronics Now* v67 p79–81 Ap '96
Total recall. J. C. Dvorak. il *PC Computing* v9 p47 Ap '96
Will Oracle's 'fantasy' come to pass? [network computers] R. D. Hof. il. *Business Week* p38 My 27 '96
INTERNET EXPLORER (COMPUTER PROGRAM) *See* Microsoft Internet Explorer (Computer program)
INTERNET MANIA (CD-ROM)
Cut your surf time on the Net. R. Schwerin. il *PC Computing* v9 p106 Mr '96
INTERNET PCS *See* Internet appliances
INTERNET PHONE (COMPUTER PROGRAM)
Free phone calls on the Net. R. C. Kennedy. il *PC Computing* v9 p66 My '96
Hey baby, call me at my IP address. P. Wayner. il *Byte* v21 p142–4 Ap '96
INTERNET PROTOCOLS
File transfer for business. M. L. Corbett. il *Black Enterprise* v26 p46+ My '96
INTERNET SEARCH ENGINES
See also
Alta Vista (Internet search engine)
Infoseek (Internet search engine)
Yahoo (Internet search engine)
Bye, Netscape. P. Somerson. il *PC Computing* v9 p45 Ap '96
Find it on the Net [cover story] R. Scoville. il *PC World* v14 p124–30 Ja '96

Source: H. W. Wilson Company, *Reader's Guide to Periodical Literature,* August 1996, Vol. 96, No. 6, p. 358

EXERCISE 11–8

Scan Figure 11–3 (p. 342) from Book Review Digest *to locate the answers to the following questions.*

1. Who is the author of a book of biographies of various artists?
2. Is Krupinski's book fiction or nonfiction?
3. What does Janice Voltzow think of Krupinski's writing in "Bluewater Journal; the Voyage of the Sea Tiger"?
4. What is the subject of the book written by Virginia L. Kroll?
5. Which book concerns itself with foreign economic relations?

Scanning Prose Materials

Prose materials are more difficult to scan than columnar material. Their organization is less apparent, and the information is not so concisely or obviously stated. And unless the headings are numerous and concise, you may have to scan large amounts of material with fewer locational clues. To scan prose materials, you must rely heavily on identifying clue words and predicting the form of your answer.

It is useful to think of scanning prose materials as a floating process in which your eyes drift quickly through a passage searching for clue words and phrases. Your eyes should move across sentences and entire paragraphs, noticing only clue words that indicate you may be close to locating the answer. As you become skilled at scanning prose material, your clue words will "pop out" at you as though they were in boldface print.

EXERCISE 11–9

Scan the article titled "Giving Viruses a Cold Reception" on pp. 332–335 and answer the following questions.

1. How many cold-related viruses are humans susceptible to?

   _____

2. What is the difference between a "productive" and a "nonproductive" cough?

   _____

3. Why are small children most susceptible to colds?

   _____

4. What effects might vitamin C have on cold viruses?

   _____

5. How does breathing steam relieve cold symptoms?

   _____

Figure 11–3 Book Review Digest

KROLL, VIRGINIA L.—*Continued*
REVIEW: *SLJ* v41 p102 Je '95. Barbara Osborne Williams (104w)

"A unique offering. Kroll creatively captures the visual essence and diversity of the African continent and the poetic gaiety of Mother Goose. . . . Full-color illustrations depict topography, urban centers, forest, jungle, desert, plain, and marketplace. Colors are rich and vibrant, reflecting the warmth of the African continent. A welcome, interesting addition."

REVIEW: *Small Press* v13 p78 Summ '95. Karima A. Haynes (150w)

"Virginia Kroll brings an African sensibility to the time-honored [Mother Goose] rhymes by setting them against a backdrop of modern African culture. 'Hickory, Dickory Dock' becomes 'Chicory Pickory Pock.' Likewise, 'The Old Woman Who Lived in the Shoe' is now 'The Old Woman Who Lived by the Nile.' Artist Katherine Roundtree brings the continent to life in a resplendent rainbow of illustrations that showcase diversity. Each page is bordered in beautiful patterns with the country of origin from which the rhymes are derived. The book also includes a map of Africa to help children identify the location of each country."

KRUEGER, ANNE O. American trade policy; a tragedy in the making. 141p $29.95; pa $12.95 1995 AEI Press
 382 1. United States—Commercial policy 2. United States—Foreign economic relations
 ISBN 0-8447-3888-3; 0-8447-3889-1 (pa) LC 95-9946

SUMMARY: "Krueger analyzes the apparent shift in US trade policy from leadership of the General Agreement on Tariffs and Trade (GATT) to administered protection where the US negotiates trade policies on a country-by-country, bilateral basis." (Choice) Bibliography. Index.

REVIEW: *Choice* v33 p662 D '95. R.L. Lucier (230w)

"The shift toward bilateralism and administered protection puts the US government in a 'good cop, bad cop' game where the administration convinces US trading partners that a bilateral resolution of a trading conflict will be preferable to the protectionist legislation which the US Congress would impose. Examples [Krueger] offers include the 'voluntary' export restraints the US negotiated in auto and steel trade. Following a discussion of bilateral trade negotiations—particularly between the US and Japan—she turns to the question of regional trading blocs. . . . In the Uruguay Round of GATT and the newly developed World Trade Organization (WTO). The monograph is well documented and displays a familiarity with recent research on world trade policies and disputes. Graduate; faculty; professional."

REVIEW: *Libr J* v120 p94 Jl '95. Lisa K. Miller (150w)

"This work is an examination of our country's trade policy and its repercussions. Over the past several years, we have been moving away from multilateralism toward bilateralism, a trend Krueger sees as dangerous. She encourages our participation in and support of the newly formed World Trade Organization, which promotes an open multilateral trading system. In fact, the book seems to be a treatise to promulgate her opinions, based on study, about the direction of world trade. She discusses the impact of NAFTA and GATT on our trade policy and devotes considerable space to the various regional trade associations, such as EFTA, ASEAN, EC, and EACM. Extensive footnotes supplement the text. Recommended for all international business collections."

KRULL, KATHLEEN, 1952—. Lives of the artists; masterpieces, messes (and what the neighbors thought); written by Kathleen Krull; illustrated by Kathryn Hewitt. 96p col il $19 1995 Harcourt Brace & Col.
 709.2 1. Artists—Biography—Juvenile literature
 ISBN 0-15-200103-4 LC 94-35357

SUMMARY: This book presents biographies for such artists as "Leonardo, Bruegel, Cassatt, Van Gogh, Picasso, O'Keeffe, Dali, Noguchi, Rivera, Kahlo, and Warhol." (Booklist) Index. "Grade six and up." (SLJ)

REVIEW: *Booklist* v92 p468 N 1 '95. Carolyn Phelan (140w)

"The subject seems well suited to Kroll's format: informative short biographies that focus on the subjects' personal lives and eccentricities rather than chronologies of their masterpieces. A few notes on major artworks follow each biography. . . . Each chapter begins with one of Hewitt's distinctive portrait paintings, handsome caricatures of the artists and a few significant or distinctive objects indicating their interests and individual traits. A lively, entertaining presentation. . . . Grades four to six."

REVIEW: *SLJ* v41 p164 O '95. Kenneth Marantz (190w)

"Tidbits flood the brief biographies: Leonardo's and Michelangelo's homosexuality, Van Gogh's 'ear episode,' Bruegel's fondness for practical jokes, Cassatt's support of women's suffrage, etc. These morsels are integrated into chapters with an easy-flowing sequence of short paragraphs, and supplemented with an 'Artworks' section that adds a few pithy comments about several specific pieces, such as O'Keeffe's bone paintings. . . . Hewitt supplies a full-page watercolor and colored-pencil portrait and vignette for each artist. These are friendly representations that also include personal objects like Matisse's fiddle, Chagall's village, Duchamp's snow shovel, etc. They add pleasant visual attractions to the lighthearted approach in this inviting introduction to a few of the Big Names in our artworld. A page of artistic terms is also included."

KRUPINSKI, LORETTA, 1940—. Bluewater journal; the voyage of the Sea Tiger. col il $14.95/Can$19.95; lib bdg $14.89 1995 HarperCollins Pubs.
 ISBN 0-06-023436-9; 0-06-023437-7 (lib bdg) LC 94-13241

SUMMARY: Based on "logbooks, journals and letters found at the Mystic Seaport Museum in Connecticut, this fictional account in diary form relates the story of young Benjamin Slocum's 1860 voyage with his family from Boston to the Sandwich Islands (present-day Hawaii). . . . The Sea Tiger, captained by Benjamin's father, races to reach Honolulu before its rival clipper ship Morning Star. . . . Grades two to five." (SLJ)

REVIEW: *Bull Cent Child Books* v48 p351 Je '95. Elizabeth Bush (200w)

"As Benjamin describes the . . . fictional 1860 voyage, readers form a vivid picture of four months at sea–the genteel but cramped nest of a stateroom, livestock for fresh milk, eggs, and meat, polite society that entertains them in Rio Janeiro and Honolulu, the treacherous waters off Cape Horn, and a race for port against the rival Morning Star. The text will entice independent readers, and the single-page journal entries will work well as a classroom read aloud; although the figures in Krupinski's ouache paintings are as still as a mainmast, . . . the audience will be fascinated by the precision of nautical details, and viewers in the back of the room will appreciate the illustrations' size and clarity. Budding navigators can use Krupinski's map to trace Sea Tiger's route."

REVIEW: *Sci Books Films* v31 p215 O '95. Janice Voltzow (120w)

"Although the [book's] premise is good, the writing is sometimes awkward and not very convincing. The text gives some insights as to what life on board the ship might have been like. Whales, seasickness, domestic animals, storms, and a race with another clipper ship add a small touch of drama, but not enough to make the story very interesting. It is never clear why the boy, his mother, and his sister are accompanying his father, the sea captain, or why, once they finally arrive in Honolulu, they leave again for Hong Kong."

REVIEW: *SLJ* v41 p65 Jl '95. Marie Orlando (180w)

"Text on lefthand pages is adorned with small watercolor pictures, while full-page or page-and-a-third paintings on the right, in gouache and colored pencil, illustrate the events of the trip which include a powerful lightning storm, a stop in Brazil, and a dramatic whale sighting. . . . An author's note, afterword, and glossary augment the information incorporated into the text and pictures. . . . Krupinski has made a fine contribution to that group of picture books that provide an accurate sense of time and place for older children."

DOCUMENTATION AND NOTE TAKING

As you read reference sources for a research paper, documentation and note taking are important. You must record carefully the sources you use and take clear and concise notes to use when writing your paper.

Documentation Format and Systems

Documentation—recording the sources you use—is necessary for preparing the footnotes and bibliography of any paper you write. As you use sources, you will need to keep a record of the complete title, author, publisher, place, date, and pages referred to. Before you begin, select the format you will use for the paper's bibliography, and use this format to record sources as you use them. Several documentation styles are available; often a particular style is preferred in a specific academic discipline. The two most common styles are those of the MLA and the APA, which are explained in the following manuals. Instructors usually require one style or the other.

Gibaldi, Joseph. *MLA Handbook for Writers of Research Papers,* 5th ed. New York: MLA, 1999.

American Psychological Association. *Publication Manual of the American Psychological Association,* 4th ed. Washington, DC: APA, 1994.

Documentation rules are complex and may seem picky and annoying, especially if you have to learn different styles for different courses, but there is good reason for them. If your source is fully documented, your reader can follow up, explore further, or research a topic in more depth. Documentation also may be useful to you. As you complete your paper, for example, you may need to return to a source to get an important date you missed or to check a name spelled two different ways in your notes.

Many researchers list their sources on 3 x 5 inch index cards, which make it possible to alphabetize rapidly when preparing the bibliography. For each source, record the library call number in addition to bibliographic information. (This will save you time should you need to locate the source again.) A sample source card is shown in Figure 11–4 (p. 344).

Note-Taking Cards

For taking notes, 5 x 8 inch or 4 x 6 inch index cards are best. Use a separate card for each subtopic or aspect of your topic. In the upper-left corner, record the author's last name and the pages you used. In the upper-right corner, record the subtopic. Be sure to write only on one side of the card. A sample note-taking card is also shown in Figure 11–4. Here are a few suggestions for taking good research notes.

Figure 11–4   Sample Source and Note-Taking Cards

Source Card

• T J
211
• C69
1995

Critchlow, Arthur J.

Introduction to Robotics

New York : Macmillan, 1995,

pp. 39-51

Note Card

Critchlow, P. 42   Payback on
investment

formula for   =   capital cost of system
payback   yearly   _   operations
savings   cost

$$\left(P = \frac{c}{s-o}\right)$$

Capital includes robot, auxiliary, safety
equipment, installation and training
Operations include overhead and maintenance,
wages and salaries of operators

Record the information in your own words instead of copying the author's words. By recording the author's wording, you run the risk of using it in your paper, perhaps without realizing that you have done so. Whenever you use an author's words or ideas instead of your own, you are required to use quotation marks and/or give proper credit by indicating the author and source from which the material was taken. Failure to give credit is known as **plagiarism.** Plagiarism is a form of theft and therefore a serious error; many institutions penalize students who either knowingly or unknowingly plagiarize.

Try to summarize and condense information. You will find that it is impossible to record all the information that appears in your sources. If you have already made a note once, do not spend time writing it again. (You might, however, want to note the fact that there is common agreement in a number of sources about the information.) Occasionally, you may need to check back through your notes to see what you already have recorded.

Record useful quotes. If you find a statement that strongly supports your thesis, you may want to include it as a quotation in your paper. Copy it down exactly and place it in quotation marks in your notes, along with its page reference. Photocopy important articles so you can refer to them while you work.

READING COLLATERAL ASSIGNMENTS

In addition to the course textbook, many professors assign collateral readings. These assignments are drawn from a variety of sources: other textbooks, paperbacks, newspapers, periodicals, scholarly journals, and reference books. Often, your professor will place the required book or periodical on reserve in the library. This means the book is held at the reserve desk, where its use is restricted to a specified period of time. Collateral assignments may present

- new topics not covered in your text
- updated information
- alternative points of view
- applications or related issues
- realistic examples, case studies, or personal experiences

Reading collateral assignments requires different skills and strategies than reading textbooks. Unless the assignment is from another textbook, you may find that the material is not as well or as tightly organized as it would be in a textbook. It may also be less concise and factual.

Analyzing the Assignment

First, determine the purpose of the assignment: How is it related to the course content? Listen carefully as your professor announces the assignment; he or she often provides important clues. Next, determine what type and level of recall are necessary. If the purpose of an assignment is to present new and important topics not covered in your text, then a high level of recall is required. If, on the other hand, an assignment's purpose is to expose you to alternative points of view on a controversial issue, then key ideas are needed but highly factual recall is not.

Choosing Reading and Study Strategies

Depending on the purpose of the assignment and the necessary level and type of recall, your reading choices range from a careful, thorough reading to skimming to obtain an overview of the key ideas presented. Before you begin, you need to select a strategy to enable you to retain and recall the information. Table 11–3 lists examples of supplementary assignments and their purposes and suggests possible reading and retention strategies for each. The table shows how strategies vary widely to suit the material and the purpose for which it was assigned.

TABLE 11-3 STRATEGIES FOR COLLATERAL READINGS

ASSIGNMENT	PURPOSE	READING STRATEGIES	RETENTION STRATEGIES
Historical novel for American history course.	To acquaint you with living conditions of the period being studied.	Read rapidly, noting trends, patterns, characteristics; skip highly detailed descriptive portions.	Write a brief synopsis of the basic plot; make notes (including some examples) of lifestyles, living conditions (social, religious, political, as well as economic).
Essay on exchange in Moroccan bazaars (street markets) for economics course.	To describe system of barter.	Read for main points, noting process, procedures, and principles.	Underline key points
Article titled "What Teens Know about Birth Control" assigned in a maternal care nursing course.	To reveal attitudes toward, and lack of information about, birth control.	Read to locate topics of information, misinformation, and lack of information; skip details and examples.	Prepare a three-column list: information, misinformation, and lack of information.

Working on Nonprint Collateral Assignments

Occasionally, a professor may ask you to view videotapes, films, lectures, or television documentaries. Approach these assignments as you would approach a reading assignment. It is particularly important to determine your purpose and to take adequate notes at the time because it is usually difficult, or impossible, to review the material later. Making notes on nonprint materials is, in some ways, similar to taking notes on class lectures. In the case of films, dramatic recreations, or performances, your notes should reflect your impressions as well as a brief review of the content.

EXERCISE 11–10

Summarize how you would approach each of the following collateral assignments. What would be your purpose? What reading and study strategies would you use?

1. Reading a *Time* magazine article about a recent incident of terrorism for a discussion in your political science class.
2. Reading two articles that present opposing opinions and evidence about the rate of the spread of AIDS throughout the United States.
3. Reading a recent journal article on asbestos control to obtain current information for a term paper on the topic.
4. Reading a case study of an autistic child for a child psychology course.
5. Reading IBM's end-of-the-year statement for stockholders for a business class studying public relations strategies.

EVALUATING SOURCES

Through your research and supplementary reading, you will encounter a variety of sources ranging from newspaper editorials to professional journal research reports. Not all sources are equal in accuracy, scholarship, or completeness. In fact, some sources may be inaccurate, and some may be purposely misleading. Other sources that were once respected are now outdated and have been discredited by more recent research. Part of your task as a researcher is to evaluate available sources and select those that seem the most reliable and appropriate. Use the following suggestions in evaluating sources.

1. *Assess the authority of the author.* In standard reference books such as encyclopedias and biographical dictionaries, you can assume the publisher has chosen competent authors. However, when using individual source materials, it is important to find out whether the author is qualified to write on the subject. Does he or she have a degree or experience in the field? What is the author's present position or university

affiliation? This information may appear in the preface or on the title page of a book. In journal articles, a brief paragraph at the end of the article or on a separate page in the journal may summarize the author's credentials. If the author's credentials are not provided, then it may be necessary to consult reference sources to establish or verify the author's qualifications. Sources such as *Who's Who, Directory of American Scholars* and numerous biographical dictionaries are available in the library reference section. By appraising the sources the author cites (footnotes and bibliography), you also can judge the competence of the author.

2. *Check the copyright date.* The date the source was published or revised is indicated on the back of the title page. Especially in rapidly changing fields such as computer science, the timeliness of your sources is important. Using outdated sources can make a research paper incomplete or incorrect. Consult at least several current sources, if possible, to discover recent findings and new interpretations. Suppose that in doing research on regulations for day care centers, you have located several articles. One was written in 1993, another in 1996, another in 2000. The 1993 and 1997 articles may be outdated because regulations change frequently.

3. *Evaluate the fulfillment of the work's purpose.* Does the work accomplish what it promises? Purposes are often stated or implied in the title, subtitle, preface, and introduction. Does the author recognize appropriate limitations, or does he or she claim the source is a complete study of a topic?

4. *Assess the intended audience.* For whom is the work intended? Some sources are written for children, others for young adults, and others for a general-interest audience. The work should suit the audience in format, style, complexity of ideas, and amount of detail. Some sources may be too technical and detailed for your purposes. For example, if a book on control of water pollution control is written for engineers, then it may be too complicated.

5. *Verify one source against another.* If you find information that seems questionable, unbelievable, or disputable, verify it by locating the same information in several other reputable sources. Ask your reference librarian for assistance, if necessary. If you do verify the information in other sources, then you can be reasonably confident that the information is acceptable. You cannot, however, assume that it is correct—only that it is one standard or acceptable approach or interpretation. For instance, in researching global warming, you might encounter several theories of its cause and many projections of its long-range effects.

Eventually, you'll recognize the more standard theories and the more widely accepted projections.

6. *Look for a consensus of opinion.* As you read differing approaches to or interpretations of a topic, sometimes it is difficult to decide what source(s) to accept. When you encounter differing opinions or approaches, the first thing to do is locate additional sources; in other words, do more reading. Eventually, you will discover the consensus.

7. *Evaluate statistics carefully.* Many students regard statistical figures as correct and indisputable and assume that no interpretation or evaluation of statistics is required. Actually, statistics must be carefully evaluated, along with the conclusions the authors draw from them. Suppose you read a statement that "at present, a recent survey indicated that 52 percent of single-parent household heads lack a high school diploma, compared to 22 percent in 1965." To evaluate this statistic, you might ask questions such as, "What year is the 'present'? How were these data obtained? How many single-parent households were surveyed? How were they surveyed? What was the survey response rate? How is a high school diploma defined? Does it include high school equivalency diplomas? How were the 1965 data obtained?" You can see that the answers to these questions can influence how the statistics should be interpreted. In general, ask questions about

   sample size (the size of the group studied)

   sample composition (who was included)

   method of obtaining the data

   definition of terms

   Approach statistics as critically, then, as you would any other type of information.

8. *Consider whether the article is fact or opinion.* Question the author's purpose, the use of generalizations, any basic assumptions, and the type of evidence presented. For a review of these criteria, refer to the sections in Chapter 4 entitled "Assess the Author's Ideas."

**EXERCISE
11–11**

What questions would you ask when evaluating each of the following sources?

1. An article in *Newsweek* reporting a dramatic increase in domestic violence in the United States.

_____

2. An article written by the president of Chrysler Corporation describing effective and ineffective business management strategies.

_____

3. An essay in a right-to-life pamphlet reporting a high incidence of injury and maternal death resulting from abortion. Other articles, using other sources, report a much lower incidence.

_____

4. An article, published in an advertising trade journal, titled "Teenage Drinking: Does Advertising Make a Difference?"

_____

5. An article in *TV Guide* titled "Should TV Stop Projecting Election Winners?"

_____

STUDY Tips Controlling Test Anxiety

Do you get nervous and anxious just before an exam begins? If so, your response is normal; most students feel some level of anxiety before an exam. However, some students become highly nervous and emotional and lose their concentration. Their minds seem to go blank, and they are unable to recall material they have learned. The following suggestions are intended to help you ease test anxiety.

1. *Be sure test anxiety is not an excuse.* Many students say they have test anxiety when actually they have not studied and reviewed carefully or thoroughly.

2. *Become familiar with the building and room in which the test is given.* Visit the room when it is empty and take a seat. Visualize yourself taking a test there.

3. *Develop practice or review tests.* Treat them as real tests, and do them in situations as similar as possible to real test conditions.

4. *Practice working with time limits.* Set an alarm clock and work only until it rings.

5. *Take as many tests as possible,* even though you dislike them. Always take advantage of practice tests and makeup exams. Buy a review book for the course you are taking or a workbook that accompanies your text. Treat each section as an exam, and have someone else correct your work.

6. *Think positively.* Send yourself positive messages. Say to yourself, "I have studied hard and I deserve to pass," "I know that I know the material," or "I know I can do it!" Remember, being well-prepared is one of the best ways to reduce test anxiety.

7. *Answer easy questions first.* To give yourself an initial boost of confidence, begin with a section of the test that seems easy. This will help you to work calmly and you will prove to yourself that you can handle the test.

SUMMARY

This chapter discusses reading strategies for nontextbook materials and presents a systematic approach for reading research sources. The steps include

- defining and focusing your topic
- devising a search strategy
- previewing sources
- defining your purpose for reading

Two alternative reading strategies will help you get the most from research materials.

- Skimming is a rapid reading technique that enables you quickly to obtain main ideas only.
- Scanning is a process of searching for a specific piece of information.

As you read reference sources, a note card system can help you with documentation and note taking. Collateral reading assignments require that you analyze the assignment and select the appropriate reading and study strategies. Finally, evaluating sources is an important step in reading research.

ENGLISH

PREREADING QUESTIONS

1. What does documenting sources mean?
2. On what three topics does this reading focus?

DOCUMENTING SOURCES

John M. Lannon

1   Documenting research means acknowledging one's debt to each information source. Proper documentation satisfies professional requirements for ethics, efficiency, and authority.

Why You Should Document

2   Documentation is a matter of ethics in that the originator of borrowed materials deserves full credit and recognition. Moreover, all published material is protected by copyright law. Failure to credit a source could make you liable to legal action, even if your omission was unintentional.

3   Documentation is also a matter of *efficiency*. It provides a network for organizing and locating the world's printed knowledge. If you cite a particular source correctly, your reference will enable interested readers to locate that source themselves.

4   Finally, documentation is a matter of *authority*. In making any claim (say, "A Mercedes-Benz is more reliable than a Ford Taurus"), you invite challenge: "Says who?" Data on road tests, frequency of repairs, resale value, workmanship, and owner comments can help validate your claim by showing its basis in *fact*. A claim's credibility increases in relation to the expert references supporting it. For a controversial topic, you may need to cite several authorities who hold various views, as in this next example, instead of forcing a simplistic conclusion on your material.

>   Opinion is mixed as to whether a marketable quantity of oil rests under Georges Bank. Cape Cod geologist John Blocke feels that extensive reserves are improbable ("Geologist Dampens Hopes" 3). Oil geologist Donald Marshall is uncertain about the existence of any oil in quantity under Georges Bank ("Offshore Oil Drilling" 2). But the U.S. Interior Department reports that the Atlantic continental shelf may contain 5.5 billion barrels of oil (Kemprecos 8).

Readers of your research report expect the *complete* picture.

What You Should Document

5 Document any insight, assertion, fact, finding, interpretation, judgment or other "appropriated material that readers might otherwise mistake for your own" (Gibaldi and Achtert 155). Specifically, you must document

- any source from which you use exact wording, or
- any source from which you adapt material in your own words, or
- any visual illustration: charts, graphs, drawings, or the like.

6 You don't need to document anything considered *common knowledge*: material that appears repeatedly in general sources. In medicine, for instance, it is common knowledge that foods high in fat cause some types of cancer. Thus, in a research report on fatty diets and cancer, you probably would not need to document that well-known fact. But you would document information about how the fat/cancer connection was discovered, subsequent studies (say, of the role of saturated versus unsaturated fats), and any information for which some other person could claim specific credit. If the borrowed material can be found in only one specific source, and not in multiple sources, document it. When in doubt, document the source.

How You Should Document

7 Borrowed material has to be cited twice: at the exact place you use that material, and at the end of your document. Documentation practices vary widely, but all systems work almost identically: a brief reference in the text names the source and refers readers to the complete citation, which enables the source to be retrieved.

8 Many disciplines, institutions, and organizations publish their own documentation manuals. Here are a few:

Style Guide for Chemists

Geographical Research and Writing

Style Manual for Engineering Authors and Editors

IBM Style Manual

NASA Publications Manual

When no specific format is stipulated, consult one of the following three general manuals: *The MLA Handbook for Writers and Research Papers,* the *Publication Manual of the American Psychological Association,* or the *Chicago Manual of Style.* (The formats in any of these three manuals can be adapted to most research writing.)

—Lannon, *Technical Writing,* pp. 188–89

VOCABULARY REVIEW

1. For each of the words listed below, use context, prefixes, roots, and suffixes, and/or a dictionary to write a brief definition or synonym of the word as it is used in the reading.

   a. ethics (para. 2) _____

   b. originator (para. 2) _____

   c. unintentional (para. 2) _____

   d. network (para. 3) _____

   e. cite (para. 3) _____

   f. claim (para. 4) _____

   g. credibility (para. 4) _____

   h. stipulated (para. 8) _____

2. Underline new specialized terms introduced in the reading.

COMPREHENSION QUESTIONS

1. Give three reasons for documenting sources.
2. What types of material should be documented?
3. In what two places should borrowed materials be cited in a paper?

THINKING CRITICALLY

1. Suppose you are doing a research paper on in-line skating. Give three examples of types of information that should be documented.
2. Explain why documentation is a matter of ethics.
3. In what types of research would authority be particularly important?
4. Describe the author's purpose for writing.
5. If you had to explain to a child in fifth grade why she should not copy information from an encyclopedia without acknowledging that she had done so, what would you say?

LEARNING/STUDY STRATEGIES

1. Write a brief outline of this reading.
2. Draw a map of this reading.

SPEECH COMMUNICATION

PREREADING QUESTIONS

1. What is plagiarism?
2. How can it be avoided?

USING SOURCE MATERIAL ETHICALLY

Bruce E. Gronbeck et al.

1   Now that we've discussed locating and generating material for your speeches, we come to a major ethical issue—plagiarism. **Plagiarism** has been defined as "the unacknowledged inclusion of someone else's words, ideas, or data as one's own." (Louisiana State University, "Academic Honesty and Dishonesty," adapted from *LSU's Code of Student Conduct*, 1981.) One of the saddest things an instructor has to do is cite a student for plagiarism. In speech classes, students occasionally quote material from *Reader's Digest, Newsweek, Time, Senior Scholastic*, or other easy-to-obtain sources, not realizing how many speech teachers habitually scan the library periodicals section. Even if the teacher has not read the article, it soon becomes apparent that something is wrong—the wording differs from the way the person usually talks, the speech does not have a well-formulated introduction or conclusion, and the organizational pattern is not one normally used by speakers. Often, too, the person who plagiarizes an article reads it aloud badly, another sign that something is wrong.

2   Plagiarism is not, however, simply undocumented verbatim quotation. It also includes (a) undocumented paraphrases of others' ideas and (b) undocumented use of others' main ideas. For example, if you paraphrase a movie review from *Newsweek* without acknowledging that staff critic David Ansen had those insights, or if you use the motivated sequence as a model for analyzing speeches without giving credit to Alan Monroe for developing it, you are guilty of plagiarism.

3   Suppose you ran across the following excerpt from Kenneth Clark's *Civilisation: A Personal View:*

> It was the age of great country houses. In 1722 the most splendid of all had just been completed for Marlborough, the general who had been victorious over Voltaire's country: not the sort of idea that would have worried Voltaire in the least, as he thought of all war as a ridiculous waste of human life and effort. When Voltaire saw Blenheim Palace he said, "What a great heap of stone, without charm or taste," and I can see what he means. To anyone brought up on Mansart and

Perrault, Blenheim must have seemed painfully lacking in order and propriety . . . Perhaps this is because the architect, Sir John Vanbrugh, although a man of genius, was really an amateur. Moreover, he was a natural romantic, a castle-builder who didn't care a fig for good taste and decorum.

Imagine that you decided to use the excerpt in a speech. The following examples illustrate what would constitute plagiarism and suggest ways that you could avoid it:

1. *Verbatim quotation of a passage* (read it aloud word for word). To avoid plagiarism: say, "Kenneth Clark, in his 1969 book *Civilisation: A Personal View,* said the following about the architecture of great country estates in eighteenth-century England: [then quote the paragraph]."

2. *Undocumented use of the main ideas:* "In eighteenth-century England there was a great flurry of building. Country estates were built essentially by amateurs, such as Sir John Vanbrugh, who built the splendid Blenheim Palace for General Marlborough. Voltaire didn't like war and he didn't like Blenheim, which he called a great heap of stone without charm or taste. He preferred the order and variety of houses designed by French architects Mansart and Perrault." To avoid plagiarism: say, "In his book *Civilisation: A Personal View,* Kenneth Clark makes the point that eighteenth-century English country houses were built essentially by amateurs. He uses as an example Sir John Vanbrugh, who designed Blenheim Palace for the Duke of Marlborough. Clark notes that, when Voltaire saw the house, he said, 'What a great heap of stone, without charm or taste.' Clark can understand that reaction from a Frenchman who was raised on the neoclassical designs of Mansart and Perrault. Clark explains English style arose from what he calls 'natural romanticism.'"

3. *Undocumented paraphrasing:* "The eighteenth century was the age of wonderful country houses. In 1722 the most beautiful one in England was built for Marlborough, the general who had won over France. When Voltaire saw the Marlborough house called Blenheim Palace, he said it was a great heap of stones." To avoid plagiarism: use the same kind of language noted under Example 2, giving Clark credit for his impressions.

4. Plagiarism is easy to avoid if you take reasonable care. Moreover, by citing such authorities as Clark, who are well educated and experienced, you add their credibility to yours. Avoid plagiarism to keep from being expelled from the class or even your school, and avoid it for positive reasons as well: improve your ethos by associating your thinking with that of experts.

—Gronbeck et al., *Principles of Speech Communication,* pp. 27–29

VOCABULARY REVIEW

1. For each of the words listed below, use context, prefixes; roots, and suffixes; and/or a dictionary to write a brief definition or synonym of the word as it is used in the reading.

   a. verbatim (para. 2, 3) _____

   b. paraphrase (ing) (para. 2, 3) _____

   c. constitute (para. 3) _____

   d. expelled (para. 4) _____

   e. ethos (para. 4) _____

2. Underline new specialized terms introduced in the reading.

COMPREHENSION QUESTIONS

1. Define plagiarism.
2. Why does plagiarism carry a severe penalty?
3. Summarize three ways to avoid plagiarism.

THINKING CRITICALLY

1. What are possible penalties for plagiarism? Do you think they are fair, too severe, or not severe enough?
2. The reading suggests how to avoid plagiarism when making speeches. How useful are these suggestions for avoiding plagiarism when writing a paper?
3. Can plagiarism be unintentional? If so, should the penalties be the same?
4. What implications does this reading have for your research note-taking techniques?
5. Suppose you needed further information about plagiarism. What sources would you consult, and how would you locate them?

LEARNING/STUDY STRATEGIES

1. Write a paraphrase of paragraph 2 of this reading.
2. Identify the overall thought pattern(s) used in this reading.
3. Draw a conceptual map (p. 302) or write a summary (p. 307) of one of these readings.

THINKING ABOUT THE PAIRED READINGS

INTEGRATING IDEAS

1. In what ways are the two readings similar?
2. In what ways are they different?
3. In what ways do the authors' purposes differ?

GENERATING NEW IDEAS

Using both readings as sources, write a tip sheet for beginning college students who are about to begin their first research paper. Include advice and information that would be helpful to them.

CHAPTER

12 | READING ONLINE

LEARNING OBJECTIVES

- ■ **To learn to locate electronic sources more effectively**
- ■ **To evaluate Internet sources**
- ■ **To develop new reading and thinking strategies for reading electronic sources**
- ■ **To use electronic study aids**

Increasingly, college students are finding the Internet to be a valuable and useful resource. The Internet is a worldwide network of computers through which you can access a wide variety of information and services. Through the Internet, you can access the **World Wide Web** (WWW), a system of Internet servers that allow exchange of information of specially formatted documents. It connects a vast array of resources (documents, graphics, and audio and video files) and allows users to move between and among them easily and rapidly. Many instructors use the Internet and have begun requiring their students to do so. In this chapter, you will learn to read and study electronic sources differently than you do print sources.

Although in most courses, your textbook is still your primary source of information, more and more instructors are expecting their students to use the Internet to supplement their textbook or obtain additional, more current information by visiting Web sites on the Internet. (Textbooks, no matter how up to date they may be, often do not contain information within the past year.)

Other instructors encourage or require their students to use CD-ROMs that accompany their textbooks or use CD-ROMs available in computer labs. Still other instructors expect their students to consult Internet sources in researching a topic for a research paper. Many students, too, are finding valuable information on personal or special interests on the Internet.

For example, Maria Valquez, a student majoring in liberal arts, over the course of a week conducted the following activities using electronic sources.

- Ordered a music CD from Amazon.com, an online book and music store.
- Visited an online writing center, www.purdue.edu, for help with an English paper.
- Searched for Web sites on the topic of tattooing for a sociology research paper.
- Used a CD-ROM tutorial to help her solve problems for her math class.
- Sent and received e-mail from friends.
- Checked the weather in her hometown in anticipation of a weekend trip.
- Visited a Latino student Web site for ideas for organizing a Latino student group on her campus.

Electronic sources are becoming increasingly important in many students' academic and personal lives. Therefore, it is important to know how Web sites are structured, how to locate useful sources, how to evaluate the sources you locate, how to understand differences from print sources, and how to navigate through them in an efficient way.

Although this chapter focuses on using electronic sources, you should realize that the Internet is not always the best source of information. Sometimes, it is easier and quicker to find a piece of information in a book or other traditional sources.

FEATURES OF A WEB SITE

A **Web site** is a location on the World Wide Web where you can obtain information on a particular subject. It is a collection of related pages linked together. Each page is called a **Web page** and stands for a set of information. (It can be any length and is not restricted to a single screen or printed page.) The first page you see when you access a Web site is called its **homepage.**

Major corporations such as Hertz, Burger King, and General Motors have Web sites, as do many universities, government agencies, nonprofit organizations, and local businesses. Web sites are created for a variety of purposes: to sell products, present information, promote a particular viewpoint, share creative work, and so forth.

Web sites have recently been established by textbook publishers and authors to provide information and activities that supplement the textbook. A Web site for a biology text, for example, may contain reviews of recent research and discoveries not included in the text. A Web site for an English composition textbook may contain additional current readings or up-to-date information on documenting electronic sources or exercises that relate to specific portions of the textbook.

EXERCISE 9–1 *Visit two of the following Web sites by typing in the Internet addresses listed below. Then answer the following questions.*

a. www.si.edu
b. www.cnn.com
c. www.nypl.org
d. www.irs.ustreas.gov

If any of the above sites is unavailable, substitute a Web site of your own choice.

1. What is the purpose of each site?
2. In what ways are they similar, and in what ways do they differ?

Parts of a Web Site

A Web site begins with a home page which is the first screen (and possibly more) of the site; it serves as the site's introduction. You can also think of it as a master directory. A sample home page for the Interamerican University Studies Institute is shown in Figure 9–1 on page 262. You can move to other pages on the site by using either navigational buttons or links. **Navigational buttons** are graphic icons such as symbols, arrows, pictures, or buttons. They usually appear at the top, bottom, or on one side of each page. Clicking on these buttons allows you to move to different pages within the site. On the sample homepage in Figure 9–1, the icon "IUSI Presents 1999 Scholarship" is a button, as is the list of items at the left side of the screen. **Links** are highlighted words or phrases within a document that take you to other pages within the site (related links) or to other Web sites (remote links). In Figure 9–1 "Need a Passport?" and "Check the Weather" are external links; they take you to another Web site.

Because it is easy to get lost when navigating through a site, many sites include buttons on all secondary pages that take the reader back to the homepage.

Well-designed Web sites tend to cluster chunks of related information together. The more important information often appears in the top left or right of the screen, since readers of English use a left-to-right eye movement pattern.

Figure 9–1 A Sample Homepage

Interamerican University Studies Institute

Dedicated to fostering cultural and educational exchange between the U.S. and Latin America

▶ Home Page

Programs:

Program Overview

High School

Undergraduate

Workshops

For Teachers

Independent

Group Tours

Host Countries:

Mexico

Costa Rica

Order Books

Contact Us:

About IUSI

Info Request

Send Us E-mail

Participants in our "Experience Costa Rica" program surrounded by children during a visit to the school of Tilarán, Costa Rica.

Welcome to the Interamerican University Studies Institute web site, offering information on IUSI's programs as well as links to Internet resources regarding Mexico and Latin America.

Click here to view the snapshots we've been collecting from our trips to Mexico and Costa Rica.

A Special Offer

Need a Passport?

Travel with Children

Suggested Reading

Check the Weather in Mexico or Costa Rica

Interamerican University Studies Institute
P.O. Box 10958, Eugene, OR 97440
Phone (541) 687-6968 / Fax (541) 686-5947
Outside area code 541, call 1-800-345-IUSI (4874)
email: office@iusi.org

**World To World Literary Translation
Creative Writing in Mexico
Professional Development**

Source: The Interamerican University Studies Institute (http://iusi.org/index.shtml)

Web Site Addresses

Each Web site has its own address, known as its **URL** (Uniform Resource Locator). Here's how to read a URL for the *San Francisco Chronicle.*

transfer format   host computer directory path file name

http: // www.sfgate.com / chronicle / index.shtml

The transfer format identifies the type of server the document is located on and indicates the type of transfer format to be used. The second names the host computer. The directory path is the "address" part of the Web site. The last is the document name.

Many sites can be contacted using only the transfer format and the host computer address. Once you have contacted the site, you can move to different locations and files within the Web site. For example, suppose you are looking for information on an author, and all you know is that she teaches at Tufts University. You could search for the URL of Tufts University and then get to the University homepage. Once there, you could look under Faculty and you might find information about the author.

Anyone can place a Web site on the Internet. Consequently, you must be cautious and verify that the sources are reliable. A Web page may contain a heading, called a header, that serves as a title for the information on that page. It often appears in bigger, bolder type than the rest of the text on the page. These headers can sometimes serve as valuable, concise descriptions of the contents of the page. If they are descriptive, use them to decide whether the page contains the information you need and if it is worth reading.

LOCATING ELECTRONIC SOURCES ON THE WEB

Begin by gaining access to the Internet. In addition to a computer, you will need a modem and a browser, such as Microsoft Explorer or Netscape Navigator. You will also need an Internet service provider (ISP) to connect your computer to the Internet. Your college's computer center, your telephone or cable company, or a commercial service provider such as America Online can connect you. You will need a name you use online, called a username, and a password. If you need help getting started, check with the staff in your college's computer lab.

Identifying Keywords

To search for information on a topic, you need to come up with a group of specific words that describe your topic; these are known as **keywords.** It is often necessary to narrow your topic in order to identify specific keywords.

For example, if you searched the topic home-schooling, you would find thousands of sources. However, if you narrowed your topic to home-schooling of primary grade children in California, you would identify far fewer sources.

There are three basic groups of search tools you can use to locate information: subject directories, search engines, and meta-search engines.

Using Subject Directories

Subject directories classify Web resources by categories and subcategories. Some offer reviews or evaluations of sites. Use a subject directory when you want to browse the Web using general topics or when you are conducting a broad search. A subject directory would be helpful if you are looking for sites about parenting issues or want to find a list of organizations for animal welfare. Here are several useful directories:

INFOMINE http://infomine.ucr.edu

Lycos top 5% http://www.lycos.com

Yahoo http://www.yahoo.com

Using a Search Engine

A **search engine** is a computer program that helps you locate information on a topic. Search engines search for keywords and provide connections to documents that contain the key words you instruct it to search for. Depending on your topic, some search engines are more useful than others. In addition, each search engine may require a different way of entering the keywords. For example, some may require you to place quotation marks around a phrase ("capital punishment"). Other times, you may need to use plus signs (+) between keywords ("home schooling" + "primary grades" + "California"). The quotes around "home schooling" will create a search for those words as a phrase, rather than as single terms. Be sure to use the "help" feature when you use a new search engine to discover the best way to enter keywords.

Useful search engines include

Alta Vista http://altavista.com

Excite http://www.excite.com

HotBot http://www.hotbot.dom

Go Network http://www.go.com

NetSearch http://home.netscape.com/home/internet-search.html

WebCrawler http://webcrawler.com

Most search engines have help sections that include instructions about how to use them.

Using Meta-Search Engines

You can search a number of search engines at the same time and combine all the results in a single listing using a **meta-search engine.** Use these types of engines when you are searching for a very specific or obscure topic or one for which you are having trouble finding information. Here a few common ones:

MetaFind http://metafind.com

DogPile http://dogpile.com

PROFUsion http://profusion.com

EXERCISE 9–2

Use one of the search tools listed above to locate three sources on one of the following topics. Then use a different tool or different search engine to search the same topic again. Compare your results. Which engine was easier to use? Which produced more sources?

1. The Baseball Hall of Fame
2. Telecommuting
3. Your favorite musical group
4. Parenting issues

EVALUATING INTERNET SOURCES

Although the Internet contains a great deal of valuable information and resources, it also contains rumor, gossip, hoaxes, and misinformation. In other words, not all Internet sources are trustworthy. You must evaluate a source before accepting it. Here are some guidelines to follow when evaluating Internet sources.

1. *Check the publisher or sponsor of the site.* If a site is sponsored or provided by a well-known organization, a reputable newspaper such as *The New York Times,* the information is apt to be reliable. One way to discover the sponsoring organization is to check the URL. The last part of a URL,

called the domain, reveals something about the nature of a Web site's sponsor. Here is a list of common domains and their abbreviation as used in a URL.

Commercial	-.com	(Internet providers, AOL, for example; companies, or anyone trying to sell something)
Education	-.edu	(public schools, colleges, universities, students' homepages, term papers)*
Government	-.gov	(State, National agencies)
Network	-.net	
Non Profit Organization	-.org	(non profit groups)
Military	-.mil	
Other countries	-.ca (Canada), -.uk (United Kingdom)	

2. *Check the author.* For Web sites, look for professional credentials or affiliations. Often, the author's professional affiliation will be included at the end of an article he or she has written. Usually, you can trust a reputable sponsor to feature only credible authors. To find out about an author through an Internet search, use a search engine. Type the author's full name in the search box. Place the full name in quotation marks, or choose phrase searching, if it is available.

   For newsgroups or discussion groups (see p. 278), check to see if the author has given his or her name and a signature (a short biographical description included at the end of messages).

3. *Check the date of the posting.* Be sure you are obtaining current information. A credible Web site usually includes the date on which it was last updated.

4. *Discover the purpose of the posting.* Many Web sites are written with an agenda, such as to sell a product, promote a cause, advocate a position, and so forth. Look for bias in the reporting of information.

5. *Check links (addresses of other sources suggested by the Web site).* If these links are no longer working, the Web site you are visiting may be outdated or not reputable.

* The .edu abbreviation used to be a good indicator of a higher education academic site, but that is no longer the case. Be sure to check the source.

6. *Cross-check your information.* If you doubt the accuracy of information you have found, try to find the same information in another source.

EXERCISE 9–3 *Evaluate each of the sites you located for Exercise 9–2. Assign a rating of 1–5 (1 = low reliability; 5 = high reliability). Be prepared to discuss your ratings.*

EXERCISE 9–4 *Visit a Web site and become familiar with its organization and content. Evaluate it using the suggested criteria. Then write a brief paragraph explaining why the Web site is or is not a reliable source.*

READING ELECTRONIC TEXT

Reading electronic text (also called hypertext) is very different from reading traditional printed text such as textbooks or magazines or newspaper articles. The term electronic text, as used in this chapter, refers to information presented on a Web site. It does not refer to articles and essays that can be downloaded from Searchbank or from an e-journal, for example. Because Web sites are unique, they require a different mind set and different reading strategies. If electronic text is new or unfamiliar to you, you need to change the way you read and the way you think when approaching Web sites. If you attempt to read Web sites the same way you read traditional text, you may lose focus or perspective, miss important information, or become generally disoriented. Text used on Web sites is different in the following ways from traditional print text.

- *Reading Web sites involves paying attention to sound, graphics, and movement, as well as words.* Your senses, then, may pull you in several different directions simultaneously. Recorded or artificial sounds may compete with animated sequences, flashing graphics, and colorful drawings or photos for your attention. Some Web sites are available in two formats—graphical and text-only. This is most common for academic sites. If you are distracted by the sound and graphics, check to see if a text-only version of the site is available.

- *Text on Web sites comes in brief, independent screenfuls, sometimes called nodes.* These screenfuls tend to be brief, condensed pieces of information. Unlike traditional text, they are not set within a context, and background information is often not supplied. They do not depend on other pages for meaning either. In traditional print text, paragraphs and pages are dependent—you often must have read and understood a previous one in order to comprehend the one that follows it. Electronic pages are often intended to stand alone.

- *Text on Web sites may not follow the traditional main idea–supporting details organization of traditional paragraphs.* Instead, the screen may appear as a group of topic sentences without detail.

- *Web sites are multidirectional and unique; traditional text progresses in a single direction.* When reading traditional text, a reader usually follows a single direction, working through the text from beginning to end as the author has written. Web site text is multidirectional; each electronic reader creates his or her own unique text, by following or ignoring different paths. Two readers of the same Web site may read entirely different material, or the same material in a different orders. For example, one user of the Interamerican University Studies Institute site in Figure 9–1 might begin by reading about the "Experience Costa Rica" program; another user might start by checking the information about IUSI; a third might begin by clicking on the group tours link.

- *Web site text requires readers to make decisions.* Because screens have menus and links, electronic readers must always make choices. They can focus on one aspect of the topic and ignore all others, for example, by following a path of links. Readers of print text, however, have far fewer choices to make.

- *Web sites allow readers the flexibility to choose the order in which to receive the information.* Partly due to learning style, people prefer to acquire information in different sequences. Some may prefer to begin with details and then come to understand underlying rules or principles. Others may prefer to begin in the opposite way. Electronic sources allow readers to approach the text in any manner compatible with their learning style. A pragmatic learner may prefer to move through a site systematically, either clicking or ignoring links as they appear on the screen from top to bottom, for example.

- *Web sites use new symbol systems.* Electronic texts introduce new and sometimes unfamiliar symbols. A flashing or blinking light may suggest a new feature on the site, or an underlined word or a word in a different color may suggest a link. Sound effects, too, may have meanings. For example, on children's Web sites where a child can have books read aloud, and auditory signal may tell the child when to turn the page. Icons and drawings may be used in place of words. (A drawing of a book, for example, may indicate that print sources are available.)

EXERCISE 9–5 | *Locate a Web site on a topic related to one of the end-of-chapter readings in this text. Write a list of characteristics that distinguish it from the print readings.*

Changing Your Reading Strategies for Reading Electronic Text

Reading electronic text is relatively new to the current generation of college students. (This will no doubt change with the upcoming generations who, as children, will learn to read both print and electronic text.) Most current college students and teachers first learned to read using print text. We have read print text for many more years than electronic text; consequently, our brains have developed numerous strategies or "work orders" for reading traditional texts. Our work orders, however, are less fully developed for electronic text. Electronic texts have a wider variety of formats and more variables to cope with than traditional texts. A textbook page is usually made up of headings, paragraphs, and an occasional photo or graphic. Web sites have vibrant color, animation, sound, and music as well as words.

Reading is not only different, but it also tends to be slower on the computer screen than on print sources. One expert estimates reading a screen is 25 percent slower than reading on paper. Your eyes can see the layout of two full pages on a book. From the two pages, you can see headings, division of ideas, and subtopics. By glancing at a print page, you get an initial assessment of what it contains. You can tell, for example, if a page is heavily statistical (your eye will see numbers, dates, symbols) or is anecdotal (your eye will see capitalized proper names, quotation marks and numerous indented paragraphs for dialogue, for example). Because you have a sense of what the page contains and how it is organized, you can read somewhat faster. Because a screen holds fewer words, you get far less feedback before you begin to read.

DEVELOPING NEW WAYS OF THINKING AND READING

Reading on electronic sources demands a different type of thinking than print sources. A print source is linear—it goes in a straight line from idea to idea. Electronic sources, due to the presence of links, tend to be multidirectional and let you follow numerous paths (see illustration on next page).

Reading electronic text also requires new strategies. The first steps to reading electronic text easily and effectively are to understand how it is different (see previous section) and realize that you must change and adapt how you read. Some specific suggestions follow.

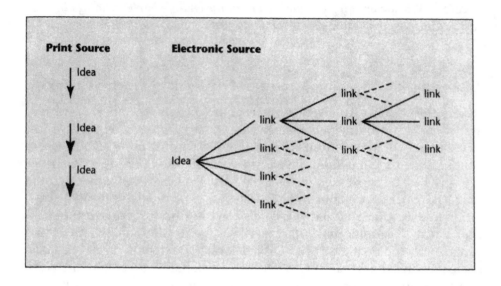

Focus on Your Purpose

Focus clearly on your purpose for visiting the site. What information do you need? Because you must create your own path through the site, unless you fix in mind what you are looking for, you may wander aimlessly, wasting valuable time, or even become lost, following numerous links that lead you farther and farther away from the site at which you began.

Get Used to the Site's Design and Layout

Each Web site has unique features and arranges information differently.

1. *When you reach a new site, spend a few minutes getting used to it and discovering how it is organized.* Scroll through it quickly to determine how it is organized and what information is available. Ask yourself the following questions.

    - What information is available?
    - How is it arranged on the screen?

2. *Expect the first screen to grab your attention and make a main point.* (Web site authors know that many people [up to 90 percent] who read a Web page do not scroll down to see the next page.)

3. *Get used to the colors, flashing images, and sounds before you attempt to obtain information from the site.* Your eye may have a tendency to focus

on color or movement, rather than on print. Because Web sites are highly visual, they require visual as well as verbal thinking. The author intends for you to respond to photos, graphics, and animation.

4. *Consider both the focus and limitations of your learning style.* Are you a spatial learner? If so, you may have a tendency to focus too heavily on the graphic elements of the screen. If, on the other hand, you are a verbal learner, you may ignore important visual elements or signals. If you focus *only* on the words and ignore color and graphics on a particular screen, you will probably miss information or may not move through the site in the most efficient way. Review your learning style (p. 8), and consider both your strengths and limitations as they apply to electronic text.

EXERCISE 9–6

In groups of two or three students, consider at least two aspects of learning style. For each, discuss the tendencies, limitations, and implications these particular learning styles may have for reading electronic text. For example, consider how a pragmatic learner would approach a Web site with numerous links and buttons. Then consider how a pragmatic learner's approach might differ.

EXERCISE 9–7

Locate two Web sites that you think are interesting and appealing. Then answer the following questions.

1. How does each use color?
2. How does each use graphics?
3. Is sound or motion used? If so, how?

Pay Attention to how Information Is Organized

Because you can navigate through a Web site in many different ways, it is important to have the right expectations and to make several decisions before you begin.

Some Web sites are much better organized than others. Some have clear headings and labels that make it easy to discover how to proceed; others do not and will require more thought before beginning. For example, if you are reading an article with 10–15 underlined words (links), there is no prescribed order to follow and these links are not categorized in any way. Figure 9–2 (p. 272) shows an excerpt from a Web site titled "Gender and Society" sponsored by Trinity University. Notice that is has numerous links built into paragraphs.

Figure 9–2

GENDER AND SOCIETY

The desire of a man for a woman is not directed at her because she is a human being, but because she is a woman. That she is a human being is of no concern to him.

--Immanuel Kant

In addition to age, gender is one of the universal dimensions on which status differences are based. Unlike sex, which is a biological concept, gender is a social construct specifying the socially and culturally prescribed roles that men and women are to follow. According to Gerda Lerner in *The Creation of Patriarchy,* gender is the "costume, a mask, a straitjacket in which men and women dance their unequal dance" (p.238). As Alan Wolfe observed in "The Gender Question" (*The New Republic,* June 6:27–34), "of all the ways that one group has systematically mistreated another, none is more deeply rooted than the way men have subordinated women. All other discriminations pale by contrast." Lerner argues that the subordination of women preceded all other subordinations and that to rid ourselves of all of those other "isms" -racism, classism, ageism, etc. -it is sexism that must first be eradicated.

Women have always had lower status than men, but the extent of the gap between the sexes varies across cultures and time (some arguing that it is inversely related to social evolution). In 1980, the United Nations summed up the burden of this inequality: Women, who comprise half the world's population, do two thirds of the world's work, earn one tenth of the world's income and own one hundredth of the world's property. In Leviticus, God told Moses that a man is worth 50 sheikels and a woman worth 30 -approximately the contemporary salary differentials of the sexes in the United States. What might be the socio-cultural implications if men were to also be the child bearers? Follow the first human male pregnancy at www.malepregnancy.com.

And the significance of the stamps above? A recent U.S. Postal Service publication, "Women on Stamps," holds some interesting methodological possibilities. Putting a deceased individual's likeness on a stamp is one way by which political immortality is conferred. Of the hundreds of Americans so immortalized only a handful are women: 16, to be precise, through 1960; 19 through 1970; and 29 through 1980 (any connection between this 50% increase with the ERA movement of the seventies?). An enterprising student may wish to investigate and compare how this female proportion of immortalized citizens varies across countries and time.

Matters of gender are scattered throughout these pages, including gender differences in household duties, in in voting during the 1996 Presidential election, and in suicide rates cross-nationally. Take advantage of this site's search engine by first entering "gender" and next "sex" as the search words.

Source: Michael C. Kearl, "Gender and Society" *A Sociological Tour Through Cyberspace* (http://www.trinity.edu/~mkearl/gender.html)

Use the following suggestions to grasp a site's organization.

1. *Use the site map, if provided, to discover what information is available and how it is organized.* A sample site map, a Web site sponsored by the U.S. Department of Energy and the National Institutes of Health, is shown in Figure 9–3 (p. 274). The site presents information about the Human Genome Project that collects information on genetic research. Notice that the links are categorized by subject: resources, education, research, meetings, and so forth.

2. *Consider the order in which you want to take in information.* Choose an order in which to explore links; avoid randomly clicking on link buttons. Doing so is somewhat like randomly choosing pages to read out of a reference book. Do you need definitions first? Do you want historical background first? Your decision will be partly influenced by your learning style.

3. *Consider writing brief notes to yourself as you explore a complicated Web site.* Alternatively, you could print the homepage and jot notes on it.

4. *Expect shorter, less detailed sentences and paragraphs.* Much online communication tends to be briefer and more concise than in traditional sources. As a result, you may have to mentally fill in transitions and make inferences about relationships among ideas. For example, you may have to infer similarities and differences or recognize cause and effect connections.

EXERCISE 9–8

Visit two Web sites on the same topic. Write a few sentences comparing and contrasting the sites' organization and design.

Use Links to Find the Information You Need

Links are unique to electronic text. Here's how to use them.

1. *Plan on exploring links to find complete and detailed information.* Links—both remote links (those that take you to another site) and related links within a site—are intended to provide more detailed information on topics introduced on the homepage.

2. *As you follow links, be sure to bookmark your original site and other useful sites you come across so you can find them again.* **Bookmarking** is a feature on your Internet browser that allows you to record Web site addresses and access them later by simply clicking on the site name.

Figure 9–3 A Website Map

Project Information

- What's New?
- FAQs
- What is the HGP?
- Goals
- Progress
- History
- Timeline
- Budget
- Benefits
- Ethical, Legal, & Social Issues
- Genome Science
- Links

Contact Information

- DOE HGP Administration
- Project Contacts
- About Us
- Site Stats and Credits

Resources

- Glossary
- Acronyms
- Images
- Videos
- Audio Files

Education

- Teachers
- Students
- Careers

Research

- Research in Progress
- Funding
- Research Sites
- Sequencing
- Sequencing Technologies
- Mapping
- Bioinformatics
- Functional and Comparative Genomics
- Ethical, Legal, & Social Issues
- Recent Abstracts
- Chromosome Launchpad
- BACs
- Virtual Library Genetics
- Microbial Genome Program

Publications

- List of all Publications
- Human Genome News
- To Know Ourselves
- Primer on Molecular Genetics
- Your Genes, Your Choices
- 1997 Program Report
- 1999 DOE HGP Abstracts
- ELSI Retrospective
- NEW Judicature Genes and Justice issue
- Judges' Journal special genetics issue
- A Vital Legacy
- 1997 DOE BER Exceptional Service Awards
- Miscellaneous

Meetings

- Meetings Calendar
- Workshop Calendar
- Meetings and Reports

Search Human Genome Project Information

Search Web pages:

[Search] [Reset]

Search Web pages plus publications:

[Search] [Reset]

Survey: After searching this web site, have you found what you wanted?

○ Yes ○ No If not, tell us what you were searching for:

[Submit]

Please do not submit questions here. Send questions via this form: caseydk@ornl.gov .

Medical Applications

- Medicine and the New Genetics
- Disease Diagnosis and Prediction
- Disease Intervention
- Genetic Counseling
- CME
- Genetic Disease Information --pronto!

Topical Fact Sheets

- Cloning
- DOE and the HGP
- Functional Genomics
- Gene Testing
- Sequencing
- SNPs

Source: Oak Ridge National Laboratory Web site wysiwyg://158http://www.ornl.gov/TechResources/ Human_Genome/home.html

Different search engines use different terms for this function. Netscape uses the term *Bookmarks;* Microsoft Explorer calls it *Favorites.* In addition, Netscape has a *GO* feature that allows a user to retrace the steps of the current search.

3. *If you use a site or a link that provides many pages of continuous paragraphs, print the material and read it offline.*

4. *If you find you are lacking background on a topic, use links to help fill in the gap or search for a different Web site on the same topic that is less technical.*

5. *If you get lost, most Internet browsers have a history feature.* It allows you to backtrack or retrace the links your followed in a search. On Netscape, for example, click on "Back," it will take you back one link at a time; "History" keeps track of all searches over a given period of time and allows you to go directly to a chosen site, rather than backtracking step by step.

EXERCISE 9–9

For one of the Web sites you visited earlier in the chapter or a new site of your choice, follow at least three links and then answer the following questions.

1. What type of information did each contain?
2. Was each source reliable? How do you know?
3. Which was the easiest to read and follow? Why?

ELECTRONIC LEARNING AIDS

In addition to the Web sites on the Internet, you may use many other electronic sources and services as well: CD-ROMs, computer tutorial software, e-mail, listservs, and news groups. Each of the following are described below, along with suggestions for how to use them.

CD-ROMs That Accompany Textbooks

A CD-ROM may be included with the textbook when you purchase it or it may be available in your college's academic computer labs. (Not all textbooks have CD-ROM accompaniments.) CD-ROMs contain a wealth of information, activities, and learning resources. Here is an example of what a CD-ROM that accompanies a psychology text contains.

- review of key topics
- a "click here" function for more information on terms, concepts, etc.

- demonstrations and experiments
- matching games and other learning activities
- review quizzes
- glossary of key terms
- student notepad (for recording your own ideas)
- reference sources

The best part of CD-ROMs is that they are interactive and engaging. The sound, dialogue, and visuals hold your interest and are well-suited if you tend to be an auditory, spatial, or pragmatic learner. They also allow you to choose what and how you want to learn. If you need to review a topic such as learning theory, you click on an icon and are guided through a learning sequence. You can access more information if you need it. When you have finished, you can choose whether or not to take a review quiz to assess what you have learned. Additionally, many of the activities are interactive—you get involved with the material by responding, rather than merely reading it.

Here are a few guidelines for using CD-ROMs that accompany textbooks.

1. *Try whatever is available.* Even if you have never used a computer before, if software is available, try it out. College computer labs are usually staffed with friendly, helpful people (sometimes other students) who can show you how to get started.

2. *Use them with, but not in place of, your text.* CD-ROMs are supplements. Although they are fun to use, you still must read your textbook.

3. *Use the CD-ROM as a chapter preview.* View the CD-ROM on a particular topic to get an overview of it before reading the corresponding text material.

4. *Use the CD-ROM for review and practice.* After you have read the text, use the CD-ROM to help you learn the material.

5. *Use the quiz or self-test modules when studying for an exam.* Use the quizzes to discover which topics you need to study further. Keep a record of your progress. Many programs will do this for you and allow you to print a progress report. This record will enable you to see your strengths and weaknesses, plan further study, and review troublesome topics.

6. *If the CD-ROM has a notepad (a place where you can write your own notes), use it.* You will learn more efficiently if you express what you have learned in your own words.

7. *Space out your practice.* Because many software programs are fun and engaging, some students work on them for hours at a time. To get maximum benefit from the time you are spending, limit your work to an hour or so. Beyond that, many activities become routine; your mind switches to "automatic pilot," and learning ceases.

8. *Consolidate your learning.* When you finish a module or program segment, do not just exit and shut off the machine. Stop and reflect on what you have learned. If you worked on an algebra module about the multiplication of polynomials, stop and recall the techniques you learned. Write notes or summarize the process in a separate section of your course notebook reserved for this purpose.

E-mail

E-mail (electronic mail) enables you to send messages to another person or place using your computer. A variety of computer programs are available that allow you to send and receive messages electronically, as well as to print them for future reference. There are many academic uses for e-mail. Students in a class may collaborate on a project or critique each others' papers using e-mail. Other times, instructors and students communicate through e-mail. In completing a research paper, it is possible to contact professors or other students doing research on the topic you are studying. You can also transmit word processing files by attaching them to an e-mail message.

Most e-mail follows a consistent format and, consequently, is easy to read. Messages begin with a memo format in which the topic of the message, date the message was sent, sender, and receiver are identified as "Subject" or "Re," "Date," "From," and "To." The message follows this introductory identifying information. Transmittal information that tracks the electronic path through which the message was sent may accompany the message. This information, if it appears, can be ignored unless you wish to verify the source of the sender.

The style of e-mail messages tends to be more casual and conversational than the traditional print forms of communication (letters and memos) but more formal than phone or in-person conversations. Because e-mail is intended to be a rapid, expedient means of communication, some formalities of written communication are relaxed. Expect to find a briefer introduction, more concise sentences, and few or no concluding remarks. Consequently, e-mail requires close attention; unlike print forms of communication, there is little repetition and fewer cues as to what is important.

Figure 9–4 A Sample E-mail Message

```
Subj:       Research on learning styles

Date:       98-02-23 11:49:34 EST

From:       Maryrod@daemon.edu (Mary Rodriguez)

Reply to:   Maryrod@daemon.edu

To:         KateApp@daemon.edu

----------------------------------------------------------

Dear Kate,

In response to your request for recent research

on the learning styles of university versus

community college students, I do know of one

article that may be useful as a starting point:

Henson, Mark and Schemeck, R.R. "Learning Styles

of Community College Versus University Students."

Perceptual Motor Skills, 76(1), 118.

Good luck on your research project.

Mary
```

Reading lengthy e-mail messages may be easier if you print them first. Figure 9–4 shows a sample e-mail message. Notice that the message is a concise yet effective form of communication.

Newsgroups

Newsgroups are collections of people interested in a particular topic or issue who correspond to discuss it. Participants post messages on a given topic; other participants read and respond. Read postings with a critical mind set. Most postings are written by average people expressing their opinions; their ideas may be informative, but they may also contain incorrect information, bias, and unsubstantiated opinion. At times, you also may find postings that are mindless ranting and raving. Here are some tips for reading newsgroup postings.

- Separate fact from opinion (see Chapter 4, p. 100). Take into account the bias, motivation, and prejudices of the author.
- Verify any information you get from a newsgroup with a second source.
- Use newsgroups to explore the range of opinion on a topic or issue.

Usually, newsgroups are open forums; anyone can lurk or "listen in" to the discussion. Newsgroups can yield additional sources of information, as well as a variety of interesting perspectives on a topic. A specialized form of newsgroup is known as a **listserv.** Participation is limited to those who have subscribed. Academic discussion groups are considered listservs. Directories are available to help you locate useful newsgroups and listservs. These include

Directory of professional and Scholarly e-conferences

http://www.n2h2.com/KOVACS/

E-mail Discussion Lists

http://alabanza.com/kabacoff/Inter-Links/listserv.html

Usenet News Groups http://www.liszt.com/news/

EXERCISE 9–10

Visit a newsgroup and either lurk or participate in the discussion. Then answer the following questions.

1. What was the topic of discussion?
2. Were the postings largely fact or opinion?
3. Did you detect bias or prejudice?
4. How useful is the newsgroup as a source of information?

EXERCISE 9–11

Working with another student, select a topic of mutual interest. Discuss it, narrow it down, and write two or three specific research questions. Working independently, use the Internet to locate answers to your research questions. When you have finished, compare your answers and the sources from which you obtained them.

416

Using a Computer as a Study and Learning Aid

A computer's word processing capability makes it a useful study and learning aid. The following are suggestions for using the computer to organize your study. To make the most of the suggestions, you will need access to a computer on a daily basis.

1. *Use a computer to organize notes from textbook reading.* As you take notes from reading, your notes tend to follow the organization of the text. At times it is useful to reorganize and rearrange your notes. For example, you may want to pull together information on a certain topic that is spread throughout one or more chapters. Once your notes are entered into a computer file, you can use the cut and paste function to rearrange and reorganize your notes or outlines easily without rewriting.

2. *Use a computer to organize lecture notes.* Lecture notes are, of course, recorded by hand as you listen to the lecture, unless you are using a laptop. Typing your notes into a computer file is a means of editing and reviewing, as well as reorganizing.

3. *Use a computer to integrate text and lecture notes.* The computer offers an ideal solution to the problem of how to integrate notes you have taken from your textbook and those you have taken in class. The cut and paste function allows you to move sections of your lecture notes to corresponding sections in your notes from your text.

4. *Use a computer to create lists of new terminology for each of your courses.* The computer's word processing capabilities allow you to group similar terms, organize them by chapter, or sort them into "know" and "don't know" files. A biology student, for example, grouped terms together into the following categories: energy and life, cells, biological processes, reproduction, biological systems, brain and behavior, and environmental issues.

SUMMARY

Reading electronic sources requires unique reading and thinking skills.

A Web site contains unique features:

- homepage
- links to other sites

Locating sources on the World Wide Web (WWW) involves identifying key words and using a search engine.

To evaluate a Web site, consider the following:

- the publisher or sponsor
- author

- date of posting
- links
- purpose of site

Web sites differ from print text in the following ways:

- Web sites involve graphics, sound, color, and animation.
- Language on Web sites tends to be brief.
- Screens are often independent of one another.
- Web sites are multidirectional, require decision-making, and allow flexibility.

Electronic text should be read differently than print text. Be sure to

- Identify the purpose of the site.
- Familiarize yourself with the site's design and layout.
- Pay attention to how the information is organized.
- Use links to find additional information.

Other electronic aids can also help you learn more effectively. These include

- CD-ROMs, which often accompany textbooks, facilitate learning and review.
- E-mail, which is useful to communicate with classmates and professors.
- Newsgroups can yield additional sources of information on a topic and can provide a variety of interesting perspectives on a topic.

ARCHAEOLOGY

PREREADING QUESTIONS

1. How do archaeologists know there might be an important artifact buried under the earth?
2. What can artifacts reveal about the past?

SLICES OF THE PAST

Alan Hall

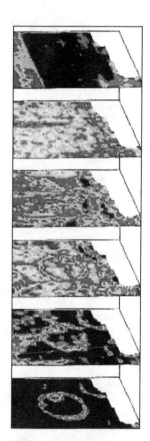

Series of Radar Images probe beneath an alfalfa field (top) in Japan to reveal the long-buried circular moat of an ancient *burial mound* (bottom).

1　When archaeologists suspect than an important find lies buried beneath the earth, they reach for their shovels, hoping to hit some clue of a buried city or important burial site; sometimes they even call in backhoes and trenching machines. But now, a University of Denver anthropology professor has come up with a ground-breaking alternative that may turn traditional archaeology upside down.

2　Lawerence B. Conyers and his colleague, Dean Goodman, have adapted a technology known as "ground penetrating radar" to pioneer a new era of "non-invasive" archaeology. By pumping radar pulses into the ground and creating images of the radar reflections on a computer,

Field Work. Conyers and his team have set up their radar base station at a site near Bluff, Utah believed to conceal an ancient ceremonial room, or *kiva*, of the ancient Anasazi people.

they can obtain detailed pictures of a potentially important site before the first shovel of dirt is lifted. Then, the researchers can decide whether to dig—and where to dig—while doing the least damage to important artifacts.

3　"Archaeologists tend to be very low-tech people," Conyers says. "They have a tendency to be more comfortable digging in the dirt than working with computers. But this radar can help to locate sites and objects that you can't see on the surface. It can help us save sites that could be destroyed with traditional escavation techniques."

4　Gound-penetrating radar has been used for decades for everything from locating buried family treasures hidden from the Nazis to finding the engines of the ValuJet crashed in the Everglades. Conyers has used the technology, and the software written by Goodman, to: map a Mayan village buried under 15 feet of volcanic ash in Ceren, El Salvador; create images of a Mayan ceremonial center buried in a sugar cane field in Coatzalmaguapa, Guatemala; located 1,700 year old kiln sites and a large village buried in wind-blown sand between two ceremonial pyraminds in Peru; and disclose details of ancient burial sites in Japan.

5   Closer to his home base in Denver, Conyers has employed the new technique to reveal the history of the ancient Anasazi people of the American West. Because of their sacred nature, the issue of whether to disturb these sites is crucial to their descendants. Near Bluff, Utah, Conyers and his colleagues pinpointed a subterranean kiva, used in ceremonial rites by the Anasazi people. "Even though the people that constructed this kiva have been dead for more than 900 years, these sites are still very sacred," says Conyers. "So radar was a method that we could use to first image what was there and then adjust out excavation procedures to dig only in certain spots to test our scientific ideas."

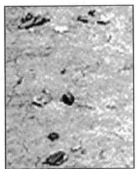

Fragments of Pottery litter the ground at a site near Bluff, Utah where Conyers and his colleagues located a village of Anasazi "pit houses". The broken ceramics were dated about AD 1100.

6   Nearby, Conyers and his colleagues also found a field littered with sherds of pottery that dated to 1100 A.D. By searching the area with radar, they located a village of Anasazi "pit houses." Archaeologists usually use this type of evidence to locate sites, but of course have no idea where they are under the gound, says Conyers. "The typical way of finding the buried houses of this sort is to randomly dig test pits or drill auger holes—or even worse use backhoe trenchers that really destroy the site.

7   Mapping these sites using traditional excavation methods would have cost millions of dollars and taken many years. Conyers, using ground-penetrating radar and 3-D imaging software developed by Goodman, can map a site for a fraction of the cost in as little as three weeks. Many buried sites would not have been discovered without the ground-penetrating radar technology and would be potentially at risk from construction and erosion.

8   The next step for Conyers is the creation of moving 3-D images that will allow people to take video "tours" of archaeological sites that have not been unearthed. Maybe those people who Conyers refers to as "dirt archaeologists" will soon retire their shovels.

Related Reading

"Gound-penetrating Radar: An Introduction for Archaeologists," by Lawrence B. Conyers and Dean Goodman, Altamira Press, Walnut Creek, California, 1997.

—Hall, "Slices of the Past," *Scientific American—Exhibit: Radar Archaeology*, June 22, 1998
(http://www.sciam.com)

[By clicking on the "burial mound" link, the following site was located.]

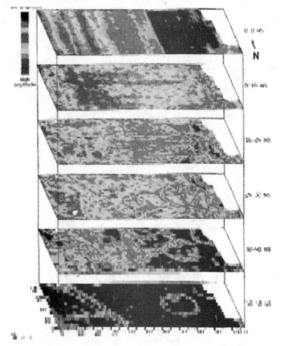

BURIAL MOUND

9   RADAR SURVEY, conducted by Dean Goodman, in Japan revealed a circular burial mound with a burial inside it, which shows up clearly in the bottom slice. The straight line at the left is probably an old fence line when the area was used for horse corrals about 500-600 years ago (Edo Period). The burial moat is much older, probably at least 1100 years old (Kofun Period). The surface is an alfalfa field. "As is usual in these surveys, there were no surface indicators of what was below the ground," says Conyers.

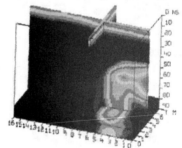

10   IMAGE is a 3-dimensional cutaway of a burial chamber that was found by Dean Goodman on a mound on the Island of Kyushu in Japan. It contained the remains of a warrior with a variety of artifacts, including bronze swords. This is a 3-D cutaway image of this chamber. It reveals a main chamber and a vertical shaft that leads to an offering below the burial.

Images: Lawrence B. Conyers and Dean Goodman, from "Ground-penetrating Radar: An Introduction for Archaeologists," Altamira Press, Walnut Creek, California, 1997.

Back to <u>Slices of the Past</u>

—"Burial Mound," *Scientific American—Exhibit: Radar Archaeology,* June 22, 1998 (http://www.sciam.com)

VOCABULARY REVIEW

1. For each of the words listed below, use context, prefixes, roots, and suffixes; and/or a dictionary to write a brief definition or synonym of the word as it is used in the reading.

a. alternative (para. 1) _____

b. potentially (para. 2) _____

c. artifacts (para. 2) _____

d. excavation (para. 3) _____

e. disclose (para. 4) _____

f. subterranean (para. 5) _____

g. sherds (para. 6) _____

2. Underline new specialized terms introduced in the reading.

COMPREHENSION QUESTIONS

1. Why is the radar procedure referred to as noninvasive?
2. Name two important advantages of using the ground penetrating radar.
3. What is the usual way of finding buried artifacts?
4. Why do archaeologists not like to use backhoe trenchers?
5. Why was it important to use radar to examine the subterranean kivas used by the Anasazi people?
6. How long does it take to map a site using this new radar technique compared to traditional excavation?
7. What did the radar survey conducted by Dean Goodman reveal?

THINKING CRITICALLY

1. What would you do if you wanted to know more about Lawrence B. Conyers?
2. What does Conyers mean by the term *dirt archaeologists*?
3. For what other nonarchaeological situation can you imagine using ground penetrating radar?
4. Do you think archaeologists should be permitted to dig up sacred sites? Explain.
5. How did this Web site differ from a textbook?
6. How useful did you find the link to "burial mound"?

LEARNING/STUDY STRATEGY

Design a study sheet explaining the different types of remote sensing.

ARCHAEOLOGY

PREREADING QUESTIONS

1. Why is the study of archaeology important?
2. What is remote sensing?

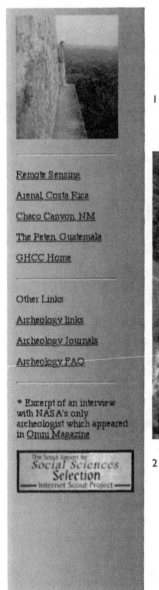

* Excerpt of an interview
with NASA's only
archeologist which appeared
in Omni Magazine

The Scout Report for
Social Sciences
Selection
— Internet Scout Project —

ARCHAEOLOGY

Tom Sever

1   Much of human history can be traced through the impacts of human actions upon the environment. The use of remote sensing technology offers the archeologist the opportunity to detect these

impacts which are often invisible to the naked eye. This information can be used to address issues in human settlement, environmental interaction, and climate change. Archaeologists want to know how ancient people successfully adapted to their environment and what factors may have led to their collapse or disappearance. Did they overextend the capacity of their landscape, causing destructive environmental effects which led to their demise? Can this information be applied to modern day societies so that the mistakes of the past are not repeated?

2   Remote sensing can be used as a methodological procedure for detecting, inventorying, and prioritizing surface and shallow-depth archeological information in a rapid, accurate, and quantified manner. Man is a tropical creature who has invaded every environment on earth successfully; now we are ready to explore, and eventually colonize, the delicate environments of Space. Understanding how ancient man successfully managed Earth is important for the success of current and future societies.

3   "The stereotype has archaeologists just digging up spearheads and pottery and anthropologists just writing down the words of primitive tribes. But we're examining how people adapted to their environment throughout time, how they experienced environmental shift, why cultures come and go. Soils associated with artifacts are as important as the artifacts themselves—probably more relevant to us than the actual objects. Now more than ever, archaeological research is interdisciplinary: botany, forestry, soil science, hydrology—all of which contribute to a more complete understanding of the earth, climatic shifts, and how people adapt to large regions. This understanding is critical to future decision making affecting the planet.

4   In Costa Rica, the culture survived repeated volcanic explosions that repeatedly destroyed the environment, explosions equal to the force of a nuclear blast. Other cultures, like the advanced Maya societies, did not survive or recover from similar eruptions. Did it have to do with the size and violence of the eruption, the way they farmed their land over time, or territorial and political struggle?"

We have not inherited the earth from our fathers, we are borrowing it from our children

Amish Farmer

Comments regarding our web service may be e-mailed to:

webmaster@wwwghcc.msfc.nasa.gov

Responsible Official: Dr. Timothy L. Miller (tim.miller@msfc.nasa.gov)
Page Author: Tom Sever
Page Curator: Diane Samuelson (diane.samuelson@msfc.nasa.gov)

Last Updated: May 12, 1998

[By clicking on the "Remote Sensing" link, the following site was located.]

—Sever, "Archaeology," Global Hyrology and Climate Center, NASA/Marshall Space Flight Center Web site (http://www.msfc.nasa.gov)

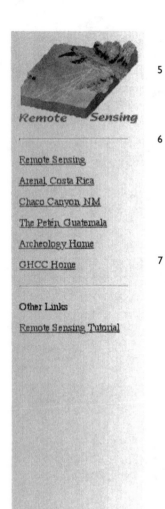

ARCHAEOLOGICAL REMOTE SENSING

5 Now more than ever, archaeological research is interdisciplinary: botany, forestry, soil science, hydrology—all of which contribute to a more complete understanding of the earth, climate shifts, and how people adapt to large regions.

6 As a species, we've been literally blind to the universe around us. If the known <u>electromagnetic spectrum</u> were scaled up to stretch around the Earth's circumference, the human eye would see a portion equal to the diameter of a pencil. Our ability to build detectors that see for us where we can't see, and computers that bring the invisible information back to our eyesight, will ultimately contribute to our survival on Earth and in space.

7 The spectrum of sunlight reflected by the Earth's surface contains information about the composition of the surface, and it may reveal traces of past human activities, such as agriculture. Since sand, cultivated soil, vegetation, and all kinds of rocks each have distinctive temperatures and emit heat at different rates, sensors can "see" things beyond ordinary vision or cameras. Differences in soil texture are revealed by fractional temperature variations. So it is possible to identify loose soil that had been prehistoric agricultural fields, or was covering buried remains. The Maya causeway was detected through emissions of infrared radiation at a different wavelength from surrounding vegetation. More advanced versions of such multi-spectral scanner (Visible & IR) can detect irrigation ditches filled with sediment because they hold more moisture and thus have a temperature different from other soil. The ground above a buried stone wall, for instance, may be a touch hotter than the surrounding terrain because the stone absorbs more heat. Radar can penetrate darkness, cloud cover, thick jungle canopies, and even the ground.

8 Remote sensing can be a discovery technique, since the computer can be programmed to look for distinctive "signatures" of energy emitted by a known site or feature in areas where surveys have not been conducted. Such "signatures" serve as recognition features or fingerprints. Such characteristics as elevation, distance from water, distance between sites or cities, corridors, and transportation routes can help to predict the location of potential archaeological sites.

9 ## Computational techniques used to analyze data.

1. sun-angle correction
2. density slicing
3. band ratioing

4. edge enhancement
5. synthetic color assignment
6. filtering
7. multichannel analysis

Remote Sensing Instruments

10   Aerial Photography:
Many features which are difficult or impossible to see standing on the ground become very clear when seen from the air. But, black and white photography only records about twenty-two perceptible shades of gray in the visible spectrum. Also, optical sources have certain liabilities; they must operate in daylight, during clear weather, on days with minimal atmospheric haze.

11   Color Infrared Film (CIR):
Detects longer wavelengths somewhat beyond the red end of the light spectrum. CIR film was initially employed during World War II to differentiate objects that had been artificially camouflaged. Infrared photography has the same problems that conventional photography has, you need light and clear skies. Even so, CIR is sensitive to very slight differences in vegetation. Because buried archaeological features can affect how plants grow above them, such features become visible in color infrared photography.

12   Thermal Infrared Multispectral Scanner (TIMS):
A six channel scanner that measures the thermal radiation given off by the ground, with accuracy to 0.1 degree centigrade. The pixel (picture element) is the square area being sensed, and the size of the pixel is directly proportional to sensor height. For example, pixels from Landsat satellites are about 100 feet (30 m) on a side, and thus have limited archaeological applications. However, pixels in TIMS data measure only a few feet on a side and as such can be used for archeological research. TIMS data were used to detect ancient Anasazi roads in Chaco Canyon, NM.

13   Airborne Oceanographic Lidar (ADI):
A laser device that makes "profiles" of the earth's surface. The laser beam pulses to the ground 400 times per second, striking the surface every three and a half inches, and bounces back to its source. In most cases, the beam bounces off the top of the vegetation cover and off the ground surface; the difference between the two give information on forest height, or even the height of grass in pastures. As the lidar passes over an eroded footpath that still affects the topography, the pathway's indentation is recorded by the laser beam. The lidar data can be processed to reveal tree height as well as elevation, slope, aspect, and slope length of ground features. Lidar can also be used to penetrate water to measure the morphology of coastal water, detect oil forms, fluorescent dye traces, water clarity, and organic pigments including chlorophyll. In this case,

part of the pulse is reflected off the water surface, while the rest travels to the water bottom and is reflected. The time elapsed between the received impulses allows for a determination of water depth and subsurface topography.

14 Synthetic Aperture Radar (SAR):

SAR beams energy waves to the ground and records the energy reflected. Radar is sensitive to linear and geometric features on the ground, particularly when different radar wavelengths and different combinations of the horizontal and vertical data are employed. Different wavelengths are sensitive to vegetation or to ground surface phenomena. In dry, porous soils, radar can penetrate the surface. In 1982, radar from the space shuttle penetrated the sand of the Sudanese desert and revealed ancient watercourses. Using airborne radar in Costa Rica, prehistoric footpaths have been found.

15 Microwave Radar:

Beaming radar pulses into the ground and measuring the echo is a good way of finding buried artifacts in arid regions (water absorbs microwaves). Man-made objects tend to reflect the microwaves, giving one a "picture" of what is underground without disturbing the site.

Selected Papers

"Remote Sensing Methods," In *Advances in Science and Technology for Historic Preservation,* edited by Ray Williamson, Plenum Press. (In Press).

"Remote Sensing," In *American Journal of Archaeology,* 99:83–84, 1995.

"Applications of Ecological Concepts and Remote Sensing Technologies in Archaeological Site Reconnaissance," with F. Miller and D. Lee. (In *Applications of Space-Age Technology in Anthropology,* edited by Clifford Behrens and Thomas Sever. NASA, Stennis Space Center, MS, 1991.)

"Remote Sensing," Chapter 14 of *Benchmarks In Time and Culture: Introductory Essays in the Methodology of Syro-Palestinian Archaeology.* Scholars Press. March, 1988.

"Cultural and Ecological Applications of Remote Sensing." Final Report of a Conference Sponsored by the National Science Foundation. With Daniel Gross and Paul Shankman. University of Boulder Colorado, Boulder. April, 1988.

"Conference on Remote Sensing: Potential for the Future." NASA, Stennis Space Center, Science and Technology Laboratory, SSC, MS., January, 1985.

webmaster@wwwghcc.msfc.nasa.gov

Responsible Official: Dr. Timothy L. Miller (tim.miller@msfc.nasa.gov)
Page Author: Tom Sever
Page Curator: Diane Samuelson (diane.samuelson@msfc.nasa.gov)

Last Updated: May 12, 1998

—Global Hyrology and Climate Center, NASA/Marshall Space Flight Center Web site (http://www.msfc.nasa.gov)

VOCABULARY REVIEW

1. For each of the words listed below, use context, prefixes, roots, and suffixes; and/or a dictionary to write a brief definition or synonym of the word as it is used in the reading.

   a. impacts (para. 1) _____

   b. demise (para. 1) _____

   c. methodical (para. 2) _____

   d. prioritizing (para. 2) _____

   e. quantified (para. 2) _____

   f. emit (para. 7) _____

   g. infrared (para. 7) _____

   h. perceptible (para. 10) _____

   i. optical (para. 10) _____

   j. camouflaged (para. 11) _____

   k. eroded (para. 13) _____

   l. morphology (para. 13)_____

   m. porous (para. 14) _____

2. Underline new specialized terms introduced in the reading.

COMPREHENSION QUESTIONS

1. Why do archaeologists need remote sensing?
2. What is the value of research that allows archaeologists to uncover previously invisible information?
3. Describe one archaeological discovery that was made using remote sensing.
4. What characteristics can predict the potential of an archaeological site?
5. Why might the ground above a buried stone wall be a little warmer than the ground surrounding it?
6. Name and briefly describe one remote sensing instrument.

THINKING CRITICALLY

1. If you did not understand the term *remote sensing,* what would you do?
2. What is the purpose of the quotation given in paragraphs 2–4?
3. Which of the remote sensing instruments might be useful in environmental preservation and conservation of wetland and coastal areas?
4. Name two advantages of reading material electronically (as opposed to a print source) that this electronic reading provided?
5. If you wanted additional information on synthetic aperture radar, how would you go about finding it?
6. Evaluate this Web site using the criteria suggested in the chapter

LEARNING/STUDY STRATEGIES

1. Locate at least three additional electronic articles on ground penetrating radar.
2. Evaluate each source you identify.

THINKING ABOUT THE PAIRED READINGS

INTEGRATING IDEAS

1. Which of the two readings do you think offers the most informaton?
2. Compare the author's purpose in both readings?
3. How do the readings differ?
4. Which of the two readings offers a more scientifically based definition of radar as used in the study of archaeology? Explain your answer.
5. If you came across these two readings online, which one would you find more "user friendly" and why?

GENERATING NEW IDEAS

1. Visit one or both of the Web sites from which these readings were taken. Search for updated information on research tools in archaeology. Write a brief summary of your findings.
2. Write a cause-effect essay explaining how technology has affected and changed the field of archaeology.